Transnational Memory

Media and Cultural Memory/ Medien und kulturelle Erinnerung

Edited by
Astrid Erll · Ansgar Nünning

Volume 19

Transnational Memory

Circulation, Articulation, Scales

Edited by
Chiara De Cesari and Ann Rigney

DE GRUYTER

ISBN 978-3-11-048601-8
e-ISBN (PDF) 978-3-11-035910-7
e-ISBN (EPUB) 978-3-11-038673-8
ISSN 1613-8961

Library of Congress Cataloging-in-Publication Data
A CIP catalog record for this book has been applied for at the Library of Congress.

Bibliographic information published by the Deutsche Nationalbibliothek
The Deutsche Nationalbibliothek lists this publication in the Deutsche Nationalbibliografie;
detailed bibliographic data are available on the Internet at http://dnb.dnb.de.

© 2014 Walter de Gruyter GmbH, Berlin/Boston
Cover image: Adrian Paci, The Column, 2013 production shot. Courtesy of the artist and
Kaufmann Repetto, Milan.
Typesetting: le-tex publishing services GmbH, Leipzig
Printing and binding: CPI books GmbH, Leck
♾ Printed on acid-free paper
Printed in Germany

www.degruyter.com

Acknowledgements

This collection was made possible by the input and support of many individuals and institutions. In the first place, we are happy to acknowledge the support of the Netherlands Organisation for Scientific Research (NWO) through their funding of the Network in Transnational Memory Studies (NITMES). The idea of putting together a collection on this topic originated in the Transnational Memory initiative of Utrecht University's Research Area Cultures and Identities, for whose generous financial and logistical support we are grateful. We would also like to thank Amsterdam University's Institute of Culture and History, which provided support in the initial editing stage. Ann Rigney is also grateful for the hospitality of the University of Toronto in the Spring of 2014, which certainly contributed both to the pleasure and the pace of the final editing.

An earlier version of Chiara De Cesari's chapter appeared in the *Journal of Social Archaeology* 10.3 (2010), and an earlier version of Ann Rigney's chapter in *New Literary History* 43.4 (2012). We would like to thank the editors of these journals for permission to re-use these materials.

To Astrid Erll and Ansgar Nünning we owe the honour of publishing this volume in their Media and Cultural Memory series, but also many wise editorial suggestions along the way. Stella Diedrich, Manuela Gerlof, and Angelika Hermann at De Gruyter were models of patience; we thank them in particular for their endless readiness to answer our questions and their willingness to cope with shifting deadlines. We are also grateful to Lori Allen for her generous advice and suggestions. A special word of thanks is owed to Tessa Super who helped us in the initial stages of this editorial process and, especially, to Sophie van den Elzen, whose quiet and efficient editorial support in the prolonged final phases was invaluable. Finally, we would like to express our gratitude to Adrian Paci and the Kaufmann Repetto gallery, Milan for their generous cooperation and the permission to use two stills from Paci's videos for our cover photo and our envoi.

Chiara De Cesari and Ann Rigney

Contents

Chiara De Cesari and Ann Rigney

Introduction

Beyond methodological nationalism

By now there is a vast literature demonstrating how collective memory is crucial for identity formation and how, particularly in the modern period, the self-
reflexive cultivation of the past has played into the formation of imagined communities (Anderson 1991; Assmann 1995). A large proportion of this scholarship has
been governed, however, like so much social science and humanities research, by
a methodological nationalism that posits the nation as "the natural social and political form of the modern world" (Wimmer and Glick Schiller 2002; see also Beck
2000). In the case of memory studies, this has meant assuming that the nation-
state is the natural container, curator, and telos of collective memory. This book
offers an alternative approach.

   The primacy of the national frame is not in itself surprising, of course, given
the co-emergence of nationalism and historicism in the nineteenth century, and
the subsequent importance of heritage, canonicity, narratives of liberation, and
commemorative rituals to the very working and legitimization of the modern
nation-state (Gillis 1994), which in turn provided the blueprint for emerging research taxonomies. Memory institutions and the cultivation of the past have been
cornerstones of ethnic nationalism in line with the principle that nations are
"grand solidarities" based both on a commitment to a shared future and identification with a shared past (Renan 1882). The intensification of interest in memory
and the emergence of memory studies in the last decades have most often been
explained by a crisis of remembrance occasioned by the horrors of WWII, decolonization, and the growth of identity politics (see Olick et al. 2012). It should also
be tied, however, to an increasing awareness of nationalism as a specifically historical formation based on a questionable congruence between cultural, political,
and territorial borders that was articulated through the cultivation of the past.
The imagined community constitutive of modern 'nationalized' France, for example, as Pierre Nora's influential *Lieux de mémoire* (1984–1992) argued, was shaped
around the shared knowledge of a limited number of highly invested and highly
mediated memory sites that served as common points of reference across the
national territory. A quarter of a century after its first publication, Nora's project
and the comparable work it inspired in other countries now appears in a double

light: on the one hand, as the production of a new canon as a way of bulwarking (ethnocentric and racialized) national traditions in face of postcolonial diversity (see Rothberg 2010; Stoler 2011); on the other hand, as a symptom of an emerging 'post-national' awareness of the contingency of nationalism. In retrospect, it can be seen that Hobsbawm and Ranger's *Invention of Tradition* (1983) and Anderson's *Imagined Communities* (1983), appearing just a year earlier, were dancing to the same intellectual tune.

Thirty years on, the time is ripe to move memory studies itself beyond methodological nationalism. Globalized communication and time-space compression, post-coloniality, transnational capitalism, large-scale migration, and regional integration: all of these mean that national frames are no longer the self-evident ones they used to be in daily life and identity formation. As a result, the national has also ceased to be the inevitable or preeminent scale for the study of collective remembrance. By now, in the second decade of the twenty-first century, it has become a matter of urgency for scholars in the field of memory studies to develop new theoretical frameworks, invent new methodological tools, and identify new sites and archival resources for studying collective remembrance beyond the nation-state. Building on emerging discussions, the present volume aims to contribute to this long-term goal.

Without claiming to be exhaustive, we nevertheless hope to have identified some of the key issues at stake in the further development of memory studies and provided a pathway to their further exploration. What new frames of collective remembrance have been emerging as alternatives to the nation? And how do new media technologies affect practices of remembrance both in local and in transnational arenas? What are the mechanisms of inclusion and exclusion that govern even seemingly all-inclusive transnational memory cultures in the digital age? Looking back, does the historical formation of national memories provide a blueprint for understanding the larger-scale processes of integration currently taking place across the world, including Europe? Do the memory cultures among migrant communities replicate those of nationalism, or work in a different way? How do memory narratives interact transnationally, specifically along the fault lines created by colonialism? Does the weakening of nationalized memory mark the beginnings of the end of historical identity (and 'roots') as the principal marker of citizenship and belonging?

Why transnational?

It might be going too far to speak already of a transnational turn in memory studies, but there are stirrings in that direction. In that sense, the present volume can
build on earlier discussions of some specific issues as well as on more general surveys. Most notable among the latter are several recent collections that thematize
the idea of a global memory culture deeply connected to the propagation of human rights and respect for the memory of the Holocaust as a moral benchmark in
a new world order. Daniel Levy and Natan Sznaider have spoken in this regard in
Kantian terms of a "global memory imperative" based on the Holocaust; conceived
as a "universal code" the memory of the Holocaust, they argue, now underpins a
global concern for human rights that changes the nature of national sovereignty
and indeed the very idea of an autonomous "bounded nation" (Levy and Sznaider
2006; 2010). In their *Memory in a Global Age: Discourses, Practices and Trajectories* (2010), Aleida Assmann and Sebastian Conrad, while less centered than Levy
and Sznaider on the Holocaust as benchmark, show a similar concern with identifying icons or narratives that have a global, universalist reach in an increasingly
convergent world – the mnemonic equivalent of UNESCO World Heritage, as it
were.

The present volume echoes these studies in proposing to focus on "nation-
transcending idioms, spanning territorial and national borders" (Levy and Sznaider 2010, 6). However, where Levy and Sznaider and others have highlighted
the ways in which "global concerns become part of local experiences" (Levy and
Sznaider 2002, 87) and advance a human rights consensus that is potentially
world-wide, the present volume will pay more attention to the multivocality that
is brought into play in the interlocking social fields connecting the 'local,' the
'national,' and the 'global' that are as often sites of dissensus and differentiation,
of productive if unequal encounters – what Anna Tsing has called "frictions"
(Tsing 2005) – as they are of convergence and agreement.

What to call this new mnemonic arena? Terms like "global memory" or "cosmopolitan memory" and "world conscience" (Beck et al. 2009) carry the risk of homogenization and of implying misleadingly that the movement of memory is uniform, unidirectional, and teleological. The term "transcultural memory" (Crownshaw 2011) resonates with many of our concerns here and is also fruitfully deployed on occasion in some of the essays which follow (see in particular Rothberg's discussion of the relative value of the terms 'transnational' and 'transcultural'). The 'transcultural' also marks a desire to move beyond traditional configurations of the field of research along the lines of discrete, nationally-defined
'container cultures.' As Astrid Erll puts it in a valuable survey article, transcultur-

ality offers a "research perspective" that is "directed towards mnemonic processes unfolding *across* and *beyond* cultures" (Erll 2011, 9). It allows one to highlight the way cultures can transcend national borders per se (as in the case, for example, of 'Anglo-American' culture). Even more crucially, it highlights the way narratives, images, and models of remembrance "travel" and circulate widely with the help of media. In this way, the concept of transcultural memory helps us to a better understanding of how certain ways of looking and recalling can actually become shared by groups at different locations across the world. While "the existence and variable permeability of borders" (Erll 2011, 14) is acknowledged, transculturality has been applied above all to the study of mobility and flows rather than the social and political factors, as well as cultural ones, that may impede them.

It is precisely on the issue of borders that transculturality seems to lose some of its analytical purchase; an approach "across and beyond cultures" invokes the idea of cultures as bounded containers at the same time as it suggests that it is the very nature of cultural production to work across such boundaries. This volume will attempt precisely to tease out more fully, theoretically as well as empirically, the nature and role of borders in cultural remembrance. This means that, while it takes on board the principle that memory 'travels' and that it does so increasingly in our age of globalized communication, it recognizes the dialectical role played by national borders (which are not just imagined, but also legally defined) in memory practices and in memory studies.

In light of these considerations, among others, we concluded that the term 'transnational,' although not without its own shortcomings (see Vertovec 2009, 17), seemed best suited to approach the multi-layered, multi-sited, and multi-directional dynamic that we are hoping to capture. 'Transnationalism' recognizes the significance of national frameworks alongside the potential of cultural production both to reinforce and to transcend them. Crucially, it opens new possibilities for examining the interplay and tensions between culture and institutions, and hence for developing a new dialogue between those approaching the field from the Humanities and those approaching it from the Social Sciences. Since nation-states in principle have hard and fast, legal boundaries, the combination of 'transnational' and 'memory' opens up an analytic space to consider the interplay between social formations and cultural practices, or between state-operated institutions of memory and the flow of mediated narratives within and across state borders. It makes it possible to move to the centre of analysis the material presence of borders in the 'flows' of globalized memories; these may be non-hierarchical and deeply democratic in appearance, but may well themselves be the sites of hegemonic and governmental processes in ways that both reproduce and alter those of older national memory forms. In this way, 'transnationalism' proves better suited than more homogenizing cognates to highlight the frictions at play at the interfaces between different social formations and cultural imaginaries, and the varieties of currents and cross-currents at work in the exchange and appropriations of travelling narratives and mnemonic forms in a world that is not seamless. Finally, it helps open up the crucial question of how practices of remembrance themselves participate in the making of hard and fast borders: for example, how does the current flurry of institutional activities geared toward the production of a new European memory relate to the hardening of Fortress Europe?

In essence, then, a transnational approach directs attention to all kinds of "sustained, cross-borders relationships spanning nation-states" (Vertovec 2009, 1) and to those phenomena not neatly captured within the borders of the latter. At an even more fundamental methodological level, transnationalism problematizes "container thinking" as such (Beck 2000; Amelina et al. 2012; cf. Gupta and Ferguson 1997) and forces us to question our ingrained understanding of appropriate spatial units of analysis. As Sanjeev Khagram and Peggy Levitt (2008, 5) have put it:

> In contrast to traditional perspectives, which see transnational phenomena and dynamics as a subset of those occurring somewhere between the national and the global, [Transnational Studies] includes another, in some cases, more productive option. What are assumed to be bounded and bordered social units are understood as transnationally constituted, embedded and influenced social arenas that interact with one another. From this perspective, the world consists of multiple sets of dynamically overlapping and interacting transnational social fields that create and shape seemingly bordered and bounded structures, actors and processes. ... By transnational, we propose an optics or gaze that begins with a world without borders, empirically examines the boundaries and borders that emerge at particular historical moments, and explores their relationship to unbounded arenas and processes.

As this passage suggests, the critique of container thinking leads into an even more fundamental critique: of the idea of scale and of the unspoken hierarchies of scale implicit in our research practices. Transnationalism allows us to grasp the *multi-scalarity* of socio-cultural processes and the fundamental "mutual construction of the local, national and global" in the contemporary world (Glick Schiller 2012, 23); as well as the proximity of the intimate and the global (Pratt and Rosner 2012). Palestinian cultural heritage preservation organizations offer a case in point (see De Cesari, this volume); they produce a form of institutionalized and materialized memory, Palestinian heritage, which can be considered simultaneously locally rooted and markedly globalized thanks to the appropriation of a globally circulating language of heritage to repurpose the local vernacular past in the service of national liberation (see also De Cesari 2010).

Crucially, rethinking scale also means rethinking the spatial imaginaries and imagined topographies of verticality (Ferguson 2004) that have shaped research practices in memory studies. Consider, for example, the common scholarly repre-sentation of 'local' or 'grassroots' memories as opposed to 'national' and 'global' memories. The former, no matter how far they reach out towards the world, are always imagined as being small-scale in scope and extremely localized, akin to a point on a map, and, most importantly, as situated below the broader configura-tions of national or global memory that are thought of as containing and subsum-ing them. Moreover, we tend to imagine 'the global' in terms of a homogeneous and steadily expanding spread across the globe (usually from a Western location) at the expense of the older mosaic pattern of national memories – and this imag-inary, in fact both spatial and temporal, has also been at the core of recent theo-rizing of memory in relation to globalization. The transnational optics adopted in this volume allows memory to be visualized differently: not as a horizontal spread or as points or regions on a map but as a dynamic operating at multiple, interlock-ing scales and involving conduits, intersections, circuits, and articulations. With its rethinking of scales and how they operate, transnationalism has fundamental methodological implications that go beyond the new attention it brings to bear, for example, on diasporic communities (Creet and Kitzmann 2011; Hirsch and Miller 2011; Glynn and Kleist 2012; Quayson and Daswani 2013).

It will be clear by now that transnationalism is not used here in a teleologi-cal sense, as synonym for an ever-widening of the frameworks of memory within some homogeneously conceived space. There is no necessary or linear 'progress' from the familial, to local, to national to global memories, because not only do we encounter movements or developments in reverse, but also different, non-linear configurations and constellations. Indeed, the term transnational itself crucially serves here as a reminder of the fact that even in a so-called post-national age, 'the national' as a framework for identity and memory-making is still a powerful one, indeed one that may be reinforced in response to calls for new types of confed-eration and integration. As a number of our chapters illustrate, the transnational dynamics of memory production operate in conjunction with the continuous pres-ence and agency of the national, with which it thus remains deeply entangled (wit-ness the harnessing of national rights to human rights; see Kennedy, De Cesari). Just as post-coloniality constitutes a break with colonialism that cannot transcend its enduring legacy, so too does post-nationality – or better, transnationality (Glick Schiller 2012) – continue to respond to national meanings and values. In some cases indeed, the globalization of memory practices has paradoxically helped re-inforce the nation as the social framework par excellence for identity and soli-darity, suggesting that the latest phase of globalization and transnational capital-ism has not led to the disappearance of the national, but rather its transformation and reconfiguration (see Gupta and Ferguson 2002; Ferguson 2006). Arguably, the unstable, tense, and discontinuous social fields of diaspora may be the most important site of national memory today (see also Khalili 2005; De Cesari 2012a). A complex feedback from the transnational to the ethnic-national, with nationalism fostered in interaction with transnational discourses, is brought out here in several chapters: most notably in Gal Kirn's analysis of post-Yugoslav memory, Christina Schwenkel's account of the deep entanglement of the national and the transnational in the celebratory internationalist-socialist remembrance of anti-colonial nationalism, and Chiara De Cesari's analysis of the work of Palestinian heritage organizations and their relations to UNESCO.

In line with a commitment to exploring such non-linear trajectories and complex temporalities, this volume does not assume that transnationalism is a recent phenomenon particular to the latest phase of globalization. As Benedict Anderson already argued, nationalism has always been transnationally constituted, because it is the very possibility of its "being transplanted" (1991, 4) into always new contexts and travelling across multiple borders that allowed for its worldwide success (as explored, for example, in the comparative study of "viral nationalisms" in Europe by Leerssen 2006; 2011). Transnationalism in memory studies helps in casting retrospective light on transnational cross-currents which were operative at the height of nationalism but which were subsequently written out of national narratives. These cross-currents included the transnational character of nationalism itself: while each nation proclaimed itself unique, the fact that they did so along remarkably similar lines has tended to be forgotten (Edwards, this volume; also Leerssen and Rigney 2014). Crucially, transnational cross-currents were also at the heart of colonialism, slavery, and other forms of exploitation by globalized capital involving the violent asymmetrical entanglement of racialized communities; this shadow side of national progress has been largely occluded from memory (Ebron, this volume; see also Stoler 2011). Along a positive vein, mention can also be made of various transnational cross-currents involving utopian projects based on the promise of transcending all borders: aimed at establishing international socialism, as Kirn and Schwenkel show in their respective essays, or at a universal visual archive that also fostered national imaginaries, as shown by Edwards in hers. The memory of such transnational interactions and cross-currents became retrospectively nationalized once placed under the purview and control of national institutions, which thereby also foreclosed the production of alternative narratives as Legêne and Eickhoff show in their analysis of the cataloguing of colonial photographs. With the help of a transnational lens, however, it is now possible to see retrospectively some of the paths not taken in the formation of dominant national narratives, and so re-open archives and reactivate the potential of certain icons and narratives to become recuperated as new sites of future memory.

Transnational dynamics

This collection of essays shows the inter- and transdisciplinarity at the heart of contemporary memory studies. The two editors come from socio-cultural anthropology and comparative literature respectively, and our contributors have been drawn in almost equal measure from the humanities and the social sciences. Combining expertise in this way will hopefully bring us closer to an outstanding desideratum: the integrated study of memory production as a cultural process embedded in social formations that it helps in turn to shape. In the case of the present topic, this has meant integrating a concern with institutions, actors, and struggles for power in concrete material circumstances with a concern for mediation, cultural forms, and the media-supported mobility of narratives across time and space. Integrating these two perspectives seemed all the more urgent given what appears to be a growing divergence between traditional state-controlled institutions of memory and 'unregulated' grassroots exchanges using digital media, and the emergence of new actors in the struggle to define collective memory.

Underlying our approach is a dynamic model of cultural memory that sees it in processual terms (as the outcome of ongoing cultural practices and unequal encounters) as well as generative ones (as an activity that is productive of stories and new social relations rather than merely preservative of legacies). As a number of recent studies have argued, and as is borne out by the essays here, cultural remembrance involves the continual production, remediation, and sharing of stories about a past that changes in relation to the new possibilities for interpreting it within shifting social frames operating at different scales and across different territories (see Erll and Rigney 2009). Mediated acts of remembrance help to create new narratives and displace or marginalize others and, by opening up fresh perspectives on the past, continuously change the grounds on which common futures are imagined (Gutman et al. 2010). The stabilizing, hegemonic role of memory narratives (Assmann 1995) and canonical "sites of memory" (Nora 1997) has deservedly received a lot of critical attention in the last half of the past century since they have such a formative influence. However, any focus on canonization needs to be offset by due concern for the parallel process whereby new acts of remembrance, spurred on by emerging groups in search of recognition, help generate new identities and contest old ones as part of a dynamic system. Seen in this way, cultural memory is always "on the move" (Rigney 2012), working as a "gyroscope that mediates trajectories from past to future through gravitational points in the present" (Olick 2010, 213). With this in mind, the present volume seeks to analyze the movement of narratives alongside the workings of power that underpin it. It will pay particular attention to those pressure points where this process becomes foreclosed, when some images and stories become territorialized, stabilized, or otherwise caught up in national or ethnic practices and meanings.

This dynamic and generative approach to cultural memory acknowledges the complex temporalities whereby past, present, and future are re-calibrated. More importantly, it allows us to conceive of the relations between memory and social identity in other ways than as an unalienable inheritance that binds groups to a particular identity fixed in the past. Ever since Maurice Halbwachs' *Cadres sociaux de la mémoire* (1925), it has been generally accepted that personal recollection is shaped by "social frameworks," since people adapt what they remember to the social contexts (in the first instance, according to Halbwachs, the family, religion, and profession) in which they conduct and imagine their lives. Although the national frame has until recently been politically the most important and academically the most theorized, it co-exists and has long co-existed with multiple others. The essays below explore a wide variety of these alternatives, from extended families (Feuchtwang, Küchler), to diasporic and mobile communities (Baronian, Kapralski), to globally-distributed publics (Erll, Kennedy), to entangled neighbors and immigrants (Rothberg), to would-be confederations (Rigney), and supranational and transnational organizations (De Cesari). Suffice it here to point out the more fundamental theoretical assumption: that social frames should not be conceived merely as 'containers' of memories, but rather as the historical outcome of acts of remembrance that help to (re)define groups – and their boundaries – and establish new modes of mutual implication (Ebron; see also Rothberg 2013).

At this point, the transnational lens on memory intersects in fruitful ways with recent discussions on the making of publics and counter-publics (Warner 2002) within the context of a transnational public sphere (Kennedy, this volume; see also Fraser 2007). If nationalizing cultures of memory (and much of the theorization that followed from it) took the borders of the mnemonic community as a given, the generative approach offered here indicates that communities and publics are created "prosthetically" (Landsberg 2004) through mediated acts of remembrance and, in line with this, shows how the borders between imagined communities become reconfigured through the agency of cultural remembrance itself. The dynamics of remembrance are thus intimately bound up with community-making since narratives about events belonging to 'our world' continuously reproduce, redraw or challenge the lines between 'them' and 'us.' And while cultural remembrance helps thus to create bonds, it is a two-edged sword whose power can also be deployed to discriminate against groups. As Michael Rothberg points out in this volume, Turkish migrants to Germany become caught in a double-bind, being simultaneously told that the Holocaust is not part of their history because they are not 'ethnically' German and then castigated for their alleged indifference to Holocaust remembrance (see also Rothberg and Yildiz 2011).

The idea of (multidirectional memory) first developed by Michael Rothberg (2009), has proved very fruitful in opening up new perspectives on the 'vectors' (Wood 2009) and modalities by which stories and icons move across space, time, and social groups – or fail to do so. The concept of 'multidirectionality' has made visible the sedimented quality of memory discourses, and the fact that multiple dialogues and exchanges with existing narratives play a constitutive role in their making. Crucially, it reveals how the memory narratives central to the identity of one group can, in travelling, help model the narrative of another group in a manner that is mutually-supportive. In this process, Rothberg has shown, memory does not have to work according to the economy of a zero-sum game whereby one narrative gains public salience only at the cost of obliterating competitors.

As several contributions to the volume demonstrate, it is indeed the case that globally circulating memories and particularly the memory of the Holocaust – which has itself emerged as a paradigm and model for memory-making worldwide – have helped provide a language in which to articulate other narratives of suffering and loss (as well as a template for subjectivity and agency, see Ebron, this volume) in an increasingly transnational yet fragmented public sphere. However, there is also evidence to suggest that the relations between memorial traditions and the effects of memory encounters do not always amount to a zero-sum game or to a power-free interaction that is equally rewarding to both parties. Memory discourses are deeply entangled; yet such interconnections are often, if not always, asymmetrical ones, as the interactions between the memory of the Holocaust and the memory of the Palestinian Nakba illustrate, or the privileging of some genocides over others as part of a global canon. A Foucauldian understanding of power as fundamentally productive, as a power that works by empowering (while also regulating and subordinating), can help further illuminate the relationship between memorial traditions and effects of memory encounters in ways that go beyond the alternatives initially offered by Rothberg. In practice, as he himself has acknowledged in recent publications (Rothberg 2011), hierarchies of suffering are a frequent, even if avoidable, effect of memory encounters; comparison and mutual mirroring are often "agonistic" (Mouffe 2005) and even antagonistic, rather than non-competitive and equal. A more elaborate understanding of the complexity of such intersections and comparisons can help advance our understanding of memory politics beyond the simple paradigm of silencing and obliteration (see also Gilroy 2004) and bring it more in line with what Ann Stoler has called "aphasia" (Stoler 2011): an incapacity to engage with some dimensions of the past and their enduring and troubling presence. Stoler's analysis bears in the first instance on France's dealing with its colonial past, but it also speaks to broader European political dynamics, opening up a way to understand the aphasia relating to the thousands of deaths at sea of migrants and asylum seekers (often from former European colonies) as they attempt to cross Europe's borders in the Mediterranean. Their lives are becoming lost, invisible, in the interstices between national commemorative spaces and within everyday affective taxonomies that organize the distinction between "grievable" and "ungrievable" bodies (see Butler 2009) along racialized and national lines.

In order to flag this blind-spot or constitutive outside of transnational memory, we have included a visual contribution in our envoi in the form of a still from the video *Centro di permanenza temporanea* (literally: Temporary Stay Center, 2007) by Albanian-Italian artist Adrian Paci. In the video, a group of migrants crowd a gangway right in the middle of a runway, but it soon becomes clear that the planes leaving the airport are not for them, so they are left waiting, their faces scarred by the betrayal of their hopes for a better life. What awaits them is clarified by the video's title, which refers to the detention centers spread across Italy and other Mediterranean countries where irregular migrants are detained, often for months and in spite of not having committed any crime, until they are 'repatriated.' The survivors of the Mediterranean crossing end up stuck in a prison-like temporal, spatial, and legal limbo – a de-territorialized national frontier, and a key site in a broader accretion of borders that is itself deeply entwined with memory processes (Rigney, this volume; see also De Cesari 2012b).

Transnational memories are commonly believed to ground and foster a new international morality based on human rights (Kennedy). Yet the use of memory as a marker of citizenship (Rothberg) or as an informal accession criterion to the EU in cases such as Turkey (Rigney) indicates that the moral politics of remembrance are ambiguous. Unraveling the tangle of memory and human rights today means acknowledging the double role of memory: on the one hand, it offers a conduit to recognition and empowerment on the part of the marginalized and dispossessed (as in the case of the Roma, see Kapralski); on the other hand, it functions as an instrument of discrimination and a measure of exclusion.

The essays below, in focusing on particular instances of border-making and border-crossing, thus uncover some of the power dynamics and power struggles that are at the heart of the contemporary production of memory. While charting the movement and proliferation of particular narratives, they also help to relaunch some 'residual' memories that were blocked or marginalized or had simply lost momentum: socialist narratives of transnational solidarity (Kirn, Schwenkel), or hopeful memories of multicultural co-existence (Erll).

Circulation

Globalized communication has meant, among other things, an observable convergence in the modes and aesthetics of remembrance practiced around the globe
and the discourses informing them. One can think here, for example, of the so-
called politics of regret and the global travels of public apologies as a cultural template (Olick 2007), the discourse of victimhood and trauma (Fassin and Rechtman
2009), and the discourse of World Heritage, not to mention the widespread famil-
iarity with the Holocaust as a memory site (see Levy and Sznaider 2006; Rothberg
2009). This convergence in the 'languages of commemoration' indicated that our
study of transnational memory should begin with the issue of 'circulation' and the
question of how stories and models for remembrance shape what is remembered
and provide conditions for the exchanges between individuals and groups. The
first set of essays in our volume address these questions from different disciplinary
perspectives and with reference to different geographical areas. Building on recent insights into the mobility or 'travelling' of memory, the four essays brought
together here examine both the mediated quality of memories and the situated
work that these perform as they move across media and between social groups. A
key concern is with the ways in which mediation is culturally and imaginatively
productive, but also socially so, shaping not only narratives but also the collective identities of the people who appropriate them. What triggers the alternation
between deterritorialization and re-territorialization (or "vernacularization," see
Merry 2006) of globally circulating memories? Are digital media fostering such a
thing as a transnational public sphere or simply the increasing interconnection
of (still) distinctly national ones? Are we heading conversely towards the growing
fragmentation and dispersion of communities of debate?

These issues have taken on fresh urgency in light of the fact that new media
technologies and the emergence of participatory cultures (Jenkins 2006) have
clearly multiplied the possibilities for reproducing, adapting, accessing, and
transmitting images and narratives on the part of non-state actors. Media are increasingly powerful agents in connecting individuals and shaping their relations
to each other and to the world (Garde-Hansen et al. 2009; Hoskins 2011). While
texts, film, and photography continue to be key to the production of cultural
memory, these media function more and more in online ecologies and as part of
what Erll here calls "plurimedial networks" that operate across the borders of
states. The emergence of a participatory culture facilitated by internet and social
media is clearly changing the conditions in which memories are produced and circulated, offering new possibilities for intervention that have a low threshold but
potential impact. This does not mean, however, that the internet should be un-

thinkingly celebrated as "digital democracy" (Kuntsman and Stein 2011); indeed, there is a growing literature on digital memories showing that despite widespread ideas linking the internet with Habermassian notions of the public sphere and communicative reason, cyberspaces and online communities of 'debate' can well turn into platforms of hatred and hate speech (Kuntsman 2010). Moreover, it is not a fully de-nationalized space (Rutten and Zvereva 2012, 2). Grassroots and non-state actors play an increasingly vocal role in producing memory in opposition to state-sponsored narratives and institutions (Kennedy, this volume offers a case in point), but also as a substitute for the latter in the context of shifting patterns of globalized governance (see Gupta and Ferguson 2002; Ferguson 2004). But do recent developments in media culture mean the end of the centrality of the nation-state as primary producer of collective memory and of hegemonic narratives about the past? And if there is a shift, what constellations of actors, forces, and resources enable the creation of cultural memory in the absence of state institutions and apparatuses?

The widespread imaginary of the 'flow' as the figure of mobility under the most recent phase of globalization overlooks, as signaled earlier, the importance of frictions and blockages in what are discontinuous memory movements. As the essays below illustrate, memory narratives indeed move with the help of media technologies, but they do so within ultimately limited circuits and along multiple pathways that, while they are sometimes a conduit to something new, may also turn out to be dead ends. How does the very metaphor of the deterritorialized and unbounded hide memory's baggage of epistemic exclusions? How are hegemonic memories being produced in the shift from the museum to the internet as a chief apparatus of memory? Stef Jansen and Staffan Löfving have emphasized that we should approach "the key concepts of sedentarist and placeless paradigms – including territorialization and deterritorialization, emplacement and displacement – as empirical issues to be investigated rather than as philosophical assessments about what characterizes our age" (2009, 5; see also Amelina et al. 2012, 7).

The opening chapter by Astrid Erll takes as its empirical focus the representations of District Six in Cape Town and, analyzing this particular case, builds theoretically on her earlier work by considering in more detail the factors that shape the palimpsestic layering and the mobility of stories. Analyzing the rich mediation of District Six – which includes poetry, a museum, performances and the science-fiction movie *District 9* – Erll shows how this location became transformed into a memory template that travelled across media and places. She highlights in particular the role of cinema in facilitating the global circulation of stories, and shows how narrativization working across plurimedial networks helped turn the history of District Six into a mobile and mobilizing figure of memory that speaks to groups elsewhere. Her analysis ends by pondering the reasons for the 'stickiness' of District 6 as an internationally-recognized figure of memory. Its global resonance was enhanced, she argues, by comparisons between the apartheid system and the Nazi regime. Ultimately, she claims however, its resilience as an icon that was picked up and reproduced in many parts of the world should be linked to the ways in which District 6 came to function as a "shorthand for lost hybridity." In other words, its role as a site of memory was entwined with its role as a site of possibility – a platform for imagining the future and for reactivating a path not yet taken in history.

In the essay following, Rosanne Kennedy examines the deterritorialization and reterritorialization, and the complex trajectories of an apparently extremely localized but in fact deeply cosmopolitan memory: Palestinian testimonies of violence. The chapter takes as case study testimonies solicited during the UN's *Fact-Finding Mission in Gaza* (2009), which was led by South African judge Richard Goldstone, to determine whether violations of human rights had been committed during the Israeli war on Gaza in December 2008–January 2009. Kennedy shows how the original testimonies were reproduced, reframed, and remediated as they were circulated in print form and on the internet by human rights institutions and activist networks. Her concern is less with the role of plurimediation as such than with the transformations incurred by the testimonies as they were brought to the attention – via a print edition, but also live readings on the part of celebrities – into a mode of address to an international public, specifically an American one. Her concept of "moving testimonies" is used to indicate that these testimonies did not merely travel 'under their own steam' as it were, but were made to move by particular actors with the intention of mobilizing publics elsewhere in support of the Palestinian people (and ultimately, via the appeal to human rights, their own right to nation-statehood). Her analysis concludes with a critical reflection on the nature of the transnational public sphere currently in the making under a human rights regime and on its impact on nation-state sovereignty or rather lack thereof. The global memory imperative, and the idea that the global circulation of memories and moving testimonies of suffering can help stop the human rights violations that caused it, is seriously called into question.

Film takes central stage in the third essay by Marie-Aude Baronian, on the work of the Canadian-Armenian artist and filmmaker Atom Egoyan. Building on Jacques Derrida's notion of "archive fever," she shows how Egoyan assumes the role of archivist for a stateless diasporic community in his audiovisual oeuvre: how his images are both grounded in particular locales (as in his recurrent depiction of the iconic Mt Ararat) and de-territorialized as internationally circulating films. His obsessive desire to fill the void of history (the double injustice of the Armenian genocide and its subsequent denial) ensure that his films work 'archivally.' Without the ambition to provide authoritative narratives, they nevertheless mimic memory work and provide an imaginary storage place and a virtual point of reference for a community without full material access to its history and its homeland. Baronian's close study of Egoyan as a creative and self-reflexive curator of diasporic memory reveals the fundamental role of images, and particularly filmic imaginaries, in the transnational making of memories as well as the complexity of the process whereby forgetfulness and erasure are written into the visualizing process itself.

Where the first three chapters explore the circulation of memories through film, reports, and photography, the final chapter by Susanne Küchler focuses on a different, often neglected, medium of remembrance: ordinary material culture, in particular, home-made domestic items. In a detailed analysis of quilt-making in the Cook Islands, Küchler discusses the agency of quilts as quintessentially cultural objects and their semantic density in the lives of the islanders, particularly women, whether resident in the Cooks or in the diaspora. In this context, quilt-making and the act of sewing appear to be deeply entangled with community building, but in ways that challenge traditional notions both of community (modeled on kinship relations, including the nation, conceived as a community of fictive kindred) and of communicative memory (grounded in co-presence and story-telling). That quilts are media of memory is a key aspect of their cultural salience in the Cook Islands, though one which is bound up in fascinating ways with their future-oriented role in creating new pathways and relations rather than merely recalling old ones. Echoing Astrid Erll, Küchler's analysis also suggests that memories travel faster across borders when they are capable of mobilizing imaginaries of the future and not just of the past.

Articulation

With their focus on mediation, the essays in the first section show how acts of re-membrance involve 'articulation' in the sense of 'giving expression' to events in the form of a narrative. Cultural memories are "articulated discourses" (see Hall in Grossberg 1986) made up of heterogeneous elements, borrowings, and appropriations from other languages and memorial traditions that are assembled together into narratives. But acts of remembrance, as the second section emphasizes, also involve 'articulation' in another sense: they help to link up ('articulate') individuals and groups through their common engagement with those narratives. It is this double meaning of the term that has given us the title of our second section.

The five essays collected here explore the various ways in which social relations are constituted and communities (re)formed through the exchange and negotiation of memories across imagined or actual borders. They offer further elaborations of the point made earlier that communities come into being by producing a coherent discourse of memory that serves both to bind the group and to demarcate it from outsiders, and that they do so often by analogy with other communities along multidirectional lines. They also provide examples of the ways in which narratives "become articulated, at specific conjunctures, to certain political subjects" (Hall in Grossberg 1986, 53): the emergence of a memory discourse is part of the constitution or coming into being of political subjects and, crucially, their inscription into (always shifting and unstable) power geographies. Circulating memories are thus both the medium and outcome of the entanglements between people and groups.

Publics and memory communities are constituted, as Kennedy shows in her study of the reception of the Goldstone report on Gaza, through the exchange of narratives in the form of borrowings, appropriations, cross-references, negotiations, and intersections. Asymmetrical as such exchanges are, they may in some situations become nevertheless an important resource in providing new avenues for subjectivity but also for citizenship and belonging. That the same memory discourse can simultaneously empower *and* marginalize some of the groups that claim it as their own is illustrated by the double bind described in Michael Rothberg's essay, which examines the ways in which German Muslim citizens are made into improper subjects of memory and therefore placed outside the inner circle of citizenship increasingly marked by memorial criteria. His essay explores the way German Muslim women and immigrants actively participate in remembering the Holocaust, and use it as a platform for performances of citizenship. His analysis offers a new view of memory practices among migrant communities: where the usual emphasis is on the way migrants cultivate memory as a resource for long-distance nationalism and homeland politics, he emphasizes instead how public acts of remembrance can be used to engage dialogically with the host community. To this end, he introduces the notions of "thickening" and "unscripted new linkages" to describe the work of articulation effected by memory exchanges, encouraging us to think of memory as a resource for building relations rather than as an exclusive legacy.

In the essay following, Paulla Ebron brings to light the transnational dialogues and unexpected encounters that have shaped the emergence of the remembrance of slavery in the US public sphere. Analyzing a sample of cinematic, narrative and material sites of memory, her analysis traces the development throughout the twentieth century of what she calls "memory projects" of slavery, which helped shape a new public. She emphasizes the ways in which these memory projects emerged at the intersection of 'grassroots' and 'official' remembrance. She also traces the multidirectional interaction between Holocaust memory and the memory of slavery from the early 1970s, in practices of remembrance and, crucially, in forms of subjectivity. Her central claim is that such interactions provided African-American activists with an "affective vocabulary" that helped to articulate the story of slavery and give public expression to its memory. The transnational spread of the Holocaust as memory site thus facilitated the multidirectional emergence into public visibility of the past and enduring legacy of slavery in the United States and, in the South, offered an extra transnational counterweight to the local emphasis on the secessionist legacy.

The availability of a transnational language for articulating suffering, trauma, and marginalization is also a central theme in the next essay by Slawomir Kapralski. Charting the history of Romani activism, Kapralski shows how the memory of Nazi persecution has been mobilized by marginalized, stateless actors to claim rights and access to citizenship. He demonstrates how recent Romani political activism has pursued 'national' identity and memory-making in the absence of state institutions and as part of an effort to fight discrimination and achieve equal status and rights in the countries where Roma live at best as second-class citizens. His analysis also illustrates the paradoxes and predicaments of a "transnational nationalism" whose strategy, in line with nineteenth-century models of nation-building, is centered on the mobilization of a collective memory, in this case, following post-Holocaust models, a collective memory of suffering and victimhood. Emphasizing the growing political role of the mobilization of memory in the framework of a politics of recognition (echoed by Rothberg), and hence its value as a conduit to inclusion and equality, Kapralski shows how Romani activists have attempted to produce a 'national' memory to claim their rights at the cost of adopting a victim role – with so far only partial success.

Christina Schwenkel's essay vividly exemplifies the way transnational (and even nationalist) memories can be mobilized to create broader communities and solidarities. She discusses the transnational socialist remembrance of the Vietnam War through an analysis of GDR (East-German) and Cuban films of the war. These produce memories that are both nation-specific and nation-transcending. She emphasizes the role of visual culture and particularly of cinematic images in the constitution of what she calls a "postnational scopic regime of memory" which positions and interpellates the viewer in compelling ways. Arguing that there are particular figurations of humanity at the core of diverse scopic regimes of memory – discourses and imaginations of what constitutes the essence of the human – she compares notions of humanity within socialist discourse and socialist iconography with liberal humanitarian ones circulating as part of the human rights regime. With her analysis of the visual culture of memory formations and of the ways in which these expose not only particular ideas of community (national vs. transnational) but also of the human, we have now come almost full circle in exploring the work of articulation and subjectification in remembrance.

The final essay in this section by Elizabeth Edwards adds an extra twist to this tale by showing, with reference to the photographic survey movement in late nineteenth-century Europe, how a utopian memory project directed towards 'humanity' could end up producing nationalized subjects in practice. Her analysis provides a reminder of the fact that the transnational, mediated circulation of memories and images is not new. More specifically, it presents the pan-European survey movement as an instance of an epochal "memorializing desire" that was nested within (and productive of) the landscape and vocabulary of nationalism at the same time as it aspired to become universal. Based on the large-scale mobilization of amateurs to capture the essence of 'national' experience with photos taken of everyday life, the ultimate aim of the survey movement was the creation of a utopian "memory bank" for a future conceived on a Europe-wide if not indeed world-wide, imperial scale. It combined organizations at local and national level, as well as a transnational network of connections and exchanges. Edwards argues that the movement was not only transnational in its organization, but also in the all-pervasiveness of a nationalizing mode of apprehension and sense of a common modernity that was brought to bear on the localized photographs. At the same time, she also shows that there was no easy fit, but rather a series of fractures and thresholds, between the local, the national, the European, and the global.

Scales

As mentioned earlier, a critical rethinking of scale and of the unspoken hierarchies of scale implicit in our research practices is one of the core challenges of a transnational approach. The issue of scale is indeed present in all of the essays in our volume, as is cross-scale intersectionality. Where several essays bear, for example, on a nationalization paradoxically aided by transnational and supranational actors (De Cesari, Kennedy, Legêne and Eickhoff, in this volume), others contribute to the deconstruction of taken-for-granted hierarchies of affective power based on the distinction (see Margalit 2002) between thick, lived, and affective 'local' or national memories and artificial, empty, and thin transnational memories (Rothberg, Schwenkel). However, the essays collected in this final section offer more overt attempts to address the politics of scale and in particular of "scale-making" (Tsing 2000). How did and do apparatuses at different scales work to nationalize memory? Do recent developments mean the end of the primacy of the nation-state as the dominant framework for collective memory?

Focusing on UNESCO's World Heritage program, Chiara De Cesari's opening essay investigates the paradoxical ways in which transnational remembrance can help reproduce and reinforce national memories and nation-state institutions of memory. It also highlights the unsuspected entanglement of World Heritage and national sovereignty. By examining the translation of UNESCO's cultural heritage policies in the context of Palestine/Israel, she shows how this project of world-wide cultural heritage preservation entails a double predicament and fundamental contradictions. On the one hand, World Heritage reinforces nation-state apparatuses' reach and control over heritage sites and processes, often at the expense of the grassroots. On the other hand, recent World Heritage reforms in the direction of a less Eurocentric approach and a stronger multiculturalism not only risk affirming and solidifying cultural differences, but also the global asymmetries between them.

Working at the scale of the cognitive, the intimate, and the familial, the next essay by Stephan Feuchtwang offers a comparative study of the Indian Sora people alongside a Russian-Jewish family living in Berlin. Challenging Pierre Nora's reductive opposition between (contemporary) sites of memory and (past) *milieux* of memory, Feuchtwang shows how kinship, trans-generational connectedness, and alternative family archives provide enduring and crucial memory environments even in more recent times, and that they involve individual subjects in intense transpersonal relations that give them the sense of an extended temporality. Using the notion of "haunting memory," his analysis shows how such *milieux* are not only alive and well today, even as they adapt themselves to changing circumstances, but are also developing in complex interaction with the narratives produced by the apparatuses of the state.

The starting point of the next essay by Susan Legêne and Martijn Eickhoff is precisely at the level of the state and its role in shaping what is considered worthy of recollection or not. Their concern is with the role of archiving practices in the Netherlands in the national framing of histories of WWII and decolonization. With an empirical focus on colonial photographs in the Netherlands Institute for War, Holocaust and Genocide Studies (NIOD), they show how the transnational history of Empire and decolonization became post-hoc nationalized through the workings of the archive itself. The national scale determined what was deemed relevant or not, and how it was catalogued, leading to an artificial separation between the history of WWII and the history of decolonization that played an important role in the post-war effacement of the fundamental transnationality of European colonialism. Since a visual archive has a potential which exceeds the stories told about it, however, those committed to re-articulating Dutch history could use these photographs in the future in a new way: as a resource for writing a new large-scale history of European colonialism that would have repercussions for both European memory and European citizenship.

If transnational histories are reduced to national ones, or displaced by them, thanks to the taxonomic and representational practices of national archives, it can also happen that transnational institutions inadvertently end up promoting ethno-nationalist memories. Gal Kirn discusses such a case with reference to the former Yugoslavia. He traces the transition from a transnational socialist towards an ethno-nationalist revisionist memory that took place in tandem with the fragmentation of the former Yugoslavia into seven different nation-states. In particular, he details what this scale reduction meant in politico-aesthetic terms, using the example of the memorials to WWII located across the former Yugoslav territory. His focus is on the remarkable socialist modernist memorials which perform a future-oriented memory and mobilize transnational aspirations, but which since 1989 have been neglected. Comparing these WWII memorials to more recent ones, Kirn's essay thematizes the deep entanglement of the new, post-conflict discourses of national reconciliation, nationalist historical revisionism, the rehabilitation of fascism, and very regressive forms of remembrance politics. Most interestingly, the paper traces the collusion between these nationalistic memory discourses and the anti-totalitarian thesis which has also been recently adopted, if only indirectly, by the EU through its policies relating to commemorative days – thus emphasizing the deep paradox of an institution such as the EU, which aims to foster new, transnational frames of memory but ends up lending legitimacy to very different kinds of locally-embedded ethnocentric remembrance.

Further reflecting on recent EU memory policies, Ann Rigney closes the volume by critically examining the assumption that European institutions should aspire to construct a new collective memory along the old national lines but on a larger-scale. She shows how ideas about the future of Europe have been articulated from the late 1940s in tandem with the gradual emergence of a master narrative that sees the EU as the outcome of an ability to overcome its past violence – an idea that found expression in the awarding of the Nobel peace prize of 2012 as well as in the planning of a "European House of History" in Brussels. Rigney's essay challenges the homogenizing top-down efforts to produce a common master-narrative as exclusivist and, literally, backward looking. She argues instead for a more forward-looking way of thinking about cultural memory that would emphasize its capacity to renegotiate the borders of communities at local, regional and macro-regional levels, and generate new "unscripted" linkages (Rothberg, this volume) at these different scales rather than merely express and enshrine existing legacies in an exclusive way. In particular, she indicates the importance of the arts, and their capacity to imagine the past differently, as potentially a key player in this process. This transformative multi-scalar view of memory is more appropriate when conceiving of new forms of citizenship within a rapidly changing and diverse EU than the ethnic-nationalist models inherited from the nineteenth century.

Envoi

The volume charts a rich production of memory taking place across and beyond national boundaries. While showing that globalization is not just new, the essays also bring into focus the massive acceleration of transnational interconnectedness and the growing "transnationalization of the political" (Balibar 2004) that is taking place today. The extent of these changes also makes it necessary to ask if the link between memory and identity is not also in the process of becoming a thing of the past as something specific to the nation-state as a particular cultural-political formation. To a certain extent this may be true. Yet the essays also reveal how the production of new narratives in the interstices between nation-states and in the transnational arena, is gradually giving rise to new modes of remembrance that are not just historicist but also forward-looking. They illustrate the potential in diverse practices of remembrance to move beyond ethno-nationalist discourses of victimhood and, with the help of artists among others (Baronian, Rigney, in this volume), provide spaces for "imagining things otherwise" (see Esche 2004) as well as resources for alternative figurations of agency and political aspirations. Non-nostalgic modes of remembrance can indeed provide avenues to democratic and emancipatory politics (see Gutman et al. 2010), hence helping put some of the future back into memory (called for by, e.g., Huyssen 2010). Several contributions to the volume thus point towards memories' ability to speak to the future, to their quality of containing *in nuce* a hint of a different condition. As Astrid Erll here suggests, it may ultimately be their future-oriented, agentive quality that makes them travel across borders.

By inviting specialists with expertise pertaining to different geographical areas, we hope to keep open a perspective on geo-political diversity in memory cultures, and on the variety of transnational pathways that are being used alongside globalized icons and modes of remembrance. Exhaustiveness was not possible, and given our own location, there is a certain provincial bias towards European themes, which is reinforced by the Euro-centered character of much work in memory studies. However, in line with our theoretical approach, the 'Europe' discussed in several contributions is marked by blurred, shifting boundaries and ramifying worldwide connections but also, crucially, by the ways in which it is constituted by its alleged 'others.' We are hopeful that the particular combination of approaches and topics will work together fruitfully to open up new lines of inquiry and conceptualization that can travel beyond their original contexts.

References

Amelina, Anna, Thomas Faist, Nina Glick Schiller and Devrimsel D. Nergiz. "Methodological Predicaments of Cross-Border Studies." *Beyond Methodological Nationalism*. Eds. Anna Amelina, Devrimsel D. Nergiz, Thomas Faist, and Nina Glick Schiller. New York: Routledge, 2012. 1–20.
Anderson, Benedict. *Imagined Communities: Reflections on the Origins and Spread of Nationalism*. 1983. London: Verso, 1991.
Anderson, Benedict. "Exodus." *Critical Inquiry* 20.2 (1994): 314–327.
Assmann, Jan. "Collective Memory and Cultural Identity." *New German Critique* 65 (1995): 125–133.
Assmann, Aleida, and Sebastian Conrad, eds. *Memory in a Global Age: Discourses, Practices and Trajectories*. London: Palgrave Macmillan, 2010.
Balibar, Étienne. *We, the People of Europe? Reflections on Transnational Citizenship*. Trans. James Swenson. Princeton: Princeton UP, 2004.
Basch, Linda, Nina Glick Schiller and Cristina Szanton Blanc. *Nations Unbound: Transnational Projects, Postcolonial Predicaments and Deterritorialized Nation-States*. Amsterdam: Gordon and Breach Science Publishers, 1994.
Beck, Ulrich. "The Cosmopolitan Perspective: Sociology of the Second Age of Modernity." *British Journal of Sociology* 51.1 (2000): 79–105.
Beck, Ulrich, Daniel Levy, and Natan Sznaider. "Cosmopolitanization of Memory: The Politics of Forgiveness and Restitution." *Cosmopolitanism in Practice*. Eds. Magdalena Nowicka and Maria Rovisco. London: Ashgate, 2009. 111–127.
Boyarin, Jonathan, ed. *Remapping Memory: The Politics of TimeSpace*. Minneapolis: University of Minnesota Press, 1994.
Butler, Judith. *Frames of War: When is Life Grievable?* London: Verso, 2009.
Creet, Julia and Andreas Kitzmann. *Memory and Migration: Multidisciplinary Approaches to Memory Studies*. Toronto: University of Toronto Press, 2011.
Crownshaw, Rick, ed. *Transcultural Memory*. Special Issue *Parallax* 17.4 (2011).
De Cesari, Chiara. "Creative Heritage: Palestinian Heritage NGOs and Defiant Arts of Government." *American Anthropologist* 112.4 (2010): 625–637.
De Cesari, Chiara. "Anticipatory Representation: Building the Palestinian Nation(-State) through Artistic Performance." *Studies in Ethnicity and Nationalism* 12.1 (2012a): 82–100.
De Cesari, Chiara. "The Paradoxes of Colonial Reparation: Foreclosing Memory and the 2008 Italy-Libya Friendship Treaty." *Memory Studies* 5.3 (2012b): 316–326.
Erll, Astrid. "Travelling Memory." *Transcultural Memory*. Ed. Rick Crownshaw. Special Issue *Parallax* 17.4 (2011): 4–18.
Erll, Astrid, and Ann Rigney, eds. *Mediation, Remediation, and the Dynamics of Cultural Memory*. Berlin: De Gruyter, 2009.
Esche, Charles. "What's the Point of Art Centres Anyway? Possibility, Art and Democratic Deviance." *Republic Art*, April 2004. Available at: www.republicart.net/disc/institution/esche01_en.htm (accessed 8 March 2013).

Fassin, Didier and Richard Rechtman. *The Empire of Trauma: Inquiry into the Condition of Victimhood*. Trans. Rachel Gomme. Princeton: Princeton UP, 2009.

Ferguson, James. "Power Topographies." *A Companion to the Anthropology of Politics*. Eds. David Nugent and Joan Vincent. Oxford: Blackwell, 2004.

Ferguson, James and Akhil Gupta. "Spatializing States: Toward an Ethnography of Neoliberal Governmentality." *American Ethnologist* 29.4 (2002): 981–1002.

Fraser, Nancy. "Transnationalizing the Public Sphere: On the Legitimacy and Efficacy of Public Opinion in a Post-Westphalian World." *Theory, Culture & Society* 24.4 (2007): 7–30.

Garde-Hansen, Joanne, Andrew Hoskins, and Anna Reading, eds. *Save As … Digital Memories*. London: Palgrave Macmillan, 2009.

Gillis, John R., ed. *Commemorations: The Politics of National Identity*. Princeton: Princeton UP, 1994.

Gilroy, Paul. *After Empire: Multiculture or Postcolonial Melancholia*. London: Routledge, 2004.

Glick Schiller, Nina. "Transnationality, Migrants and Cities: A Comparative Approach." *Beyond Methodological Nationalism*. Eds. Anna Amelina, Devrimsel D. Nergiz, Thomas Faist, and Nina Glick Schiller. New York: Routledge, 2012. 23–40.

Gluck, Carol, and Anna Lowenhaupt Tsing, eds. *Words in Motion: Toward a Global Lexicon*. Durham: Duke UP, 2009.

Gluck, Carol. "Words in Motion." *Words in Motion: Toward a Global Lexicon*. Eds. Carol Gluck and Anna Lowenhaupt Tsing. Durham: Duke UP, 2009. 3–10.

Glynn, Irial and J. Olaf Kleist, eds. *History, Memory and Migration: Perceptions of the Past and the Politics of Incorporation*. London: Palgrave Macmillan, 2012.

Grossberg, Lawrence. "On *Postmodernism and Articulation*: An Interview with Stuart Hall." *Journal of Communication Inquiry* 10.2 (1986): 45–60.

Gupta, Akhil and James Ferguson. "Beyond Culture: Space, Identity, and the Politics of Difference." *Culture, Power, Place: Explorations in Critical Anthropology*. Eds. Akhil Gupta and James Ferguson. Durham: Duke UP, 1997. 33–51.

Gutman, Yifat, Adam Brown, and Amy Sodaro, eds. *Memory and the Future: Transnational Politics, Ethics and Society*. London: Palgrave Macmillan, 2010.

Halbwachs, Maurice. *Les cadres sociaux de la mémoire*. 1925. Paris: Albin Michel, 1994.

Hirsch, Marianne, and Nancy K. Miller, eds. *Rites of Return: Diaspora Poetics and the Politics of Memory*. New York: Columbia UP, 2011.

Hoskins, Andrew. "Media, Memory, Metaphor: Remembering and the Connective Turn." *Transcultural Memory*. Ed. Rick Crownshaw. Special Issue *Parallax* 17.4 (2011): 19–31.

Huyssen, Andreas. "Present Pasts: Media, Politics, Amnesia." *Public Culture* 12.1 (2000): 21–38.

Hobsbawm, Eric and Terence Ranger, eds. *The Invention of Tradition*. Cambridge: Cambridge UP, 1983.

Insin, Engin F. *Citizens without Frontiers*. London: Continuum, 2012.

Jansen, Stef and Staffan Löfving. "Introduction: Towards an Anthropology of Violence, Hope and the Movement of People." *Struggles for Home: Violence, Hope and the Movement of People*. Eds. Stef Jansen and Staffan Löfving. London: Berghahn Books, 2009.

Jenkins, Henry. *Convergence Culture: Where Old and New Media Collide*. New York: New York UP, 2006.

Levitt, Peggy and Sanjeev Khagram. "Constructing Transnational Studies: An Overview." *The Transnational Studies Reader: Intersections and Innovations*. Eds. Sanjeev Khagram and Peggy Levitt. London: Routledge, 2008. 1–18.

Khalili, Laleh. "Virtual Nation: Palestinian Cyberculture in Lebanese Camps. " *Palestine, Israel, and the Politics of Popular Culture.* Eds. Rebecca L. Stein and Ted Swedenburg. Durham: Duke UP, 2005. 126–149.

Kuntsman, Adi. "Webs of Hate in Diasporic Cyberspaces: The Gaza War in the Russian-language Blogosphere." *Media, War and Conflict* 3.3 (2010): 299–313.

Kuntsman, Adi and Rebecca L. Stein. "Digital Suspicion, Politics, and the Middle East." *Critical Inquiry*, 2011. Available at criticalinquiry.uchicago.edu/digital_suspicion_politics_and_the_middle_east (accessed 8 March 2013).

Landsberg, Alison. *Prosthetic Memory: The Transformation of American Remembrance in the Age of Mass Culture.* New York: Columbia UP, 2004.

Leerssen, Joep. "Nationalism and the Cultivation of Culture." *Nations and Nationalism* 12.4 (2006): 559–578.

Leerssen, Joep. "Viral Nationalism: Romantic Intellectuals on the Move in Nineteenth-Century Europe." *Nations and Nationalism* 17.2 (2011): 257–271.

Leerssen, Joep and Ann Rigney, eds. *Commemorating Writers in Nineteenth-Century Europe: Nation-Building and Centenary Fever.* London: Palgrave Macmillan, 2014.

Levy, Daniel, and Natan Sznaider. "Memory Unbound: The Holocaust and the Formation of Cosmopolitan Memory." *European Journal of Social Theory* 5.1 (2002): 87–106.

Levy, Daniel, and Natan Sznaider. *The Holocaust and Memory in the Global Age.* Trans. Assenka Oksiloff. Philadelphia: Temple UP, 2006.

Levy, Daniel, and Natan Sznaider. *Human Rights and Memory.* University Park: Pennsylvania State UP, 2010.

Margalit, Avishai. *The Ethics of Memory.* Cambridge: Harvard UP, 2002.

Merry, Sally Engle. "Transnational Human Rights and Local Activism: Mapping the Middle." *American Anthropologist. New Series* 108.1 (2006): 38–51.

Mouffe, Chantal. *On the Political (Thinking in Action).* Abingdon: Routledge, 2005.

Nora, Pierre, ed. *Les lieux de mémoire.* 3 vols. 1984–1992. Paris: Gallimard, 1997.

Olick, Jeffrey K. "The Politics of Regret: Analytical Frames." *The Politics of Regret.* New York: Routledge, 2007. 121–138.

Olick, Jeffrey K. "Afterword." *Memory and the Future: Transnational Politics, Ethics and Society.* Eds. Yifat Gutman, Adam Brown, and Amy Sodaro. London: Palgrave Macmillan, 2010. 209–213.

Olick, Jeffrey K., Vered Vinitzky-Seroussi and Daniel Levy, eds. *The Collective Memory Reader.* Oxford: Oxford UP, 2011.

Pratt, Geraldine and Victoria Rosner, eds. *The Global and the Intimate: Feminism in Our Time.* New York: Columbia UP, 2012.

Quayson, Ato, and Girish Daswani, eds. *A Companion to Diaspora and Transnationalism.* Oxford: Wiley-Blackwell, 2013.

Renan, Ernest. "Qu'est-ce qu'une nation?" 1882. *Oeuvres complètes d'Ernest Renan.* Ed. Henriëtte Psichari. Paris: Calmann-Lévy, 1947–1961. 886–907.

Rigney, Ann. "Plenitude, Scarcity and the Circulation of Cultural Memory." *Journal of European Studies* 35.1 (2005): 209–226.

Rigney, Ann. *The Afterlives of Walter Scott: Memory on the Move.* Oxford: Oxford UP. 2012.

Rothberg, Michael. *Multidirectional Memory: Remembering the Holocaust in the Age of Decolonization.* Stanford: Stanford UP, 2009.

Rothberg, Michael. "Introduction: Between Memory and Memory: From *Lieux de mémoire* to *Noeuds de mémoire.*" *Yale French Studies* 118/119 (2010): 3–12.

Rothberg, Michael. "From Gaza to Warsaw: Mapping Multidirectional Memory." *Criticism* 53.4 (2011): 523–548.

Rothberg, Michael and Yasemin Yildiz. "Memory Citizenship: Migrant Archives of Holocaust Remembrance in Contemporary Germany." *Transcultural Memory*. Ed. Rick Crownshaw. Special Issue *Parallax* 17.4 (2011): 32–48.

Rothberg, Michael. "Implicated Subjects." Utrecht University. June 2013. Lecture.

Rutten, Ellen and Vera Zvereva. "Introduction: Old Conflict, New Media: Post-Socialist Digital Memories." *Memory, Conflict and New Media: Web Wars in Post-Socialist States*. Eds. Ellen Rutten, Julie Fedor and Vera Zvereva. London: Routledge, 2013. 1–17.

Stoler, Ann Laura. "Colonial Aphasia: Race and Disabled Histories in France." *Public Culture* 23.1 (2011): 121–156.

Tsing, Anna. "The Global Situation." *Cultural Anthropology* 15.3 (2000): 327–360.

Tsing, Anna Lowenhaupt. *Friction: An Ethnography of Global Connection*. Princeton: Princeton UP, 2005.

Vertovec, Steven. *Transnationalism*. London: Routledge, 2009.

Warner, Michael. "Publics and Counterpublics." *Public Culture* 14.1 (2002): 49–90.

Wimmer, Andreas and Nina Glick Schiller. "Methodological Nationalism and Beyond: Nation-State Building, Migration and the Social Sciences." *Global Networks* 2.4 (2002): 301–334.

Wood, Nancy. *Vectors of Memory: Legacies of Trauma in Postwar Europe*. Oxford: Berg, 1999.

Part I: **Circulation**

Astrid Erll

From 'District Six' to *District 9* and Back: The Plurimedial Production of Travelling Schemata

Aliens in Johannesburg: 'District Six' in international cinemas

In the year 1982, an alien spaceship appears over the South African city of Johannesburg. The extra-terrestrials are in a state of utter destitution, many of them dead, sick, or malnourished, and obviously unable to find their way home again.[1] A camp is set up for these aliens just outside Johannesburg: District 9. In the decades that follow, the camp deteriorates into a slum area, ripe with violence, drug-abuse and inter-species prostitution. Because of their crustacean-like appearance, the aliens are derogatorily called 'prawns,' and all humans in Johannesburg seem to agree that "the prawns must go." In 2010, the South African government decides on a relocation scheme and contracts Multi-National United (MNU), a private company mainly interested in alien weaponry, to transfer the aliens into a new camp at a safe 200 kilometers' distance from the city. Wikus van de Merwe (Sharlto Copley), a simple Afrikaner clerk at MNU, is to lead this operation, assisted by a brutal armed force, but he fails; while handing out eviction notices to the inhabitants of District 9, he accidentally touches a spray with alien DNA, mutates into an alien, is hunted by his own government, finds refuge in District 9, and learns to sympathize with the outcasts whom he finally helps to escape in their spaceship.

This is the story of *District 9*, an alien movie directed by the South African filmmaker Neill Blomkamp and produced by Peter Jackson. It came out in 2009, to great international acclaim. The movie starts as a mock-documentary, combining fictional interviews, television news footage, and videos from surveillance cameras (see Figure 4). This fictive footage, all edited at a rapid pace, reconstructs

---

1 I had the opportunity to present this piece at the universities of Utrecht, Tübingen and Frankfurt, and I am grateful for all critical comments and suggestions I received. My special thanks go to my colleague Frank Schulze-Engler for his generosity in sharing his knowledge of Africa with me.

Fig. 1. The alien spaceship over Johannesburg; screenshot, *District 9* (dir. N. Blomkamp, 2009).

Fig. 2. District 9 (shot on location in Chiawelo, Johannesburg); screenshot, *District 9* (dir. N. Blomkamp, 2009).

from the vantage point of a near future the fictional history of aliens in Johannesburg since 1982 and provides 'evidence' of Wikus van de Merwe's actions and whereabouts up to the point at which he disappears off the radars of MNU and the South African government into District 9. Halfway through the movie, the mock-documentary mode changes into a conventional cinematic narrative. Wikus' unrecorded further fate, his transformation into an alien, is represented much in the style of alien movies from the 1980s.

   District 9, the alien movie set in Johannesburg, does something that seems worth drawing attention to in a collection on transnational memory, which has to do with the obvious reference, in the movie's title, to Cape Town's District Six.

With its focus on a government scheme that aims at moving aliens dwelling in an inner-city slum area to an internment camp outside the city, the movie clearly refers to the history of apartheid and the ways in which it was acted out in South African cities. In enormous relocation schemes, the country's less-privileged people, mostly 'black' and 'colored,' were forcibly moved from inner city compounds to townships at the fringes of the cities.

In a science fiction setting and an allegorical framework, the movie re-enacts the violent history of apartheid, which, although it belongs to the past now, has permanently shaped the face of South African cities. It does so by substituting a present-day story about speciesism for South Africa's history of racism: humans of all races fight against the aliens.² While in postcolonial studies, there has been work on how alien movies, from *Alien Nation* (1988) to *Independence Day* (1996), address, articulate, and reframe ideas and anxieties about race (see, for example, Sardar and Cubitt 2002) and it would certainly be interesting to study how this tried and tested allegorical pattern is transformed in *District 9* – which leaves the spectator feeling utterly alienated by the violence and mercilessness of the human beings – the main aim of this chapter is to address a somewhat different question. If a contemporary alien movie is set in Johannesburg, if it half-mockingly, half-critically refers to segregation as it was practiced in South Africa, if it shows the inhumanity of an apartheid-legislation that enables forced removals, if, in fact, the movie is shot on location in a part of Soweto, the squatter camp of Chiawelo – why is such a movie not called 'Aliens in Soweto,' or, for that matter, 'Aliens in Sophiatown,' thus referring to the inner-city districts and townships that actually belong to the city of Johannesburg and its apartheid-history? Why 'District 9'?

It seems that, rather than Sophiatown or Soweto, it is Cape Town's District Six, which has, over the past two decades or so, been turned into a powerful transnationally available schema to draw on when it comes to giving form to issues of racism, segregation, victimization, and the forced removal of people from their original place.

According to cognitive psychology, schemata are patterns and structures of knowledge on the basis of which we make assumptions regarding specific objects, people, situations and the relation between them. Schemata reduce real-

---

2 In this fictional fight, those acquainted with South Africa's history of apartheid will find many ironic echoes: an interviewee's wish to kill all aliens with a 'selective virus;' Wikus' wholesale promotion of abortion in District 9 (once a fantasy of radical white Afrikaners); the ubiquitous boards prescribing segregation (see Figure 3); the MNU's hypocritical justification for evicting aliens on humanitarian grounds; the fact that the alien language features clicking sounds, which are also typical of Bantu languages, spoken, for example, by the Xhosa people who were victims of South African apartheid.

Fig. 3. Apartheid between humans and aliens; screenshot, *District 9* (dir. N. Blomkamp, 2009).

world complexity and guide perception and remembering. As Frederic Bartlett already showed in his *Remembering*, schemata are always culture-specific (Bartlett 1932) and emerge from socially shared knowledge systems. In our age of global media cultures and transnational migration, the circles, or social frameworks (Halbwachs 1925), of this sharing are ever expanding. With migrants and mass media as their carriers, cultural schemata are set to 'travel' and may thus acquire transnational and transcultural dimensions (see Erll 2011b). They appear and are used in different local contexts across the world. In the form of travelling schemata, patterns of knowledge cut across boundaries of language, cultural communities, or nations.[3]

In order to describe the transnational dynamics of remembering connected with 'District Six,' I will, in the following, distinguish between two categories of schemata: visual schemata (icons), which are the result of iconization, and story-schemata (narratives), which are the result of topicalization and narrativization. The focus will be on the medial – more precisely: plurimedial – production of key icons and narratives about District Six. The goal is to understand how the 'District Six'-schema has been set to travel: from Cape Town to Johannesburg, from South

[3] The transnational and transcultural dynamics of memory has been studied by memory scholars in recent years, most notably by Levy and Sznaider (2001), Huyssen (2003), Rothberg (2009), and Crownshaw (2011). What their different approaches, despite different accentuations, have in common is that they make it possible for memory studies to move beyond methodological nationalism and notions of bounded culture.

Fig. 4. Forced removals viewed form surveillance cameras; screenshot, *District 9* (dir. N. Blomkamp, 2009).

Africa to worldwide cinemas, from the serious, and violent, history of apartheid to the half-mocking imagination of an alternative alien present.[4]

District Six and the history of South African apartheid

When the apartheid regime came into power in South Africa in 1948, an array of new laws was introduced. The Prohibition of Mixed Marriages Act of 1949 put a ban on marriages between white people and people of other races. The Immorality Amendment Act of 1950 prohibited extra-marital sexual relationships between white and black people. The Population Registration Act of 1950 meant that every person's race was classified and recorded in a national register. This register knew

---

4 District Six can of course also be understood as a *lieu de mémoire*, a site of memory in Pierre Nora's sense. With my focus on the district as a schema, however, I want to highlight the medializations of District Six, the importance of cognitive processes for collective memory, and the insight that contents of memory can be set to travel only once they have been transformed into highly condensed patterns – which have been variously conceptualized in memory studies as schemata, symbols, narrative abbreviations, memory figures, or pathos formulas (see Erll 2011a, 146).

the categories of four racial groups: 'native,' 'white,' 'colored,' and 'Asian.' The Group Areas Act of 1950 put all these forms of segregation into spatial practice. It created apartheid within the city itself, segregating people of different 'races' into different urban spaces.

The aim of the Group Areas Act was to exclude non-whites from living in the most developed and attractive urban areas. They were forcibly removed from their neighborhoods and dumped in townships which were often far away from the city centers. Cape Town's District Six was declared a 'white area' under the Group areas Act in 1966. In 1968, the forced removals started. The district's inhabitants were relocated in the Cape Flats township complex, in an until then uninhabited flat and sandy area more than twenty kilometers south-east of Cape Town often called 'the dumping ground of apartheid.' The forced removals stretched over a period of more than fifteen years. In the end, with the exception of some places of worship, all of the old houses were bulldozed. Even today, District Six is an empty space within the city. Ironically, the district was never 'redeveloped' into a white area. In the 1980s, the Hands Off District Six Campaign was formed and exerted strong pressure on the government. In 1994, with the end of apartheid, the National Congress recognized the claims of former residents and started to organize their return, which, however, is still in process.[5]

The specificity of District Six is that it was a multi-ethnic quarter with a long history. Already in the late nineteenth century it was a mixed community of former slaves, immigrants, merchants and artisans. Many so-called 'Cape Malays,' descendants of people who were brought from Malaysia to South Africa by the Dutch East India Company in the seventeenth century, had settled in the area. Next to them lived Xhosa people, Indians, and, in less large groups, Afrikaners, white people of British descent, and Jews. District Six, in short, featured almost all of the ethnic communities living in that part of South Africa at that time.[6]

In the 1960s, according to the South African government, District Six had deteriorated into a slum area which had to be cleared. The government portrayed the district as a dangerous place, full of crime, gambling, drinking, and prostitution. This may have been true (the stories by Alex La Guma, for example, suggest that District Six was certainly not a convent), but for the government – with its obsession with racial purity and segregation – the 'mixedness' of District Six seems to have been the greatest outrage. Furthermore, the area's location near the city cen-

---

5 For an extensive social history of Cape Town, see van Heyningen, Worden and Bickford-Smith (1999); on memories of apartheid and forced removals in Cape Town, see Field, Meyer and Swanson (2007); on the Hands Off District Six Campaign, see Jeppie and Crain (1990).
6 On the urbanism of District Six and its long history, see Pistorius et al. (2002).

tre, Table Mountain, and the harbor meant that District Six could be turned into a valuable residential area for rich white people.

Mediations of 'District Six'

How, then, did District Six turn from such a specific historical place into a travelling schema? The clue is mediation. This can already be sensed in the prime site of District Six remembrance, the District Six Museum, which was founded in 1994 and is located in the District's Central Methodist Church in Buitenkant Street, a former "sanctuary for political opponents and victims of apartheid" (Coombes 2003, 126).[7] Using the terms introduced by Jay David Bolter and Richard Grusin in their theory of remediation (1999), the District Six Museum can be said to bring back the disappeared quarter by means of hypermediation. Dating from its inaugural exhibition in 1994, *Streets: Retracing District Six*, its ground floor is covered with the painting of a large street map of District Six. There are columns of original street signs from the old district and large-scale photographic portraits of well-known former residents. The museum collection features more than 8,500 photographs of District Six and its families. It provides audio-visual material and oral history recordings. In 2000, the exhibition *Digging Deeper* created soundscapes out of the voices of ex-residents.[8] Some of these various media of cultural memory are also available online on the museum's webpage, including a virtual walk through the district.

Arguably, the museum has become such a powerful site of memory because it connects these manifold mediations with various forms of social performance. This social embeddedness can be traced back to the museum's origins in the

---

7 In 1989, the District Six Museum Foundation emerged from the Hands Off District Six Campaign. For a history of the museum, see Rassool and Prosalendis (2001). For a discussion of its uses of media and memory, see the chapter "District Six: The Archeology of Memory" in Coombes (2003) and the chapter "Working With Memory: The District Six Museum in the New South Africa" in McEachern (2002). On memory, space and identity in Cape Town, see Murray, Shepherd and Hall (2007).

8 See Rassool (2006, 15). See also the description of *Digging Deeper* and its multi-mediacy on the Museum's webpage: "The form of the exhibition is both multi-media and interdisciplinary, combining simple direct techniques (the immediacy of material, hand-mixed color and hand-generated processes), with documentary, digital, and sound elements, digital and sound elements. The voices of narrators and transcribed life histories of ex-residents are the major resource and departure point for the choice of exhibition themes" (www.districtsix.co.za/, accessed 18 May 2012).

Hands Off District Six Campaign, and is still testified to today in the museum's self-description as a "a living memorial" with an archive that is "a living organism,"[9] and by its strong reliance on visitors' and ex-residents' active participation as well as its emphasis on being a "community museum."[10] According to the historian Ciraj Rassool, one of the museum's trustees and most prolific scholars, the District Six Museum can thus be described as "a hybrid space," which combines "scholarship, research, collection and museum aesthetics with community forms of governance and accountability, and land claim politics of representation and restitution" (Rassool 2006, 15). By offering a rich texture of medial representations, material traces of the past, and their various social uses, the museum (hyper-)mediates the district's history and seems to recreate the real to the extent that "soon after its creation, many visitors began to refer to the museum simply as 'District Six'." The site of the district's memorialization and commemoration, "had to perform the work of satisfying the desire for the real" (Rassool 2006, 13).

But also beyond this particular museum, there is a long history of District Six mediations. In painting, for example, artists such as John Dronsfield, Gregoire Boonzaier, Gerard Sekoto and Kenneth Baker, have captured versions of life in the district. Professional photographers, such as Cloete Breytenbach, Jillian Edelstein, Paul Grendon, Jan Greshoff, George Hallett, Jackie Heyns, Jimi Matthews, and Jansje Wissema, have substantially shaped the imagination of District Six. Various forms of entertainment also play a key role in the memory of District Six: Hybrid Cape Jazz, for example, can be understood as a medial self-expression of the district's creole realities. A District Six musical was produced by David Kramer and Taliep Petersen in 1986. Short films about District Six, such as Lindy Wilson's documentary *Last Supper at Horstley Street* (1983) and Yunus Ahmed's *Dear Grandfather, Your Right Foot is Missing* (1984) represent the time during and after the forced removals and their impact on resident families.[11]

Literature has had its share in the representation of District Six memories, too; poetry on the topic was written by James Matthews, Adam Small, Dollar Brand (Abdullah Ibrahim), and Cosmo Pieterse. Peter Abraham's *Path of Thunder* (1948) is arguably (Rive 1990, 113) the earliest published novel about District

---

9 www.districtsix.co.za/ (accessed 18 May 2012).

10 "The museum's use of 'community' is not naive, but conscious and strategic. The museum insists on utilizing this concept as an organizational device, in asserting a particular politics of governance and institutional orientation, and in expressing a particular commitment to social mobilization, and to constructing and defending independent spaces of articulation and contestation in the public domain" (Rassool 2006, 17).

11 For more extensive accounts of representations of District Six, see Richard Rive's essay "District Six: Fact and Fiction" (1990) as well as McCormick (2002, 202–206).

Six. The most famous works, however, emerged from the authors of the *Quartet* group,[12] most notably Alex La Guma's detective story *A Walk in the Night* (1962) and Richard Rive's fictional communal biography of the forced removals in *Buckingham Palace, District Six* (1986). In *Waiting for Leila* (1981), Achmat Dangor tells a love story against the backdrop of the district's destruction. More recently, different forms of life writing about District Six, often collective memoirs of families and communities, have gained critical attention.[13]

Plurimedial constellations

The above-mentioned representations of District Six together constitute a rich medial network, or what I call a 'plurimedial constellation of memory.'[14] The term emphasizes that it is never one single medium which 'makes' a memory schema, but a complex constellations of different media, which may refer to, imitate, or comment upon another. An integral part of such constellations is the social dimension: media of memory can only have an effect through their social performance, the way they are produced, received, discussed, and handed on.

According to this model, I imagine the movie *District 9* as one of the most recent additions to the plurimedial constellation which creates and constantly redefines the memory of 'District Six'– a constellation which is not only made up of different media, produced and received at different times, and of the social practices connected to them, but is increasingly transnational in its scope. Worldwide political discussions about apartheid, the international news coverage of the transition, and the promotion of truth and reconciliation in South Africa, as well as the far-reaching media attention to the new ideal of the 'Rainbow Nation,' which gained added momentum during the 2010 FIFA World Cup, have provided a medial framework within which representations of the memories of specific locales,

---

12 Alex La Guma, James Matthews, Richard Rive and Alf Wannenburgh, whose short stories were collected and edited by Richard Rive in *Quartet: New Voices from South Africa* (New York: Crown Publishers 1963) and immediately banned by the apartheid government.

13 For example, Hettie Adams's and Hermione Suttner's *Williams Street District Six* (1988), Andrina Dashwood-Forbes *Birds on a Ledge* (1992), Linda Fortune's *The House in Tyne Street: Childhood Memories of District Six* (1996), Nomvuyo Ngcelwane's *Sala Kahle District Six: An African Woman's Perspective* (1998), and Noor Ebrahim's *Noor's Story: My Life in District Six* (1999); see McCormick (2002, 203f.).

14 This term has first been worked out by the contributors to a volume on film and memory (Erll and Wodianka 2008); see also Erll (2011a, 138).

such as that of 'District Six,' can be received and understood in mnemonic communities across the globe.

As they illustrate the important role that literary representations have played in the creation of 'District Six' as a travelling schema, the following two examples serve to show how plurimedial networks extend into a transnational space. Firstly, in the 1990s, South African poet and novelist Tatamkhulu Afrika, a former District Six-resident, ANC member and political prisoner under the apartheid regime, wrote the poem "Nothing's Changed" about his return to District Six after the end of apartheid, only to find that segregation and the unequal distribution of wealth were still in place: "new, up-market, / haute cuisine, / guard at the gatepost, / whites only inn." The poem ends with the return of anger when the speaker realizes that "nothing's changed:" "I back from the glass, / boy again, / leaving small mean O / of small mean mouth. / Hands burn/ for a stone, a bomb, / to shiver down the glass. / Nothing's changed" (Afrika 1994, 33–4).

In the United Kingdom, this poem is part of the GCSE English syllabus. It was included in 2009 under the topic of "poems from different cultures."[15] British youngsters from all over the country study this piece for their exams. This is a striking example of some of the processes typically involved in the generation of travelling schemata: the production of powerful media representations, their movement or transportation across the globe, and their social use in new local contexts. The case of "Nothing's Changed" raises the question of what it is that actually constitutes a transportable impact-medium. Although there are no general properties which make some media more memorable, moveable, usable, or effectual than others, in the case of Tatamkhulu Afrika's poem, major factors seem to be that it offers a concise and rather easily 'translatable' representation of 'District Six,' both in terms of the linguistic register and the experience evoked; that it allows for authenticity to be ascribed to the poem by readers who are acquainted with its author's life; and the fact that the reading and discussion of the poem have been firmly and strategically institutionalized in the educational sector.[16] Indeed, alongside the patterns of attention that are generated through global mass media and the new media, 'old' mnemonic strategies, such as the formation of canons

---

15 See www.teachit.co.uk/armoore/anthology/differentcultures.htm (accessed 17 March 2014).
16 Sally E. Merry's observation that "[a]s ideas from transnational sources travel to small communities, they are typically vernacularized, or adapted to local institutions and meaning" also works the other way around (2006, 39); as ideas or memories emerge from a local context and enter the transnational arena, they are remade for transnational audiences – *transnationalized* – translated from local specificities into languages and practices that render those memories widely intelligible and relevant, so that the work of vernacularization can commence in new local contexts.

and syllabi, are still a major factor in the movement of memory across time and space.

A second example is the short story collection *Rosa's District 6* (2004) by Rozena Maart, a South African writer living in Canada. On the one hand, these short stories are part of a growing body of South African memory literature;[17] on the other hand, they testify to the increasing importance of literary remembrance that emerges in contexts of migration. Diasporic writers may become carriers as well as mediators of transnational memory.[18] That this role is recognized and fostered in at least some parts of the world is shown by the fact that the collection's first story, "No Rosa, No District Six," originally published in 1991, won the Canadian *Journey Prize* in 1992. Such awards exemplify the strategic social uses of media of memory. They are a way of steering the economy of attention, by highlighting one topic of memory and not another.[19]

Iconization: Cloete Breyetenbach's *The Spirit of District Six*

The idea of plurimedial constellations implies that representations of memory are in many ways interconnected through forms of cross-reference and thus gain visibility and strength in international arenas of remembrance. Interestingly, Rozena Maart's collection participates in this mnemonic cross-referencing in the way in which the book's cover is fashioned. It features one of Cloete Breytenbach's famous photographs of District Six ("Seven Steps," see Figure 5). Breytenbach (b. 1933) is a South African news photographer who worked, among others, for *Life Magazine*, the *Daily Telegraph* and *Bunte*, and covered events in Africa, Europe, the US, Vietnam, and Israel. His photographs of District Six were taken over a period of more than a decade, from 1959 to 1970.[20] His "District Six Collection" was

---

17 For accounts of contemporary forms of literary memory in South Africa, see Nuttall and Coetzee (1998); Nuttall (2009).

18 On diaspora and cultural memory, see Baronian et al. (2007) and Hirsch and Miller (2011).

19 Clearly, these types of promotion as well as the above-mentioned forms of institutionalization and canonization are key components of a power dynamic that makes certain memories travel and not others. As my examples show, much of the power of selecting and highlighting items of memory still resides on the national level, thus giving evidence of the significance of national boundaries and frameworks in the dynamic of transnational memory as it is outlined in the introduction to this volume.

20 Personal correspondence with Cloete Breytenbach (18 May 2012).

Fig. 5. "Seven Steps;" Cloete Breytenbach, *The Spirit of District Six* (1970); reproduced with permission.

published as a book in 1970, under the title *The Spirit of District Six* (Cape Town: Purnell), with an accompanying text by Brian Barrow. This book has since seen six editions.

With the choice of one of Breytenbach's photographs as an illustration of her literary memories of District Six, Rozena Maart's collection clearly takes part in a larger, and indeed transnational, trend. In fact, it seems that today, almost no representation of District Six can work without using this body of iconic images. Other examples of this phenomenon include the new edition of Alex La Guma's *A Walk in The Night* in the Trent Editions (2006), whose cover features Breytenbach's "Tram Ride" (see Figure 6). The cover of Richard Rive's *Buckingham Palace: District Six*, in the new edition of the German Cornelsen Senior English Library of 2006, shows Breytenbach's image of "Richmond Street" (see Figure 7) – while the novel's original edition of 1986 (Cape Town: David Philip Publishers) had displayed a water-color linocut by the South African painter Gregoire Boonzaier ("District 6," 1978), presumably a then-iconic representation of life in the district.

It seems as if Breytenbach's photographic collection has become a nodal point in the plurimedial constellation constituting 'District Six' as a memory schema.

Fig. 6. "Tram Ride;" Cloete Breytenbach, *The Spirit of District Six* (1970); reproduced with permission.

The images' tremendous, virtually worldwide significance as media of memory appears to have been established in the late 1980s, perhaps with the reissuing of the 1970 collection in 1987 and 1997, which coincided with the international attention to the Hands Off District Six Campaign and the end of apartheid. Another important factor are international exhibition tours, in the course of which these photographs have travelled from Cape Town to Europe, Asia, and the United States.[21]

Breytenbach's photos have thus played a crucial role in the iconization and international circulation of the history of District Six, and its meaning within cultural memory. These images appear whenever a concise impression of past life in the district is required; they 'travel' and materialize in intermedial combination with life writing, novels, and scholarly articles alike.[22] To study iconization as a

---

21 To the question whether he has found increased attention to his collection in recent years, Cloete Breytenbach replies: "There are increasing requests from TV producers, media publications etc. worldwide, for the use of images from the collection" (personal correspondence, 18 May 2012).

22 For example, Breytenbach's "Tram Ride" and other photographs can be found in Ciraj Rassool's academic article "Making the District Six Museum in Cape Town" (2006). It seems that the historian Rassool uses them here not so much as historical sources in a strict sense, but as a

Fig. 7. "Richmond Street;" Cloete Breytenbach, *The Spirit of District Six* (1970); reproduced with permission.

process of transnational memory, I draw on a definition recently proposed by the
sociologist and memory scholar Claus Leggewie:

> Iconization is an exaggerated form of visualization. An issue or process is represented in
> a particularly concise and sustained manner, and possibly surrounded with an aura. This
> is what the origin of the term 'icon' suggests: an icon used to be a transportable cult im-
> age showing biblical scenes … The *iconability* of images is enhanced by their historical sig-
> nificance, certain visual properties, and by the durable modalities of their reproduction …
> Icons mobilize collective affects, they concentrate public attention, and they shape individ-
> ual and collective memories. They have the power to do so, because they are displayed in a
> particularly intense, frequent, permanent, and widespread way, because they stand out of a
> mass of images due to their potential to be quickly recognized, and because they transgress
> social, political and cultural boundaries.[23]

'shorthand' for the richness of a past life in District Six that he wants to convey to the international
readership targeted by the journal *Museum International*.

23 Leggewie (2009, 9–10), my translation. The original is: "Ikonisierung stellt eine zugespitzte
Visualisierung dar: Ein Sachverhalt oder Vorgang wird besonders prägnant und nachhaltig
dargestellt, womöglich mit einer Aura umgeben. Darauf deutet die Herkunft des Begriffs Ikone
hin, die ursprünglich ein transportables Kultbild mit biblischen Szenen war … Zur *Ikonabil-
ität* von Bildern tragen historische Signifikanz, spezifische Bildeigenschaften und die Modal-
itäten ihrer Reproduktion bei … Ikonen mobilisieren kollektive Affekte, binden öffentliche

Cloete Breytenbach's photographs, which have come to stand for life in District Six before the forced removals, are clearly such icons in Leggewie's sense. They visualize, in a concise, memorable, and recognizable way, certain ideas about the past of District Six, for example its multiculturality and *joie de vivre* (see Figure 8). They highlight art, music, carnival, and street life as essential characteristics – or 'the spirit' – of District Six. Arguably, the quality of these black-and-white photographs creates a certain aura around past events. Having mainly been taken at the end of the Golden Fifties and in the Sixties, i.e. before the start and during the first phase of the forced removals, these photographs function for today's viewers as symbolically charged medial 'traces' of, or 'witnesses'[24] to, the district's lost past.[25] By virtue of their specific visual and contextual properties, these photographs have mobilized affects and shaped the transnational memory of District Six in a pronounced way.

Topicalization and narrativization: stories of urban futures past

While iconization is a key process of transnational memory in the field of the visual, in the realm of language, powerful ideas about the past are often crystallized into topoi – concise commonplaces, often in the form of metaphors or clichéd phrases (see Erll 2011a, 70–72). One example of such topicalization is that of District Six's 'lost multiculturality.' Contained in this topos is a story-schema that can be unfolded by narrativization. To understand these processes, it is worth looking once more at Rozena Maart's collection *Rosa's District 6*. Maart's short stories

Aufmerksamkeit und modellieren individuelle und kollektive Erinnerungen. Sie können dies, weil sie besonders intensiv, häufig, dauerhaft und breit gestreut gezeigt werden, sich damit auf Grund ihres raschen Wiedererkennungspotenzials aus einer gewaltigen Menge von Bildern herausheben und dabei auch soziale, politische und kulturelle Grenzen überschreiten."

24 I use these terms in the sense of ontological theories of photography, e.g. by Roland Barthes and Susan Sontag, whose work revolves around analogue photography's indexical relationship to the past. In memory culture, photographs are often understood as 'traces' or 'witnesses' of the past (see also Ruchatz 2010). Powerful photographs are inscribed, moreover, with a symbolic potential; they are understood to stand for, or capture the meaning of, historical events and processes.

25 This after-the-fact significance is typical for photography as a medium of memory. Accordingly, Breytenbach states that "only towards the end of my reportage of the area, by which time most of the structures in the district had been demolished, did I realize that the photographs could be of historical value" (personal correspondence, 18 May 2012).

Fig. 8. "Carnival in District Six;" Cloete Breytenbach, *The Spirit of District Six* (1970); reproduced with permission.

unfold and put into narrative form those condensed topoi and icons that have become staple elements in the imagination of District Six. In the short story "The Green Chair," for example, the reader is presented with a description that elaborates the idea of a creole past:

> Pickled fish was a traditional District Six dish that was often eaten during the year but especially on Good Friday ... Christian families attended the three-hour mass in the morning, and returned home to eat their pickled fish. Muslim families went to mosque in the morning and they too would go home to enjoy their pickled fish ... Food in District Six was not divided along religious lines. Many families kept halal homes because they had extended family that were Muslim, and eating was such an important part of District Six life, everyone wanted their friends and families to be able to eat at their homes. (Maart 2004, 16, 17)

District Six appears here as a site of happy multicultural living-together. In fact, this claim is repeated incessantly, across the spectrum of available media. Again and again, District Six is called a 'lively quarter,' a 'vibrant quarter,' a 'cosmopolitan place,' or, to quote from the text accompanying Cloete Breytenbach's photographs, "a happy, generous wonderful community" which "simply disappeared" (Breytenbach and Barrow 1997, 7).

Does this sound too good to be true? What could be the function of such a recurrent and highly schematized representation? As Sandra Prosalendis, curator of the District Six Museum, explains:

> District Six is remembered by many who had lived there as a place where they were able to cross religious, class and social boundaries. As a place where they were able to share their everyday experiences and to live not as 'colored,' 'whites,' 'Africans' or 'Indians' but as South Africans. District Six occupies a special place in the history of South Africa. (Prosalendis 1999, 141; quoted in Coombes 2003, 212)

In her pertinent study *Visual Culture and Public Memory in a Democratic South Africa* (2003, 123), Annie E. Coombes describes District Six as "a location that to all intents and purposes no longer exists in its former physical form, but that as a memory and a concept embodies all the attributes of a vibrant 'community' that refused the 'logic' of the apartheid state." But she also makes sure to emphasize that such a memory presumes "an (impossibly) harmonious and unified population prior to apartheid and possibly colonialism" (126).

It is indeed remarkable that, as Richard Rive muses, "so much attention has been focused on District Six and not on the many other similarly affected areas. What about Pageview in Johannesburg, South End in Port Elizabeth and Claremont and Simonstown in the Cape Peninsula?" (Rive 1990, 110). Rive also makes clear that District Six was not a romantic "fairyland," as a famous graffiti on one of its houses suggested, but "a ripe, raw and rotten slum. It was drab, dingy, squalid and overcrowded" (1990,111). However, it seems that, compared to other forced removals in South Africa, "this removal had more dramatic or melodramatic qualities than the others" (110), not least because "District Six had a mind and a soul of its own. It had a homogeneity that created a sense of belonging. ... It cultivated a sharp urban inclusivity, the type which cockneys have in the East End of London and black Americans in Harlem" (112). Therefore, in District Six, "there was no observable apartheid since the District was one, big apartheid" (112).

What all this suggests is that, today, 'District Six' serves as a shorthand for lost hybridity and a creole reality burgeoning in a multicultural urban space. It refers to a 'past potentiality,' to possibilities that existed in South Africa's past before the advent of apartheid, and that might have unfolded had history only turned out differently – in short, to a yearned-for urban future past.[26]

---

26 On the concept of 'futures past,' see Koselleck (1985). What, in our case, such a romanticizing vision of an urban future past tends to forget, however, is that the history of South African racism and segregation actually predates 1948. As early as 1901, after an outbreak of the bubonic plague, black South Africans were forcibly removed from District Six to Ndabeni (see Sambumbu 2010).

As a complex, over-determined memory schema which operates backwards and forwards in time, 'District Six' is highly important for today's imagination of South Africa. It implies a narrative that is both a warning *and* a promise; it explains at once what must never happen again *and* what might have been. With its nostalgic focus on what might have been (i.e. a future past), it creates a model for what might still come into being (i.e. a utopian future present). Much in this vein, ANC member Jeremy Cronin asserts that "[w]e should certainly not romanticize the pre-apartheid past of Cape Town, but neither should we lose sight of the *proto-non-racialism* that was forged unevenly in localities all about our city, as Capetonians went about their daily lives" (Cronin 2005, 49, my emphasis).

Connective schemata: Holocaust and apartheid

Travelling schemata are connective schemata.[27] Their movement across time and space enables – and is arguably enabled by – their capacity to connect with other memories. And indeed, the images and narratives associated with District Six today resonate with, enable and are enabled by discourses about lost multiculturality, racism and injustice all around the world.[28] In recent years, for example, the memory of District Six has increasingly been invoked, in South Africa and elsewhere, in critical discourses about urban gentrification.[29] Most powerfully and repeatedly, however, 'District Six' has been linked to that other "floating signifier" (Huyssen 2003, 99), the Holocaust.

The linkage between the experience of South African apartheid and German Nazism can most prominently be found in Richard Rive's well-known novel of District Six, *Buckingham Palace, District Six* (1986). It is embodied in the character of the Jewish landlord Solomon Katzen. The novel tells the story of a mixed community living in Buckingham Palace, the mock-name for a row of dilapidated houses in District Six. The narrative traces the history of the people living in those houses from the hey-day of multicultural life in District Six in the 1950s, all the way to the forced removals starting in 1968 and the final breaking-up of the community fifteen years later. Halfway through the novel, it turns out that the owner of Buck-

---

27 For a discussion of comparative and connective work in memory studies see Hirsch and Miller (2011, 8).

28 See Levy and Sznaider's (2001) work on the Holocaust as a global symbol or Michael Rothberg's studies on the multidirectionality of memory (2009).

29 See, for example, the German documentary, directed by Alexander Kleider and Daniela Michel, *Im Schatten des Tafelbergs* (When the Mountain Meets its Shadow, 2010).

ingham Palace, Solomon Katzen, is a German Jew who fled the Nazi regime. Ironically, he finds himself now in a similar constellation, only with a reversal of roles:

> It is very funny for me. In Germany they treated me as an *untermenschen*. Here they force me to be part of the *herrenvolk*. But I cannot forget what they did to us in Germany. So my heart is with all the *untermenschen*, whoever and wherever they are ... They tell me that if I want to sell my houses in the District, I can only sell them to white people. If I want to sell my business, I can only sell it to white people. If anyone moves out of any of my houses, only white people can move in. So I have decided that while this evil law remains I will never sell my houses. (Rive 2006, 139)

It has been argued that such combinations and comparisons in memory discourse obscure the historical singularity and specificity of events such as the Holocaust. However, the travels of and links between memory schemata may also create a greater visibility and understanding of injustice beyond local and national contexts (consider, for example, the significance of Rive's novel in the German schoolbook edition mentioned above) and potentially engender solidarity among victims across the world.

District 9 and back: fluidity and stability of the travelling schema

Blomkamp's *District 9* taps the resources of travelling schemata much in the way described above. The movie's tacit allusion to 'District Six' will be understood at least by parts of its international audiences, and for those viewers the actualization of the memory schema will add a semantic dimension to the film. Moreover, *District 9* uses the connective possibilities of the District Six-schema, for example, when "District 10," the place where the aliens are to be relocated, is described as a "concentration camp."

However, although the movie's title and part of its storyline clearly refer to District Six, *District 9* actually resists filling the schema according to the now widely conventionalized model. First of all, it does not describe District 9 as the site of a multicultural community harmoniously living together, but instead as home to a more or less homogeneous mass of aliens, which is 'diversified' only by a group of fierce Nigerians who are both profiting from and fighting against the extra-terrestrials. The movie does not romanticize slum dwellers. On the contrary, the aliens are shown, in their majority, to be rather witless, unruly, and violent. They seem utterly incapable of integrating into human society. Secondly, the movie's representation of District 9 seems to point not so much to a romanticized past, but more to the difficult present situation in South Africa, with its waves of immigrants and refugees like those from Zimbabwe, who have been greeted by South Africans with great distrust and xenophobic violence and put into camps much like the movie's aliens.[30] Finally, the film seems to be a comment on how the reality in South African slums such as Johannesburg's Chiawelo, where the film was shot on location and from where many extras were recruited (see Figure 2), is still drab. The South African newspaper *Global Post* comments: "In *District 9*, Chiawelo is depicted as a place so dire that it is only fit for alien refugees who landed in Johannesburg from another planet." For the inhabitants of Chiawelo, the movie thus produces the bitter "irony of living in what was shown in the movie as only habitable for aliens" (Conway-Smith 2009).

District 9 draws on the recognizability and power of the travelling schema 'District Six,' but it actualizes the schema in rather complex and at times contradictory ways. It transforms the icons and narratives conventionally connected with the schema. It creates new images and tells new stories about new challenges.[31] This, too, is a key process of memory in transnational media cultures. Instead of becoming inert by repetition, powerful travelling schemata are characterized by their ongoing transformation, by the way in which they are put to ever new uses, the way in which they enable ever new discourses and stories – ranging, in the case of 'District Six,' all the way from Richard Rive's novelistic comparison of Holocaust and histories of apartheid to the science fiction movie that comments on immigration and social tensions in present-day Johannesburg.

With this vital fluidity of the successful travelling schema, however, comes an equally important degree of stability. From Richard Rive to Neill Blomkamp, the 'District Six'-schema essentially remains a tool to tell stories of multiculturalism

---

30 Another dimension of the immigration-theme in the movie is the very unfavorable representation of Nigerian immigrants. The Nigerians dwelling in District 9 are depicted as criminals and warlords, with strong leanings towards witchcraft and cannibalism. The chief of the Nigerian gangster gang in *District 9* is called Obasanjo, a name that is certainly reminiscent of the past Nigerian president, Olusegun Obasanjo. As a result, the Nigerian Minister of Information and Communications, Dora Akunyili, officially protested to the South African government about the movie and demanded an apology from its makers. However, many Nigerian commentators have also pointed to the role that 'Nollywood' (Africa's greatest film factory which mainly produces cheap and not very sophisticated videos about life in Nigeria) plays in the worldwide dissemination of unfavorable images about Nigerians. This again emphasizes the great significance of travelling schemata for forms of representation.

31 But of course, despite all its critical overtones, Blomkamp's movie is first of all a medium of entertainment, an action-based alien film with many comical effects. This freedom and levity in the use of the 'District Six' schema seems to suggest that at least part of the memory work and reconciliation process in South Africa may have been successful.

and racism, of victims and perpetrators, of displacement and return, of injustice
and reconciliation, of futures past and futures present.

A how memory schema travel through different forms of media (intertextuality)

References

Afrika, Tatamkhulu. "Nothing's Changed." *Maqabane*. Belville, South Africa: Mayibuye Books, 1994. 33–34.

Bartlett, Frederic C. *Remembering: A Study in Experimental and Social Psychology*. Cambridge: Cambridge UP, 1932.

Baronian, Marie-Aude, Stephan Besser, and Yolande Jansen, eds. *Diaspora and Memory: Figures of Displacement in Contemporary Literature, Arts and Politics*. Amsterdam: Rodopi, 2007.

Bolter, Jay David and Richard Grusin, eds. *Remediation: Understanding New Media*. Cambridge: MIT Press, 1999.

Breytenbach, Cloete and Brian Barrow. *The Spirit of District Six*. 1970. Cape Town: Human & Rousseau, 1997.

Conway-Smith, Erin. "*District 9* Puts Spotlight on South Africa's Housing Crisis." *Global Post* 17 September, 2009. http://www.globalpost.com/dispatch/south-africa/090916/district-9-hits-south-africa (accessed 16 June 2014).

Coombes, Annie E. *History after Apartheid: Visual Culture and Public Memory in a Democratic South Africa*. Durham: Duke UP, 2003.

Cronin, Jeremy. "Creole Cape Town." *A City Imagined*. Ed. Stephen Watson. Johannesburg: Penguin Books, 2006. 45–54.

Crownshaw, Rick, ed. *Transcultural Memory*. Special Issue 'Parallax 17.4 (2011).

District 9. Dir. Neill Blomkamp. TriStar Pictures, 2009.

Erll, Astrid. *Memory in Culture*. Basingstoke: Palgrave Macmillan, 2011a.

Erll, Astrid. "Travelling Memory." *Transcultural Memory*. Ed. Rick Crownshaw. Special Issue *Parallax* 17.4 (2011b): 4–18.

Erll, Astrid and Stephanie Wodianka, eds. *Film und kulturelle Erinnerung: Plurimediale Konstellationen*. Berlin: De Gruyter, 2008.

Field, Sean, Renate Meyer and Felicity Swanson, eds. *Imagining the City Memories and Cultures in Cape Town*. Cape Town: Human Sciences Research Council (HSRC) Press, 2007.

Halbwachs, Maurice. *Les cadres sociaux de la mémoire*. Paris: Alcan, 1925.

Hirsch, Marianne and Nancy K. Miller, eds. *Rites of Return: Diaspora Poetics and the Politics of Memory*. New York: Columbia UP, 2011.

Huyssen, Andreas. *Present Pasts: Urban Palimpsests and the Politics of Memory*. Stanford: Stanford UP, 2003.

Jeppie, Shamil and Soudien Crain, eds. *The Struggle for District Six: Past and Present*. Cape Town: Buchu Books, 1990.

Koselleck, Reinhart. *Futures Past: On the Semantics of Historical Time*. Cambridge: MIT Press, 1985.

La Guma A. *A Walk in the Night and Other Stories*. 1962. Ed. Nahem Yousaf. Nottingham: Trent Editions, 2006.

Leggewie, Claus. "Von der Visualisierung zur Virtualisierung des Erinnerns." *Erinnerungskultur 2.0. Kommemorative Kommunikation in digitalen Medien*. Ed. Erik Meyer. Frankfurt: Campus, 2009. 9–28.

Levy, Daniel and Natan Sznaider. *Erinnerung im globalen Zeitalter: Der Holocaust*. Frankfurt: Suhrkamp, 2001 (Trans: *The Holocaust and Memory in the Global Age*. Philadelphia: Temple UP, 2006).

Maart, Rozena. *Rosa's District 6*. Toronto: TSAR, 2004.

McCormick, Kay. *Language in Cape Town's District Six*. Oxford: Oxford UP, 2002.

McEachern, Charmaine. *Narratives of Nation: Media, Memory and Representation in the Making of the New South Africa*. New York: Nova Science Publishers, 2002.

Merry, Sally Engle. "Transnational Human Rights and Local Activism: Mapping the Middle." *American Anthropologist* 108.1 (2006): 38–51.

Murray, Noléen, Nick Shepherd and Martin Hall, eds. *Desire Lines: Space, Memory and Identity in the Post-Apartheid City*. London: Routledge, 2007.

Nuttall, Sarah, and Carli Coetzee, eds. *Negotiating the Past: The Making of Memory in South Africa*. Cape Town: Oxford UP, 1998.

Nuttall, Sarah. *Entanglement: Literary and Cultural Reflections on Post-Apartheid*. Johannesburg: Wits UP, 2009.

Pistorius, Penny, Marco Bezzoli, Rafael Marks, and Martin Kruger. *Texture and Memory: The Urbanism of District Six*. 2nd edn. Cape Town: Sustainable Urban and Housing Development Research Unit, Dept. of Architectural Technology, Cape Technikon, 2002.

Prosalendis, Linda. "District Six – Kanaladorp." *Nordisk Museologi* 1 (1999): 135–146.

Rassool, Ciraj. "Making the District Six Museum in Cape Town." *Museum International*. 58 (2006): 9–18.

Rassool, Ciraj and Sandra Prosalendis, eds. *Recalling Community in Cape Town: Creating and Curating the District Six Museum*. Cape Town, South Africa: District Six Museum, 2001.

Rive, Richard. *Buckingham Palace, District Six*. Berlin: Cornelsen, 1986.

Rive, Richard. "District Six: Fact and Fiction." *The Struggle for District Six: Past and Present*. Eds. Shamil Jeppie and Soudien Crain. Cape Town: Buchu Books, 1990. 110–116.

Rothberg, Michael. *Multidirectional Memory: Remembering the Holocaust in the Age of Decolonization*. Stanford: Stanford UP, 2009.

Ruchatz, Jens. "The Photograph as Externalization and Trace." *A Companion to Cultural Memory Studies*. Eds. Astrid Erll and Ansgar Nünning, in collaboration with Sara B. Young. Berlin: De Gruyter, 2010. 367–378.

Sambumbu, Sipokazi. "Reading Visual Representations of 'ndabeni' in the Public Realms." *Kronos: 'n geleentheidspublikasie van die Wes-Kaaplandse Instituut vir Historiese Navorsing* (2010): 184–206.

Sardar, Ziauddin and Sean Cubitt. *Aliens R Us: The Other in Science Fiction Cinema*. London: Pluto Press, 2002.

Van Heyningen Elizabeth, Nigel Worden and Vivian Bickford-Smith. *Cape Town in the Twentieth Century: An Illustrated Social History*. Claremont, South Africa: D. Philip Publishers, 1999.

Rosanne Kennedy
Moving Testimony: Human Rights, Palestinian Memory, and the Transnational Public Sphere

Testimony, a transnational cultural form, is today crucial to the process of documenting violations, constructing memories, and soliciting witnessing publics in human rights campaigns.[1] The Holocaust has "shaped the discourse on collective, social, and cultural memory, serving both as touchstone and paradigm," and has introduced the idiom of witness testimony (Hirsch and Spitzer 2010, 390). The Eichmann trial, in particular, has been identified as a landmark event for "legitimating testimony as a form of 'truth telling' about the past" (Wieviorka 2006, 88), and consequently, for producing a collective memory of the Holocaust (Felman 2002).[2] While testimonies demonstrate the uniqueness of the witness's perspective, they do so "using the language of the time … and in response to questions and expectations motivated by political and ideological concerns" (Wieviorka 2006, xii). Thus, testimony is not simply personal nor does it have the detached perspective required of law or historiography; rather, it contributes to collective memory (Felman 2002; Wieviorka 2006, xii). The Holocaust paradigm, which is grounded in the presumption that memories of the Holocaust will act as a moral and legal justification for humanitarian intervention in present conflicts, has had significant impact both on memory studies and on human rights.[3] Indeed, it has been a potent justification – if not raison d'etre – for the post-WWII memory apparatus. In human rights contexts, the approaches that have been developed to collect, archive, and present Holocaust testimony in legal courts, museum exhibitions, documentary films and the like, continue to inform processes for recording and remembering genocides, atrocities, and human rights violations today (Wieviorka 2006, xxiii; see also Felman 2002).

---

[1] On the concept of witnessing publics, see McLagan (2003, 609).

[2] For an account of the emergence of the Holocaust survivor as a bearer of historical truth, see Wieviorka (2006). On the Eichmann trial and Holocaust memory, see also Douglas (2001); Felman (2002); and Kennedy (2013). On the contribution of Holocaust scholarship to memory studies, see Hirsch and Spitzer (2010).

[3] For a summary of the impact of the 'Holocaust metanarrative' on the development of human rights, see Hapgood (2013).

Within memory studies Daniel Levy and Natan Sznaider have been leading proponents of the Holocaust paradigm as a basis for human rights. "Memories of the Holocaust," they argue, "facilitate the formation of transnational memory cultures, which in turn, have the potential to become the cultural foundation for global human rights politics" (2006, 4). In theory, if not always in practice, Holocaust memory, with its mantra of 'never again,' functions as an ethical prompt to nations to intervene in crisis situations to prevent atrocities. In *Human Rights and Memory* (2010), they extend this argument to consider the impact of the global human rights regime on national sovereignty. They identify the consolidation of a transnational Holocaust memory in the 1990s with the emergence of a "global memory imperative." Fuelled by memories of past genocides and violations, the "global memory imperative" is "transforming nation-state sovereignty by subjecting it to international scrutiny," and empowering the human rights regime to intervene into current sites of violation (Levy and Sznaider 2010, 149). Their argument should be regarded as aspirational, for it is not yet clear whether the human rights regime is in fact transforming national sovereignty, nor in what direction – whether it is making states more open or more fervently nationalistic.[4] The Israeli-Palestinian conflict, in which human rights non-governmental organizations (NGOs) have been deeply involved for the past twenty-five years, provides an especially rich site for considering the political and humanitarian effectiveness of the Holocaust paradigm and the global memory imperative.

The global memory imperative and the Israeli-Palestinian conflict

In an era of human rights and of rapid media transmission, human rights reports are an important site for the production and transnational circulation of testimonies, and the construction of a transnational memory of human rights violations. In this chapter, I take as my case study the Goldstone Report, and in particular, testimonies that were produced in conjunction with the UN's Fact-Finding Mission on the Gaza Conflict in 2009 (hereafter, the Goldstone Mission). The Goldstone Mission, headed by South African judge Richard Goldstone, was appointed by the United Nations Human Rights Council (UNHRC) to investigate breaches of human rights and humanitarian law by the Israel Defense Forces (IDF) that were

---

4 Israel regarded the Goldstone Report as an attack on its very existence as a state, and responded by threatening human rights organizations working within Israel.

alleged to have occurred during "Operation Cast Lead" – Israel's name for its attack on Gaza in the final days of 2008. The Goldstone Mission submitted its final report – *Human Rights in Palestine and Other Occupied Arab Territories: The Report of the United Nations Fact-Finding Mission on the Gaza Conflict*, known as the Goldstone Report – to the UNHRC in September 2009 (see UN 2009; hereafter 'the official report'). Goldstone, a South African lawyer and judge of Jewish descent, has been a leading figure in promoting the Holocaust as a metanarrative of human rights (Hapgood 2013, 53). The Goldstone Mission, during which Goldstone put the Holocaust paradigm into practice by holding public hearings that generated testimony, provides a revealing case study of human rights, transnational memory, and national sovereignty. In addition, the Goldstone Report was remediated for a North American audience in 2011 by the progressive American publisher, The Nation, which published an abridged and supplemented edition. Selected testimonies from the Goldstone hearings were edited and included in the American edition, which invites analysis of how they are framed and remediated for a North American audience, and what effects and affects they have had on that audience.

The Israeli occupation of the Palestinian territories and its blockade of Gaza have produced an ongoing legal and humanitarian crisis in which human rights NGOs have become deeply embedded, especially since the 1990s. Consequently, the Israeli-Palestinian conflict has become a touchstone for scholarship on human rights, humanitarianism, witnessing and testimony, especially in relation to Palestinian national aspirations. Didier Fassin argues that the Israeli-Palestinian conflict, especially since the second intifada, "enlightens many of the issues humanitarian workers are confronted with when they want to transform their witnessing into advocacy and make themselves spokespersons for the supposed voiceless" (2008, 534). The testimonies that were produced in conjunction with the Goldstone Mission, and later edited for an American public, provide an opportunity to consider how testimony is framed for different audiences. In this chapter, I introduce the concept of 'moving testimonies' to track the remediation of Palestinian testimony as it travels from Gaza and Geneva to English-speaking audiences in the West, especially in the United States. Both meanings of 'moving' – as travel and affect – are relevant to my analysis.

Human rights institutions and activists facilitate the movement of testimonies into the global public sphere. There are, as Gillian Whitlock (2007) points out, "well-established conduits for the production, authentication, and cultural transmission of testimony, and these are available to nurture ... testimony in ... campaigns for human rights" (74). Human rights organizations and the social and cultural practices they generate and support constitute a "circulatory matrix, or dedicated communications infrastructure, out of which human rights claims are generated and through which they travel. Comprising multiple layers – commercial, nonprofit, nongovernmental, intergovernmental, and community ... these circuits provide the scaffolding for the making public of human rights violations" (McLagan 2006, 192). The concept of a "circulatory matrix" provides a useful framework for analyzing how human rights testimonies travel transnationally, and in the process, contribute to the construction of a "prosthetic" (Landsberg 2004) or "cosmopolitan" memory (Levy and Sznaider 2002) of Operation Cast Lead.

'Moving' is also a useful term to describe the affective dimension of testimony. It is widely recognized that human rights and humanitarian activists use testimonies of suffering as a means of soliciting a compassionate response from audiences, with the anticipation of moral, political and financial support. Testimony is premised on a belief that pain is a universal that crosses social, economic, and geographic boundaries (McLagan 2003; Allen 2009a). Meg McLagan argues that testimonies of suffering are an "inter-cultural technology" that connects "individuals ... from different worlds through the medium of pain, creating solidarity out of difference" (2003, 607). This affective dimension of testimony, which informs my use of the term 'moving testimonies,' is presumed to be crucial to the effectiveness of human rights reports in stimulating public memory and humanitarian advocacy.

My interdisciplinary framework brings together scholarship on human rights, testimony, and publicity – particularly but not exclusively in the Palestinian context – with scholarship on transnational memory. Two methodological approaches inform my analysis: analysis of the semiotics and poetics of testimony, and analysis of the mediation and framing of testimony in different contexts and for different audiences. McLagan proposes that "analysis of the relation between human-rights testimonies and transnational publicity ... involves bringing aesthetic questions about formal semiotic properties and generic conventions to bear on considerations about how testimonies generate action outside the textual event itself" (2007, 306). It is precisely this conjunction of the textual and the extra-textual dimensions of testimony that I undertake. On an empirical level, my aim is to analyze the circulation and mediation of Palestinian testimonies, and the memories they produce, as they travel "across and beyond ... territorial and social borders" (Erll 2011, 8). Specifically, I am interested in how they are mediated for national and transnational "witnessing publics" (see McLagan 2003, 609), and how they sustain or challenge the concept of a global memory imperative. Conceptually, I suggest that engagement with public sphere theory, and particularly with the concept of the transnational public sphere, would enrich the study of transnational memory and human rights.

Publicizing the Goldstone Report: from the UN to the US

On April 2, 2009 the UNHRC initiated a fact-finding mission, the Goldstone Mission, in the aftermath of Israel's attack on Gaza in late 2008. 'Operation Cast Lead' lasted from 27 December 2008 to 17 January 2009, and resulted in approximately 1,400 Palestinian and 13 Israeli casualties. The government of Israel refused to cooperate with the mission. While reporting the casualties' figure of the Israeli army too, the Goldstone Mission accepted assessments from various Israeli, Palestinian, and international human rights groups that the vast majority of the Palestinian deaths were of civilians, including more than 300 Palestinian children (UN 2009, 90–91).[5] The number of civilian casualties was one of the 'serious concerns' raised by the Goldstone Mission. In the months afterwards, several human rights NGOs produced reports that documented violations of international humanitarian and human rights law by the IDF, particularly relating to the illegal use of white phosphorus (see e.g. Human Rights Watch 2009). The UNHRC tasked the fact-finding mission, which included three international lawyers – Christine Chinkin, Hina Jilani, and Colonel Desmond Travers – with investigating breaches of international law during Operation Cast Lead. In its searing final report, the Goldstone Mission documented numerous incidents, particularly by the IDF but also by Hamas, which potentially constituted war crimes and crimes against humanity, and recommended that the IDF and Hamas investigate these incidents. Particularly contentious were allegations that the IDF deliberately targeted civilians, and that the destruction of civilian infrastructure resulted from a deliberate Israeli policy of "collective punishment" of the people of Gaza for their support of Hamas.

The Goldstone Report, as text and event, has generated enormous controversy (see Falk 2010).[6] It has been read, debated, and critiqued not only by academics in

---

5 The number of Palestinian deaths, and particularly deaths classified as 'civilian,' has been contentious. An Israeli report that rebuts the Goldstone Report reinstates the Israeli army's figure of 1,166 Palestinian casualties (Meir Amit, 323), and claims that over 100 were Palestinian police officers who were also active in 'terrorist' organizations (316–323). It cites the number of civilian deaths as being 'only' 20% of total deaths. By contrast, Raji Sourani, from the Palestinian Centre for Human Rights, states that "1,419 Palestinians were killed. The overwhelming majority of the dead – 1,167 or 82 percent – were civilians, the so-called protected persons of international humanitarian law. A further 5,300 Palestinians were injured, of whom approximately 2,400 were women and children" (Sourani 2011, 329). Sourani's figures are consistent with those of other human rights organizations.

6 See also articles on the Goldstone Report in *Global Governance* 16 (2010).

international law, politics, philosophy, and history, but by media commentators, activists, and public intellectuals. Numerous websites, blogs, journalistic essays and academic articles evaluated, celebrated or rebutted the Goldstone Report.[7] For instance, in March, 2010, the Meir Amit Intelligence and Terrorism Information Centre produced a response to the Goldstone Report, *Hamas and the Terrorist Threat from the Gaza Strip*, purporting to compare the "Goldstone findings" with "factual findings" (Meir Amit 2010). It accused the Goldstone Report of "vilifying" the IDF's conduct in Operation Cast Lead, by claiming that the IDF targeted civilians rather than terrorist organizations. It also charged the Goldstone Report with ignoring issues that arise in "asymmetrical warfare" (Meir Amit 2010, 324).[8] Criticisms of the Goldstone Report have also come from supporters of Palestinian human rights. For example, Richard Falk (2011) and others have pointed out how most of its conclusions had already been reached by other respected international studies and reports on international law in the occupied Palestinian territories. Moreover, crucially, the Goldstone Report "proceeds on the basis of Israel's right of self-defense without bothering to decide whether in a situation of continuing occupation a claim of self-defense is ever available under international humanitarian law" nor did it "examine whether the factual conditions prior to the attacks supported any security claim" (Falk 2011). Also, some critics have suggested that the report and the various discourses on the 'war' in Gaza represented Operation Cast Lead as an exception and thus obscured the protracted and systematic violence of the occupation (Allen 2012).

In April 2011, controversy was further inflamed when Goldstone wrote a bombshell op-ed in *The Washington Post* in which he withdrew the charge, made in the Goldstone Report, that the IDF deliberately targeted civilians, and noted that Israel had begun internal investigations of allegations, whereas Hamas had done nothing (Goldstone 2011). Israeli authorities celebrated Goldstone's statement as a 'retraction' of the report. In response, the other members of the fact-finding mission re-affirmed their commitment to the findings of the report, and insisted that the documented violations should be investigated thoroughly (Jilani et al. 2011; see Pilkington and Urquhart 2011). Goldstone's equivocations, they pointed out, had to be viewed in the context of the immense personal pressure on him, which extended to threats against his family and caricatures of him as a 'self-hating Jew.'[9]

---

7 These are too numerous to list, but many sources are referenced in the articles in Horowitz et al. 2011.

8 For another take on the 'asymmetrical' nature of the conflict, see Allen (2012).

9 See responses by Mondoweiss (2011); Montell (2011); Pogrebin (2011).

Human rights organizations produce and circulate their reports not only to document specific violations, but also to publicize breaches and to solicit the support of the international community to hold states and individuals accountable for their actions. Michael Ignatieff (2003) observes that "... in the context of a state's stubborn refusal to cooperate, the monitoring bodies have only the power of publicity" (53).[10] Given the global significance of the Gaza conflict, and the UN's support for the fact-finding mission, its report was destined to attract significant publicity. A year after the report was published, Richard Falk (2010) suggested that despite its hefty 575 pages and legal language, the report had achieved "remarkable salience" and had "touched the raw nerve of global moral and political consciousness" (173). Acknowledging that it was never likely that members of the IDF would be prosecuted in the International Criminal Court (ICC), he contends that the most significant audience for the Goldstone Report is not international law but global civil society, as demonstrated by the growing 'Boycott, Divestment and Sanctions' (BDS) campaign. Launched in 2005 by Palestinian civil society, the global BDS campaign uses economic and political strategies to pressure Israel to end the occupation, to recognize Palestinian rights, and to comply with international law. Rashid Khalidi contends that the report has had an "unprecedented reception," especially amongst young Americans, and is "both a product of an evolving consciousness and a vital contributor to it" (2011, 376). For the report to reach a wider spectrum of global civil society, however, it needed to be made accessible and relevant to audiences despite its length and density.

In 2011, The Nation published an abridged and supplemented version of the Goldstone Report, thereby facilitating its transit to an English-speaking humanitarian and activist public. Entitled *The Goldstone Report: The Legacy of the Landmark Investigation of the Gaza Conflict* (2011), The Nation's edition (hereafter the American edition) is edited by Adam Horowitz, Lizzy Ratner, and Philip Weiss. It frames an abridged version of the Goldstone Report with a preface by Bishop Desmond Tutu, an introduction by Naomi Klein, a timeline of the conflict since 1947, maps, and a suite of articles by public intellectuals, academics, and journalists, mostly located in the United States, but with ties to Palestine and Israel. Available in paperback and as an e-book from Amazon, the American edition has

---

10 Where violations of human rights are concerned, 'publicity' cuts in multiple directions. Numerous reports, commentaries, and blogs challenge and seek to discredit the findings of The Goldstone Report. See *Hamas and the Terrorist Threat from the Gaza Strip* (Meir Amit, 2010). Available at: www.terrorism-info.org.il/en/article/19298; also linked on Right Side News, http://www.rightsidenews.com/2010031528688/world/israel/hamas-and-the-terrorist-threat-from-the-gaza-strip-goldstone-report.html; and on the IDF's official blog, www.idfblog.com/facts-figures/rocket-attacks-toward-israel/ (all accessed 17 January 2014).

achieved unusual visibility in the American public sphere. For instance, publicity for the American edition was generated in May 2011, when the activist art group, Culture Project, as part of its 'town hall' series, *Blueprint for Accountability*, held a public event in New York city to discuss the fallout from Goldstone's *Washington Post* op-ed article, and to call for an end to Israeli impunity.[11] The event – *Gaza, Goldstone and the Crisis of Impunity* – was sponsored by the Culture Project and Mondoweiss. The latter identifies itself as a "news website devoted to covering American foreign policy in the Middle East, chiefly from a progressive Jewish perspective," and is hosted by Horowitz and Weiss, editors of the American edition of the Goldstone Report.[12]

The American edition, together with associated events, has created an opening for a public conversation, especially in the United States, on the Israeli-Palestinian conflict. Along with Weiss and Ratner, Naomi Klein and several other celebrity activists – many of them young American Jews – participated in *Gaza, Goldstone and the Crisis of Impunity*, which included readings of Palestinian testimonies from The Nation's edition of the Goldstone Report.[13] The involvement of a younger generation of North American Jews in promoting *The Goldstone Report* conveyed the message that Jews can be critical of Israel's treatment of Palestinians, and of the United States government's unqualified support for Israel, without being anti-Semitic. This validation is important for changing the politics of the Israeli-Palestinian conflict in the United States, which has long been a strong moral and economic supporter of Israel. While it is difficult to trace changes in public opinion directly to the Goldstone Report, the publication of the American edition has coincided with increased activism on the conflict on university campuses and on the internet, including growing support for the BDS campaign.[14] A sign of its

---

11 For further information, see blueprint.cultureproject.org/gaza-goldstone-and-the-crisis-of-impunity (accessed 17 January 2014).
12 See mondoweiss.net/about-mondoweiss (accessed 17 January 2014).
13 Trudie Styler read the testimony of Mahmoud Abd Rabbo al-Ajrami at the event, see blueprint.cultureproject.org/category/past-events/ (accessed 21 March 2014). Al-Ajrami's testimony is included in The Nation's edition of the Goldstone Report (Horowitz et al. 2011, 174–176).
14 See for instance: jewishvoiceforpeace.org/campaigns/young-jewish-and-proud; electronicintifada.net/tags/students-justice-palestine; electronicintifada.net/blogs/nora-barrows-friedman/victory-campus-free-speech-us-dept-education-throws-out-anti-semitism; www.theasa.net/caucus_activism/item/academic_and_cultural_boycott_campaign/; mondoweiss.net/2013/12/association-convention-resolution.html; www.nytimes.com/2014/01/12/us/another-academic-group-considers-israel-censure.html (all accessed 17 March 2014). For commentary on the reception of the report in the United States, see Khalidi (2011).

increasing visibility, the BDS campaign has been discussed at academic conferences in the United States – including the American Studies Association (2013) and the Modern Language Association (2014) – and is increasingly reported on in the mainstream news.[15]

The editors of the American edition of the Goldstone Report rhetorically positioned it as a transformative event in the collective memory of the Israeli-Palestinian conflict. The cultural politics of the American edition are signaled by two aspirational words in the subtitle – 'legacy' and 'landmark.' A 'landmark' implies that the commission's report has been instrumental in bringing about a significant change, not so much in the conflict itself, but in the public perception of it. Raja Sourani, from the Palestinian Centre for Human Rights, comments that "[f]or Palestinians, the Goldstone Report represents an acknowledgement of their suffering and of the systematic nature of Israel's illegal actions … what had been known in the Occupied Palestinian Territories for years but had never been brought up so sharply on the international level" (Sourani 2011, 330). The preface and introduction suggest that the report is contributing to "a new accountability," a phrase that recurs in the preface, introduction, and commentaries in the American edition. Former chair of the South African Truth and Reconciliation Commission, Bishop Tutu (2011) advocates that: "once we have read it [the report], we must pursue its … calls for accountability" (ix). The introduction also refers to the end of the "myth of Israeli exceptionalism" – the ideology that Israel, in its occupation of Palestinian territories and its violations of Palestinian rights, is exempt from being held to the same standards of international law that apply to other nations. The anticipated 'legacy' is one in which Israel will be under increased pressure as a result of the scrutiny of its human rights violations. In short, the editors rhetorically presume the outcome they hope the report will produce – that it will be a 'landmark' and have a 'legacy' – and in so doing, implicitly position the report within the ambit of a global memory imperative.

Of particular significance from the perspective of transnational memory, Naomi Klein's introduction to the American edition demonstrates how the "global memory imperative" is used in practice. Klein (2011) quotes a 2001 article by Goldstone, written with reference to the South African Truth and Reconciliation Commission, in which he writes: "If future perpetrators of genocide, crimes against humanity, and serious war crimes are brought to justice and appropriately punished then the millions of innocent victims who perished in the Holocaust will not

---

15 See, for instance, "Netanyahu Promotes Efforts Towards a Peace Deal," 7 March 2014. www.nytimes.com/2014/03/05/world/middleeast/netanyahu-promotes-efforts-toward-a-peace-deal.html (accessed 7 March 2014).

have died in vain. Their memory will remain alive and they will be remembered when future war criminals are brought to justice" (Goldstone 2001, as quoted by Klein 2011, xiv). Klein's remediation of Goldstone's 2001 article exemplifies the way Holocaust memory functions as a moral justification and prompt to prosecute human rights violations in the present. For instance, she comments that "[i]t is this theory of justice – a direct response to the Nazi Holocaust – that Justice Goldstone brought to his work in Gaza in 2009, insisting that his fact-finding mission would examine the crimes committed by both Israelis and Palestinians" (xiv-xv). In transposing Goldstone's comments on Holocaust memory to his work on human rights violations in the Gaza conflict, she demonstrates just how mobile and "multidirectional" (Rothberg 2009) Holocaust memory can be in an era of human rights. But this raises an urgent question: what is the evidence that the global memory imperative, in the context of the Israeli-Palestinian conflict, will have the desired long-term effect of ending the occupation and securing human rights for Palestinians? Before returning to this issue, I offer a close reading of two linked testimonies from the Goldstone hearings, by a father and son, to consider the discourses they used in communicating their horrific experiences to the Goldstone Mission, to listeners in Gaza, and to a transnational public.

A humanitarian discourse of suffering

As a judge in South Africa, Goldstone was familiar with the powerful and moving effects of testimony, and its value as a means of publicizing human rights violations. As chair of the fact-finding mission in Gaza, Goldstone, together with the other commissioners, determined to hold public hearings during which Palestinian and Israeli victims could testify, thereby extending the Holocaust testimonial paradigm to the Gaza conflict. In providing a public stage for survivors, the mission enabled the transmission of Palestinian and Israeli memories of violent conflict to local and transnational publics. The commissioners wished to hold all of the hearings on site in Gaza, but Israel refused to allow witnesses from Israel and the West Bank to enter Gaza; consequently, they testified at hearings in Geneva, while residents of Gaza testified in Gaza City. The Gaza hearings, held on 28–29 June 2009, were broadcast live to a hall in Gaza City that was open to the public and the media, with simultaneous translations into English and Arabic, and were televised. The hearings in Geneva on 6–7 July 2009 were translated into English, Arabic, and Hebrew. Transcripts and webcasts of the hearings are available on the UN Human Rights Council website, constituting a unique public archive of the proceedings. Of equal, if not more importance, are the afterlives of testimony, for instance in activist campaigns, films, museum exhibitions, artworks, and digital installations. Through these afterlives, which keep memory and testimony alive for new audiences, testimony contributes to and shapes collective memory.

In Palestine, local NGOs and UN agencies, through the ubiquitous use of a discourse of suffering, are re-shaping the language and nature of political struggles in the Israeli-Palestinian context (see Khalili 2007; Fassin 2008; Allen 2013). Laleh Khalili argues that with the rise of a liberal discourse of rights and development at the end of the Cold War, and the associated emergence of NGOs in Palestine, political claim making was increasingly couched in a language of trauma, victimhood, and human rights, thereby appealing to international audiences and actors – especially in Europe and North America – for sympathy and support. Revolutionary armed struggle ceded to human rights, and the heroic narrative gave way to the tragedy of abject victims in need of transnational support (Khalili 2007, 39). Along with many others, Khalili observes that the theme of suffering in human rights discourse is linked to "the centrality of Holocaust narrative and symbols of trauma" (35). What she calls "trauma drama" – the performance of a "drama of suffering for an audience whose sympathy is sought" – has had a profound impact on contemporary nationalist discourse in Palestine (34–35). On the basis of recent ethnographic research in Palestine, Lori Allen argues that since the second intifada, suffering has come to permeate Palestinian political discourse even more intensely than it had previously. In the transnational human rights community, suffering is perceived to be the basis of a 'common humanity' and, as such, is presumed to give rise to political entitlement (Allen 2009a, 162). The discourse of suffering produces the "rights-bearing suffering subject" (Allen 2009, 162) and the discourse of trauma, closely aligned with that of suffering, produces a "suffering subject" (Fassin 2008). The "suffering subject" position is more palatable to a Western audience and more likely to generate compassionate responses than an overtly political subjectivity, such as "the suicide bomber" or the "youthful stone thrower." The discourse of suffering and trauma, however, obscures a more overtly political discourse of occupation, colonization, and the struggle for national self-determination (Fassin 2008).

Many international human rights lawyers and humanitarian advocates regard the minimum aim of human rights as the reduction of human suffering (see Baxi 1998). Appealing to the transnational discourse of suffering, Goldstone aligned the hearings with the aim of exposing and alleviating suffering. "The aim of holding these public hearings," he declared, "was to show the human side of the suffering; to give a voice to the victims so that they are not lost among statistics" (UN press release, 7 July 2009). At the same time, he cautioned that the testimonies did not constitute evidence in the legal sense; they were not subject to a judi-

cial process of proof, and were "not in any way similar to truth and reconciliation commissions." Goldstone's comments indicate that the primary addressee
of the testimonies was not international law but a humanitarian audience – that
is, global civil society. Despite his disclaimer that the testimonies did not constitute legal evidence, testimony produces truth effects and truth claims. Goldstone's comments, which reinforce the presumption of authenticity, are an example of what Lori Allen (2009a), drawing on Mazzarella, calls "immediation". In the
Palestinian context, immediation refers to the way human rights institutions obscure their own role in mediating testimonies, and instead prime audiences to receive testimonies as "authentic experience and truth" (Allen 2009a, 162). Allen argues that in the Palestinian context, in which political and social change has been
stalled, "the immediacy of pain – and sympathy for it – has become a weak core
of politics" (162). At the public hearings in Gaza and Geneva witnesses recounted,
in the now ubiquitous language of trauma, victimhood, and human rights, their
grief, loss, and outrage at the violent attacks that killed beloved family members
and members of the community.

Moving testimony

The testimony collected by the Goldstone Mission has been framed and re-framed
for different audiences, as it has travelled from one geopolitical context to another,
in the different registers of the public hearings, the official UN report, and the
American edition of the report. To consider these differing contexts I have selected
a single incident: a missile attack on the al-Maqadmah mosque, which is on the
outskirts of Jabaliyah camp. Although informed by testimony that was delivered
at the public hearings, the official report provides a de-subjectified description of
the bombing:

> On the evening of 3 January 2009, between 5 and 6 p.m., a large number of people had gath-
> ered in the mosque for evening prayers. Witnesses indicate that between 200 and 300 men
> had gathered on the first floor. A number of women had also congregated in the basement at
> that time. Witnesses explained that in time of fear or emergency it was the tradition to com-
> bine sunset and evening prayers. ... The witnesses indicated that prayers had ended and
> the sermon was just beginning. At that point there was an explosion in the doorway to the
> mosque. One of the two wooden doors was blown off its hinges and all the way across the
> prayer area to the opposite wall. As a result of the explosion at least 15 people died. Almost
> all were inside the mosque at the time. One of the casualties was a boy who had been sit-
> ting at the entrance. His leg was blown off by the missile strike and found afterwards on the
> roof of the mosque. A large number, around 40, suffered injuries. (UN 2009, para. 824–825,
> footnotes omitted)

The official report, which records the incident in a clinical, forensic style, and avoids graphic or personalizing details about the deaths, exemplifies the 'de-subjectified' style characteristic of human rights reports.[16] As Wilson (1997) observes, "accounts of human rights violations are characterized by a literalism and minimalism which strip events of their subjective meanings in pursuit of objective legal facts" (134). In the example above, the doors become a proxy for the devastating effects of the missile strike on human bodies: the boy's leg, like the doors, was "blown off;" boy and doors are rendered interchangeable. As Wilson points out, "the 'just give us the facts' approach inherently implies ... excising personal biography, the filter of memory and the performative dimensions of the speech act" (146). He has advocated that human rights reports should try "to capture the nature of the subject matter" – extreme violence with resulting shock and trauma – "through engaging with the existential circumstances of the victims, bystanders, even the perpetrators" (156). He argues that authors of human rights reports could learn how to represent the subjective experience of trauma from discussions about representing the Holocaust.

In contrast to the de-subjectified account provided in the official report, the testimony that was presented at the public hearings conveyed the subjective perspective of witnesses and survivors. For instance, at the hearing in Gaza on 28 June 2009, 91-year-old Moussa Al-Silawi testified about the attack on the mosque that killed his son and several other family members.[17] He is a "superstes" witness – someone who "lived through the ordeal and suffered it," and who testifies in the first person from a subjective perspective (Fassin 2008, 535). His testimony, grounded in a specific geographical location and conflict, exemplifies what Bhaskar Sarkar and Janet Walker (2010) call 'situated testimony:' testimony delivered at the site of a catastrophic event by a witness who was present. Al-Silawi begins with a ritual address to God, and locates himself as a member of a specific community:

> In the name of God, the compassionate, the merciful, I am Moussa Al-Silawi. I live in Jabaliyah Camp, on the eighth block. On the day of the event ... I went to the mosque ... After evening prayer we heard a shell hit the mosque. And we have no idea what we saw at the moment. It was absolutely incredible and we started screaming. We screamed and we called for God ... And after that, and after, I heard, I was told that your son Ibrahim, your son Ibrahim Moussa Isa Ibrahima Al-Silawi, he was carried to the hospital and he became a martyr. He died. He has seven daughters ... Altogether they are ten who became orphans, without any-

---

16 For analyses of the rhetoric and genre of human rights reports, see Cohen (1996); and Dudai (2006).
17 The testimonies of Moussa Al-Silawi and Moteeh Al-Silawi are archived at: www.un.org/webcast/unhrc/archive.asp?go=090628 (accessed 17 March 2014).

body to, to give them assistance. And moments later I heard … "Ahmed, Ahmed Al-Silawi, he is also dead. He's a martyr." He was completely disintegrated in the mosque. [Al-Silawi also lost a nephew and two grandchildren.]

Moussa Al-Silawi suffered devastating losses. Attempting to articulate this loss in front of both the immediate audience in Gaza, and a global legal and humanitarian audience, it is striking that he uses both national and transnational discourses to communicate his traumatic experience and his understanding of the political significance of the events. He uses the Islamist nationalist discourse of the martyr, which has become prevalent among Palestinians especially since the 1980s (Khalili 2007, 6).[18] Since the second intifada, the discourse of the martyr has expanded to include not only suicide bombers, but also any Palestinian killed by Israeli fire (Fassin 2008). Thus, while recalling his shattering experience of the attack on the mosque, Moussa Al-Silawi's testimony, framed within a nationalist discourse of martyrdom and self-sacrifice (Kahlili 2007), contributes to a collective memory that places Palestinian deaths during Operation Cast Lead within the longer history of the Palestinian national struggle.[19]

Al-Silawi speaks in the familiar terms of transnational humanitarian and moral discourses – including a discourse of dignity, a discourse of Palestinian rights and justice, and a discourse of duty and obligation – to make an ethical claim on Arab and Western nations to intervene in the conflict and to end Palestinian suffering. In an echo of Holocaust memory, he laments that Palestinians have been abandoned both by Arab and Western nations, despite the ethical imperatives of Islam and international law:

may God protect us … may He … punish also all the Arabs that have allowed this to happen. The governors, the rulers who have let us down … and I call on you … Where is rule? Where is justice? Where is Islam? Where is the government? Where is the whole world?

His testimony exemplifies Khalili's observation that "the affinity of local nationalism with broader transnational discourses negates the idea that Palestinian nationalist practices are sui generis products of a static and unique Palestinian culture" (3). Rather, with its rhetorical questions, Al-Silawi's testimony demonstrates

18 Khalili (2007) argues that since the 1960s, Palestinian nationalist discourse has undergone a shift from a heroic to a tragic mode. The image of the guerilla fighter has been replaced by that of abject martyrs and victims, and the heroisms of the nationalist movement have given way to tragedies of endured losses (6–7).
19 On the gendered dimensions of the discourse of the martyr, see Khalili (2007); and Allen (2009b).

that Palestinian discourse is transnational and multidirectional, incorporating both global and nationalist discursive trends.

Al-Silawi's son, Moteeh Al-Silawi, the sheikh of the mosque, also testified at the Gaza hearings. Whereas the official report described the effects of the bombing on inanimate objects such as the doors, he graphically details the carnage on human bodies caused by the missile attack:

> It was a terrible, terrible shock … people go to the mosque for safety, and we saw bloodshed … I saw legs, I saw legs and arms uh, I saw the, the leg of a small child, and I stepped on it, even … I saw this blood being shed in the mosque. The mosque, the safe place where everybody should feel safe.

> There was a lot of uh, action and everybody running around in the mosque. At that moment I cannot describe to you what I felt. It was frightful … I – with my own foot I stepped on the head of a small child. Where is the world? Where is international law? Is this what the Palestinian people deserve, our children screaming?

Lori Allen contends that the representation of suffering and damaged bodies "remains central to Palestinian nationalist representations" (Allen 2009a, 162). Palestinians use images that depict the effects of Israeli violence – bodies that are reduced to "blood, guts, and flesh" – as a means of "staging claims to a humanity shared in common with the international community and, therefore, to their status as deserving of human rights …" (162). When Al-Silawi describes stepping on a child's head "with my own foot," he immerses listeners, as well as himself, in the horror of the scene. Testimony is a mode of address that presumes a response. As Felman and Laub observe, "to testify … before an audience of readers or spectators – is more than simply to … relate what has been lived, recorded and remembered. Memory is conjured … in order to address another … to appeal to a community" (1992, 204). Through his testimony, Al-Silawi solicits listeners to share his shock and outrage at wanton killing, and to empathize with the suffering of victims and their families.

In addressing the international legal community and global civil society, Moteeh Al Silawi's testimony inevitably uses the language of suffering. Testimonies of suffering, presumed to be universal and to be a basis for political entitlement (Allen 2009a, 162), make "ethical claims on viewers and cultivate … potential actors" to intervene in the conflict (McLagan 2003, 609):

> I tell the world, the world listening to me now: where is the law of international protection? Where … are the Geneva Conventions on the protection of civilians in time or war? Where is democracy? Where is the right to worship that the European countries call for? Where is international law? … A dog would die in one of the European countries or in Israel and there is upheaval because of the dog, but we see sheikhs dying, their body parts scattered around

in a place of worship, and nobody looks at them. Where is justice? Where is justice? Where are human rights? The issue, the question of Palestine – and we hear about international law, about human rights, about Geneva Conventions – where is all of that?

His appeal to the international community in the language of dignity, suffering, and human rights indicates "the profound influence of global politics on the production and reproduction of local memories …" (Khalili 2007, 5). International humanitarian law provides him with a political subjectivity, and human rights discourse provides the moral justification to make claims. He uses his testimony, however, to point to the limits of the human rights regime, and its failure to prevent Palestinian suffering and death.

As the above examples demonstrate, the official report and the public hearings differ dramatically in their accounts of the same incident. Whereas legal evidence requires precise details of events, the testimonies make a moral appeal for support and intervention. While the official report privileges the language of fact, the testimonies evoke emotion and produce affect. Yet the split between fact and emotion is not absolute, since legal claims for justice and recognition of rights are increasingly made in the language of emotion, suffering, and dignity, as demonstrated in the Al-Silawis' testimonies. The distinctive rhetorical and affective registers of the official report and the testimonial archive are reinforced through form.

While the fact-finding mission was tasked with documenting breaches of international law, it also, like all human rights reporting, aimed to reach a broader humanitarian public as a means of preventing future violations. For a legal audience, the report needed to conform to juridical expectations of rationality, neutrality, and proof supported by material and testimonial evidence. For a humanitarian audience, emotions and morality – not law and rationality – are at the core of the enterprise (Dudai 2006, 790). To satisfy a humanitarian audience, the producers of human rights reports often include first-person unedited testimonies from victims and witnesses in the text. Testimonies provide the reader with "the emotional, non-legal, language that the authors feel compelled not to insert themselves" (Dudai 2006, 790). The UN fact-finding mission was, however, tarred with allegations of anti-Israeli bias even before it got underway.[20] In this sensitive political context, the otherwise standard human rights practice of including graphic and emotion-laden first-person testimony – with its aim of conveying the suffer-

---

20 Some critics argued that one of the commissioners, Christine Chinkin, should have been rendered ineligible to serve because she had signed a petition supporting an academic boycott of Israel. See e.g.: blog.unwatch.org/index.php/2009/07/05/why-goldstone-mission-member-must-resign/; www.jpost.com/Opinion/Op-Ed-Contributors/As-biased-as-their-UN-masters (both accessed 10 December 2013).

ing of victims – in the body of the report may have been seen as inflammatory. Perhaps as a compromise solution, the report draws on these testimonies to document its findings, but the transcripts of the hearings are not included in the official report. Instead, they are archived, together with a webcast, on a UN website.[21] As a supplement to the report, the testimonies do not directly challenge the report's detached legal realism, but they are available to humanitarian activists for use in campaigns.

Domesticating testimony: the familial trope and intercultural witnessing

The shift that I have been mapping from a legalistic documentation of events in the official report to a humanitarian approach was, I have suggested, evident in the discourse of suffering Goldstone used to justify holding the public hearings. The American edition of the Goldstone Report, which incorporated fifteen testimonies from the hearings, signals a further shift from a juridical conception of testimony as evidence to the politics of advocacy, and from a focus on prosecuting human rights violations to witnessing Palestinian suffering. This act of witnessing underpins the global memory imperative – the belief that witnessing Palestinian suffering will generate support from global civil society, which will in turn pressure Israel to end the occupation. The American edition of the Goldstone Report offers the opportunity to examine the remediation and circulation of these testimonies as they move from one geopolitical context – the public hearings held in Gaza and Geneva six months after the conflict – to another, the United States nearly two years later. Given support for Israel by the United States government, American citizens – who can be regarded as 'implicated subjects' (Rothberg 2013) – are an important audience for human rights publicity about the conflict.

Packaged in the American edition, the testimonies from the Gaza hearings are de-territorialized – they are removed from the Palestinian sites where the events occurred and from the hall in Gaza (or Geneva) where they were originally performed.[22] These narratives exemplify the concept of 'moving testimonies:' they are positioned in the American edition of the report to add an affective, humanizing dimension, which creates possibilities for audiences in the West to identify em-

---

21 Webcasts of the hearings are available on a UNHRC webcast archive site: www.un.org/webcast/unhrc/archive.asp?go=090628 (accessed 17 March 2014).

22 For a discussion of territorialization and deterritorialization, see Kennedy et al. (2013).

pathically with Palestinians on the basis of a shared humanity, claimed through the presumed universality of bodily and psychological suffering, and especially, of grief at the destruction of families and the random deaths of civilians, especially children and the elderly. The circulatory matrix of human rights – the NGOs, the UN, activist networks, publishers, and the internet – move the testimonies materially and virtually across national borders. Both meanings of 'moving' – affective and literal – are crucial for soliciting the support of transnational publics that could increase scrutiny of Israel's activities and potentially pressure Israel to change its behavior, for instance, through civil society initiatives such as the BDS campaign.

As a result of their publication in the United States, the testimonies were re-territorialized and even domesticated for an American audience. The process of domestication occurs through the selection of testimonies that are included in the report, how they are framed and edited, the discourses they use, and the tropes they exemplify – all of which humanizes Palestinians and potentially makes it easier for Americans to identify with them. Moussa Al-Silawi's testimony, the first testimony in the American edition, is reported seamlessly in English, without any hesitations or repetitions in speech, no awkward English expressions, and no sign of translation, thereby erasing an important symbol of linguistic and cultural difference.[23] The testimonies included in the American edition foreground certain issues for an American audience while omitting others. For instance, Moteeh Al-Silawi's testimony included disturbing and graphic details of dismembered bodies, which are omitted in the American edition.[24] What is included, however, is his appeal to a global public: "Where is the world? Where is international law? Is this what the Palestinian people deserve, our children screaming? Where are the Arab countries?" His condemnation of both Arab and Western nations may make his plea more acceptable to Americans. His testimony thus functions both as a reminder of a failure on behalf of the international community to prevent human rights abuses, and as prod to intervene in the ongoing conflict.

In human rights advocacy, the figure of the innocent child is "the humanist foundation stone" (Hapgood 2013, 69). Stephen Hapgood argues that the suffering child – "the central figure of liberal humanism" – is a "proxy for naturalness (guilelessness, blamelessness). In this way both compassion and justice can be anchored on the child. Nothing is more authentic" (71). Whereas the Israeli report that rebuts the Goldstone Report downplays the deaths of civilians (Meir Amit 2010), in the testimonies selected for the American edition the figure of the child –

---

23 Excerpts from Moussa Al-Silawi's testimony are printed in Horowitz et al. (2011, 15).
24 Excerpts from Moteeh Al-Silawi's testimony is included in Horowitz et al. (2011, 136).

who has been killed, dismembered, and orphaned as a result of the attack – is prominent. Moussa Al-Silawi, for example, articulates his shock explicitly in relation to the deaths of children: "I have lived 91 years, I have seen everything, but ... I have never seen such a catastrophe. We see our children dead ... We transport them to the hospital ... and then we carried them to the cemetery." His repeated references to children resonated with concerns about Israel's assault on Gaza that were expressed in the media during the attack. By drawing attention to the killing of children and parents, and the shattering of family bonds, the Palestinian testimonies make a moral case that the IDF showed a reckless and callous disregard for Palestinian life and the families that sustain it. Images of the brutal separation of parent (usually the mother) and child – which following Clare Kahane I call 'the familial trope' – are often used to solicit identification and compassion from an audience (see Kahane 2001). The figure of the child and the familial trope work rhetorically to facilitate testimony as an "intercultural technology" that brings people together across cultural and social differences, positioning them in "relationship with one another in such a way that obligations are put into play and communities of solidarity are formed" (McLagan 2006, 193).

Another dimension of the American report – its implicit endorsement of psychology, and specifically trauma discourse – merits attention for its transnational reach. On the basis of his ethnographic research with humanitarian mental health workers in Palestine and Israel, Didier Fassin argues that a "new language of trauma" has replaced the language of oppression, and the image of the suffering victim has taken the place of the liberation fighters of the past (see Fassin 2008, 532). This new language "adds psychological and cultural representations to the political and moral representation of the facts" (Christian Lachal, as quoted in Fassin 2008, 532). In the political arena "trauma produces the suffering being just as humanitarianism produces the victim" – and in this way the presence of psychologists and psychiatrists enables and makes necessary a particular form of subjectification (Fassin 2008, 533). Fassin, together with Richard Rechtman, has analyzed the effects of teams of psychiatrists and psychologists, who see it as their task to bear witness to Palestinian suffering. They place the Palestinian case in the broader context of the development of humanitarian psychiatry, which, as a clinical and moral diagnosis, is used worldwide to communicate the suffering of victims to the world (Fassin and Rechtman, 2009). The forms of subjectivity that are produced through humanitarian psychiatry, in Palestine as elsewhere, enable individuals to exist not only as victims, but also politically. Indeed, victims are compelled to use the language of human rights and trauma if they hope to make political claims that have a chance of being heard in the transnational public sphere. This is precisely what we see in the testimony of Moussa and Moteeh Al-Silawi.

Humanitarian psychiatrists and psychologists working in Gaza and Israel have been crucial in moving testimonies into the global public sphere. Fassin argues that the Israeli-Palestinian conflict, especially since the second intifada, is "the site where the politics of testimony has relied most on psychiatrists and psychologists" (Fassin 2008, 535). Of the fourteen testimonies included in The Nation's edition of the Goldstone Report, several are by psychiatrists and psychologists, working on both sides of the conflict. Dr. Rony Berger, for example, testifies that 28.4% of the population of Sderot, an Israeli town, "suffer from PTSD as a result of constant exposure to rocket fire from Hamas" (Horowitz et al. 2011, 53). Dr. Tawahina testifies that the Gaza war had "led to many, many psychological disorders, the treatment of which and the rehabilitation of the victims will need a very long time …" (Horowitz et al. 2011, 37). "Recourse to the concept of trauma," Fassin argues, "expand[s] the range of victims considerably…. Potentially the entire Israeli population is susceptible to suffering from posttraumatic stress symptoms." He adds a caveat: "But the farther away the individual is from the attack, the less clinical the description …" (Fassin 2008, 550). In other words, the primary use of trauma discourse is not only or not even necessarily to achieve a clinical diagnosis. Rather, "to talk of suffering in order to speak about domination is to do morals and politics with new words" (Fassin 2008, 532). The Goldstone Report repeatedly uses the psychological language of trauma to draw attention to the long-term effects of violence on the affected populations. The mission, for example, states that it believes that "the Israeli armed forces arbitrarily prevented the evacuation of the wounded from the al-Samouni area, thereby causing … severe psychological trauma in at least some of the victims, particularly children" (Horowitz et al. 2011, 124). Through such statements it legitimates trauma – "a new language of the event" – as the moral discourse for understanding and interpreting violence in our time. It does so, however, at the expense of speaking in the explicitly political terms associated with an older vocabulary of liberation struggle – a vocabulary of violence, domination, oppression and liberation (Fassin and Rechtman 2009).

The American edition of the Goldstone Report further domesticates Palestinian testimony for a US audience through its concluding essay, "Messages from Gaza," by Laila El-Haddad. At the time of the assault on Gaza, El-Haddad was living in North Carolina with her husband and two young children. A journalist from Gaza, she is the author of a blog, "Gazamom," and a memoir, *Gaza Mom: Palestine, Politics, Parenting and Everything in Between* (2010). Through her self-fashioning as "Gazamom," El-Haddad positions herself as a 'rooted cosmopolitan' – tied to specific places but also crossing territorial and national borders. By joining together the American familial idiom 'mom' with the remote 'Gaza,' she brings her identities as Palestinian and American into intimate proximity, and temporarily collapses the cultural, geographic and political distance between Gaza and the US.

During Operation Cast Lead, El-Haddad reported on her daily and sometime hourly conversations via Skype with her father and mother, moving seamlessly between the American domestic and the Gaza domestic under siege. Her essay opens with a poignant memory: "When I spoke to my father over Skype the night of January 16, 2009, from Durham, North Carolina, it was with the very real possibility that we might never see or speak to each other again. He was in his home in Gaza City, in the heart of Israel's assault on Gaza" (El-Haddad 2011, 417). She tells readers that during the assault she and her father did back to back interviews on CNN, which legitimates their speaking positions in the United States. "I called my parents every hour; sometimes every few minutes when I saw renewed bombardment on my television screen, my eyes fixed on Al Jazeera English a good part of the day despite my son Yousuf's nagging to switch to cartoons" (418). Skype brings distant places into intimate proximity; cartoons and missile strikes compete for visual space. When El-Haddad daughter's first birthday occurred during the siege, she "couldn't help but think: Who was born in bloodied Gaza on that day?" (419). Representing Palestinians in familial terms valued by Americans, El-Haddad challenges media images of Palestinians as anti-Western terrorists. Instead, Gaza becomes a place peopled with moms, dads, and kids, and Americans are invited to identify with their terror.

El-Haddad's essay – a diary of transnational familial conversations during Operation Cast Lead – constitutes a personal and now public memory. While the first part humanizes Palestinians for an American audience, the second half provides a history lesson. El-Haddad explains that "Gaza is an occupied territory that has been subject to a premeditated, methodical siege since the free and fair parliamentary elections in 2006" (420). She proposes that "the siege is not about food and sustenance … it is about freedoms: freedom to move in and out of Gaza … freedom to learn, to work, to farm, to build, to live, to prosper." Her strategic appeals to freedom, a cherished American value, create a basis for American readers to identify compassionately with Palestinians trapped in Gaza, and to respond to *The Goldstone Report's* call "for action, for accountability" (421). The overwhelming message is one of Palestinian humanity and dignity: "we Palestinians are human, like you."[25] Her essay – another example of how testimony functions as an 'intercultural technology' – invites Americans to demand that Israel respects Palestinian human rights to live in dignity and free from occupation.

---

25 For an incisive account of how life writers from conflict zones in the Middle East produce identification with Western audiences, see Whitlock (2007, 34–35).

The Goldstone Report, informed by the Holocaust paradigm and the global memory imperative, exemplifies the way memory travels transnationally. It has documented and publicized violations committed during Operation Cast Lead, it has contributed to collective memory, and it has attracted significant publicity transnationally. But to return to the question I asked earlier, how effective is the Goldstone Report as a form of transnational memory in achieving the ultimate end of human rights – to end human rights abuses against Palestinians? Here, the concept of the transnational public sphere may provide some insight into the obstacles blocking the effectiveness of the human rights regime.

Conclusion: the transnational public sphere and the limits of memory

The concept of transnational memory implies, as its corollary, a transnational public sphere. Michael Warner (2002) argues that a public exists by virtue of being addressed, and that "texts that can be picked up at different times and in different places by otherwise unrelated people" are "crucial in constructing publics" (51). As texts that publicize violations and shape public opinion, human rights reports such as the Goldstone Report address "otherwise unrelated people" and thereby bring into being a transnational humanitarian public. As Nancy Fraser (2007) has argued, the concept of the public sphere has implicitly assumed a Westphalian frame, in which the public sphere was "a bounded political community with its own territorial state" (8). As was evident in the case of the Goldstone Report, however, "current mobilizations of public opinion seldom stop at the borders of territorial states" (Fraser 2007, 14). Thus, public sphere theory and memory studies are both confronting significant conceptual and empirical issues as they shift focus from a national to a transnational frame. It may therefore be beneficial to memory studies to consider how public sphere theory responds to the challenges raised by the transnational as a field of operation.

Fraser argues that while the concept of a transnational public sphere is today both taken for granted and empirically plausible, it poses conceptual challenges to the theory of the public sphere. The public sphere has been envisioned as a site for democratic discussion of ideas that do not necessarily agree with those of the national government. In the political theory of democracy, a public sphere is concerned with the legitimacy and efficacy of "public opinion as a political force" (Fraser 2007, 7). In this context, "publicity is supposed to hold officials accountable and to assure that the actions of the state express the will of the citizenry. Thus, a public sphere should correlate with a sovereign power" (7). These issues go to the very heart of the legitimacy and efficacy of a transnational regime such as human rights, which works to generate public opinion in contexts in which the interlocutors are not fellow members of a national political community. For instance, in the case of the Gaza conflict, transnational public opinion is mobilized not to hold Israel accountable to its citizens, but rather, to the moral standards of global civil society (8). But how effective is the transnational public sphere, supported by the human rights regime, in pressuring a sovereign power? Fraser observes that rather than "institutionalizing debate among citizens who share a common status as political equals, post-Westphalian publicity appears in the eyes of many observers to empower transnational elites, who possess the material and symbolic prerequisites for global networking" (11). This criticism has been repeatedly leveled at the human rights industry, which despite its ubiquitous presence in the occupied Palestinian territories, has failed to alleviate Palestinian suffering and end the occupation.

Rather than jettison the concept of a transnational public sphere, Fraser proposes that it needs to be reformulated to take account of the conditions that prevail in a post-Westphalian world. To this end, she articulates the "all-affected principle:" in a transnational world, "public opinion is legitimate if and only if it results from a communicative process in which all potentially affected can participate as peers, regardless of political citizenship" (Fraser 2007, 11). In the case of the Gaza conflict, this would mean that Palestinians, even though they are stateless, should participate as peers in a communicative process of making claims of abuses and constructing memories that circulate in the transnational public sphere. The public hearings held by the Goldstone Mission enabled Palestinians some small participation, not simply as victims but as political subjects, in the process of generating public opinion about the conflict, and demanding that Israel, and indeed 'the world,' be held accountable.

What relevance do these observations have for transnational memory studies? Levy and Sznaider presume that memories of atrocity, and I have argued, the circulation of testimonies of ongoing violations, will generate publicity and a response from global civil society. "Publicity," Ignatieff points out (2003, 53), "is only effective to the extent that others report and care about the exposed shortcomings of the government in question." In the case of the Gaza conflict, documentation of human rights violations alone is not enough to compel international intervention. There are also geopolitical realities that determine whether nations or international bodies will intervene. Florian Hoffman argues that human rights discourse is now facing competition from an expanding "human security discourse" (2006, 403). Israel defends its punitive actions in Gaza on the grounds that Hamas poses a terrorist threat to Israel's citizens, and Operation Cast Lead was necessary for Israel's security. In a context in which human rights competes with human security, it does not follow that scrutiny from the human rights regime is transforming Israel's national sovereignty – its sense of itself as an inviolable nation. Indeed, Israeli leaders have interpreted the Goldstone Report as an attack on the legitimacy of the nation itself and as an 'existential threat.' In its wake, the government of Israel has become more defensive, and demanded greater patriotic loyalty from its citizens to counteract international criticism, especially of the IDF. Moreover, to the extent that human rights actors and institutions support claims for a sovereign Palestinian nation, the human rights regime is not working against the concept of the nation-state or national sovereignty per se. Rather, it is working against the ways in which Israel invokes national sovereignty to oppress Palestinians and legitimate violence against them. It is also worth recalling that a nation's right to self-determination is a foundational principle of international law. Thus, what we see in human rights discourse is a tension between subverting nationalism in defense of universal rights and protecting nationalism as a state right. Nation-states would not, of course, join the international human rights system if their own rights were invalidated.

The American edition of the Goldstone Report, which addressed American readers both as citizens of the United States, and as potential members of a transnational public sphere, raises additional considerations concerning the effects of the transnational human rights regime on national sovereignty. The American edition aimed to generate public opinion and to spur debate not only on Israeli policies towards Palestinians, an issue that had long been censored in the United States by claims of anti-Semitism. It also invited debate on the American government's unconditional support for Israel. In lobbying the American government to change its policies on Israel, Americans operate as members a national public sphere. Their criticism of American support for Israel would need to go "through the institutions and agencies of the nation-state." Thus, a transnational network such as the human rights regime needs "to work with and through … nationalism to achieve maximum political effectivity" (Cheah 2006, 43). Rather than human rights contributing to the demise of national sovereignty, as Levy and Sznaider propose, it may be more accurate to recognize that the publicity generated by human rights campaigns and reports is a case of "nationalism operating in a cosmopolitical [or transnational] force field" (Cheah 2006, 42). As members of a transnational public sphere, American readers could also choose to participate in global civil society initiatives, such as the BDS campaign, to pressure Israel to change its policies towards Gaza, but these campaigns also work, at least some of the time, on and through national governments.

Rather than assume that the human rights regime is transforming national sovereignty, then, the Israeli-Palestinian conflict, as illustrated through the case of the Goldstone Report, compels us to consider the limits of the global memory imperative in a geopolitical system in which nation states still hold sovereign power. The Goldstone case, which generated significant publicity, demonstrates that human rights reports do indeed create a form of transnational memory of events. The Goldstone Report has been effective at producing a temporary mobilization of global civil society, as indicated by the *Blueprint for Accountability* event. Indeed, the growing BDS campaign against Israel suggests the possibility of a longer-term mobilization. Although the Holocaust paradigm was invoked both explicitly and implicitly in the Goldstone Mission, the global memory imperative – i.e. stimulating a public memory and awareness of human rights violations – did not achieve the intended aim of ending human rights violations and changing Israeli policy towards Palestinians in Gaza and the Occupied Territories. Referring to the human rights industry, Lori Allen asks a pressing question: "how [does] … a system that so obviously does not deliver on its promise continue to grow, functioning as if it could fulfill those ideals" (Allen 2013, 20)?

The optimistic claims of 'never again' – made for both the Holocaust paradigm and the global memory imperative – are clearly overstated. While the fact-finding mission public hearings did not lead to the prosecution of members of the IDF or Hamas for war crimes, the public hearings did create a testimonial archive of Palestinian and Israeli testimonies, which is now available to activists, filmmakers, writers and historians to mine for political purposes and for cultural memory. Contemporary technologies, such a live video streaming and audio and visual recording, have transformed these 'live' testimonies into recorded memories that are now preserved on the internet for posterity. In contributing to a local and global memory, this archive constitutes an important legacy of the Goldstone Mission. It can be used to preserve memory until such time as there is a national or transnational community ready to receive and act upon it (Gutman 2011). But this result is a far cry from the claims of preventing violations that are routinely made on behalf of the global memory imperative.

References

Allen, Lori. "Martyr Bodies in the Media: Human Rights, Aesthetics, and the Politics of Immediation in the Palestinian *Intifada*." *American Ethnologist* 36.1 (2009a): 161–180.

Allen, Lori. "Mothers of Martyrs and Suicide Bombers: The Gender of Ethical Discourse in the Second Palestinian *Intifada*." *Arab Studies Journal* 17.1 (2009b): 32–61.

Allen, Lori. "The Scales of Occupation: 'Operation Cast Lead' and the Targeting of the Gaza Strip." *Critique of Anthropology* 32.3 (2012): 261–284.

Allen, Lori. *The Rise and Fall of Human Rights: Cynicism and Politics in Occupied Palestine.* Stanford: Stanford UP, 2013.

Al-Silawi, Moteeh. Testimony 6. *The Goldstone Report: The Legacy of the Landmark Investigation of the Gaza Conflict*. Eds. Adam Horowitz, Lizzy Ratner, and Philip Weiss. New York: Nation Books, 2011. 136.

Al-Silawi, Moussa. Testimony, presented in Gaza on www.un.org/webcast/unhrc/archive.asp?go=090628 (accessed 30 December 2012).

Al-Silawi, Moussa. Testimony 1. *The Goldstone Report: The Legacy of the Landmark Investigation of the Gaza Conflict*. Eds. Adam Horowitz, Lizzy Ratner, and Philip Weiss. New York: Nation Books, 2011. 15.

Baxi, Upendra. "Voices of Suffering and the Future of Human Rights." *Transnational Law and Contemporary Problems* 128 (1998): 125–169.

Cheah, Pheng. *Inhuman Conditions: On Cosmopolitanism and Human Rights*. Cambridge: Harvard UP, 2006.

Cohen, Stanley. "Government Responses to Human Rights Reports: Claims, Denials, and Counterclaims." *Human Rights Quarterly* 18. 3 (1996): 517–543.

Douglas, Lawrence. *The Memory of Judgment: Making Law and History in the Trials of the Holocaust*. New Haven: Yale UP, 2001.

Dudai, Ron. "Advocacy with Footnotes: The Human Rights Report as Literary Genre." *Human Rights Quarterly* 28 (2006): 783–795.

El-Haddad, Laila. "Messages from Gaza." *The Goldstone Report: The Legacy of the Landmark Investigation of the Gaza Conflict*. Eds. Adam Horowitz, Lizzy Ratner, and Philip Weiss. New York: Nation Books, 2011. 417–421.

El-Haddad, Laila. *Gazamom: Palestine, Parenting, Politics and Everything in Between*. Charlottesville: Just World Books, 2010.

Erll, Astrid. "Travelling Memory." *Transcultural Memory*. Ed. Rick Crownshaw. Special Issue *Parallax* 17.4 (2011): 4–18.

Falk, Richard. "The Goldstone Report: Ordinary Text, Extraordinary Event." *Global Governance* 16 (2010): 173–190.

Falk, Richard. "What Future for the Goldstone Report? Beyond the Name." 20 April 2011. richardfalk.wordpress.com/2011/04/20/what-future-for-the-goldstone-report-beyond-the-name/ (accessed 28 February 2014).

Fassin, Didier. "The Humanitarian Politics of Testimony: Subjection Through Trauma in the Israeli-Palestinian Conflict." *Cultural Anthropology* 23.3 (2008): 531–558.

Fassin, Didier, and Richard Rechtman. *The Empire of Trauma: An Inquiry into the Condition of Victimhood*. Trans. Rachel Gomme. Princeton: Princeton UP, 2009.

Felman, Shoshana. *The Juridical Unconscious: Trials and Traumas in the Twentieth Century*. Cambridge: Harvard UP, 2002.

Felman, Shoshana and Dori Laub. *Testimony: Crises of Witnessing in Literature, Psychoanalysis, and History*. New York: Routledge, 1992.

Fraser, Nancy. "Transnationalizing the Public Sphere: On the Legitimacy and Efficacy of Public Opinion in a Post-Westphalian World." *Theory, Culture and Society* 24.4 (2007): 7–30.

Goldstone, Richard. "Reconsidering the Goldstone Report on Israel and War Crimes." *Washington Post*. 1 April 2011. articles.washingtonpost.com/2011-04-01/opinions/35207016_1_drone-image-goldstone-report-israeli-evidence (accessed 17 January 2013).

Goldstone, Richard. "From the Holocaust: Some Legal and Moral Implications." *Is the Holocaust Unique? Perspectives on Comparative Genocide*. 2nd edn. Ed. Alan S. Rosenbaum. Boulder: Westview Press, 2001.

Gutman, Yifat. "Transcultural Memory in Conflict: Israeli-Palestinian Truth and Reconciliation." *Transcultural Memory*. Ed. Rick Crownshaw. Special Issue *Parallax* 17.4 (2011): 61–74.

Hapgood, Stephen. *The Endtimes of Human Rights*. Ithaca: Cornell UP, 2013.

Hirsch, Marianne and Leo Spitzer. "The Witness and the Archive." *Memory: History, Theories, Debates*. Eds. S. Radstone and B. Schwarz. New York: Fordham UP, 2010. 390–405.

Hoffmann, Florian F. "'Shooting into the Dark': Toward a Pragmatic Theory of Human Rights (Activism)." *Texas International Law Journal* 41.3 (2006): 403–414.

Horowitz, Adam, Lizzy Ratner, and Philip Weiss, eds. *The Goldstone Report: The Legacy of the Landmark Investigation of the Gaza Conflict*. New York: Nation Books, 2011.

Human Rights Watch. *Rain of Fire: Israel's Unlawful Use of White Phosphorus in Gaza*. New York: Human Rights Watch, 2009. www.hrw.org/reports/2009/03/25/rain-fire (accessed 15 April 2009).

Ignatieff. Michael. "Human Rights, Sovereignty, and Intervention." *Human Rights, Human Wrongs: The Oxford Amnesty Lectures, 2001*. Ed. Nicholas Owen. Oxford: Oxford UP, 2003.

Jilani, Hina, Christine Chinkin, and Desmond Travers. "Goldstone Report: Statement Issued by Members of UN Commission on Gaza War." *The Guardian* 14 Apr. 2011. www.guardian.co.uk/commentisfree/2011/apr/14/goldstone-report-statement-un-gaza (accessed 28 April 2011).

Kahane, Claire. "Dark Mirrors: A Feminist Reflection on Holocaust Narrative and the Maternal Metaphor." *Feminist Consequences: Theory for the New Century*. New York: Columbia UP, 2001. 161–188.

Kennedy, Rosanne, Jonathan Zapasnik, Hannah McCann, Miranda Bruce. "All Those Little Machines: Assemblage as Transformative Theory." *Australian Humanities Review* 55 (2013): 45–66.

Kennedy, Rosanne. "Memory, History and the Law: Testimony and Collective Memory in Holocaust and Stolen Generations Trials." *Memory and History: Understanding Memory as Source and Subject*. Ed. Joan Tumblety. London: Routledge, 2013. 50–67.

Khalidi, Rashid. "Palestinian Dispossession and the U.S. Public Sphere." *The Goldstone Report: The Legacy of the Landmark Investigation of the Gaza Conflict*. Eds. Adam Horowitz, Lizzy Ratner, and Philip Weiss. New York: Nation Books, 2011. 375–386.

Khalili, Laleh. *Heroes and Martyrs of Palestine: The Politics of National Commemoration*. Cambridge: Cambridge UP, 2007.

Klein, Naomi. "Introduction." *The Goldstone Report: The Legacy of the Landmark Investigation of the Gaza Conflict*. Eds. Adam Horowitz, Lizzy Ratner, and Philip Weiss. New York: Nation Books, 2011. xi-xvii.

Landsberg, Alison. *Prosthetic Memory: The Transformation of American Remembrance in the Age of Mass Culture*. New York: Columbia UP, 2004.

Levy, Daniel and Natan Sznaider. "Memory Unbound: The Holocaust and the Formation of Cosmopolitan Memory." *European Journal of Social Theory* 5.1 (2002): 87–106.

Levy, Daniel and Natan Sznaider. *The Holocaust and Memory in the Global Age*. Trans. Assenka Oksiloff. Philadelphia: Temple UP, 2006.

Levy, Daniel and Natan Sznaider. *Human Rights and Memory*. University Park: Pennsylvania State UP, 2010.

McLagan, Meg. "Principles, Publicity, and Politics: Notes on Human Rights Media." *American Anthropologist* 105.3 (2003): 609–612.

McLagan, Meg. "Introduction: Making Human Rights Claims Public." *American Anthropologist* 108.1 (2006): 191–195.

McLagan, Meg. "Human Rights, Testimony, and Transnational Publicity" *Nongovernmental Politics*. Eds. Michel Feher, Gaëlle Krikorian, and Yates McKee. New York: Zone Books, 2007. 304–317.

Meir Amit Intelligence and Terrorism Information Centre. *Hamas and the Terrorist Threat from the Gaza Strip: The Main Findings of the Goldstone Report versus the Factual Findings*. Israeli Intelligence and Heritage Commemoration Centre, March 2010.

Mondoweiss, "What the Goldstone Op-ed Doesn't Say." *Mondoweiss* 5 April 2011. mondoweiss. net/2011/04/what-the-goldstone-op-ed-doesn't-say.html (accessed 18 January 2013).

Montell, Jessica. "Beyond Goldstone: A Truer Discussion about Israel, Hamas and the Gaza Conflict." *Washington Post Opinions* 5 April 2011. articles.washingtonpost.com/2011-04-05/opinions/35230405_1_goldstone-report-judge-richard-goldstone-israel (accessed 18 January 2013).

Pilkington, Ed. and Conal Urquhart. "UN Gaza Report Authors Round on Goldstone." *The Guardian* 14 April 2011. www.guardian.co.uk/world/2011/apr/14/un-gaza-report-authors-goldstone (accessed 28 April 2011).

Pogrebin, Letty Cottin. "The Unholy Assault on Richard Goldstone." *The Goldstone Report: The Legacy of the Landmark Investigation of the Gaza Conflict*. Eds. Adam Horowitz, Lizzy Ratner, and Philip Weiss. New York: Nation Books, 2011. 409–416.

Rothberg, Michael. *Multidirectional Memory: Remembering the Holocaust in the Age of Decolonization*. Stanford: Stanford UP, 2009.

Rothberg, Michael. "Beyond Tancred and Clorinda: Trauma Theory for Implicated Subjects." *The Future of Trauma Theory*. Eds. Gert Buelens, Sam Durrant, and Robert Eaglestone. London: Routledge, 2013. xi–xviii.

Sarkar, Bhaskar and Janet Walker, ed. *Documentary Testimony: Global Archives of Suffering*. New York and London: Routledge, 2010.

Sourani, Raji. "The Right to Live in Dignity." *The Goldstone Report: The Legacy of the Landmark Investigation of the Gaza Conflict*. Eds. Adam Horowitz, Lizzy Ratner, and Philip Weiss. New York: Nation Books, 2011. 329–336.

Tutu, Desmond. "Foreword: A Call to the Community of Conscience." *The Goldstone Report: The Legacy of the Landmark Investigation of the Gaza Conflict*. Eds. Adam Horowitz, Lizzy Ratner, and Philip Weiss. New York: Nation Books, 2011. vii-ix.

UN. *Human Rights in Palestine and Other Occupied Arab Territories: Report of the United Nations Fact-Finding Mission on the Gaza Conflict*. Human Rights Council Twelfth Session [A/HRC/12/28]. 29 September 2009. www2.ohchr.org/english/bodies/hrcouncil/docs/12session/A-HRC-12-48.pdf (accessed 28 February 2014).

Warner, Michael. "Publics and Counterpublics." *Public Culture* 14.1 (2002): 49–90.

Whitlock, Gillian. *Soft Weapons: Autobiography in Transit*. Chicago: University of Chicago Press, 2007.

Wieviorka, Annette. *The Era of Witness*. Trans. J. Stark. Ithaca: Cornell UP, 2006.

Wilson, Richard. "Representing Human Rights Violations: Social Contexts and Subjectivities." *Human Rights, Culture, and Context: Anthropological Perspectives*. Ed. Richard Wilson. London: Pluto Press, 1997. 134–160.

Marie-Aude Baronian

Archive, Memory, and Loss: Constructing Images in the Armenian Diaspora

"You can always go back to an image but not to a land" (Naficy 1997, 215). These words by Canadian Armenian filmmaker Atom Egoyan allude to the impossibility of his ever returning to a homeland or Origin; unprecedented mass destruction has radically affected the ancestral territorial locus and resulted in a large diasporic community, whose members remain deeply perturbed and expropriated in the multi-layered sites of their existence. The Armenian genocide of 1915, initiating the systematic annihilation of a people, was followed by a long and persistent campaign of denial that continuously agitates the Armenian community in their search for a sense of home. The planned destruction of a people has thus been pursued and amplified in this active policy of denial and negation: every trace of the Catastrophe was meant to disappear. As a result, Armenians in diaspora have to struggle to defend their memory and continuously feel the need to adduce visual evidence in order to legitimate their inherited historical past.

The aim of this chapter is to question the assumed co-substantiality of images, archives, and memory, by showing how the relation between these elements is based in loss and destruction. I want to show that the production of memory in transnational movements requires, first and foremost, a critical understanding of the process of destruction that underlies the compilation of any archive. Focusing on the nature of archives will ultimately prove to be a fundamental tool for studying collective remembrance in the case of dislocated histories, specifically that of the Armenians. While it is generally accepted that all memory cultures are in some sense dynamic, a dynamic that in contemporary times is increasingly linked to the mobility of people, such dynamics become all the more relevant when discussing cultures that have undergone drastic displacements along with the widespread destruction of the evidence pertaining to their experience (see also Hirsch and Miller 2011). This suggests the interest of analyzing the diasporic memory of the Armenian genocide through the idea of archival dynamics.

The purpose of this chapter is accordingly twofold: to disclose, echoing Jacques Derrida, the inherent tension and complexity of the archive in the case of the Armenians and its effect on remembering practices, and to position the audio-visual work of filmmaker and artist Atom Egoyan in relation to the distinctive work of the (professional) archivist. In particular, as I shall show, his artistic practice creates archives that respond to the experience and memory of displacement, and turns them into *imaginary archives.*

The term 'archive' has multiple meanings and can be used to refer to a document, a place, an institution, or a process; it can also be used metaphorically. But in all cases, its usage is linked to memory. There is no doubt that archives, in the literal sense of repositories of knowledge, are decisive for memory formation and for giving people access to history. Nevertheless, despite our reliance on archival objects, the force of the archive is always already crossed by silences, obscurities, breaks, ruptures or frustrations, and tensions. In the same way that images are, ontologically speaking, always lacunary and incomplete, and never absorb the reality they represent, the archive is cut through by lacunae. While this is true of all archives and all images, it becomes of critical importance in the case of those dealing with an historical catastrophe that suffers a lack of (political) recognition in the phenomenal or social space.

In order to articulate this inextricable link between archive, image, and destruction, I will closely consider Derrida's account of the archive alongside Atom Egoyan's multiple (filmic) images. While the French philosopher has demonstrated 'fever' as constitutive of all archives, Egoyan has translated this same fever into an obsessive desire to fill the void of history by creating and constructing alternative archives. Egoyan's work translates a commitment to, even an obsession with, remembering the loss of history and home that is symptomatic of Armenians who live (or were born) outside the homeland Armenia. As Gregory Goekjian has argued:

> Put simply, the Holocaust constituted a symbolic end to the Jewish diaspora, whereas the Genocide is the symbolic origin of the Armenian diaspora: in actuality, of course, an enormous and powerful Jewish diaspora remains after the Holocaust, and Armenia had a significant diaspora for centuries before the Genocide. But whereas the Holocaust resulted in the creation of a concentrated, modern centre for Jewish historical discourse, the Armenian Genocide erased that centre, creating a 'nation' that has had to exist in exile and memory – in diaspora. (Goekjian 1998, 3)

Most Armenians living in diaspora were not born in Armenia per se, but they were born with the loaded tragic legacy of Armenia: an extremely heavy inheritance that forces the concept of the archive (within its multifaceted definitions) to be carefully examined.

From his very first feature films to his latest, as well as in his video work, installations, theatre plays, short films and films for television, Egoyan always 'talks' about the scars of Armenian history or deals with themes that relate to this particular history, for instance, the recurrent topic of loss. His Armenian references are sometimes oblique and hermetic (linked to narrative structure and visual style); at other times they are more overt (linked to proper names, cultural or political references, symbolic images, musical motifs, and physical appearances). As I will show, Egoyan's filmic and visual practices are also caught up with acts of remembering, originating from diasporic experience and perception that are fraught with an inextricably ambivalent desire to archive. In order to make this point, it is necessary to elaborate in more detail on the (epistemological and ethical) foundations, as well as the existential conditions, of archiving.

Archives and Destruction

While archives are central for preserving memory, there is no denying that they are also inevitably the products of selection, suppression, and the exercise of control. Certain pasts are sanctified, glorified, and canonized, where others are buried, neglected or even denied with power dynamics involved in remembering at every stage.[1] As Jane Taylor writes: "every act of codification is an act of selection" (Taylor 2002, 243). In the process of mediating memory, technology and its ability to enhance or to modify our remembering of the past also plays a role; as we will see, this is an issue that is abundantly present in Egoyan's work where the characters viscerally and even obsessively depend on audio-visual technology for freezing or controlling time, experience, and memories.

Ann Stoler has identified an "archival turn" in the humanities (Stoler 2002, 92–95), observing that a "move from archive-as-source to archive-as-subject gains its contemporary currency from a range of different analytic shifts, practical concerns, and political projects" (Stoler 2002, 93). She indicates a certain inflation of the concept in cultural theory, where it is too often used metaphorically to refer to any corpus of selective omissions and collections. Yet, as she specifies, all these studies engaging with the concept of the archive have one theme in common: the legitimation or validation of knowledge and its link to truth and political forces (Stoler 2002, 95). The result of this widespread interest is a general acceptance of the fact that archiving is never a neutral operation but one that involves ongoing transformations and the operation of different agendas. Who forms the archive and what are the processes, policies, and protocols of an archive's establishment and further maintenance?

This general 'archival turn' in the humanities can also be linked to a widespread fear of forgetting and to the "public panic of oblivion" characteristic of the current culture of amnesia (Huyssen 2000, 28). This explains the urge to col-

---

1 On the inaccessibility of (e.g. French national) archives, see Combe (2001).

lect, to store, and to gather: to *archive*. The "memory boom" characteristic of contemporary culture reflects our fear of amnesia, according to Huyssen, and makes us search, desperately and at times artificially, for any object that plays a role in modes of remembering and that can help constitute an archive of apparently incontrovertible facts. Nevertheless, in the case of a catastrophic event that has been denied, the desire for incontrovertible facts is profoundly compromised by the ways the event has been recorded, modulated, and presented. In what follows, I will argue that Egoyan's work attempts to step outside the realm of facts and historical truth, while the genocide remains nevertheless in desperate need of recognition. There is definitely more at stake than the mere establishment of and access to facts. As Derrida has deftly explained, "the perpetrator tries not only to kill, but to erase the memory of the killing, that is, to do, to act in such a way that no archive is left. … We know that the perpetrators, sometimes in an industrial way, in a massive way, try to kill not simply their victims but the memory, the names of their victims" (Derrida 2002, 66). Being suppressed and expelled from an official shared history, the genocide logically entails all sorts of discussions around the archive as a source of both knowledge and acknowledgment.

Disputing the value of Ottoman archives for facts about the Armenian genocide, which was actually engineered by the Turkish state and its agents, is still part of an active and vicious campaign in the denial of this event.[2] Marc Nichanian explains that this denial starts with the role of the archive in the rationalization of history and in memory: "At the very heart of his action, the genocidal executioner has already placed the denial, he has already thought of erasing all traces of his crime. He would have never done this if he had not found himself committed from the start to the archive's sphere of influence" (Nichanian 1994, 79). The denial of the Armenian Catastrophe starts with the very workings of the archive; the deniers have always already infected the archive with negation, and afterwards use the authority of the same archive to pursue their politics of denial. As a result, to discuss the archive strictly as a historiographic object and discourse in the case of the Armenians entails a vicious and perverted agenda. In the persistent (historical and political) denial, the status of the archive is thus very much at stake – not only its value and use as a repository of reliable historical documents, but more profoundly the logic and the dynamics behind it.

In the Armenian case, the necessity to inscribe the past with evidence of the original destruction of an archive produces the desire for another archive and the quest to establish one. The deniers, however, have an investment in destroying traces of the original event whilst creating an archive provided with power and

---

2 For a more detailed discussion on this controversy, see Sarafian (1999).

authority. But if one follows dictionary definitions, an archive always remains related to identifiable places; be this a 'small' object, such as a document, or an 'imposing' object, like a monument, an institution, or a venue to visit. In this sense, archives are understood as material and tangible, even if they remain inaccessible. Archives are there, and are meant to be 'touched.' Such a definition becomes complicated, however, when an archive is missing or at least seriously questioned. If we investigate the diasporic remembrance of the Armenian genocide, those concerns come to the fore.

Thanks to the emergence of the new field of archival science, we have become increasingly aware of the ways in which archives are involved in producing collective memory and cultural heritage, and how they function as instruments for constructing identity; contemporary archivists are not only 'technicians' who assemble information, describe data, and classify objects, they are also increasingly self-reflective subjects engaged in the responsible observation of the world they live in and enjoying a certain privilege in assigning value and visibility. As Dutch archive theorist Eric Ketelaar has demonstrated, archivists tell stories that are part of the bigger narratives of a societal context (Ketelaar 2001, 131–41).

Even though Derrida's reflections on archives can be seen as metaphorical or a-historical,[3] his seminal work *Archive Fever* (1995) nevertheless provides useful insights for understanding both the erasure of archival objects in the denial of historical pasts, and the artistic desire to create alternative archives. Derrida, and Ketelaar after him, critically engage with positivist notions of the archive, deconstructing the commonplace idea of the archive as something static.[4] Putting the archive at the centre of a psychoanalytical investigation,[5] Derrida shows how archival science is concerned with issues of memory and forgetting, desire, re-

---

3 Derrida is not, strictly speaking, an archive theorist, even if his work on the archive dating from the mid-nineties has deeply influenced archive theory and archival science. Prominent archivists and archive theorists, such as Eric Ketelaar, Terry Cook, Joan Schwartz, Wendy Duff, Verne Harris and Theo Thomassen have turned to Derrida for re-considering their practice within the paradigm of postmodernism, as social changes have confronted them with the need to re-orient their profession; and, indeed, their perception of the "new" archival practice owes much to the philosopher's ideas; see, for example, Cook (2000); Ketelaar (2001).
4 Before Derrida, Michel Foucault already argued in his *Archeology of Knowledge* (1969) that the archive is not simply an institution, but rather constitutes the law of what can be said or not; archives are both 'documents' of exclusion and 'monuments' to particular configurations of power.
5 The subtitle of the book *Archive Fever: A Freudian Impression* makes clear its psychoanalytical underpinnings; moreover, *Archive Fever* was originally meant to offer an etymological and psychoanalytical analysis of the concept while linking it to Judaism, and ultimately to show that psychoanalysis is a Jewish science.

pression, and so forth. Specifically, the compulsion to maintain and to store runs parallel to the instinct of destruction: the *death drive*. Derrida thus discusses the psychic dimensions of memory formation and, by digging into the unconscious forces underling the formation of archives, discloses and underlines their ambivalence; an archive is at once a solid place for storage and accumulation, and an unstable or fluid site that is subject to change. The original French version of *Archive Fever* or *Mal d'archives* includes an insert, in which Derrida explicitly touches upon the contemporary relevance of his topic. In these two additional pages, while still rejecting any facile identification of archive and memory, he admits that the archive does translate a profound desire and longing for memory, especially in the case of archives that have been concealed or destroyed for some perverted historiographic reason. This note clarifies the meaning(s) of the title and the French expression *mal d'archives*: translated into 'fever' in English, it refers to our need for archives in terms of a desire, drive, passion or repetitive compulsion, while in French *mal* also means 'evil.' Thus, 'archive fever' conjugates the sickness, the passionate burning, or the compulsive, repetitive and nostalgic desire for an archive: a desire to return to the most indisputable Origin, the absolute place of commencement.

Derrida's sophisticated analysis enables us to reflect on the pivotal position of the archive in the process of genocidal violence and its remembering. Obviously, Derrida's text is not a practical handbook for archivists; nor is it a guide to mnemonic practices. It does not apply to any identifiable institution in particular, but rather discloses the latent or hidden forces underlying the concept of archive itself. In order to understand the core position of archives in the Armenian genocide and to grasp the motivation behind diasporic archival practices attached to a fragile legacy and memory, one needs to scrutinize the dynamics of the archive – its *raison d'être*.

Central to Derrida's work is the idea that archives always remain open and incomplete, since new repositories of information could always emerge from private, even secret spheres. Even more profoundly, archives are characterized by a strongly provisional dimension since they are impossible to interpret in a definitive way. In this sense, they are dynamic and mobile, with every new meaning assigned to an archive supplementing and enriching it. Archives are open "infinitely to readings, interpretation, contestation" (Derrida 2002, 76).

Derrida insists that remembering and forgetting are not oppositional. On the contrary, forgetting is always co-present in any act of remembering since at the very moment of archiving something will always remain lost. The trace is both a mnemonic element and an erasure. "Therefore the work of the archivist is," in the end, "not simply a work of memory. It's a work of mourning" (Derrida 2002, 54). One needs to archive in order to forget, at least if to forget means to consign and keep safe – *somewhere, sometime.* "When I handwrite something on a piece of paper, I put it in my pocket or in the safe, it's just in order to forget it, to know that I can find it again while in the meantime having forgotten it. If there is pure forgetting, it's because the archive, in order to be safe, in a safe, should be external to me" (Derrida 2002, 54). In this way, the archive is to be understood in terms of an open-ended dynamic of remembering, forgetting, and mediating.

We associate archives, almost naturally and logically, with the idea of preservation, but we too often overlook the very fact that archives are always already bound to destruction. This is the "archive fever," as Derrida puts it, which is always related to death. Forgetfulness and erasure are part of the archival process, and, in some cases, radical evil may traverse it and create radical disappearances. Ultimately, "the death drive is not simply at work in killing, in producing death, but in trying to save, in a certain way, the memory" (Derrida 2002, 68). This dialectical aspect of the archive as a site of remembering and erasure is omnipresent in Egoyan's work, as we shall see; his aesthetics, his narrative or his protagonists constantly point to the liberating and yet destructive nature of archiving technologies and reflect on his own role in this process.

If destruction is always already part of the archiving process, power is also always at stake, as was mentioned earlier. According to Derrida, "there is no political power without control of the archive, if not of memory" (Derrida 1996, 41). Indeed, in the Armenian case, the perversion of the archive was a constitutive part of the genocidal machine:

> In the Armenian case, as in the Jewish case, we know that the perpetrators did not publish, nor did they leave behind them, any official or hidden document that would announce their intentions and their decisions! In the Armenian case, one must know that they have done better: they have put to work the genocidal machine as a denegating machine, true to modern exigencies regarding validation by way of the archive, exigencies that were, of course, diverted and perverted but thereby, and for the first time, confirmed and revealed. (Nichanian 2009, 26–27)

In this way, the genocide depended on the destructive power of the archive, which Nichanian calls an "historiographic perversion." "The archiviolithic power," as Derrida puts it (Derrida 2002, 42), represents a radicalization of the selectivity at the core of all memory. Building on this point in a crucial way, Derrida emphasizes that the archive is "not simply a recording of the past, but also something which is shaped by a certain power, a selective power, and shaped by the future, by the future anterior" (Derrida 2002, 40). It is always open to what he calls the "future to come," an unpredictable future. Actually, and here comes his conceptual twist to the archive as we usually conceive it, archives do not exclusively concern the past, but are instead oriented towards the future. Their meaning(s) is always yet to come, along with our responses to it. "The archivist produces more archive, and that is why the archive is never closed. It opens out of the future" (Derrida 1996, 68). Indeed, "this future-oriented structure of the archive is precisely what confronts us with a responsibility, an ethical and political responsibility" (Derrida 2002, 46). Derrida underlines the messianic component of this future orientation: "if we want to know what that will have meant, we will only know in times to come. Perhaps. Not tomorrow but in times to come, later on or perhaps never" (Derrida 1996, 36). This unpredictability and openness of the archive is also to be found in Egoyan's images which never seem to depict the past as much as to question its haunting and imposing traits. The spectrality and the unforeseeable nature of the archive haunt his multiple images in the same way that the unpredictable future of the archive ineluctably occupies and animates the work of the archivist.

Egoyan and the archives of loss

If *Calendar* (1993) is Egoyan's most direct reflection on what it means to 'be' Armenian (and to shoot in Armenia), and if *Ararat* (2002) most explicitly addresses the tragic Armenian past, his preoccupation with his Armenian roots is also present in other projects such as his first feature *Next of Kin* (1984) and his second *Family Viewing* (1987),[6] as well as in video installations.[7] Indeed, most of his works reveal Egoyan's concern with Armenia's tragic history of genocide, a legacy that implies both a complex personal and political responsibility and an endless desire to find ways to represent it. This type of filmmaking can best be described using Laura Marks' notion of "intercultural cinema." This is "constituted around a particular crisis: the directly political discrepancy between official history and 'private' memory" and is crucially characterized by the fact that it "uses experimental means to arouse *collective* memories" (Marks 2000, 60 and 62).

In one work after another Egoyan continuously raises questions. How can the Armenian past be remembered (or not)? What scars or imprints did this history leave us? Moreover, he expresses a fascination with memory in a broader sense, and specifically, with the link between memory and technology. His entire oeuvre questions the (im)possibility of remembering, as well as our access to what must be (or cannot be) remembered, generating ongoing reflection on the uncertain and open future of the Armenian catastrophic legacy. Over and again he produces images and territories to recall and anchor this past.

---

6 For a close analysis of this film, see Baronian (2005).
7 See, for example, *Return to the Flock* (1996) or *America, America* (1997).

It is not surprising, then, that traumatic memory is a frequent theme in Egoyan's oeuvre,[8] and that most of his filmic characters are confronted with it. It is because some events (or the Event) have always somehow defeated their inscription into the archives that they keep returning under the form of a transgenerational trauma.

The irrepressible and recalcitrant trace of some trauma (e.g. a personal or a collective loss) is not only marked into the characters' moves and behavior, but also pervades Egoyan's authorial position as he constantly returns, reiterates, and repeats the spectral motifs of loss. As Derrida insists, "it is because this radical drive to destruction is always at work ... that the desire for archive is a burning one" (Derrida 2002, 44). This drive is adopted not only by the diegetic characters, but by Egoyan as well.

The filmmaker's approach to the legacy of genocide is highly reflective in that it endlessly questions the power of the visual while lamenting the lack of images and media with which to transpose the Catastrophe into the realm of the visible. As Georges Didi-Huberman has written in relation to the Shoah: "we often ask too much or too little of the image. Ask too much of it – 'the whole truth' for example – and we will quickly be disappointed ... we ask too little of images: by immediately relegating them to the sphere of the *simulacrum* – admittedly something difficult in the present case – we exclude them from the historical field as such" (Didi-Huberman 2008, 32–33). In the light of these remarks, Egoyan's filmic gesture would appear not to be motivated by the need to reach the signs of the Catastrophe in its wholeness, but rather by the ineffable dialectics of rendering it present and acknowledging its absence. His oeuvre is not concerned with exposing the factual truth of the Catastrophe or with replicating archival documents since it does not deal with proving the actual occurrence of the genocide. Instead, a film such as *Ararat* visually discusses it without entering into the repetitive perversity of justification and explanation, of collecting material evidence and legitimating the Event. Such 'perversity' is what the perpetrator wants: for the victims and their heirs to have to prove over and over again that 'It' happened. If the filmmaker were to bring evidence and substantiate the collective mass murders, then this would merely serve the demands of the perpetrator, who would claim that the absence of authentic images means that there is no proof that the genocide actually took place.

---

8 Traumatic memory, following Barbara Misztal's definition, "has its origin in some terrible experience and which is particularly vivid, intrusive, uncontrollable, persistent and somatic" (Misztal 2004, 161).

The plot of *Ararat* is constructed around the present-day making of a spectacular Hollywood-style epic film to depict the tragedy, which is directed by a famous filmmaker – the fictional character of Edward Saroyan played by the famous French-Armenian singer Charles Aznavour. As Saroyan's shooting of a film on the Armenian genocide is being depicted, other characters appear to contribute to its production by projecting their own perception and/or expertise onto the traumatic theme. Next to film director Edward Saroyan, other protagonists are indeed tied to the genocidal legacy and its denial. Ani is an art historian of Armenian descent who is writing a book on the Armenian painter and genocide survivor Arshile Gorky while also working as a consultant for Saroyan's film. Her son Raffi, a young man assisting Saroyan on the set, is desperately trying to understand the meaning of his dead father's extreme commitment to the recognition of the genocide (his father was killed by the police while attempting to assassinate a Turkish diplomat). There is also the character of an actor of Turkish descent who plays the 'bad guy' in Saroyan's film and cannot acknowledge, despite his involvement in the making of the film, the existence of the genocide. What ties these characters together is the inheritance of the genocide, its historical, temporal, generational and filial displacement.

Egoyan juxtaposes and edits various temporalities and narratives as *Ararat* jumps between different times, locations, and narratives, even to the extent of including scenes in the studio of artist Arshile Gorky (1904–1948). Mostly known as an American Abstract Expressionist, Gorky was also a survivor of the genocide and an iconic figure of the Catastrophe circulating in the Armenian diaspora.[9] With the 'film within the film,' Egoyan opens up and complicates our approach to this particular dislocated history; in doing so, he brings into focus what cannot be viewed otherwise. It shows that "to remember one must imagine" (Didi-Huberman 2008, 30). By proposing two films (Saroyan's and his own) Egoyan underscores simultaneously the necessity and the impossibility of reaching the Event. The first minutes of the two-hour film display the diasporic framing of this process of remembering. It starts by portraying Gorky's art studio (with close-ups of some meaningful material attributes); then we see the face of Saroyan at Toronto airport, immediately followed by video footage of Mount Ararat. The first sequences of the film thus combine three different visual trajectories epitomizing three Armenian emblems or hallmarks of the diasporic memory: Gorky the painter, the singer Aznavour, and the Mount Ararat. The issue of multiplicity and displacement, concentrated in this way in the opening sequences, is pursued throughout the film by crystallizing multiple mnemonic codes, figures, and prac-

---

9 For a closer look at Gorky in contemporary diasporic artistic practices, see Baronian (2013).

tices and showing their operation in translating the feeling of loss and belonging characteristic of Armenian diasporic communities.

Ararat deploys a plurality of visual media, since every character is involved in the process of making images or at least responding to images. Each character tries to make sense of the genocidal past and its legacy by interacting with visual media: there is the 'film within the film' (from the filmmaker, the actor, and the film's scriptwriter to the driver/production assistant and the consultant, everyone is confronted with the denial of the Catastrophe), a painting by Gorky, and an amateur video by the young Armenian Raffi. Each medium permits, albeit artificially and partially, a coming to terms with the traumatic past with the help of images. In this process, *Ararat* does not recycle any archival images. Instead, the images we see *become* an archive. They 'recycle' history in a new, more 'visible' light, which offers the possibility of envisioning the scars of the Catastrophe. The film thus produces its own found footage in order to remind us, in a rather reflexive way, that such footage and evidential documentation has not yet been unearthed or publicly shown. By including Saroyan's epic film, Egoyan underscores the need for representation; this filmic *mise-en-abyme* puts forward an immense question about representation itself, since the Armenian Catastrophe is characterized by its suspension. To represent genocide is a challenge, because of the ontological and phenomenal discrepancy between the horror of mass murders and the means available to depict it; all the more so in this case since filmic representations of the Armenian genocide remain rare. Borrowing Lipovetsky and Seroy's terms, we might conceive *Ararat* as symptomatic of 'memorial cinema' since it problematizes our capacity to understand the past in the present and offers a contrast to character Saroyan's classical historical film (Lipovetsky and Serroy 2007, 178). Although Saroyan and Egoyan's films do not become conflated, they both operate as archival film practices by pointing to the occlusion of the Event. Their difference lies in the way they aesthetically translate the archival drive.

Ararat clearly deals with the trans-generational trauma of the genocide and its filmic representation, and does not offer a one-dimensional depiction of the Armenian genocide in its historical circumstances. It critically reflects on different aspects of the archive. Firstly, it recalls its selective and 'disorienting' nature; the genocide is nowhere to be located, seen, or touched in the film. Secondly, Egoyan resists the temptation to equate the archive with a site of pure memory or with an undisputed narrative incorporating the magnitude of what is at stake. Thirdly, the film suggests the ongoing addition of layers of perceptions and experiences to the framing of the genocide across generations. Raffi's character, for example, decides to go to Turkey (to those parts that used to be Armenia) to shoot natural footage of the land on video in order to counter the artificiality of Saroyan's filmic reconstruction. Raffi comments: "When I see these places, I realize how much we've lost. Not just the land and the lives, but the loss of any way to remember it. There is nothing here to prove that anything ever happened." The ruins, as he refers to the land, might refract death and are at the same time the cipher of what constitutes Armenianness in the community's constant longing for archives. Moreover, as Naficy has observed, "[i]n accented films, certain aspects of nature and culture such as mountains, ancient monuments and ruins, are used as powerfully cathected collective chronotopes that ... condense the entire idea of nation 'particularly in the case of those nations whose' status is in dispute, as with Palestinians, Kurds and Armenians" (Naficy 2001, 160). The mountain of Ararat, which we see on Raffi's video and reproduced (artificially) on Saroyan's film set, is an example of such a collective fetishized symbol that condenses certain mythologies circulating in the diaspora.

The multitude of memorial and mnemonic artifacts in *Ararat* (e.g. a photograph, a painting, a film, a video diary) and the use of various filmic surfaces and textures, together conjure up multiple possibilities for anchoring the catastrophic legacy as well as the impossibility of capturing it 'for good' in a unique and transparent visual surface. Moreover, the film reveals the chronotopic effects of objects as they travel from different times and spaces through generations. The Event, as Elena del Rio has written, "cannot be found in any single isolated performance, story, or medium, but, more productively, in the resonating effects between different media performances and in the affects generated therein" (del Rio 2008, 19). Egoyan's filmic association of (visual) objects, territories, and media thus refracts the imaginary relationship between Armenians in diaspora and what is lost. In ways that echo the quote from Egoyan with which I began, images come to fill in a deserted locus. Images duplicate the experience of displacement – the displacement of a people, of a history, and of a territory. In other words, the scattering and de-territorializing experience is somehow re-territorialized in new imaginary sites that translate the paradoxical desire to return in a virtual and not actual way.[10]

Ararat disseminates and accumulates various filmic plots and sub-plots, together with multiple characters, within a series of scenes, cutting rather quickly from one to the other. The result is a plethora of filmic spaces, narratives, and visual possibilities that do not merely function as aesthetic devices to 'torture' the uncomfortable spectator, but instead develop into a very conscious construction that, with the help of a wide range of strategies, accords with the density and complexity of the issue at stake. These strategies are adopted by the characters themselves, who, in turn, mirror the in-between spaces of the Armenian postmemory condition.

---

10 On this 'spiritual' and subjective sense of belonging to the homeland, see Panossian (1998).

In his burning desire to provide a space for this imposing traumatic narrative within his oeuvre, Egoyan's cinema takes up the accents of *diasporic filmmaking*, juxtaposing personal, intimate history with contested History. As Hamid Naficy reminds us, "every story is both a private story of an individual and a social and public story of exile and diaspora" (Naficy 2001, 31). Egoyan is obviously aware that archives are pivotal for the 'inscription' of both the catastrophic event and a certain cultural mythology that is somehow promoted and intensified when approached from a diasporic angle. Armenians in the diaspora manifest their longing and desire for a past or a homeland that can only exist in their imagination. In Naficy's terms, Egoyan is to be counted among the *accented filmmakers*, whose "style demonstrates their dislocation at the same time that it serves to locate them as authors" and whose diasporic films are accented by multiplicity, plurality, and the performativity of identity (Naficy 2001, 22, 14–15).

Indeed, Egoyan, fascinated and obsessed with images, looks to any possibility to capture the fractures of the experience of fracture, be this collective or personal. As most of his characters find neither a single peaceful moment to mourn nor a site of storage for their grief, Egoyan's cinema accommodates an imaginary place where those fractures might be discerned, sometimes subtly or elliptically. Ultimately, those images become a barometer for loss, functioning like archival objects given their artificial, technological, and prosthetic character. Egoyan's "you can always go back to an image but not a land" suggests that the audio-visual and technological aspects of memory become reinforced or over-invested in the diasporic experience. To remember the Armenian genocide is a displacement in itself: to remember it outside the original and natal loci, and to remember it outside its original historical time. Egoyan's multiple visual works not only translate an obsession with the way that genocide haunts Armenians in diaspora, but also with the way that the heritage of the Catastrophe can only be *imagined*. Constructing a memory of the genocide binds Armenians in diaspora together, and this is expressed by archival needs refracted in the production and preservation of certain visual lexicons and iconographies.

The filmmaker's visual enterprise can thus be seen as an archival one, that conflates remembering and forgetting as constitutive of the same "fever," and attempts "not simply to forget that the violence has taken place, but simply to forget the effects, the suffering, the pain, and so on and so forth, the violence itself, the intensity, the quality of the violence" (Derrida 2002, 80). The eagerness to film – to grasp images, to voice the silences – is to construct an archive in order to locate memory somewhere where it can be restfully forgotten. A similar struggle with "moving on" and escaping the burden of a haunting past is shared among the characters in Egoyan's films, who also rely on audio-visual means and technology for coping with their loss and their grief.

Egoyan's cinema (and his many filmic or visual projects) is characterized by repetitive perspectives in its representation, transmission, and experience of the past. His images as well as his filmic characters are deeply concerned with finding ways, be they productive or counter-productive, to penetrate the past and to store and convey private and collective experiences. His speaking position or his strategy of "postmemory," as Marianne Hirsch defined this,[11] is conjured up in an ongoing fascination for recalling past events and experiences in the present. It is as though Atom Egoyan himself takes over the role of archivist and assigns a similar role to most of his filmic protagonists. They are obsessively preoccupied with collecting, gathering, ordering and evaluating objects, experiences or events by means of ritualistic behavior and recording technologies.

Egoyan is captivated not only by the memorial marks that we carefully and compulsively collect, but above all by the place and space these nostalgic objects occupy, their physical, emotional, and mental texture, and their role in shaping experience through the substance they provide or hauntingly withhold. Indeed, most of his filmic characters gather, accumulate, and consign archival objects in order to ensure their emotional or filiative territory. Those archiving acts prosthetically invest objects and images with the value, meaning, and order necessary for transmission and what could be called 'reparative kinship' to take place. In *Next of Kin*, Azah preciously safeguards a family album. In *Family Viewing* the main character Van acts like the archivist of his own life story when he saves and re-classifies the home video tapes of his Armenian childhood, while his father is obsessed with recording his adult sex games on tapes. In *Speaking Parts* (1989), Clara keeps visiting a videographic public mausoleum where she can access and watch footage of her deceased brother. In *The Adjuster* (1991), Noah,[12] an insurance adjuster, indexes the (material) value of his traumatized clients' destroyed goods by listing those objects and their values, while his wife Hera is a censor working for a company (whose offices are clearly depicted on screen as a huge archive) that examines, defines, evaluates and classifies pornographic films and magazines according to strict censorship criteria. In *Calendar*, a photographer travels to Armenia to

---

11 Postmemory "is distinguished from memory by generational distance and from history by deep personal connection. Postmemory is a very powerful and very particular form of memory precisely because its connections to its object or source is mediated not through recollection but through an imaginative investment and creation ... Postmemory characterizes the experience of those who grow up dominated by narratives that preceded their birth, whose own belated stories are evacuated by the stories of the previous generation shaped by the traumatic events that can be neither understood nor recreated" (Hirsch 1997, 22).

12 Note the significance of this proper name in Armenian mythology and Christian culture; Noah's ark ended up on top of Mount Ararat, where the earth was reborn.

take pictures of churches, which he will use to make a wall calendar intended to document and to anchor those national emblems for Armenians in diaspora. In *Felicia's Journey* (1999), Hilditch not only collects, classifies, and labels old cookery TV show tapes starring his mother; he also collects his young female victims literally like a serial killer. In *Ararat*, as we have seen, an actor, a filmmaker, and a scriptwriter all gather archival accounts to historically document and support the film they are producing on the Armenian genocide. In *Adoration* (2009), the young Simon, whose parents both died when he was only a child, devotedly treasures his father's original designs and his mother's letters. More generally, all of Egoyan's characters are involved in acts of recording and filming, which obviously feeds a need to capture and leave traces of what was once there, or to substantiate what they perceive and experience. Indeed, Egoyan's fictionalized characters all record, document, memorialize. What is more, Egoyan directed a film adaptation of Samuel Beckett's theater play *Krapp's Last Tape* (2000), which clearly deals with archival materials and recording technology; he even expanded this project into two other video installations that also touch on the archiving of past experience.[13]

Egoyan's entire oeuvre translates an obsessive desire with what has been or might be lost – a place, a home, an object or a loved one. Images are shown to provide a safe location or a refuge where, even if only in a temporary and prosthetic way, remembering and forgetting merge. His dislocated narrative and montage, together with his disconnected characters, reveal the authorial signature of a subject seeking a sense of home that would peacefully protect the various memorial attributes of images, as well as the memory of the Armenian people.

Egoyan's practices and his concerns resemble those of the (postmodern) professional archivist. His multifaceted oeuvre (in terms of media, strategies, themes, genres, and presentation contexts) involves collecting words, images, symbols, and sounds. His awareness of mediality becomes evident in a fascination for the material qualities of his medium that leads him to exhibit the dispositif at the center of his films and other works. He also recycles footage from his earlier work. The feature film *Calendar*, for example, starts with the image of an endless, fast-moving flock of sheep, which is simultaneously a symbolically condensed figure of the idyllic, timeless, pastoral image of the (lost) homeland and a historical reference to the thousands of Armenians who were forced on death marches into the Syrian Desert or drowned in the Black Sea. The image of sheep then recurs

---

13 For the installations *Steenbeckett* (2002) and *Hors d'usage* (2002), see Romney (2003, 158–170). For Romney, this consistent interest is actually in "the graven image, the trace of thought and memory as inscribed in physical material, whether paper, celluloid or audiotape" (158).

in some of his other works such as the experimental short film *Diaspora* (2000) and the video installation *Return to the Flock* (1996): this not only provides an allusive visual depiction of actual geographical places, but also gives a metaphoric impression of displacement and endless movement, and a diasporic feeling that includes the transnational movement of memory.

Egoyan also uses images from films that were inspirational for him, and were, so to speak, part of his own film archive. In the short film *Diaspora*, he recycles footage by the Turkish-born Greek exile director Elia Kazan's *America, America* (1963), a film that also inspired Egoyan when he made *Calendar*. The story of *America, America* delves into the epic and exilic adventures of a young Anatolian Greek immigrant pursuing his dream of going to America. In *Diaspora*, Egoyan selects from *America, America* the scene in which an Armenian church sheltering an Armenian community is burning. Just as he recycles the scene of the flock of sheep in a number of films and installations, Egoyan re-uses Kazan's image of the burning church for one of his video installations, also entitled *America, America* (1997, Venice Biennale, Armenian Pavilion). The burning church scene in *Diaspora* stresses the circular and endless movement of the fire and of people running all over the place trying to save themselves, which gives the viewer an impression of intense movement that coincides with the repetitive aesthetics of the film (consisting of two images from his previous films *Calendar* and *The Adjuster* that are reiterated in various formats and colors).[14] This emphasis on circularity and movement reminds us that history in this case cannot be characterized in terms of a seamless, intact, and transparent linearity; because of its prohibited, traumatic, and never self-evident nature, it can only be represented in an obsessively repetitive manner. Egoyan challenges the classical ideas of temporality and the past-present dichotomy by digging up the surfaces of cinema and other visual practices. In so doing, he generates "anomic archives" that do not abide by any rules,[15] except that of their own ineluctable bond to loss and destructiveness.

By putting himself at the center of certain works (as in *Calendar*, the short film *A Portrait of Arshile*, (1995) and the video diary *Citadel* (2003)), or by creating characters who echo his own biography (as Peter in *Next of Kin*, or Van in *Family Viewing*), Egoyan inevitably questions the meaning and weight of the catastrophic legacy that has been transmitted to him. His filmic posture engages both his displaced biographic Self, as someone of Armenian descent, and his filmic quest

---

14 For other elements of analysis on this film, see Baronian (2007).

15 I borrow this term from Ernst van Alphen (2008). In his "Visual Archives as Preposterous History," he discusses the effects of transforming the detainees of the Nazi concentration camps into archived objects, not as individuals but as traceable classified objects with a number: "selecting and sorting on the basis of a fixed set of categories are basic archival activities" (69).

for capturing and chasing images. As a result, Egoyan displaces and replaces the manifest and latent layers of the images he uses. This game of contextualizing and de-contextualizing, of recycling and bracketing, and thus of selecting and presenting, permits a reconfiguration of the invisibilities of the genocidal history in the same way that a consideration of the ideological context of the archival process would, according to Ketelaar, permit the disclosure of the "tacit narratives" of the archive. Without misappropriating the images and footage he plays with, Egoyan thus raises the issue of authorship and ownership in relation to images and history. The filmmaker's role in selecting images resembles the political responsibility of archivists charged with preserving painful historical events. In Egoyan's case, however, his use of images cannot be detached from his experimenting with narrative devices and his excavating perceptions of cultural history and identity. Nevertheless his reconfiguration of meanings and (un)certainties engages the spectator in the same way that contemporary archival practices often require the user's 'look' for generating meaning and value.

As an Armenian Canadian filmmaker, Egoyan is responsible for indicating a future-to-come as he obsessively returns to images that may replace or restore, prosthetically, the 'lands' of the Loss. In all of his films, he exposes the ambivalence inherent in recording technology, especially the videographic medium, which reveals as much as it conceals. In *Family Viewing*, Van can only access his Armenian roots through video footage, mostly home videos of his childhood, while his WASP father ritualistically erases the videos by taping over his sex games with his new wife. This is the "properly in-finite movement of radical destruction without which no archive desire or fever would happen" (Derrida 1996, 94). Armenians, in particular, are caught up in an inextricable archival dilemma: the need to produce evidential visual accounts out of the always already occluded and destroyed 'documentary' objects. And because the genocide heavily impregnates Armenian cultural heritage in diaspora, the archival drive is somehow intensified and amplified as it points to the eagerness to restore and replace what has been lost for many generations.

This simultaneous and ongoing persistence of the presence and absence of the genocidal history upholds Egoyan's filmic death drive, as he obsessively and repeatedly seeks and constructs alternative imaginary archives for the Event to be remembered, *some day somewhere.*

References

Adoration. Dir. Atom Egoyan. Sony Pictures, 2008.

Ararat. Dir. Atom Egoyan. Miramax, 2002.

Baronian, Marie-Aude. *Mémoire et image: Regards sur la Catastrophe arménienne*. Lausanne: L'Age d'Homme, 2013.

Baronian, Marie-Aude. "Image, Displacement, Prosthesis: Reflections on Making Visual Archives of the Armenian Genocide." *Photographies* 3.2 (2010): 205–223.

Baronian, Marie-Aude. "History and Memory, Repetition and Epistolarity." *Image and Territory: Essays on Atom Egoyan*. Eds. Monique Tschofen and Jennifer Burwell. Waterloo: Wilfrid Laurier UP, 2007. 157–176.

Baronian, Marie-Aude. "Archiving the (Secret) Family in Atom Egoyan's *Family Viewing*." *Shooting the Family*. Eds. Patricia Pisters and Wim Staat. Amsterdam: Amsterdam UP, 2005. 147–162.

Calendar. Dir. Atom Egoyan. Zeitgeist Films, 1993.

Citadel. Dir. Atom Egoyan. Ego Film Arts, 2006.

Combe, Sonia. *Archives interdites: L'histoire confisquée*. Paris: La Découverte, 2001.

Cook, Terry, and Joan M. Schwartz. "Archives, Records, and Power: From (Postmodern) Theory to (Archival) Performance." *Archival Science* 2.3/4 (2002): 171–185.

Cook, Terry. "Archival Science and Postmodernism: New Formulations for Old Concepts." *Archival Science* 1.1 (2000): 3–24.

Del Rio, Elena. "Ararat and the Event of the Mother." *Canadian Journal of Film Studies* 7.2 (Fall 2008): 18–34.

Derrida, Jacques. *Archive Fever: A Freudian Impression*. Trans. E. Prenowitz. Chicago: University of Chicago Press, 1996.

Derrida, Jacques. "Archive Fever" (A seminar by Jacques Derrida, transcribed by Verne Harris). *Refiguring the Archive*. Eds. C. Hamiton, V. Harris, J. Taylor, M. Pickover, G. Reid, and R. Saleh. Dordrecht: Kluwer Academic Publishers, 2002. 38–80.

Derrida, Jacques, and Bernard Stiegler. *Echographies of Television: Filmed Interviews*. Trans. Jennifer Bajorek. Cambridge: Polity Press, 2002.

Didi-Huberman, Georges. *Images in Spite of All: Four Photographs from Auschwitz*. Chicago: University of Chicago Press, 2008.

Duff, Wendy, and Verne Harris. "Stories and Names: Archival Description as Narrating Records and Constructing Meanings." *Archival Science* 2.3/4 (2002): 263–285.

Family Viewing. Dir. Atom Egoyan. Cinephile/Angel Films, 1987.

Felicia's Journey. Dir. Atom Egoyan. Artisan, 1999.

Foucault, Michel. *L'Archéologie du savoir*. Paris: Éditions Gallimard, 1969.

Goekjian, Gregory. "Diaspora and Denial: The Holocaust and the 'Question' of the Armenian Genocide." *Diaspora* 7.1 (Spring 1998): 3–24.

Hirsch, Marianne. *Family Frames: Photography, Narrative, and Postmemory*. Cambridge: Harvard UP, 1997.

Hirsch, Marianne, and Nancy K. Miller, eds. *Rites of Return: Diaspora Poetics and the Politics of Memory*. New York: Columbia UP, 2011.

Huyssen, Andreas. "Present Pasts: Media, Politics, Amnesia." *Public Culture* 12.1 (2000): 21–38.

Ketelaar, Eric. "Tacit Narratives: The Meaning of Archives." *Archival Science* 1 (2001): 131–141.

Krapp's Last Tape. Dir. Atom Egoyan. RTÉ/Channel 4/Irish Film Board, 2000.

Lipovetsky, Gilles, and Jean Serroy. *L'Ecran global: Cultures-médias et cinéma à l'âge hyper-moderne*. Paris: Seuil, 2007.

Marks, Laura. *The Skin of the Film: Intercultural Cinema, Embodiment, and the Senses*. Durham: Duke UP, 2000.

Misztal, Barbara. *Theories of Social Remembering*. Maidenhead: Open University Press, 2003.

Naficy, Hamid. *Accented Cinema: Diasporic and Exilic Filmmaking*. Princeton: Princeton UP, 2001.

Naficy, Hamid, "The Accented Style of the Independent Transnational Cinema: A Conversation with Atom Egoyan." *Cultural Producers in Perilous States: Editing Events, Documenting Change*. Ed. G. E. Marcus. Chicago: University of Chicago Press, 1997. 179–231.

Next of Kin. Dir. Atom Egoyan. Connoisseur Video, 1984.

Nichanian, Marc. *The Historiographic Perversion*. New York: Columbia UP, 2009.

Nichanian, Marc. "L'Archive et la preuve: Les procès de la visée génocidaire". *L'Intranquille* 2.3 (1994): 79–84.

Panossian, Razmik. "Between Ambivalence and Intrusion: Politics and Identity in Armenia-Diaspora Relations." *Diaspora* 7.2 (Autumn 1998): 149–196.

Portrait of Arshile. Dir. Atom Egoyan. Ego Film Arts, 1995.

Romney, Jonathan. *Atom Egoyan*. London: BFI Publishing, 2003.

Sarafian, Ara, "The Ottoman Archives Debate and the Armenian Genocide." *Armenian Forum* 2.1 (Spring 1999): 35–44.

Speaking Parts. Dir. Atom Egoyan. Zeitgeist Films, 1989.

Stoler, Ann Laura. "Colonial Archives and the Arts of Governance." *Archival Science* 2 (2002): 87–109.

Taylor, Jane. "Holdings: Refiguring the Archive." *Refiguring the Archive*. Eds. C. Hamiton, V. Harris, J. Taylor, M. Pickover, G. Reid, and R. Saleh. Dordrecht: Kluwer Academic Publishers, 2002. 243–281.

The Adjuster. Dir. Atom Egoyan. Orion Classics, 1991.

Van Alphen, Ernst. "Visual Archives as Preposterous History." *About Mieke Bal*. Ed. Deborah Cherry. Malden: Wiley-Blackwell, 2008.

Susanne Küchler
Relational Maps in the Cook Islands Transnational Communities

Small island communities such as those in the Pacific have always been prone to explore life and establish trading posts someplace else. Famous illustrations of large scale pre-historic migration movements across wider Oceania are Lapita pottery and the Maori Whare Wanuga traditions whose large-scale distribution in space and time has led scholars to hypothesize the existence of "voyaging corridors" sustaining vast networks of trade and exchange (Pearce and Pearce 2011). Conducting fieldwork today in the Pacific islands, the unpredictable presence of key informants who are regularly on tour to relatives living in the metropolises of the Pacific Rim, Asia, America or even Europe, confronts one directly with the dominance in peoples' lives of new kinds of voyaging corridors made possible by air travel. What emerges from ethnographic research conducted among the thriving transnational communities of Eastern Polynesia as described in this chapter is the importance of maps charting biographical relations that enable people to establish and maintain relations of affinity at a distance.

The Cook Islands, an archipelago of fifteen tiny islands, eight of them inhabited, are a prime example of the heightened state of mobility among a population that has always accepted inter-island migration as a way of life. The total land area of the country is only 240 square kilometers, while its exclusive economic zone covers a maritime region of nearly 2 million square kilometers in Eastern Polynesia, stretching between Tonga and Samoa, on the one hand, and French Polynesia on the other. Since 1901 the group has been included within the boundaries of New Zealand, and its people, who are culturally close relatives of the Maoris of New Zealand, are citizens of that country. With the building of an airport in 1992 there has been a net outflow of Cook Islanders. In 2006, the number leaving for overseas was 969; the highest annual exodus was that of 2000, when 1,429 people left the islands, prompted by the economic reform program of 1995–1996, when large numbers of Cook Islanders took permanent residency in New Zealand, Australia, and the US. Today, more than 50,000 Cook Islanders reside in New Zealand and an estimated 15,000 in Australia.

Cook Island migrants have strong and lasting socio-economic ties to the homelands, and most want to return there after retirement to die and be buried on the islands. The nurturing of socio-spatial ties through a two-way flow of remittances and goods has been well studied for the Pacific (Evans 2001; Siikala 2001; Bennardo 2002; Addo 2013). What emerges from these studies is the importance of the knowledge of biographical relations as pathways for the movement of ideas and goods between communities. Even more importantly, relations of affinity are not constituted just by birth or marriage but are also 'elective,' resulting from friendships or collegial relations, with elective paths being remembered across generations and continuing to be of importance even if persons are not living in proximity with one another. This chapter will discuss the question of how such knowledge of biographical relationships is codified and transmitted when the effects of persons' lives are distributed, to be drawn upon and activated at different times for different reasons, thus resisting a simple model of commemoration that presupposes a shared 'canon' of memory derived from inter-subjectively recognized and anticipated actions.

The data from the Cook Islands exemplified here bring to the fore the use of combinatorial and fractal imagery in artifacts that serve as gifts essential to mark all life cycle stages and bind people to one another across generations in ways that are mirrored in the assemblage of motivic parts so that a single element allows for the spontaneous reconstitution and recognition of wholes. The empathy with images that is embedded in the intuitive grasp of a logic of image composition paves the way, it is argued, for distributed biographical relations to be activated in flexible ways, combined and recombined in a manner that is both open-ended and mutable, and yet stable. This modular logic of image composition harbors and sustains a de-centered and third-person conception of personhood whose distributed effects are gathered in a fashion that is reminiscent of Deleuze and Guattari's (1978) concept of the *rhizome*, that is, via a map that must be constructed, a map that is always detachable, connectable, reversible, modifiable, and has multiple entranceways and exits.

Rather than assuming that persons know their place in the world and command distributed social relationships common to transnational communities by personal conjecture or trial and error, this essay will thus advance the hypothesis that persons intuit such knowledge through images whose logic commands modular ways of being and thinking and supports what Casey (1998, 301–8), leaning on Deleuze and Guattari's distinction, has called "striated" space. Striated space refers to the conception of a landscape composed of distinct points or sites that are stable landmarks when navigating from one point or location to another. "Smooth" space, on the other hand, has indefinite extensions and people reside and move within it rather than toward fixed points. With striated space, containment, permanence, and renewal of spatial relations over time are paramount. The making and activation of the spatial loci of kinship that sustain the transnational communities of the Cook Islands is supported, I will argue, by modular, stitched patchwork maps that allow people to navigate co-variant relations of kinship by utilizing exclusively temporal images as landmarks. The distributed effects of persons that constitute the political economy of the household, from children to *taunga* (culturally sanctioned knowledge and its material articulation) to bank accounts, are marked to be gathered and rooted back in the homeland with the death of a member of a household. Lowered into the grave that sits right next to the house whose actions it recalls, the layers of patchwork wrapped around the body recall the fragile presence of a social body that is invisible in people's lives and that demands to be recollected over and over again.

Although much has been written with reference to the Pacific about the importance of culture in the fashioning of identity and of relations to the homeland, little attention has been paid so far to cultural differences in the conceptualization and transmission of politically and economically effective relations of kinship (Lee and Francis 2009). Mike Evans has described for Tonga the embedding of culture in a transnational context in which potential kin and kin-like relationships are actualized and maintained through exchange (Evans 2001, 58). Others, such as Cathy Small (2011) in her book on Tongan migration and transnationalism and Tevita O. Ka'ili (2005), capture the far-reaching exchange and social networks that are sustained by the cherished knowledge of socio-spatial ties. The mass movement and the multidirectional flows of people, ideas, and goods have been most richly described with reference to Tonga. It has been shown how reciprocal exchanges at all levels of Tongan society are organized through a socio-spatial ontology, which allows for space-defining artifacts such as woven mats to make manifest relations between persons in a non-random and predictable manner (see Ka'ili 2005, 91). The material translation of woven mats into stitched patchwork, which has occurred throughout Eastern Polynesia including the Cook Islands, allows us to see the role of composite images in the extension of personal agency and the fashioning of transnational household economies that control the flow of property, of ideas and of people in ways that are both predictable and memorable, yet also open-ended.

From Tonga, over to the Cook Islands, Tahiti and Hawaii, patchwork quilts known as *tivaivai* (tifaifai) have formed an incremental part of exchange economies throughout the twentieth century and have begun to replace artifacts made from plant fiber at important life cycle ceremonies (Jones 1973; Arkana 1986; Hammond 1986; Pogglioli 1988; Rongokea 1992; Shaw 1996; Küchler and Eimke 2009). While this essay restricts itself to the analysis of Cook Island patchwork, the findings should be seen in comparative perspective, raising questions as to the differential relational logic of transnational communities and its long-term and far-reaching effects.

Cook Islands patchwork in the making

The association of the patchwork quilt with memory, with protection and with the sustaining of connections hidden from plain view has inspired generations of scholars and practitioners.[1] The quilt in the Cook Islands may appear to us to inspire nostalgia as it comes as a tangible thing, one that has been crafted, altered, and used by people and that is telling of times gone past in ways which is matched possibly only by narrative. However, this interpretation would only capture the most overt expression of what quilts make possible in this society.

As Judy Elsley has argued in her book on *Quilts as Text(iles)*, the general topos of the patchwork quilt can be compared to a text which takes shape in blocks that form an ever larger pattern "whose central motif is change" (1996, 1). While the analogy with writing is not one I want to pursue here, it is useful in allowing us to discern a unique feature of the activity of quilting which lies in the patterning of a surface: like pen on paper, the pieces which compose the quilt serve to draw ideas together in a manner that speaks of a synergy of making and knowing which the final product carries forth as a potential. In the same way as we readily accept that the writing down of a narrative makes its content portable as well as comparable and combinable with other narratives that are written both before and after, patchwork made of stitched fabric pieces lifts the resulting pattern onto a spatial

Fig. 1. Tivaivai taorei stitched by Vereara Maeva; collected by the Rarotongan Hotel; photograph (2008) Susanne Küchler.

---

1 Sections of this text have been originally published in Küchler and Eimke (2009).

and temporal plane where it functions no longer as a singular, but as a multiplier, as a provocateur or agent of transmission.

Patchwork as a technique has its roots in European decorative sewing used to embellish clothing, bedding, and other textile items, either by itself or in combination with quilting, which is a different process all together (see Horton 2005, 17). The two techniques may be combined, as they have been in American colonial history, yet they can also be used on their own to create planar surfaces where patterns appear through stitching. In quilting, two or more textiles are layered through stitches that penetrate all layers and that form a design through an alignment of rows of stitches. Patchwork, on the other hand, involves combining small pieces of fabric to create a surface pattern; this additive process may either take the form of piecework, in which fabric pieces are sewn directly onto each other, or the form of appliqué, in which fabric pieces are arranged and sewn onto a fabric background that is part of the pattern.

Where patching occurs on its own, superimposed onto a second layer of fabric, as is the case in Eastern Polynesia, the resulting artifact is fragile and impractical for daily use, as any washing would be likely to shrink top and bottom layer in different ways; in the Cook Islands, moreover, the impracticality of the resulting sewing is heightened by the size of the quilt, and by the type of cloth used, which is not colorfast and is selected for properties that have more to do with the mode of fabrication, sometimes involving the tearing of cloth into pieces, than its durability. Were one to use these as bedcovers, the time invested in stitching tiny pieces into place would stand in no relation to the brevity of use the artifact would afford; unlike other forms of quilting, patchwork must be motivated by non-utilitarian considerations.

In fact, we get at the motivations behind patchwork when we ask what does the sewing of fabric 'do' when carried out ostensibly *not* for everyday use. What it does is brought out well in studies, mostly from the US, which use entire collections of quilts and their patterns to shed light on relations of kinship that have connected women to each other and to the homes they have inhabited (O'Bagy Davis 1990, 1993; Horton 2005). Patchwork appears to encode in its patterns a map of social relations that animates genealogical information by allowing the quilt to stand in for the maker and occasionally the person it was made for.

Beyond genealogical information, quilted patterns have been shown to document a microscopic perspective on attitudes to material culture within the home that can be compared to the macroscopic perspectives that are generally captured by historical studies of wider societal patterns of consumption and identity construction. Patchwork allows us to get a glimpse of preferences for texture, color, and even the print or the smell of cloth, its weight and its sounding when unfolded, which speak as much about the time and place inhabited by members of a household as the patterns which are created through patching pieces of cloth together. Patchwork thus makes tangible the wider material relations, evoking the character of a place and a time and carrying it to other lands and times. In the Cook Islands, patchwork is stitched by women throughout their married life to be sent away as a gift to the many overseas places where members of the household reside, and beyond these places via a network of friends and work colleagues whose lives have touched the household. Folded in cupboards and stored in trunks, patchwork is an invisible reminder of places and relations that call up a possible future, rather than just a known past.

The patchwork draws one into its own world by virtue of the simplicity by which it represents the lived-in material world, presenting it to us as retention that we can use to think with when comparing here and there, now and then, and when plotting the future course of our lives. Yet more than anything, it may be the pattern that attracts our attention, as it is suggestive of the maker in ways that are very difficult to fathom. There is the stitch, the size, and the shape of the pieces of cloth and the preference for ways of aligning them into a regular pattern, all elements that draw together a polyphony of relations that make up a person's identity. By drawing discrete elements together into a tightly structured composition, patchwork schematizes and thus enables the recall of biographical time, itself made up of manifold relations coming together in ways that projects an *idea* of relation.

We can thus assert that patchwork, wherever it is made, is likely to possess a distinct socializing and historicizing potential, as it encapsulates as composite the idea of relationality and serves as an instrument for the conversion of value into intangible values which are synonymous with the moral economy of the household. Such a conversion can be seen as the *qualisign* of a quilt, one that is inherently linked to its importance as agent of transmission: in other words, the fact that a patchwork is made of fragments of cloth is more than a metaphoric allusion to the quilt's capacity to 'gather' the distributed and relational elements of a person's life into a single frame, very much like a written biography, but must also be seen as an indicator of the political economy of the household.

The prevalence of patchwork in households, therefore, does not speak so much of economic necessity or virtue, but of a value placed on fabric as a material that is uniquely able to blend together distributed resources and relations, which gathered together make up a person's identity. Patchwork quilts are stored and treasured the world over, rather than sold and bought, and hold their value over time as a result of their ability to personalize the value of the cloth. The reason for the fabric's apparent capacity to transcend the socialness of things, which binds value into patterns of consumption, is unlikely to be explained, however, just by its materiality; the fact that a patched quilt is made from fabric would not adequately distinguish it from a host of other valuable fiber-based products such as weaving or clothing. Rather, it is to the technique of assemblage and the manner of composition that we must look to understand how patchwork can convert cloth into a measure that, at certain times, can be used to gauge and to reckon the relations between persons as well as between persons and things.

The patchwork quilt already denotes in its name the laborious task of the technique of 'patching' that captures the success and efficaciousness of the household economy. The fragility of the patchwork is a tangible reminder of the work of detaching, connecting, reversing and modifying that it demands. Patchwork is indicative of a surplus of fabric, but also of a surplus of time – suggesting a division of labor within and between households which enables the conversion of a tangible commodity into the manifestation of an intangible resource. When patchwork are sold or gifted in life-cycle events, their value is not measured in terms of the original cost of the fabric used for the manufacture, but in terms of a monetary value placed on the time it took to sew. As it is surprisingly less the material value of the fabric than the embedding of time into the folds of the fabric which matters when patchworks come to market, such patched quilts may be best described as a *sewing* – a notion which expresses the temporal performativity of patchwork whose material life is punctuated by moments of airing, inspecting, unpicking and re-stitching.

What is that time, however, which is thus measured by the technique of patching? Is it an abstract notion of time, a quantifiable entity of fragmented durations of a specified kind? Or is it an experienced measure of time, a moment in a woman's life that may be as long or as short as it appears in recollection? Both notions of time are grounded in experience and may be incited by the patchwork quilt, yet neither tells the full story, because time itself is transformed into a pattern in sewing patchwork, the combinatorial, fractal, and relative nature of which projects a map of biographical relations as a foothold for the navigation of trade and exchange relations sustained by households.

There is perhaps no better example for the work done by time maps in the fashioning of effective transnational relations than Cook Islands quilts. There are three different grand types of technique found in Cook Islands' sewing which I shall be introducing in this chapter, each with its own characteristic *durée* which comes to resonate in complex ways with the biographical relations people draw on when making claims to identity, land, and knowledge, and engaging kin in the many satellite communities overseas or back in the homelands in the passing back and forth of ideas, moneys, and goods of all kinds. Being gifted a patchwork obliges one to maintain a specific relation with the maker and members of her household, the nature of it is visible in the composition of its imagery.

The most important and rarest patchwork in the Cook Islands is known as *taorei*, and involves the creation of self-referential and replicated patterns by shredding fabric and restitching often several thousands of tiny pieces of cloth (see Figure 1). Each such pattern is known by its distinctive numerical combination of colored patches. The pattern is stitched by a number of women working together, each stitching a rectangular segment of a composite motif, which is then assembled into the patchwork. Women assisting the maker have a share in the pattern and are able to reproduce it in future patchwork, yet only the maker is able to pass it on to a selected granddaughter who inherits with the patchwork the *taunga* or knowledge of her grandmother, of which patchwork is just one articulation. The second technique, known as *ta taura*, involves cutting out composite parts of plants and arranging them symmetrically on the surface of the cloth – usually rotationally and in a replicative fashion – before affixing and revealing the depicted plant's identity through embroidery. *Ta taura* are gifted between members of the same generation and as such move beyond the furthest reaches of the household to be returned eventually and placed into the grave around the body of the maker. The third technique, known as *manu*, involves the symmetrical and repeated folding of a piece of cloth, the cutting of the shadow cast by a plant into the folded cloth, and the superimposition of the unfolded symmetrical cut out onto a piece of cloth of different coloration. *Manu* are gifted to friends and work colleagues, or to sons and daughters in support of their exchange obligations, and are often lost in the course of their rapid passage from one house to another.

Patchwork is hugely popular across Eastern Polynesia and a must have in the ceremonies that punctuate the life cycle, from significant birthdays and first haircuts, to weddings and funerals. Almost to underscore its role in cementing and crafting the transnational relations in support of a mobile population, patchwork sewing here is utilizing 'new' material, detaching thereby the materiality of the quilt from personal associations that worn and reused fabric may harbor. As sewing in the Cooks uses store-bought cloth, and as quilts are rarely stored or circulated in exchanges for longer than a generation, the retrospective which the patchwork quilt invites so clearly in the US is turned into a prospective enterprise. New cloth and new sewing is demanded for the many events that punctuate the calendar of households, making new communities and new extended tentacles of the household come alive through the inherently compositional actions of shredding and restitching cloth into always new and yet recognizable configurations.

We cannot understand the resonances provoked by such sewing, however, unless we note that its pattern is not the result of a random assemblage of scraps of cloth, but one that documents a consciously executed plan which started prior to the purchase of the material; a pattern, moreover, whose complex process of creation surpasses the functionality of the sewing as a decorative cover and situates it squarely in matters of direction-finding and future-directed thinking. The Polynesian quilt, and Cook Islands sewing in particular, we may note with surprise, is thus not just a documentation of something that we may verify externally by recourse to history, oral narrative, or written or remembered genealogies. Rather, it is the means by which such discourses about history and biographical memory are made possible through recourse to an abstract map of distributed personhood, revealing the logic by which relations are traced and connections are asserted that extend across time and space.

Time-maps

To visualize how *tivaivai* may effect the gathering of distributed effects and relations of the household in ways that sustain transnational communities unfolding between diaspora and homeland, it is useful to recall how they are made. As in weaving, it is impossible to arrive at a product which displays at least a certain amount of surface regularity or a definite size without making a prior plan, meaning that decisions need to be made about the type and quantity of the material, into what shapes it is to be cut, and in what order the pieces of fabric are to be assembled. When starting to work on the quilt, the needle effects the threading of the pieces, with the eye following the course of the needle, very much in the same way as the eye will traverse the surface of the finished work, taking a course that will effect what we may call the recognition of its pattern. Looking at this planar surface, or anticipating it in production, utilizes mental images that are derived from our experience of space, which is of course as much embedded in culture as in certain cognitive universals, given that our predisposition to experience space walking upright in a directional manner is limited by the material environment around us (see Johnson 1987). The translation of a mental image of space bounded by things into an image in which space is limitless, teasing the eye to move from point to point to search for connections between visual fields that cluster around points, is a task we call mapping.

Mapping, of course, will lead to different kinds of maps, depending on preconceptions about the nature of the connections between the points. A medieval map of the world, for example, placed emphasis on the biblical connections between points, thus creating a hierarchical map of continents and places radiating outward from the point of creation. Although it does not correspond to our experience of the world today, we can still 'read' this map with the knowledge of the cultural conventions that pertained at the time of making. The claim that Polynesian quilts are mappings of space-time calls for an investigation of the particular cultural conventions on which they are based.

Much has been written in psychology and anthropology about the conception of space, the representation of which appears to fall into two types: as either point fields or as automatically bounded 'containers.' The latter is the most widespread used the world over; the lack of an explicit name for this representation of space as a box filled with matter, despite our colloquial use of it (as people talk about space 'as a place in which something is located'), may indicate that it serves as a kind of default mechanism for thinking about space. It is only in modern, relativistically-oriented physics and cosmology that we adopt a point-field manner of representing space as essentially a *relation on points*, with distance being derived from the acceleration of particles *over time*.

Contemporary physics, in its attempts at understanding the nature of nonlinear and topological space/time in which boundaries are defined by the symmetrical overlap of adjacent topological fields rather than existing as axiomatic constituents of a given space, provides support for the common intuition that in the lived world, time and space cannot be disentangled. Surprisingly, however, only a few anthropologists have paid much attention to this fact, most notably Granet (1968) in his important account of Chinese conceptions of time and space. Granet's study provides strong evidence for the importance of temporal conceptions to the mapping of the world since they enabled the Chinese to navigate the oceans effectively long before people from the West. For in fact, the Chinese had figured out a way of calculating units of space to correspond to (accurately measured) standard units of time.

The preoccupation with keeping time in the linear and cumulative manner exemplified by the clock, however, is not necessarily found across cultures, even among cultures, like those of the South Pacific, whose livelihood depends upon successful navigation. A famous example of skilled navigation using maps of a kind that do not require the element of linear time, but which elevate a notion of fields of relative temporal motion, is known as the 'stick-chart' of the Micronesian Islanders (Ascher 2002). Such charts are a geometric arrangement of sticks and shells that depict the interplay of oceanographic phenomena such as wind and sea interaction around the atolls and landmasses. Using a relational and analogical mode of representation that depicts the interaction of shapes and motions in the sea and at the sea-land interface, the islanders deploy both an idealized version for teaching and an actual version for navigation across a complex topography that even includes the underwater landscape.

Time that is depicted in images of constricting or expanding motion between connected points thus feeds into an experience of space as de-centered and relational, rather than relative or egocentric. Jürg Wassmann (1994) has pointed to

Pacific artifacts such as knotted cords, which, like the stick-charts of Micronesian seafarers, direct attention to a topological conception of space that appears to be prevailing in the ocean-dominated landscape of the Pacific. Nowhere else may the practical significance of mapping topological relations of space-time be more straightforwardly important to people as in the Pacific where a constellation of island communities are dotted across the ocean expanse, covering over one-third of the world's surface area, while its total landmass, once Australia is excluded, equates to less than one-eighth of that of Europe. The Cook Islands are in fact a typical example of an island community in the Pacific: its tiny islands and atolls are dotted across an area the size of Europe, inhabited, in some cases, by just a few hundred people. Despite their lack of proximity, the people who inhabit these island communities are culturally and linguistically linked, and are known to have had longstanding and extensive trade and kinship connections with other even more remote island communities, such as the Society Islands some 2,000 miles to the north-east. In this environment, water is the predominant feature and resource, and is a pathway along which people, their produce, and ideas can travel.

In a world dominated by the ocean, like the Pacific, it is thus not surprising that artifacts of navigation have attracted a good deal of attention from anthropology and related disciplines (Gell 1985; Hutchins 1996; Stürzenhofecker 1998; Bennardo 2002). Surprisingly, however, the importance of sewing in the Pacific has so far been discussed without any attention being paid to spatial and temporal conceptions and their representation in an ocean-dominated landscape. This is perhaps because quilts fall so awkwardly between categories of things, between the useful and the valuable, that it is difficult to treat them in any other than straightforward terms – as material proof of the devotion of 'free' time to oneself and one's family.

And yet, it is precisely this observation which must force us to look more closely at what is done with this 'free' time, how it is made materially graspable and clad in images that fill the empty hours of the day as much as they fill the gaps between the points at which the needle is inserted in the cloth. It is by attending to these images as maps of distributed personhood that Cook Islanders are able to engage effectively with the fractured and scattered household that spans the many communities living in diaspora today. The *tivaivai* is thus not just capturing a restrospective of the household, but enables it to be replicated generatively in many places at the same time while retaining its distinctive identity.

There are no historical data that document the take-up of sewing and the fashioning of patchwork *tivaivai* across the island nations of Eastern Polynesia, from Tonga and the Cook Islands to Tahiti and Hawaii. For the Cook Islands we do know that cotton cloth was a sought-after trade item, and that cotton planting and printing were well established on the main island around 1850, barely

25 years after the London Missionary Society had arrived on the islands (Gilson 1980, 44–47). The emergence of patchwork in the Pacific has often been linked to the influence of missionary wives in light of the value ascribed to cotton fabric in the heyday of missionary activity. An alternative and interesting hypothesis advanced by Robert Shaw (1996) has argued instead that the inspiration for patchwork quilting happened prior to and independently of missionary activity. Writing about the history of the Hawaiian quilt, Shaw questioned the link between patching, which was indeed taught by missionary wives to foster domestic attitudes and time management, and patchwork, which in Hawaii resulted in a block-style quilt that involved the cutting of cloth into snow-flake patterns (Arkana 1986). Noting the absence of this type of sewing in the US during the early part of the nineteenth century, with the exception of Pennsylvanian missions who taught German paper-cut techniques at mission schools and only set foot in Hawaii in 1860, Shaw points out that Hawaiians may already have been familiar with sewing, clothing, and even quilts thanks to sailors on the trading ships that preceded missionary influence in the Pacific. In 1800, you could already buy almost everything on the shores of Hawaii, as the booming trade in sandalwood had brought Chinese silks, cotton, and costumes, transported by scores of Russian and Chinese ships. There is no literature to substantiate a link with the take-up of patchwork in the Pacific Islands, but we do know from maritime collections that sailors did not just engrave whale teeth, known as scrimshaw, but also practiced macramé, a type of lace-making, as well as patchwork to while away the long hours of idleness at sea. There indeed appears to be a tantalizing link between the idea of the mobility of home where sewing binds together distributed relations and the sailing ships' use of cordage to bind together the technical means of controlling forward motion within the ships' material frame.

The idea that sewing enables the literal 'stitching up' of space-time, by giving it a material frame where it is experienced as an uninterrupted flow punctuated only by landmarks, is a powerful one in the Pacific where the voyages of trading ships between islands would have lasted weeks at a time, always ending at a definite destination. Still today, the time it takes to move from point to point across the ocean is one that is felt deeply by islanders, often waiting weeks in bad weather for their trading ship to bring fresh loads of flour and petrol to drive electricity. The desire to make time connect more effectively with points beyond the horizon may thus quite feasibly have guided the interest of both sailors and Pacific Islanders in manipulating cloth in a manner that came to take on the form of patchwork (Siikala 1991, 3).

Much of the organization of the home that was set up during the nineteenth century by the London Missionary Society as part of their effort to inculcate new ways of thinking and being still exists today. The household is the microcosm of the Cook Islands economy and its foundation, but to imagine nucleated isolates striving to maintain a balance sheet of work and leisure would be entirely wrong, for the scattered parts of nucleated households dispersed across the islands and elsewhere are connected to one another both at the level of the social organization of production and at the level of consumption. The connections, which bind households together at the economic and social level, are founded upon sewing bees in which women participate on grounds of friendship, rather than genealogical connection. Such friendships may develop in and around activities organized in relation to the Church, but they may also be based on memories of working together or running communal affairs such as girls' scouts. Memories of events or of certain relations may prompt particular quilting patterns that forever after are associated with these moments that mark women's biographies. Once-off encounters and events such as collective visits by a church group to Australia may prompt a new sewing as much as the careful planning of events such as the first haircut of a son, a wedding or a funeral.

The timing of patchwork carried out by such sewing bees punctuates the hectic yearly calendar of every woman; there is the date set by the minister's wife for the annual or bi-annual competitive display of sewing, the group trips to workshops or visits, each requiring the need to carry sewing as a gift, as well of course as the many household specific ceremonies marking birthdays, weddings, funerals, and commemorative events. Women's sewing groups usually have a joint bank-account, stocked regularly from the sale of sewing at exhibitions and from other sources, used both to finance the purchase of new material and to update the material culture of their homes, the women taking it in turn to shame their husbands by purchasing a new cooker, a new set of dishes or whatever else may need replacing or adding to a house.

Timing one's sewing work is of great importance to fit in with the calendar of competitions and ceremonies that punctuate life in the Cook Islands. Finding time for sewing is not always easy as many women also have to attend to paid employment, to gardening, and to participating in the many year-round village sports as part of their daily chores. Many women resort to employing the services of others, either because these women are known to be expert cutters of cloth or particularly good at stitching a fine and regular line, or else because they themselves are going through a hectic phase in their lives at a time when their peers have settled down. Yet others have not learned to sew the fine stitches required for the making of quilts in the Cook Islands and deeply regret having to rely on other women's time to supply their house with quilts.

The timing of sewing, however, also constitutes the value of each quilt, as well as the labor costs it incurs. Thus women can estimate with ease the expense incurred in purchasing each other's time or skill, in asking others to do the stitching or the cutting to complete a quilt in time. Several women also have reciprocal arrangements to gift each other's time, which is in any case a prerequisite for the collaborative sewing of a large patchwork quilt, whose triangular sections are stitched by different women who expect as remuneration the return of such favors when it comes to the construction of their own quilt. By joining such cooperative ventures resulting in a patchwork quilt, women also inherit the pattern, which forever is associated with the circle of women and the circumstances that brought them together.

The quilt in a woman's life

Inspired by fiber-based techniques of lattice-work, the patchwork of the Pacific have emerged as key loci of a tacit knowledge of how to manage socially effective biographical relations in ways that resonate with genealogical relations, but which are nevertheless quite independent of kinship. Quilting is of interest to people in the Cook Islands, not because it sheds light on existing relations created through marriage or birth which regulate the transmission of land and of entitlement to positions of influence and power, but because new relations – of friendship, of adoption, and of acquaintance – can develop in the vicinity of a sewing which link the makers to each other. This glue, which binds across time and space people who have otherwise no other relation with one another, is the act of patching itself which translates actual events in time into abstract geometric patterns.

Overtly it is biographical events of the maker that are traced in the stitched patterns of the large and elaborate appliqué and piecework quilt patterns (Rongokea 2001). Akaiti Ama was the eldest of five children in an important noble family on Rarotonga. On her mother's side, she descended from Potiki Taua, a high priest appointed by Tangiia Nui Ariki to perform priestly functions, especially concerning the investiture of *ariki* (high chiefs) at the *koutu ariki* (chiefly court) named Arai-te-tonga-vare-roa-paa. On her father's side, she descended from an important chiefly line from Tahiti, Tamarua Nui. Akaiti Ama gave birth to nine children, but also taught throughout her married life: first as a schoolteacher and then as a high-school principal. In her later years she performed the important function of Justice of the Peace. Alongside her busy public life, she managed to design and sew *tivaivai* for her children. When she was pregnant with her last-born son, Akaiti kept her husband company in the family's pineapple plantation, an experience that inspired her to design and sew an unusual *tivaivai taorei*, which has survived her death as part of a collection of *tivaivai* owned by the Rarotongan hotel (see

Fig. 2. Tivaivai hanging on the line at the Rarotongan Hotel: from left to right, tivaivai ta taura and two tivaivai manu; photograph (2003) Susanne Küchler.

Figure 2). The pattern was shared by the other women who partook in the sewing of this quilt and passed on to the granddaughter of Akaiti's younger sister.

Stored, folded in treasure boxes or sent out those who have departed from the islands to take up work in distant lands, patchwork quilts are the tangible reminders of relationships that are thought to be integral to a person, while being distributed and externalized throughout life. It is symptomatic of this biographical aspect of patchwork that most women start sewing around the birth of their first child, as they begin to be active in the many exchanges that will connect their own household to as many other households as possible in the course of their life. As every quilt is made to be gifted, and is often sewn with a specific occasion and even a person in mind as recipient, such relations are externalized into patterns that become iconic of events and relations. Patterns related to specific events may be later recalled in the making of new quilts, its memory reflected in the flowers or plants depicted, the symmetry used, and in the case of a *taorei* quilt, which is composed of many thousand small pieces, the design (*pu*) which is repeated across the surface of the quilt in a fractal fashion.

Quilt patterns that have been gifted to and sometimes are buried with deceased relatives, such as a son or daughter, are particularly strongly remembered and may be re-made by a woman, in anticipation of her own death, to be given to her eldest surviving child for use in her own burial. While visually the pattern may be seen to serve as a memento of an event or a relationship specific to the biography of the makers, the compositional structure of the pattern transcends this personal space of biography in giving material expression to a de-centered vision of social relations which guides and directs the life-course of individuals through its logic. Fanned out during life, the individual parts composing Cook

Island personhood are brought back together again at death, when those who received quilts from the household return gifts of patchwork to be lowered in the grave. This grave is tiled and covered by a cement foundation and a roof, and, sitting like a miniature next to the house, is the manifestation of the social body governed by a fractal logic by which the many are but one.

Much has been written about 'fractal personhood' in the Pacific where typical 'Western' oppositions between individual and society, parts and wholes, singular and plural do not apply, but where persons, things, and the relations between them, are all thought to be effected through acts of multiplication and decomposition (Strathern 1986; Wagner 1992). No other image has denoted as powerfully such ideas of fractality as the Cook Islands Staff-God and the Rurutan treasure chest in the shape of a figure of which notable examples are held in the British Museum, both collected in the mid-nineteenth century during the early period of missionary influence in the Cook Islands. Like the fractal image of personhood presented to us in these historic sculptures, the Cook Islands quilt is an entity with relationships integrally implied in the ways motifs are serially enchained, 'budding' out of one another in a depiction of human life. Constructed from layers of criss-crossing strips of fabric that are cut and stitched into regular crystalline patterns on a plane, the Cook Islands patchwork in fact presents the temporal equivalent of a spatial map in the form of a lattice of possible worlds.

The idea of a person being composed of distinct layers of biographical relations impresses itself on the mind imagining the layering of quilts that are wrapped around and folded on top of a person buried in the grave. We could thus think of patchwork as an old, yet also new, means of effectively gathering relations into a single fold in a move that has enabled Cook Islanders to sustain relations across time and space. Old, because it binds together those who live apart, and new, because it acknowledges that effective relations incorporate today not just relations that are based on birth or marriage, but also all those many circumstantial relations that life tends to fashion when it straddles the many places that mark the connections between diaspora and the homelands.

As Elizabeth Arkana writes with reference to Hawaiian quilts, "quilts contain much *mana*. If one should die and leave much spirit behind, it could be damaging and might never be able to achieve real rest" (1986, 5). The intense attachment of person and sewing means that patchwork are only separated temporarily from the maker, eventually being returned at death. As quilt-like sewings are in effect the burial shrouds of their maker, anticipating a future state of being where all possible past and present temporal worlds coalesce, a deep association – which traverses the production, the circulation, and the 'style' of the quilt – exists between biographical time and patching. The patchwork in fact resonates with temporal logic in generic ways that go beyond individual recollections of biographical time to the non-causal, but *modalized*, that is logically describable, enchainment of events in what Alfred Gell called "B-series time" (Gell 1992, 238–241).

B-series time, according to Gell, reflects the temporal relationships between events as they really are, out there, while the A-series provides subjective and tensed perceptions of events that happen in the B-series' temporal territory. In order to know how to act in a "timely" manner, to plan and anticipate what might happen, but also to defend claims about the past, we have to construct representations of B-series time, so called time-maps, that allow us to "navigate" in time based on an understanding of how possible worlds are connected with one another (Gell 1992, 235–236). Time-maps, like the maps we use to navigate in space, rely on images to be generated that correspond to how the world appears to us. This translation of non-indexical space-time beliefs into images and back into maps creates what Gell called "indexical fixes" or perceptual beliefs which give rise to our inward sense of time (236–237). Image-based maps of B-series time are not the 'real thing,' but as no experience is possible of 'real' four-dimensional space-time we are forced to rely on such reconstructions in mastering time.

The mastering of time as genealogical knowledge is of fundamental importance in the Cook Islands where land is at a premium and where locating oneself in a time-map of social relations is the prerequisite for being granted right to land. Where sometimes more than 48 generations can be recounted as coming together in one person, a fractal map that depicts the enchainment of social relations serves as a model of relationality that can be used to make decisions whenever matters of attachment are at stake.

Patchwork thus evokes both a world of images that are derived from subject-centered time awareness (in that they are in and of a specific place and time), and yet, they also match these images against invariant templates derived from the underlying cognitive maps of the B-series (Gell 1992, 254). As maps, image-based representations such as the quilts of the Cook Islands draw out as temporal beliefs the logic of an internal, template-like representation of time. The symmetry specific to each of the three Cook Islands quilts displays precisely such a modal time-map; they do not reflect subjective and tensed perceptions of events or culturally specific beliefs of how events in the past, present, and future are disposed towards one another, but *a generalized temporal logic*; and it is because the mapping of time is *logical*, while reflecting specific local beliefs and attitudes to biographical time, that Cook Islands quilts are recognizable and distinctive across Eastern Polynesia and beyond.

The linear arrangement of the cut-out pattern (*manu*) recalls the linear enchainment of possible worlds in which specific paths are singled out that connect past, present, and future. The cognitive activity of 'projecting' that is involved in giving time-maps linearity in this manner is fundamental to the production of the cut out, which, when folded, requires one to envision the cut lines projected symmetrically across the missing planes in order to arrive at a recognizable image of a flower or plant when the fabric is unfolded. In contrast to the cut out, no unique past, present, and future is represented in the appliqué quilt (*ta taura*): here repeated, identical images, usually of flowers, are arranged, mostly in rotational or diagonally offset symmetry, to depict the reflexive, transitive, but symmetrical relation between possible and co-existing worlds, visualizing equivalences between images as a singular, repeated motif. In contrast to the relational symmetry of the appliqué quilt, images are arranged in an asymmetric manner in the piecework quilt (*taorei*): here interconnecting paths (*tiare*) mirror the before and after relation between successive images (*pu*) of possible worlds that, as in the appliqué quilt, are identical to each other. Past, present, and future are depicted as relational, but not unique, and as reflexive, transitive and progressive.

The quilt as time-map is more than a projection of an individual biography, but enables women to project an understanding of their lives in ways that speak to others. One could even go further and say that it is because quilts comprehend time by locating subjective images, sometimes recalling specific datable events, in a logical and non-indexical map, that they can figure as the quintessential inalienable exchange object which enables one to keep while giving (Weiner 1992). We can now begin to imagine how patching may enable women to manage and remember relations unfolding in time, in ways that are made effective in the performativity of exchange, when quilts not only connect persons but enchain past, present, and future in ways that resonate with temporal beliefs.

Conclusion

As agents for the navigating of time, patchwork has real consequence for people's lives, as it makes effective transnational communities manageable by offering the household a tangible expression of a thought that is directed at gathering its distributed relations back into a single place. Much of what can be said about the spatio-temporal logic underlying patchwork could be extended to mats. However, the visual and material differentiation facilitated by the sewing techniques of *tivaivai* amplifies some of the more salient practical reasoning surrounding the making of things that are meant to move as tokens of distributed personhood, connecting persons to one another in a lasting manner. Sewing, in fact, has enabled time-maps to be modalized and distributed, charting temporal worlds predictably and accurately.

The modal logic of composite and fractal images that is found in Cook Islands patchwork projects a conception of personhood and sociality that seems perpetually under construction, while framed by clear landmarks that invite and direct navigation. Kinship aided by patchwork is open-ended and multidirectional in conception, suggestive of ways to balance the dynamic of distribution and containment, of multiplicity and singularity that makes life as a transnational society full of prospect and surety.

Patchwork in the Cook Islands thus has features that are broadly comparable to patchwork made elsewhere, while nevertheless affording insight into how social relations are managed in these islands in ways that are quite distinctive. We saw in this essay how patchwork fuels an economy run on 'past'-time in which generalized commodity value is converted into an asset that sustains and extends the economy of the household beyond the here and now.

More than fashioning a memory that can be mobilized in several places at once as a uniting force, patchwork carries in its distinctive and culturally motivated techniques of composition the shared and anticipated actions that express and sustain the fragility and potential of the ontology of transnational community seen as composite relations under construction. What may appear to the innocent eye as an ostentatious craft made by the busy hands of women thus confounds our expectations with an astonishing testimony to the tooling of indexical relations fit to fashion lives lived between home and elsewhere.

References

Addo, Ping-Ann. *Creating a Nation with Cloth: Women, Wealth and Tradition in the Tongan Diaspora*. Oxford: Berghahn, 2013.

Arkana, Elizabeth. *Hawaiian Quilting: A Fine Art*. Honolulu: Hawaiian Children Society, 1986.

Ascher, Marcia. *Mathematics Elsewhere: An Exploration of Ideas Across Cultures*. Princeton: Princeton UP, 2002.

Bennardo, Giovanni. *Representing Space in Oceania: Culture in Language and Mind*. Canberra: Australian National University, 2002.

Casey, Edward S. *The Fate of Place: A Philosophical History*. Berkeley: University of California Press, 1998.

Deleuze, Gilles and Félix Guattari. *A Thousand Plateaus*. Trans. Brian Massumi. Minneapolis: University of Minnesota Press, 1987.

Elsley, Judy. *Quilts as Text(iles): The Semiotics of Quilting*. Berkeley: University of California Press, 1996.

Evans, Mike. *Persistence of the Gift: Tongan Tradition in Transnational Context*. Waterloo: Wilfrid Laurier UP, 2001.

Gell, Alfred. "How to Read a Map: Remarks on the Practical Logic of Navigation." *Man* (ns) 20.2 (1985): 271–286.

Gell, Alfred. *Art and Agency: An Anthropological Theory*. Oxford: Oxford UP, 1998.

Gilson, Richard P. *The Cook Islands 1820–1950*. Ed. Ron Crocombe. Wellington: Victoria University of Wellington, 1980.

Granet, Marcel. *La pensée chinoise*. Paris: Albin Michel, 1968.

Hammond, Joyce. "Polynesian Women and Tifaifai Fabrications of Identity." *Journal of American Folklore* 99.393 (1986): 259–279.

Hanson, F. Allan. "When the Map is a Territory: Art in Maori Culture." *Structure and Cognition in Art*. Ed. Dorothy K. Washburn. Cambridge: Cambridge UP, 1983.

Horton, Laurel. *Mary Black's Family Quilts: Memory and Meaning in Everyday Life*. Columbia: University of South Carolina Press, 2005.

Hutchins, Edwin. *Cognition in the Wild*. Cambridge: MIT Press, 1996.

Jones, Stella M. *Hawaiian Quilts*. Honolulu: Hawaii UP, 1973.

Johnson, Mark. *The Body in the Mind: The Bodily Basis of Meaning, Imagination, and Reason*. Chicago: University of Chicago Press, 1987.

Ka'ili, Tevita O. "Tauhi Va: Nurturing Tongan Sociospatial Ties in Maui and Beyond." *Contemporary Pacific* 17.1 (2005): 83–114.

Küchler, Susanne and Graeme Were. *Pacific Pattern*. London: Thames & Hudson, 2005.

Küchler, Susanne and Andrea Eimke. *Tivaivai: The Social Fabric of the Cook Islands*. London and Wellington: British Museum and TePapa Press, 2009.

Lee, Helen and Steven Tupai Francis eds. *Migration and Transnationalism: Pacific Perspectives*. Canberra: ANU Press, 2009.

Lippard, Lucy R. *The Lure of the Local: Senses of Place in a Multicentered Society*. New York: New Press, 1997.

Marston, Gwen and Joe Cunningham. *Mary Schafer and her Quilts*. East Lansing: Michigan State University Museum, 1990.

Mukerji, Chandra. *From Graven Images: Patterns of Modern Materialism*. New York: Columbia UP, 1983.

O'Bagy Davis, Carolyn. *Pioneer Quiltmaker: The Story of Dorinda Moody Slade, 1805–1895*. Tucson: Sanpete Publications, 1990.

Pearce, Charles E. M. and Frances M. Pearce, eds. *Oceanic Migration: Paths, Sequence, Timing and Range of Prehistoric Migration in the Pacific and Indian Ocean*. Frankfurt: Springer, 2011.

Pogglioli, Vicki. *Patterns from Paradise: The Art of Tahitian Quilting*. Pittstown: Main Street Press, 1988.

Rongokea, Lynnsay. *The Art of Tivaevae: Traditional Cook Islands Quilting*. 1992. Honolulu: University of Hawaii Press, 2001.

Shaw, Robert. *Hawaiian Quilt: Masterpieces*. New York: Hugh Lauter Leven Associates Inc. distributed by Macmillan, 1996.

Siikala, Jukka. *Akatokamava: Myth, History and Society in the Southern Cook Islands*. Auckland: Polynesian Society in Association with the Finnish Anthropological Society, Helsinki, 1991.

Siikala, Jukka. ed. *Departures: How Societies Distribute their People*. Helsinki: Finnish Anthropological Society, 2001.

Small, Cathy A. *Voyages: From Tongan Villages to American Suburbs*. Ithaca: Cornell UP, 2011.

Strathern, Marilyn. *The Gender of the Gift: Problems with Women and Problems with Society in Melanesia*. Berkeley: University of California Press, 1988.

Stürzenhofecker, Gabriele. *Times Enmeshed: Gender, Space, and History Among the Duna of Papua New Guinea*. Stanford: Stanford UP, 1998.

Wagner, Roy. "The Fractal Person." *Big Men and Great Men: Personifications of Power in Melanesia.* Eds. Maurice Godelier and Marilyn Strathern. Cambridge: Cambridge UP, 1992.

Wassmann, Jürg. "The Yupno as Post-Newtonian Scientists: The Question of What is 'Natural' in Spatial Conception," *Journal of the Royal Anthropological Institute* 29.3 (1994): 645–666.

Weiner, Annette B. *Inalienable Possessions: The Paradox of Keeping-While-Giving.* Berkeley: University of California Press, 1992.

Part II: **Articulation**

Michael Rothberg
Multidirectional Memory in Migratory Settings: The Case of Post-Holocaust Germany

Immigrating into the past

On November 6, 1959, ten years after returning to West Germany in the wake of the Nazi period and Holocaust, Theodor W. Adorno addressed teachers from the Society for Christian-Jewish Cooperation with a lecture in Wiesbaden whose central question continues to echo more than a half-century later: "Was bedeutet: Aufarbeitung der Vergangenheit?" – "What does working through the past mean?" In his lecture, the philosopher Adorno distinguished between different modalities for confronting the difficult history of National Socialism and argued powerfully against the desire he saw in the German society of the 1950s to "close the books on the past and, if possible, even remove it from memory" (Adorno 1998, 89; cf. Adorno 1963, 125). Much has changed in the last fifty years. Adorno's argument that post-totalitarian justice requires "seriously working upon the past" has been affirmed globally as part of a new human rights regime, although this demand is most often honored in the breach. More locally, commemoration of National Socialism and the Holocaust has made its way to the center of the official national identity of a unified Germany, even if the path has most definitely been a twisted one and that centrality continues to be contested.

But other things have changed as well. Although Adorno could not have known it in 1959, the present in which Germany's difficult past would be negotiated and renegotiated over the next decades was in the process of significant transformation. Although it has rarely if ever been remarked, Adorno posed his question about *Aufarbeitung* during the early years of postwar *Arbeitsmigration* or labor migration. Under the guise of the 'guest worker program' (1955–1973), transnational labor migration brought workers and later their families to West Germany from a number of nations, including Italy, Yugoslavia, Spain, Portugal, Morocco, and Greece; the largest number of workers came from Turkey. Turkish Germans now number close to three million in the Federal Republic and constitute the nation's largest ethnic minority.[1] What would it mean to bring together the histories of *Aufarbeitung* and *Arbeitsmigration*, the legacies of the past and the complexities of the present?

Almost exactly thirty years after Adorno posed his famous question about working through the past, and just two months after the fall of the Berlin Wall, Turkish-German writer Zafer Şenocak penned a short essay with the Munich-based publisher Bülent Tulay, which addresses precisely this unlikely conjunction as well as the more general issue of transnational memory. In an essay titled "Germany: A Home for Turks?," they ask: "Doesn't immigrating to Germany also mean immigrating into Germany's recent past?" (Şenocak 1993, 16).[2] Şenocak and Tulay's challenge might be seen as a contemporary variant of Adorno's question. Set against the transnational and transcultural transformation of the German national context, they pick up where Adorno left off and put forward a double agenda. As the question about immigrating into the past suggests, they call on German Turks to engage with German history – in particular with German Jewish history and, as the phrase "recent past" implies, with Nazism and the Holocaust. But, at least as urgently, they also seek to spark the reflection of dominant German society on its own relation to difference, both historically and in the present.

Writing fifteen years after unification, Şenocak sees the problem in similar terms. In *Das Land hinter den Buchstaben*, a 2006 collection of essays addressing Islam, Turkey, and German society and culture, he restates the need for a new approach to recent German history: "It is time to connect German dealings with the National Socialist past and the questions of today. Not because sixty years of coming to terms would be enough, but rather because remembering must today become again an experience that – beyond the rituals of German *Vergangenheits-bewältigung* (mastering the past) – also reaches young people and can effect an important corrective against romanticizing and archaic imaginations of identity" (Şenocak 2006, 144). Such imaginations of identity result in what Şenocak calls "ethnic labeling" [*ethnische Etikettierung*] and block the source of memory's vitality, its connection of past and present: "Those who occupy themselves with the Holocaust and its aftermath rarely arrive in the Multiethnic Republic of Germany [*Vielvölkerrepublik Deutschland*], seldom see a connection between the persecution of Jews in Nazi Germany, between the debates about German-Jewish identity in the Wilhelminian Reich, and the current discussions about double citizenship, immigration law, and questions of integration" (Şenocak 2006, 143). As these formulations suggest, Şenocak raises questions in his various essay collections – as

---

1 For a social and intellectual history of the 'guest worker' program, see Chin (2007).
2 I have slightly altered Adelson's translation in this case. Cf. Şenocak (2000, 6).

well as in novels like *Gefährliche Verwandschaft* (Perilous Kinship, 1998) – that parallel those discussed in contemporary memory studies about what the proper frames of reference should be for the study of remembrance. By placing immigration at the center of concern, Şenocak indicates that the field of memory studies needs to think *simultaneously* about national, transnational, transcultural, and transgenerational inflections – all of which overlap and none of which is reducible to the others.

Despite the German specificity of his approach, the issues Şenocak raises have a broader compass in an age in which movements of people across borders are ubiquitous. How *should* immigrants think about the history of the nation into which they have moved? How *does* immigration transform the relation between history and memory for those born into a national community as well as for those who move across national contexts? There are no obvious answers to such questions, but reflecting on them ought to occupy a significant place in any account of the ethics and politics of transnational memory. In Germany, as in all other countries where it has been a significant factor, migration transforms the conditions of social, communicative, and cultural memory; it brings disparate histories into contact with each other, reconfigures individual and collective subjects, and produces novel constellations of remembrance and commemoration in which heterogeneous pasts jostle each other in an unsettled present. Understanding transnational and transcultural constellations of memory – which are catalyzed by such factors as media networks, imperial projects, and global economic flows in addition to migration – entails developing new conceptual frameworks for cultural memory studies. For all their ongoing usefulness, most of the inherited frameworks either derive from methodologically nationalist presumptions or rely on assumptions of continuity, closure, and homogeneity that fail to register the impact of phenomena that break apart the borders of individual and group identity. These phenomena are not themselves new – in Germany or elsewhere – even if they are being intensified under contemporary conditions of globalization. Rather, we have lacked the conceptual vocabulary and flexibility to grasp them.

Taking a cue from Şenocak, I pursue the conjunction of migration and Holocaust remembrance as a way of thinking through the emergent transnational turn in memory studies. This conjunction also offers the opportunity for me to reflect further on my own concept of multidirectional memory, a concept meant to capture the dialogic emergence of hybrid memories in transnational and multicultural contexts. The mobility of peoples is one of the primary catalysts for such a dialogic process, yet many spheres of German public culture as well as inherited scholarly models in memory studies remain resistant to recognizing the multidirectionality of collective memory. Astrid Erll has identified a Herderian conception of "container-culture" at work in the founding theories of collective memory, which blocks recognition of transcultural dynamics. In these theories, "cultures … remain relatively clear-cut social formations, usually coinciding with the contours of regions, kingdoms, and nation-states;" there is, in other words, "an isomorphy between territory, social formation, mentalities, and memories" (Erll 2011, 7). Erll's diagnosis has a particular resonance in the German context, where the Herderian legacy remains especially strong. The power of this isomorphic conception, I would add, derives from strong affective investments in an understanding of group identity as emerging from 'organic' and 'natural' forms of belonging; these forms of belonging are often imagined and lived as ethnicity. In such understandings, common in scholarly as well as popular conceptions, memory is a form of communal *property* that, in circular fashion, reconfirms the identity of the group.

In contrast to this organic conception of collective remembrance, I attempted to show in my book, *Multidirectional Memory*, that memory is not the exclusive property of particular groups but rather emerges in a dynamic process of dialogue, contestation, and exchange that renders both memories and groups hybrid, open-ended, and subject to renegotiation (Rothberg 2009). As I revealed in readings of Holocaust remembrance especially in black Atlantic and French colonial contexts, memory of the Holocaust is not simply a form of Jewish memory, just as memory of slavery or colonialism is not limited to the victims or descendants of slavery and colonialism.[3] Rather, the histories of these apparently autonomous memory traditions are interlaced with each other in ways that are productive, if often tense. How can this concept of multidirectional memory be translated for the German sphere? Because of the legacy of the Holocaust, among other factors, the link between memory, property, and historical responsibility has been especially strong in Germany and thus especially resistant to the recognition of multidirectional openings. Nevertheless, I argue, considering under-explored migrant engagements with the Holocaust and the National Socialist past allows us to demonstrate that German memory cultures can open themselves to a redefinition of German identity that takes into account the fundamental demographic transformations and transnational flows of the postwar period without jeopardizing German responsibility for the Holocaust. However, a new understanding of the dynamics of memory is a prerequisite for that redefinition.

Inspired by the case of migration and Holocaust memory in Germany, I argue here that the transnational turn cannot simply leave behind national memory if it

---

3 See also Alison Landsberg's important study of "prosthetic memory," which suggests that in the wake of modernity and the development of the mass media, memory is no longer linked to "organic" communities but becomes available for creative adaptation and sharing across identity categories (Landsberg 2004).

is to offer a new approach, for such a move would only repeat modernity's logic of abstraction and supersession, essential components of national memory.[4] Rather, the new transnational memory studies must think about how different layers and scales of memory coexist and interact in a non-teleological, non-progressive fashion (see also the Introduction to this volume). The migrant/German case also bears implications for thinking about memory's multidirectionality; it suggests that grasping multidirectionality means not only linking different *layers* of memory – that is, different traditions and historical or cultural legacies – but also mediating between different *scales* of memory (local, national, transnational, etc.) without subordinating one to the other. Attending to the articulation between these layers and scales, I argue, also suggests the need to distinguish analytically between *transcultural* and *transnational* memory dynamics. Furthermore, such attention can help reveal the relations of power that contour practices of memory; power appears not merely as hierarchical or repressive (although it can be that), but also as productive and open to rearticulation from below. The forms of mediation and articulation between different historical legacies and scales of remembrance include diverse materials: technical media and flows of money, but also embodied practices such as touch and mobility. Before turning to a resonant example from migrant/German civil society that illustrates this process of mediation and articulation – the Berlin-based Neighborhood Mothers project – I first consider what a theory and ethics of memory might look like in a transnational age defined by mass migration. Engaging with a variety of theorists of memory and migration, I will argue that such an ethics must be *located* and attentive to the forms of *thickening* that take place in transcultural encounters without reimporting the organic visions of collectivity that often accompany imaginations of locality and community.

A transcultural ethics of memory for an age of transnational migration

As memory studies has become increasingly institutionalized – through the establishment of research centers and journals and the publication of synthesizing and canonizing anthologies – its focus has, paradoxically, begun to move beyond

---

4 That is, national memory seeks to create an abstracted "imagined community" that unites citizens across their differences and supersedes local and other forms of attachment that might stand in the way of that unification (although, in Hegelian fashion, some of those local attachments might also be preserved and prove useful for national identifications).

the conceptual parameters of its founding texts and methodologies. The rich and heterogeneous works that have become 'classic' in that process of institutionaliza- tion – by Maurice Halbwachs, Pierre Nora, and Jan and Aleida Assmann, among others – emphasize *milieux de mémoire* centered on small-scale groups and com- municative transmission across tightly-knit family generations, on the one hand, and *lieux de mémoire* and canons of cultural memory anchoring national pasts, on the other (e.g. Halbwachs 1992; J. Assmann 1995; Nora 1996–1998; Nora 2001– 2006; A. Assmann 2008). While continuing to draw on the rich legacies of this transdisciplinary heritage – itself still in the process of development, as the on- going work of the Assmanns, especially, indicates (Assmann and Conrad 2010) – new currents in memory studies have begun to engage critically with these fore- bears; they have sought to move from static to dynamic, from organic to mediated, and from parochial to cosmopolitan models of memory (Rigney 2005, 2008; Levy and Sznaider 2006; Erll and Rigney 2009). This new emphasis on multidirection- ality and *noeuds de mémoire* (knots of memory) – as I have called it in my own work and in collaborative projects – also tends to be transcultural and transna- tional (Rothberg 2009; Rothberg et al. 2010; cf. also Crownshaw 2011; Craps and Rothberg 2011).

With the new move beyond the boundaries of national culture, however, have come voices of caution. In an important intervention, Susannah Radstone draws attention to the simultaneous *institutionalization* and cross-border *expansion* of memory studies and worries that their increasing fluidity reproduces too perfectly the neoliberal utopia of a globalized, borderless world (Radstone 2011). For Rad- stone, "there remains something more than a little paradoxical, as well as instru- mental ... about the attempt to produce a fully 'globalizable' version of memory studies, for memory research, like memory itself (notwithstanding possibilities for transmission and translation) is always located – it is ... specific to its site of production and practice" (113–114). Radstone warns against asserting too quickly memory's transnational and transcultural scope by virtue of its association with new media or globalized practices of cultural consumption: "Whether we focus on the ways in which memory might 'travel' via the cinema, or the Internet, for instance, that travel remains only hypothetical, or an unrealized potential, until a particular individual goes to a specific website, or a particular audience watches a specific film" (117). Radstone's emphasis on particularity corresponds to a con- cern with *power* in its "intellectual, economic, institutional" forms (114), which she understands as contouring the production, circulation, and consumption of cultural memory – as well as scholarship on it. Drawing attention to "the *located- ness* of memory" and memory research (114) in practices that must be "*instanti- ated* locally, in a specific place and at a particular time" (117) helps to ground the transnational turn in memory studies in uneven material conditions. It encourages scholars to focus on the "*processes* that can be tracked within and across locations, instances, texts, narratives and events of memory" (120). As Radstone concludes, "[t]he idea that memory 'travels,' stands in for the articulation of these processes" (120). In making a transcultural or transnational turn, scholars should foreground located articulations of remembrance embedded in uneven relations of power and not simply celebrate what Radstone calls "'high speed' travels across the globe" (114).

Radstone's foregrounding of *locatedness* as a response to the transnational and transcultural turn in memory studies should be distinguished from a return to some notion of the purely *local*. Firstly, location can never be reduced to a point in space. Indeed, as Sharon Macdonald writes in a study of a seemingly very local case – the memorial legacies and material remnants of the Nazi Party Rally Grounds in Nuremberg – the "situations and frames" of remembrance

> are simultaneously local and beyond local. That is, they involve specific local conditions and actors but these never act in a vacuum, even when they are actively producing 'locality.' Instead … local actions are frequently negotiated through comparisons with other places, through concepts and ideas produced elsewhere and that may even have global circulation, and through the sense of being judged by others. They are also negotiated in relation to legislation, political structures and economic considerations which are rarely exclusively local. (Macdonald 2009, 4)

Although focused predominantly on a very particular case of the instantiation and articulation of memory, Macdonald's study of the negotiation of "difficult heritage" in Nuremberg reveals how the transnational turn can be important even for work at other, smaller scales. Secondly, Radstone's desire to "brin[g] memory's 'travels' back home" (Radstone 2011, 120) must be accomplished with care, since, as a feminist scholar like Radstone knows well, 'home' is a contested terrain that can easily come to serve patriarchal, nationalist, and racist ideologies. In returning to the locations of memory we should lose track neither of how nation-states seek to retain hegemony by producing purified memories of home, homeland, and *Heimat*, nor of the ways in which transnational and transcultural processes can 'unhome' the homogenous conceptions of local and national community that ground the founding French and German texts of memory studies.

Appeals to the realms of the transnational and transcultural do not automatically challenge the hegemonic politics of memory, however – no matter whether such a politics is enacted at the national, subnational, or supernational level. As memory studies moves into a new phase, it will be necessary to distinguish analytically between the categories of the transnational and the transcultural, for they do not refer to identical phenomena even if they often overlap. Both categories refer to the crossing of borders, but the borders to which they refer – those of nation-states and those of cultures – are by no means strictly isomorphic. Transnational phenomena may not be transcultural – as the homogenizing effects of cultural imperialism (e.g. Hollywood cinema) illustrate. Inversely, transcultural phenomena may take place within the frame of the nation-state – for instance, in visions of domestic multiculturalism characterized by overlapping hyphenated identities (e.g. Italian Americans, Irish Americans, etc.). Although no simple formula exists, distinguishing these two axes (the national and the cultural) can help illuminate acts of remembrance and clarify when practices of memory offer alternatives to hegemonic formations and when they reproduce dominant visions. In the vocabulary I have started to develop above, transcultural memory refers to the hybridization produced by the *layering* of historical legacies that occurs in the traversal of *cultural* borders, while transnational memory refers to the *scales* of remembrance that intersect in the crossing of *geo-political* borders. Because classical memory studies tended to be both mono-cultural and nation-bound in its conception of collective memory, these distinctions have not always been visible. But both transcultural and transnational lenses are needed to provide a new orientation that does not simply rewrite hegemonic forms of belonging for a globalized age.

The movement of peoples across the globe has been a major catalyst for the production of transcultural and transnational dislocations. Yet, because memory studies scholars often share the bounded visions of national and cultural collectives, the impact of migration on local and national memory cultures often remains obscure. Sometimes, migration is even considered antithetical to remembrance. As part of his provocative argument that modernity "tends to generate cultural amnesia," Paul Connerton proposes that "[t]he history of mass migration is part of the history of modern forgetting, and of forgetting places in particular" (Connerton 2009, 135–136). While true for certain cases (such as, arguably, turn of the twentieth-century Jewish migration from Europe to the US), Connerton's argument does not necessarily hold true for more contemporary migrations where modernity also provides various technologies, such as the internet, satellite television, and inexpensive air travel, that help maintain – or forge new – links to the country of origin. Perhaps even more significant, linking memory and forgetting to "local roots" and "place[s] of origin" (135) also reveals that while Connerton's lens here may be transnational (insofar as movement across national borders is said to produce amnesia about roots and origins left behind), it is definitely not transcultural. The argument linking transnational migration with forgetting leaves out the new types of *transcultural* memory that are produced *through migration*: for both migrants and "natives" in the country of destination – and for those who remain in the country of emigration and may receive not only financial remittances but also new imports of mnemonic material.

The transnational and transcultural dimensions of migration pose challenges and offer opportunities for the ethics of memory, but the most influential account of such an ethics is founded on a foreclosure of the transcultural (and underplays the transnational). Considering the limits of philosopher Avishai Margalit's *The Ethics of Memory* will lead to the hypothesis of a new 'setting' for the ethics of migrant memory. Margalit asks significant, fundamental questions: whether there is an obligation to remember "people and events from the past" and whether "remembering and forgetting [are] proper subjects of moral praise or blame" (Margalit 2002, 7). His response takes the form of a series of correlated binary distinctions: between ethics and morality, thick and thin relations, and those people who are close to us and those who are strangers. Margalit argues that there *is* in fact an ethics of memory and an obligation to remember, but that it involves only communities that possess "thick relations" by virtue of living closely together or considering themselves part of an "imagined" collective (in Benedict Anderson's sense). Margalit gives no definition of what thick relations are, but attempts instead to describe the situations that foster them: "Thick relations are grounded in attributes such as parent, friend, lover, fellow-countryman. Thick relations are anchored in a shared past or moored in shared memory" (7). As Margalit's examples imply, these ethical communities vary in scale from the family to the nation, although at other times they also seem to include religiously- and ethnically-defined groups that are transnational in scale; in either case, they seem to be, by definition, monocultural. In contrast to this ethical terrain of memory, Margalit suggests, "there is very little morality of memory" (7), because morality concerns "thin" relations characteristic of our associations with "humanity" at large – a category so vast and abstract that it cannot easily be a subject or object of remembrance or commemoration. As with thick relations, Margalit gives no direct definition of what is thin: "Thin relations ... are backed by the attribute of being human. Thin relations rely also on some aspects of being human, such as being a woman or being sick. ... Thin relations are in general our relations to the stranger and the remote" (7). Margalit considers a morality of memory relevant only when the events to be remembered concern a fundamental definition of human being, such as "gross crimes against humanity" like genocide (9).

Although Margalit describes modern society as characterized by a complex division of labor, this complexity does not carry over into his understanding of communities of memory. Instead, he models his notion of the "thick relations" of community on the family: "What do we imagine when we imagine a community with whom we are supposed to have thick relations? My answer is that we imagine an extension of family relations that would include relatives we have not met" (Margalit 2002, 75). Families come in many forms, of course, but Margalit seems to have a very traditional notion in mind, as becomes clear when he moves from the level of the family to the level of the nation: "The true issue in assessing national relations in ethical terms is whether or not, in claiming to be an extended family, they are a natural extension of the family metaphor. Not all nations pretend to be 'organic nations' with a shared myth of common origin, but those that do should be ethically scrutinized as to whether their purported thick relations are sufficiently family-like. ... The resemblance to the family tests whether the relation is really thick" (103). While Margalit's use of scare quotes around the term "organic nations" seems to indicate skepticism about claims to organic unity, his perspective on ethics ends up confirming just such a way of thinking about human communities. Rather than questioning the premises of national (or other) organic thinking, Margalit proposes instead to test whether such organically conceived entities really possess "thick" relations. At this point it becomes clear how circular Margalit's argument is: pre-given, monocultural understandings of family and nation confirm each other by reference to the predicate "thickness." Nations are like families if their relations are thick; their relations are thick if they are like those of families. Nations are not like families, however, whatever their self-conceptions suggest, and families are not organic entities but are hybrid, social-biological formations whose relations vary both within and across cultural contexts.

Margalit's monocultural and generally nation-based imagination of community and collectivity limits the usefulness of his ethics of memory for contexts marked by immigration – that is, for almost all known modern human contexts. Margalit's tendency to conceive human relations through binary models (thick vs. thin, etc.) risks reproducing homogenous and potentially nativist notions of community, which remain powerful despite long-term movements and mixings of people. In an interview published in the German-Jewish journal *Babylon* a few years before *The Ethics of Memory* appeared but when he was already trying out its argument, Margalit denies that his understanding of community is based on an assumption of homogeneity or what he calls "tribal thinking" (Margalit 1999, esp. 110–111). Yet, in the book, the commitment articulated in the interview to understanding communities of memory as composed of "multiple loyalties" and "dispute over what is important" does not manifest itself (Margalit 1999, 110–111). The binary mode of thinking in the book leads him to polarize human relations into two (and only two) camps. Making reference to "Heidegger's recognition that everyday ontology should distinguish between objects with which we are involved and those just present to us," Margalit argues for a "parallel" "distinction with regard to human beings. There are those with whom we are involved – that is, with whom we have thick relations – and others of whom we have only a thin idea of their existence. ... This distinction between the two types of humans is part of our fundamental ontology" (Margalit 2002, 142–143). Margalit's distinction all too easily reproduces a nativist ideology of national community in which immigrants are merely "present to us" but not actually "involved" in "our" lives. Taking account of migration as a fundamental – potentially transnational and transcultural – phenomenon, and of migrants as also part of the communal "we," would reveal a much more dynamic picture of human relations than this reductive, binary understanding of ontology allows, and would thus necessitate a new ethics of memory not premised on the opposition between 'thick' and 'thin.'

While Margalit's imagination of ethical communities of memory is premised on an *a priori* exclusion of all that might disrupt the bordered world of monocultural collectives (including, especially, nations), it is also true that there is no script for the transcultural impact of transnational migration on preexisting landscapes of memory. As Radstone would rightly caution, migration is a located process involving relations of power and concrete articulations of diverse experiences and material conditions; but it is precisely the *unscripted new linkages* created by migration that characterize its locatedness and constitute its interest for rethinking practices and ethics of remembrance. Migration creates, in the words of Murat Aydemir and Alex Rotas, "migratory settings" (Aydemir and Rotas 2008). Aydemir and Rotas's concept of migratory settings provides an alternative starting point for reflecting on the mutual impact of migration and memory that is more promising than Connerton's equation of modernity and forgetting or Margalit's definition of the ethics of memory with reference to family-like thick relations. Aydemir and Rotas's notion

> invites a shift in perspective from migration as movement from place to place to migration as installing movement within place. Migration not only takes place between places, but also has its effects on place, in place. In brief, we suggest a view on migration in which place is neither reified nor transcended, but "thickened" as it becomes the setting of the variegated memories, imaginations, dreams, fantasies, nightmares, anticipations, and idealizations that experiences of migration, of both migrants and native inhabitants, bring into contact with each other. Migration makes place overdetermined, turning it into the mise-en-scène of different histories. (Aydemir and Rotas 2008, 7)

Aydemir and Rotas's proposal that migration "thickens" place by concatenating histories, memories, and fantasies and thus rendering culture as a multidirectional setting, offers the possibility of a new ethics of memory for a transnational and transcultural age precisely because it challenges the binary between "thick" national-familial relations and 'thin' relations with strangers. Their notion of thickening makes no reference to organic metaphors or genealogical understandings of collectivity; to the contrary, thickening is a process without either origin or endpoint that takes place precisely when imagined communities experience an unsettling interruption. An ethics derived from such a setting would ignore neither the concreteness of location nor the (potential) effects of oblivion associated with migration, but would leave behind assumptions of cultural homogeneity that sometimes seep back into scholarship and public memory.

Starting from the experience of migration can help cultivate the multidirectional critical sensibility needed to engage ethically with the locatedness of remembrance, a locatedness expressed in the interplay of both diverse historical layers and legacies, and disparate scales and temporalities. In order to demonstrate concretely what an ethics for a migratory setting would look like, I turn in the remainder of this essay to an example from contemporary Germany – a country of immigration in which a dominant monocultural, national frame continues to inflect the work of memory but fails to limit all of its expressions.

Neighborhood Mothers: multidirectional memory in migratory settings

In February 2009, more than two hundred immigrant and minority women – many of them wearing headscarves – filled an auditorium in Berlin's impoverished Neukölln neighborhood. They had come to listen to presentations by the Neukölln Neighborhood Mothers (*Neuköllner Stadtteilmütter*) – women from their community who work with an organization dedicated to the social welfare of immigrant families.[5] The projects presented by the Neighborhood Mothers did not, however, concern the issues of health, nutrition, and education that the organization had been founded to address when it was established by a church-affiliated association, the Diakonisches Werk Neukölln-Oberspree. Instead, one by one, the women spoke of their exploration of Germany's National Socialist past.

---

5 I discuss the *Stadtteilmütter*/Neighborhood Mothers project in a somewhat different context in a joint essay, see Rothberg and Yildiz (2011). Parts of the following section are adapted from that article, but revised and expanded here. This discussion is also part of a larger, book-length study in progress of immigrants and coming to terms with the past in contemporary Germany, co-authored with Yildiz. The event, "Miteinander statt übereinander – Geschichte in der Einwanderungsgesellschaft," took place on 25 February 2009 in Berlin's Werkstatt der Kulturen. For self-presentations by the Mothers along with essays by ASF workers and scholars, see Aktion Sühnezeichen Friedensdienste (ASF) 2010. The Neighborhood Mothers have attracted some attention for their social welfare work, but their less well known historical engagement is one of the most crucial and original aspects of their program and one of the most suggestive for rethinking cultural memory in a transnational/transcultural context. See also the brief and sympathetic discussion of the project in Partridge (2010, esp. 842–844).

The women's desire to understand both the history of the country in which they live as immigrants or refugees and that country's memory culture – which they had recognized as a powerful social force in the present – had led to the creation of a project in 2006 in partnership with *Aktion Sühnezeichen Friedensdienste* (ASF: Action Reconciliation Service for Peace), a German peace and volunteer service organization. The purpose of the partnership between the ASF and the Neighborhood Mothers, which has been running ever since, was to allow the women – many of whom were not educated within the German educational system – to find out more about the Holocaust and its legacies and to create their own modes of participation in German memory culture.

At the gathering in 2009, they reported on their meetings with Jewish and Sinti survivors of Nazi genocide, their visits to memorial sites commemorating the Holocaust, and the effects that those encounters had on them. The event culminated with the screening of *Aus unserer Sicht* (From Our Perspective), a film the women had made about their recent visit to Auschwitz. This lively and emotionally charged gathering received hardly any coverage in the local press, although it showcased what conventional wisdom asserts does not exist: a group of mostly 'Muslim' immigrants who engage with the Holocaust and the German past in serious ways and become bearers and transmitters of a historical memory ostensibly not their own. The Neukölln public forum and other aspects of the project illustrate how the Neighborhood Mothers and their institutional partners help produce a 'thickening' of German memory cultures. This thickened remembrance is just one example of a larger, underappreciated phenomena in contemporary Germany: activism and cultural production that links engagement with the National Socialist and Holocaust past and the migratory dynamics of the present.[6]

The Neighborhood Mothers project results from a collaboration that enables the articulation of different layers and scales of memory. The interplay between layers and scales moves in multiple directions – neither simply from the 'bottom up' nor from 'top down.' That is, while the project arose out of the interests of a group of mothers in Neukölln – most of whom had a Turkish background but two of whom came from Arab countries[7] – it developed within a framework shaped by the ASF. The ASF is a non-profit organization founded by mainstream Protestants critical of the church's role under National Socialism and in its aftermath. It was established to take responsibility for Nazi crimes and is run almost exclusively by non-migrant Germans. Since the late 1950s, the ASF has been involved in inter-

---

[6] For a brief evocation of further examples, see Rothberg and Yildiz 2011, esp. 37–38, as well as our forthcoming collaborative book-in-progress.

[7] Future groups of Mothers have included women from Sri Lanka, Iraq, Algeria, Poland, and many other countries.

national exchange and contact in countries throughout Europe and in Israel and the USA as part of their effort to translate "the engagement with National Socialism and its crimes" into "concrete action in the present."[8] The encounter with the Neighorhood Mothers allowed them to develop a focus on "interculturality" that they had already begun but that had not been at the center of their (nevertheless) decidedly transnational projects.[9] In this sense, members of the ASF have, in recent years, been engaged in addressing the deficit Zafer Şenocak indicts; that is, they have for the last decade begun seeking to bridge the gap between what they call the "obligations" of the past that come from the "recognition of guilt" and the challenges of the multicultural present.[10] And, of course, the very existence of the Mothers as a group with a collective identity owes a debt to the Diakonisches Werk, the charitable organization of the Protestant church. This organization also includes a commitment to intercultural work in its programming; on its homepage, it describes itself as "aspiring to intercultural opening in all services," and states that it "regards diversity as an important societal resource."[11]

The encounters and knowledge produced by the Neighborhood Mothers program – not to mention what is made of the project by the women involved, the two NGOs, and society at large – are in no way solely the effect of the ASF's or the Diakonie's programming; yet they have offered a necessary basis for the Mothers' memory work. Within the space created by this interplay between grassroots actors possessing diverse local, national, and transnational personal histories, and organized NGOs with a local, national, and international scope, different layers of memory are 'inter-activated'; personal memories of trauma and displacement from dispersed contexts interact with commemorative paradigms 'made in Germany' and create new forms of transmission. The result is not an additive process but a thickening of memory in which already existing, but frequently overlooked, constellations of remembrance become visible and articulate with canonical forms of commemoration.

This thickening of remembrance has both transnational and transcultural dimensions. It simultaneously arises out of, and makes visible, a quintessential migratory setting with all the ambivalences Aydemir and Rotas outline. In transcending its status as a local community-education program through forms of mediation such as film, publication, and public meetings, the Neighborhood Mothers

---

8 See the ASF website: www.asf-ev.de/de/ueber-uns/ueber-uns.html (accessed 17 March 2014).
9 For the purposes of this essay, I am considering the "intercultural" focus of the ASF and the Diakonisches Werk as roughly equivalent to what I have been calling the "transcultural."
10 Cf. www.asf-ev.de/de/ueber-uns/ueber-uns.html (accessed 17 March 2014).
11 See the Diakonisches Werk website: www.diakonisches-werk-berlin.de/ (accessed 17 March 2014).

project becomes a vector for participation by minoritized and marginalized subjects in various public spheres where memory culture plays a significant role. At
the same time, however, structural features of German public life – such as pe-
jorative assumptions about immigrants from 'Muslim' countries (see Yildiz 2009;
2011) and an "ethnified" Holocaust memory culture (Diner 1998, 303) – limit the
degree to which the project 'travels' and transforms dominant frameworks. Keeping these forms of limitation in view can grant us access to the power configurations that accompany and inflect acts of memory, albeit without preventing the
unexpected from arising.

Indeed, the activities of the Neighborhood Mothers are all the more remarkable for taking place in a context that strongly correlates culture and memory with
monocultural, nation-based understandings of ethnic belonging and in which,
as Şenocak has already informed us, the troubles of the past remain cut off from
the debates of the present. Two dominant social logics in unified Germany regulate who inherits the past and what rights and responsibilities accompany that
inheritance: a *German paradox*, in which ensuring responsibility for the crimes of
the recent past seems to require preservation of an ethnically homogeneous notion of German identity, even though that very notion of ethnicity was one of the
sources of those crimes; and a *migrant double bind*, in which migrants are simultaneously told that the Holocaust is not part of their history because they are not
'ethnically' German and then castigated as unintegratable for their alleged indifference to Holocaust remembrance (see Rothberg and Yildiz 2011). In the words
of Havva Jürgensen, a Neighborhood Mother and self-identified Turkish-German
"guest worker child," "we often hear that the topic of National Socialism is not
for us because we're migrants. Just as often it's insinuated that in any case we are
too antisemitic to be interested in this topic" (ASF 2010, 54). While the German
paradox and the migrant double bind evoke actually existing social attitudes that
powerfully shape the transmission of cultural memory and the possibilities of full
citizenship for non-ethnically German immigrants, they do not exhaustively describe the social landscape of remembrance in contemporary Germany. Rather,
they amount to an ideological redescription and occlusion of existing practices
of memory – including innovative collaborations such as those involved in the
Neighborhood Mothers project.

Precisely because of the lack of public recognition that greets most immigrant
engagements of this sort, the work of memory initiated by the Mothers bears implications for theories of memory in a transnational and transcultural age. The Mothers' engagement with National Socialism and the Nazi genocide has both rendered
visible and facilitated the production and transmission of new memories – in intimate as well as public settings. For instance, Havva Jürgensen describes growing
up in Berlin's Wedding neighborhood with Jewish neighbors who gave her a copy

of Anne Frank's diary as a gift. Like many Germans, this migrant subject "first concerned [herself] intensively" with the Nazi genocide through the television series *Holocaust* in the late 1970s (ASF 2010, 53). Decades later, she recounts how her involvement with the Neighborhood Mothers project has led to new forms of prosthetic, postmemorial transmission: "The impressions from the seminars often had aftereffects that lasted for days. Sometimes, as I was cooking in the evening, I still thought about the experiences of the seminar, a visit to a memorial site, a film, a conversation, a document. Then tears would roll down my face, something that my twelve-year old son would sometimes notice. Because of that I often also talked with him about the seminar" (ASF 2010, 54).[12] Feeling addressed by some of the most canonical popular texts of Holocaust memory, having had everyday neighborly exchanges with German Jewish survivors, taking part in dialogue with an Israeli survivor about the "possibilities for cohabitation among Jews and Arabs in Israel," and passing on a history not considered her own to her son, Havva Jürgensen is in some ways the prototype of the ethical secondary witness of traumatic history (ASF 2010, 54). Like many of the Mothers' self-portraits, her story is fascinating both for its ordinariness and for the insight it gives into the multidirectional transmission of memory that has taken place in Germany throughout the decades of the most active Holocaust remembrance, albeit with scant public awareness or official recognition. Her ethical engagement with the past derives neither from a thick and organically conceived link with a memory community, nor from a thin moral concern for humanity at large. Rather, the encounters she describes exemplify the 'thickening' produced in migratory settings; they include transnational connections to events beyond Germany (such as the Middle East conflict) facilitated by a Germany-based, internationally active organization (ASF), as well as the transcultural blurrings and identifications that result from neighborly contact and mass media products.

Not all of the mothers have had the same experience of intimate transmission as Jürgensen, yet their accounts also reveal unexpected layers of transnational memory culture nonetheless. Some of those who were educated outside of Germany bring with them the kinds of comparative perspectives on Holocaust remembrance and education that scholars in recent decades have valued. Regina Cysewski, a *Spätaussiedlerin* from Poland (an ethnic German who came to Berlin in 1981) reports having learned much about the fate of Polish Jews during WWII, but little about National Socialism as such (ASF 2010, 48). Meanwhile, Perwin Rasoul

---

12 In referring to this transmission as both prosthetic and postmemorial, I draw on Landsberg (2004) and Hirsch (1997, 2008). For more on the relation of postmemory and migrant memories, see Seidel-Arpacı (2006).

Ahmad, a Kurd from Iraq, recounts that Jews and Hitler were topics in school, as was the "emergence of dictatorships ... even though the Saddam-regime was itself also a dictatorship" (ASF 2010, 45). Such accounts exemplify the degree to which 'national' memory cultures are in fact assemblages of inter- and transnational exchange and highlight how attention to migration can make such exchange more visible.

Other women from the group who did not grow up in Germany confess to having known very little about National Socialism and the Holocaust before joining a Neighborhood Mothers' seminar. But even those women with little pre-existing knowledge about the past offer narratives that nonetheless provide access to aspects of postwar German life that do not always show up in the official public discourse of 'coming to terms with the past.' For instance, Binnur Babig, who came to Germany from Turkey as a twenty-five year old tourist and stayed after marrying a German man, recounts how, before the seminar, she knew "as good as nothing about the topic [of] National Socialism," except for the tales of German suffering told by her mother-in-law of "how the Russians came, how her father was taken away, and what hardship they suffered. She never mentioned that Jews had been persecuted and murdered" (ASF 2010, 43). Besides this privileged peek into the private sphere – testimony to a persistent discourse of German suffering and Holocaust relativization confirmed by scholars as well as other migrants – the women's stories also hint at continuities that mark post-National Socialist German society. Aylin Teker, born in Berlin and raised in both Germany and Turkey, describes having a history teacher in the *Oberschule* (high school) who was a "wanna-be Hitler," and who "greeted us sometimes with the Hitler greeting and cursed us that we should go back to Turkey" (ASF 2010, 51).

As the experiences of these Mothers suggest, drawing attention to transcultural and transnational dynamics does not imply that memory work in migratory settings only involves harmony. To the contrary, because of the overlapping layers and scales of memory at stake, friction often results.[13] The form of conflict that most frequently emerges in accounts of the Neighborhood Mothers project involves the Israeli-Palestinian struggle – a flashpoint almost everywhere, but particularly charged in Germany, where support of Israel has been understood as part of the country's post-Holocaust efforts at *Wiedergutmachung* (reparations or, literally, 'making good again').[14] Indeed, integral to the ASF's mission has been

---

13 For a theory of the productivity of friction in transnational exchange, see Tsing (2005).
14 Another obvious flashpoint for the predominantly Turkish-German Neighborhood Mothers project is the Armenian genocide – a genocide denied by the Turkish state and much of the Turkish diaspora. For better or worse, the Armenian question has largely been kept off the Mothers'

reconciliation work in Israel, which it has undertaken since 1961.[15] With the ASF's turn toward the inclusion of 'intercultural' projects starting in 1999, such a mission necessarily became more complicated as the organization began to work with immigrants to Germany who might have different relations to the history and politics of the Middle East, including Palestinian refugees and other people with a Muslim background.[16] Working not just transnationally (i.e. in other countries, such as the Netherlands or Israel) but also transculturally (i.e. with 'intercultural' difference within Germany) has shifted the kinds of memory work in which the ASF participates, as events around the February 2009 public forum in Neukölln illustrate.

The Mothers who took part in that forum were part of a group whose project on National Socialism and the Holocaust overlapped with Israel's 2008–2009 bombing of Gaza. Eike Segen, an ASF staff-member who was leading the seminar with the Neighborhood Mothers at the time, reports that there was "massive conflict" about the events in Israel/Palestine.[17] Yet, even despite such conflict – and perhaps, precisely, *out of* such conflict – the Neighborhood Mothers project opens up possibilities for rational political discussion. In the ASF-produced brochure that recounts the experiences of this same group of women, Emine Elçi, a religious Neighborhood Mother born in Berlin to a Kurdish family from Turkey, provides more direct access to the women's perspective. She recounts how "the time in which our seminar took place was overshadowed by the war between Palestinians and Israelis in Gaza. We talked a lot about that. When Inge Deutschkron [a Holocaust survivor] told us that she had felt accepted for the first time in Israel, we also thought of the Palestinians who suffer under Israeli occupation" (ASF 2010, 41).

---

agenda – and there are some signs of resistance on the mothers' part to linking that genocide to the remembrance of the Holocaust. However, the collective project with Yasemin Yildiz in which I am engaged has turned up significant, dissident memory work around the Armenian genocide in other Turkish-German circles. This memory work – which takes place in civil society as well as cultural spheres – seems to find an impetus in the productive dynamics of German Holocaust memory culture, but seeks to avoid falling into an ethnicizing 'Turkish paradox' by forging collaborations with non-Turkish actors, including immigrants of Armenian and Kurdish background.

15 On their website, the ASF writes: "The work in Israel could be begun after the Eichmann Trial in 1961." www.asf-ev.de/de/ueber-uns/geschichte/shnezeichen-ost-und-west/asf-geschichte-bundesrepublik.html (accessed 17 March 2014).

16 My point is by no means that immigrants with a Muslim background are 'naturally' anti-Israel – indeed, the evidence presented here shows a much more complicated picture not often represented in dominant media, which stereotypes 'Muslim immigrants' as anti-Israel and antisemitic. Rather, the point is that such immigrants have points of reference beyond the German context that allow them different – and sometimes more cosmopolitan – perspectives on the Israeli-Palestinian conflict.

17 Interview with Eike Segen, Berlin, 11 December 2011.

At the same time, Elçi also describes how participation in the group's "engagement [*Auseinandersetzung*] with National Socialism" has made her more "sensitive" to "differentiation" within groups: "At a demonstration during the Gaza War I discovered a flyer from a Jewish group that was against the war. The flyer was signed 'Not in our name.' Earlier I wouldn't have noticed these differences" (ASF 2010, 41). A similar movement from potential conflict to emergent solidarity took place during the public forum shortly after the end of the war (but still during the blockade of Gaza), at which the Mothers' film about their trip to Auschwitz was screened.[18] Echoing the exchange between the Mothers and Segen in the group's preparatory meeting, a Palestinian woman rose from the audience and asserted that what was happening in Gaza was much worse than what happened to Jews during the Holocaust. Her intervention prompted a Holocaust survivor in the audience to stand up and challenge her comparison. A tense interchange followed, but led, ultimately, to an agreement between the two women to begin a Jewish/Muslim discussion group to address such competitive memories (although it is not clear whether such a group ever emerged).[19]

As this account of events around the 2009 public forum suggests, the memory work of the Neighborhood Mothers project involves – like all memory work – both embodied practices and multiple forms of mediation. At its most powerful, the project reveals how the combination of contact and mediation fosters the transmission of new multidirectional memories. This interaction becomes visible especially in a film made by ASF about the Mothers. While *From Our Perspective*, the film about the Auschwitz trip, focuses on one particular experience (which other iterations of the project have not repeated), *Es ist auch meine Geschichte* (It's Also My History, 2011) provides an overview of the Neighborhood Mothers project. The film follows three of the Mothers – Memduha Yağli, Hanadi Mourad, and Emine Elçi – as they visit memorial sites and a synagogue, take part in public and small group discussions, and meet Jewish Holocaust survivors as well the daughter of a Sinti survivor. In addition to the overarching media framework of film itself, various other forms of mediation are at play. For instance, the Mothers encounter memorial sites – such as the Sinti memorial in Marzahn and the well-known *Stolperstein* (Stumbling Block) project of artist Gunter Demnig – and several scenes of reading are highlighted: Elçi speaks (like Havva Jürgensen) of having read Anne Frank as a girl; Petra Rosenberg reports learning the full story

---

18 I rely here on the field notes of Yasemin Yildiz. See also Partridge's account of this event (2010, 842–844).

19 For an attempt to theorize the ethical and political valences of different types of multidirectional memory through the example of comparisons between the Holocaust and the Israeli Occupation, see Rothberg (2011).

of her father's persecution as a Sinti only from his 1998 book; and survivor Margot Friedlander reads to the Mothers from her memoirs.

Despite the foregrounding of mediation, the themes of touch and 'authentic' locations also play a significant role in this film. As Friedlander describes a Nazi raid, while the women stand together in the courtyard of her former home, the survivor and the two Mothers (who are of Turkish and Lebanese background) link arms in a moving gesture of care and solidarity. Touch, however, can also be a site of difficult transcultural translation; when Mourad and Elçi – both of whom wear headscarves and are observant Muslims – meet survivor Rolf Joseph outside of a synagogue, Elçi says she does not shake hands with men to whom she is not related, but Mourad ignores that proscription and takes Joseph's hand. Once inside the orthodox synagogue, however, Elçi also finds points of identification; observing the separation of men and women, she declares, "it's exactly like with us [*genau wie bei uns*]!" The unselfconscious solidarity that Mourad shows in her interactions with Friedlander and Joseph, meanwhile, may result not only from such transcultural identification, but also from her own transnational experiences of trauma; she describes growing up in the midst of war in Lebanon and living for eight years in a German refugee home, which she likens to having been in "prison." Throughout the Neighborhood Mothers project, diverse pasts, which may have only tenuous connections according to a historical logic, but make up the over-determined terrain of migratory settings in the present, are brought into contact.

Conclusion: toward a new ethics of memory

The Neighborhood Mothers are not an exception, but one example of a multifaceted and underexplored memory culture that has emerged in a Germany which is simultaneously post-Holocaust and postmigrant. As the project exemplifies, the major concern of immigrant memory work is neither to respond to society's demands on them to 'integrate' nor to adhere to German cultural pieties. Rather, immigrants who address Nazism and the legacies of the Holocaust in cultural production or activism often do so in order to locate their own place in relation to a national past marked by genocidal violence towards groups considered 'other.' Working with non-immigrant partners, they develop new forms of cultural memory that are simultaneously vernacular and cosmopolitan. Even if dissensus and conflict remain ever-present possibilities, such collaboration tends to break the property-based, nation-state framework of collective memory and opens up multidirectional constellations of remembrance with a transnational scope instead.

So, what does it mean to immigrate into a history? Şenocak and Tulay's question has no single answer, but considering practices of remembrance from the perspective of migration has the potential to reframe theories of cultural memory at a moment when inherited models are being called into question. The Neighborhood Mothers project – which includes small-scale seminars and encounters, public forums, publications, and other forms of publicity, such as their film – displays how both immediacy and mediation facilitate contact between past and present, between local and distant histories, between familiar and allegedly foreign cultures. Such contact can produce solidarity, but it also sometimes leads to tension or even conflict. Memory in migratory settings is simultaneously multidirectional and thickened. There are no guarantees that it will also be ethical, but the Neighborhood Mothers project demonstrates that we can only begin to think seriously about an ethics of memory once we acknowledge the interweaving of different scales and layers of the past in the conflicts of the present.

References

Adorno, Theodor W. *Eingriffe: Neun kritische Modelle.* Frankfurt: Suhrkamp, 1963.

Adorno, Theodor W. *Critical Models: Interventions and Catchwords.* Ed. and trans. Henry Pickford. New York: Columbia UP, 1998.

Aktion Sühnezeichen Friedensdienste (ASF), *Neuköllner Stadtteilmütter und ihre Auseinandersetzung mit der Geschichte des Nationalsozialismus.* Berlin: Aktion Sühnezeichen Friedensdienste, e.V., 2010.

Assmann, Aleida. "Canon and Archive." *Cultural Memory Studies: An International and Interdisciplinary Handbook.* Eds. Astrid Erll and Ansgar Nünning. New York: De Gruyter, 2008. 97–107.

Assmann, Aleida and Sebastian Conrad, eds. *Memory in a Global Age.* London: Palgrave Macmillan, 2010.

Assmann, Jan. "Collective memory and Cultural Identity." Trans. John Czaplicka, *New German Critique* 65 (1995): 125–133.

Aus unserer Sicht. Berlin: Kiezfilme, 2009.

Aydemir, Murat and Alex Rotas, eds. *Migratory Settings.* Amsterdam: Rodopi, 2008.

Chin, Rita. *The Guest Worker Question in Postwar Germany.* New York: Cambridge UP, 2007.

Connerton, Paul. *How Modernity Forgets.* New York: Cambridge UP, 2009.

Craps, Stef and Michael Rothberg, eds. *Transcultural Negotiations of Holocaust Memory.* Special Issue of *Criticism* 53.4 (2011).

Crownshaw, Richard, ed. *Transcultural Memory.* Special Issue of *Parallax* 17.4 (2011).

Diner, Dan. "Nation, Migration, and Memory: On Historical Concepts of Citizenship." *Constellations* 4.3 (1998): 293–306.

Erll, Astrid. "Travelling Memory." *Transcultural Memory.* Ed. Rick Crownshaw. Special Issue *Parallax* 17.4 (2011): 4–18.

Erll, Astrid and Ann Rigney, eds. *Mediation, Remediation, and the Dynamics of Cultural Memory*. Berlin: De Gruyter, 2009.
"Es ist auch meine Geschichte": *Stadtteilmütter auf den Spuren des Nationalsozialismus*. Berlin: ASF, 2011.
Halbwachs, Maurice. *On Collective Memory*. Trans. Lewis Cosner. Chicago: University of Chicago Press, 1992.
Hirsch, Marianne. *Family Frames: Photography, Narrative, and Postmemory*. Cambridge: Harvard UP, 1997.
Hirsch, Marianne. "The Generation of Postmemory." *Poetics Today* 29.1 (2008): 103–128.
Landsberg, Alison. *Prosthetic Memory: The Transformation of American Remembrance in the Age of Mass Culture*. New York: Columbia UP, 2004.
Levy, Daniel and Natan Sznaider. *The Holocaust and Memory in the Global Age*. Trans. Assenka Oksiloff. Philadelphia: Temple UP, 2006.
Macdonald, Sharon. *Difficult Heritage: Negotiating the Nazi Past in Nuremberg and Beyond*. New York: Routledge, 2009.
Margalit, Avishai. "'Es ist leichter, Erdbeeren zu verändern als Nationen': Gespräch mit Avishai Margalit." *Babylon: Beiträge zur jüdischen Gegenwart* 19 (December 1999): 106–118.
Margalit, Avishai. *The Ethics of Memory*. Cambridge: Harvard UP, 2002.
Nora, Pierre, ed. *Realms of Memory: The Construction of the French Past*. Ed. Lawrence D. Kritzman. Trans. Arthur Goldhammer. New York: Columbia UP, 1996–1998. 3 vols.
Nora, Pierre, ed. *Rethinking France*. Trans. Mary Trouille. 4 vols. Chicago: University of Chicago Press, 2001–2010.
Partridge, Damani. "Holocaust *Mahnmal* (Memorial): Monumental Memory amidst Contemporary Race." *Comparative Studies in Society and History* 52.4 (2010): 820–850.
Radstone, Susannah. "What Place is This? Transcultural Memory and the Locations of Memory Studies." *Transcultural Memory*. Ed. Rick Crownshaw. Special Issue *Parallax* 17.4 (2011): 109–123.
Rigney, Ann. "Plenitude, Scarcity and the Circulation of Cultural Memory." *Journal of European Studies* 35.1 (2005): 11–28.
Rigney, Ann. "The Dynamics of Remembrance: Texts between Monumentality and Morphing." *Cultural Memory Studies: An International and Interdisciplinary Handbook*. Eds. Astrid Erll and Ansgar Nünning. New York: De Gruyter, 2008. 345–353.
Rothberg, Michael. *Multidirectional Memory: Remembering the Holocaust in the Age of Decolonization*. Stanford: Stanford UP, 2009.
Rothberg, Michael. "From Gaza to Warsaw: Mapping Multidirectional Memory." *Transcultural Negotiations of Holocaust Memory*. Special Issue of *Criticism* 53.4 (2011): 523–548.
Rothberg, Michael, Debarati Sanyal, and Max Silverman, eds. *Noeuds de mémoire: Multidirectional Memory in French and Francophone Culture*. Special issue of *Yale French Studies* 118/119 (2010).
Rothberg, Michael and Yasemin Yildiz. "Memory Citizenship: Migrant Archives of Holocaust Remembrance in Contemporary Germany." *Transcultural Memory*. Ed. Rick Crownshaw. Special Issue *Parallax* 17.4 (2011): 32–48.
Seidel-Arpacı, Annette. "National Memory's Schlüsselkinder: Migration, Pedagogy, and German Remembrance Culture." *German Culture, Politics, and Literature into the Twenty-First Century: Beyond Normalization*. Eds. Stuart Taberner and Paul Cooke. Rochester: Camden House, 2006. 105–119.
Şenocak, Zafer. *Atlas des tropischen Deutschland*. Munich: Babel Verlag, 1993.

Şenocak, Zafer. *Gefährliche Verwandschaft*. Munich: Babel, 1998.
Şenocak, Zafer. *Atlas of a Tropical Germany: Essays on Politics and Culture, 1990–1998*. Trans. and ed. Leslie A. Adelson. Lincoln: University of Nebraska Press, 2000.
Şenocak, Zafer. *Das Land hinter den Buchstaben*. Munich: Babel Verlag, 2006.
Tsing, Anna Lowenhaupt. *Friction: An Ethnography of Global Connection*. Princeton: Princeton UP, 2005.
Yildiz, Yasemin. "Turkish Girls, Allah's Daughters, and the Contemporary German Subject: Itinerary of a Figure." *German Life and Letters* 62.3 (2009): 465–481.
Yildiz, Yasemin. "Governing European Subjects: Tolerance and Guilt in the Discourse of 'Muslim Women.'" *Cultural Critique* 77.1 (2011): 70–101.

Paulla A. Ebron
Slavery and Transnational Memory: The Making of New Publics

> At the turn-of-the-century, Sea Island Gullahs, descendants of African Captives, remained isolated from the mainland of South Carolina and Georgia. As a result of their isolation, the Gullah created and maintained a distinctive, imaginative, and original African American culture. Gullah communities recalled, remembered, and recollected much of what their ancestors brought with them from Africa [...]. (*Daughters of the Dust*, 1991)

The film *Daughters of the Dust* opens with sounds and images crafted to evoke a sense of memory and communal recollection.[1] Set in 1902, the film shows several generations of the Gullah community grappling with the problem of memory: is the legacy of the past that which moves one forward or what must be left behind? Today, the community featured in the dramatic setting of the film is part of a larger commemorated region, recently named the Gullah Geechee National Heritage Corridor. In support of this recognition, residents work to make their cultural heritage visible with objects that represent their place in the region and their rights to the land. The region's historical importance provides a place from which to discuss public memory and the making of new publics.[2]

I use the term *public memory* to signal the process by which a group of people who were once dismissed and never thought of as part of a 'public' might become visible to themselves and to others – a public – through their use of memory. I invoke public memory in conversation with more commonly recognized terms, such as *collective memory* and *social memory*. In contrast to the fields these terms evoke, my interest is in the very processes of making communal identity and in the formation of emergent subjectivities. This requires an explicit departure from understandings of memory that assume a basis in personally experienced, remem-

1 I wish to express my appreciation to the participants of the Sea Island Field School, to Ms. Georgette Mayo, Ms. Deborah Wright and the team at the Avery Research Center for African American History and Culture and to Dr. Dale Rosengarten of the College of Charleston. I am grateful to Dr. J. Herman Blake who inspires critical thought about the place of the scholar in public debates. I appreciate the editors' careful attention and thoughtful suggestions. Their efforts have made an invaluable contribution to the development of this essay. Finally, I thank Kathryn Chetkovitch, Anna Tsing, and Claudia Engel for their generous and considerate comments.
2 For further information on the Heritage Corridor, see the official website: www.gullahgeecheecorridor.org (accessed 21 March 2014).

bered events. Rather than evoking actual events of history from which subjects enact their past, public memory directs our attention to the very process whereby new publics come into being and the ways in which new subjectivities are formed by public cultural forms and by an ever-circulating set of ideas that turns into an emergent possibility.[3]

Jürgen Habermas' notion of the public sphere is relevant (1989), but my use of public memory extends his idea of publics as well as Michael Warner's idea of counterpublics (2002). In contrast to Habermas' notion, in which the public is already assumed, my attention is drawn to those, such as the Gullah Geechee community, who were rarely included in normative ideas about who counts as a member of the public sphere. The ability of this community to gain recognition, and to recognize itself in a new way, comes about in part through interventions such as Julie Dash's film, which evoke new publics through cinematic images and the crafting of broadly circulating memories. Publics are created through technologies of practice and performance that are inspired by consumable, vernacular forms. Performative gestures, acts and style, for example, can make one see oneself through the reactions and responses of others. Public cultural forms inspire, and indeed coax, a sense of identity. Collective imaginaries are always in process.

My concern with memory, then, is targeted at the mobilization of the past to motivate contemporary outlooks and newly emerging publics. Such mobilization occurs in and through what I call 'projects,' that is, more or less coherent sets of discourses and practices. Projects draw from both official and vernacular sources; they may work simultaneously as discipline and as rebellion. They need not pit 'the state' against 'society.' Instead, to use the terms of Raymond Williams and Antonio Gramsci, they emerge in structures of feeling and emergent hegemonies. Memory projects require articulation in both its senses (Hall 1980a; 1980b). On the one hand, they create *links* between once-neglected pasts and presents-in-the-making; on the other hand, they *express* subjectivities appropriate to carry such pasts into the future. Within such articulations, tensions and contradictions come to inhabit memory projects, and these both give memory projects their traction and refuse to let them transcend the moment. Thus memory projects shift historically, and one of the purposes of this essay is to discuss some important changes in the memory of slavery in the twentieth and twenty-first centuries. Rather than assume an opposition between state and society, the concept of memory project allows me to see such oppositions, themselves, as developments within particu-

---

3 A number of recent volumes use the term 'public memory' in ways that resonate with collective and social memory; see, for example, Phillips (2004); Phillips and Mitchell (2011); Demo and Bradford (2012).

lar memory formations, which shift with political struggles and the meaning of historical events.

Expressive practices form elements within memory projects. In this essay, I examine several such practices within turn-of-the-century projects for mobilizing black American memories: a film, a place for contemplation, and a heritage tour. Each of these shows how articulations work within memory: pasts are brought to bear on evolving presents, and in the process, tensions both specify and energize potential audiences. Specification creates divisions between those interpellated and those left outside particular memory projects. Specification also sets up relations with others – whether institutional others, such as the state, or other configurations of personal identity. The dynamics of specification mean that memory projects are always sites of struggle as inclusion and exclusion are negotiated.

The specificity of those included in a memory project is also a sleight of hand. Memory projects only work because of resonance with other related projects. This resonance makes memory projects legible, and it allows them to simultaneously call out a specific group and make a claim on a universal ethics. In this way, too, they are always transnational even as they make national, regional, and local claims. Memory projects require transnational resources to make specific pasts meaningful as "engaged universals" (Tsing 2005). In this essay, the resonance between memorializations of the Holocaust and of slavery illustrates this point.

Each memory project also resonates with earlier ones. In the US, the Holocaust-slavery resonance depends on a previous memory project from the early twentieth century, associated with the New Deal's Works Progress Administration and its attempt to document American folk cultures. This mobilized a tension between black and white memories at the heart of populist memorialization, and this tension, I argue, is the ground upon which later memory projects build.

The focus of much of my discussion is the regional site that opens this essay, the Southeastern coast of the US where Gullah Geechee communities reside. This area has particular significance in US American history, for it is the region where much of the early accumulation of the capitalist wealth of the US happened – mostly thanks to the large-scale coerced-labor system and the ingenuity of African and African diasporic enslaved peoples who worked plantation crops such as rice and cotton. Their efforts upheld the US national economy up through the nineteenth century.[4] As the area with the largest concentration of enslaved Africans in the US, the Sea Island people have been represented as a community with distinctive cultural practices, as Dash suggests in the opening quote from her film.

---

4 For a discussion of the distinctive cultural and economic importance of African Americans to the history of this region, see Carney (2001) and Stewart (1996).

This was not always a celebrated history. Many of the local cultural practices were considered by the wider community as antithetical to the progress narratives of modernization. But this very fact made the Sea Islands look like a research laboratory to social scientists including ethnographers and linguists. They generally portrayed this place as a culture under glass, a place deeply entrenched in 'African' traditions, and memory was typically cast as preserved material, contained and embodied.[5] Stories of the remoteness of the region and the 'isolation' of many of the islanders have consequently made the Sea Islands the *Ur* site of memory for black Americans.

A good deal of our contemporary understanding of Gullah Geechee culture comes from records collected by the Works Progress Administration during the New Deal. As soon as we recognize how these materials were gathered, it becomes obvious that they were themselves part of a memory project, and not merely neutral collections. Thus, it seems important to begin my investigation of contemporary memorialization that enrolls Gullah Geechee materials with this earlier project, the contradictions and tensions of which are the architecture of more recent initiatives.

Memory work and the WPA

The first public memory project I focus on then is a national initiative from the 1930s, in which ordinary citizens helped invent the nation. Their recollections and reflections on everyday practices helped make places and regions part of national identity. This model of national memory making took inspiration from European romantic ideas of folk culture and its importance in the making of a national identity.[6]

The Works Progress Administration (WPA) was a US government project that became a major part of Depression-era President Franklin Roosevelt's effort to put a burgeoning number of unemployed citizens to work as public works employees. Many New Deal workers were tasked with rebuilding the nation's infrastructure,

---

5 Gullah Geechee culture was by definition transnational for enslaved Africans' journey to the New World, the Caribbean, and the US hinged on the mixing of remembered practices with their new cultural encounters. See Dow Turner (1949); Herskovits (1958); and Jones-Jackson (1987) for a discussion of linguistic retentions.
6 See Anderson (1983) for a discussion of the rise of nationalism and the role of culture in that process. Also see Filene's (2000) discussion of the influence of late eighteenth- and early nineteenth-century European ideas about folk culture and the impact this had on twentieth-century US American ideas about folk culture.

including roads and public buildings. More pertinent to this discussion, artists and writers were also employed under the New Deal programs, some of them recruited to work under the Federal Writers Project as fieldworkers, writers, artists, and photographers who documented the folkways and stories of ordinary people. Their efforts led to the production of local cultural history. In terms of my concept, this may be seen as a public memory project, simultaneously state-initiated and grassroots. A number of WPA guides to US states were written, which included stories about ways of life based on remembered practices. Neglected rural communities were particularly prominent in this ethnographic project. Those whose memories had not previously been considered significant were central to it. New publics were in the making.

Yet the project was full of contradictions and tensions. The WPA researchers encountered difficulties in attempting to include certain groups within the general body. One contributor, writer James Agee, noted in 1936 that southern white American interviewees refused to participate if blacks were included in the project (Agee and Evans 2013). As a consequence, a separate set of interviews gathered together black Americans' stories, documenting cultural practices whose categories were very similar to those of their white counterparts. One exception to these similarities in accounts of everyday vernacular practices were the interviews with elderly black Americans who had lived part of their lives as enslaved children. The question of African cultural continuities and what interviewees remembered about Africa drew the attention of many researchers.

The Federal Writers project both sustained segregation and became a resource for black American writers such as Zora Neale Hurston who was, for a brief period, employed as a field researcher for the WPA. Hurston went on to become famous for her novels about southern black culture. Hurston's work as a folklorist and novelist drew attention to black southern culture and in turn became a resource that later cultural producers could draw upon. The WPA collection was also available for Julie Dash, who drew upon early interviews in writing the script for *Daughters of the Dust*.[7] The WPA collection, which consisted of transcriptions of interviews, helped later cultural producers generate a sense of what the early informants might have recalled about their lives.[8] More significantly, pieces of these accounts could be fashioned into something beyond an account of the actual incidents that were already long removed from immediate recollection. These materials and stories contributed greatly to a new moment of public memory.

---

7 See Dash's (1992) discussion of the making of the film.
8 See Georgia Writers' Project (1940); Chandler (2008).

New public memory projects in the US followed the big changes initiated by WWII: decolonization, the formation of new international governance regimes, and, as of the 1970s, the spread of the memory of the Holocaust. In the memory projects of the late 20th century, national integration through ethnography was no longer the point. Instead, international recognition stood out as both a goal and a strategy for making these projects legible. These new projects, then, were always transnational in their composition, even as they made claims to reworking national spaces. Ethical questions imagined as universal were at the heart of this turn, which centered around the politics of recognition. To unravel the contours of this shift in my discussion of transnationally inflected memory, the next section introduces analytic tools that are useful for my discussion of three projects that show the interface between the Holocaust and black American memory.

Transnational chains of recognition

How are memory projects made at different scales, including the local, national, and transnational? One notable discussion about memory's transnational entanglements is offered by Michael Rothberg, whose work *Multidirectional Memory* (2009) highlights the kinds of transnational dialogues that take place across memorial communities. In particular, Rothberg's work makes visible the dynamic intellectual exchange between postcolonial and Holocaust studies. The transnational discussions that followed WWII reveal the productive working of conversations that move across geographic regions and communities. My analytic approach for this essay takes inspiration from Rothberg's critique of the inherent problems with competitive memory projects that depend upon hierarchies of trauma and his focus on what these memorial disputes conceal, namely, resonances and borrowings, which are a key feature of remembrance processes. Furthermore, he pays special attention to how publics are formed in dialogues across memory projects:

> The understanding of collective remembrance that I put forward in *Multidirectional Memory* challenges the basic tenets and assumption of much current thinking on collective memory and group identity. Fundamental to the conception of competitive memory is a notion of the public sphere as a pregiven, limited space in which already-established groups engage in a life-and-death struggle. In contrast, pursuing memory's multidirectionality encourages us to think of the public sphere as a malleable discursive space in which groups do not simply articulate established positions but actually come into being through their dialogical interactions with others; both the subjects and spaces of the public are open to continual reconstruction. (Rothberg 2009, 5)

My reading is further enriched by Anna Tsing's toolkit for analyzing globalization processes (2005). Her term "friction," which at first sight appears counterintuitive, refers not so much to tensions and conflicts, but to "global connections" that in turn show the "grip" of encounter. "Rubbing two sticks together produces heat and light; one stick alone is just a stick. As a metaphorical image, friction reminds us that heterogeneous and unequal encounters can lead to new arrangements of culture and power" (Tsing 2005, 5).

I draw upon the insights of Tsing, who proposes ways to analyze global processes and highlight things coming into being. While Rothberg reads the relationship between memories and groups as conversations and dialogues, Tsing's use of such concepts as "gaps," "contingencies," and "articulations" proves particularly useful for my exploration into the performative elements of vernacular culture. Attention to the emergent and enacted possibilities found in performances allows for an appreciation of how vernacular audiences are drawn into debates about memory. In contrast to *Multidirectional Memory*, my work includes a full variety of cultural productions, from elite writings to folktales, and from state directives to everyday performances. I focus on practices and cultural forms that mobilize both local and global publics.

The emergence of new publics

How did the Holocaust become a stimulus for public memory? It took cultural work, both local and global, to reconceptualize the Holocaust so that it could function as an agreed-upon focus for traumatic memory; only from the 1970s onwards, according to Levy and Sznaider (2006), did the Holocaust come to serve as a referent for other public memory projects. Levy and Sznaider provide a helpful chronology, showing that, after a postwar decade of relative silence, the Holocaust became important as a signpost of ethical citizenship in Europe in the 1960s, and was used to keep European nationalism in check. In Levy and Sznaider's scenario, the Holocaust as a framework for discussion of the horrors of the past only spread beyond Europe in the 1970s. These authors further argue that by the 1990s, the Holocaust had been reconfigured as a decontextualized event oriented toward nation-transcending symbols.

It is at that point, too, that the history of transatlantic slavery entered discussions of public memory. What proved distinctive about emergent publics in the 1970s is that these historical events, and the ways they had come to be 'remembered,' that is, mobilized for the present, enabled a range of groups to narrate their own group's experience in a particular way. A key departure in how the past could be remembered, and more specifically, framed, was the introduction of an affective vocabulary that allowed the significance of a particular trauma to spread to a wider group. Words such as genocide, trauma, Holocaust, victim, memory, and testimony entered public discourse and helped groups across a wide spectrum insert themselves in history (see e.g. Fassin and Rechtman 2009). In the subsequent formation of multiple memory projects, new publics formed dialogically – and in friction. Thus even Holocaust memories must be understood through wider dialogue. Moving beyond Levy and Sznaider's analysis, Rothberg's approach allows us to look at concrete histories of interplay in the making of each of these public memories; in the late twentieth century, Holocaust and slavery memory projects had significant effects on the way each project was shaped.

Fourteen years before Dash's film appeared, the television miniseries *Roots* (1977) captivated the attention of audiences in the US and beyond. Based on a novel by Alex Haley (1976), the story's main character, Kunta Kinte, vividly brought to life the reality of an enslaved person. Over the course of several evenings, Kinte's story brought presence and an immediacy to the experience of slavery. Viewers watched as Africans were snatched away from their lives in The Gambia and put on ships to the New World. The captives arrived in chains, only to find that they would be further subjected to harsh treatment under the 'peculiar institution' that was the US system of slavery. The same director, Marvin J. Chomsky, was responsible for both *Roots* and *Holocaust* (1978), a second television miniseries that followed a year later. The latter was to become one of the key triggers and sites of the new memory of the Holocaust. Once again, over the course of several evenings, a story of erasure was told; in this case, the story of Jews being rounded up and put into camps and eventually put to death in gas chambers drew the attention of wide-ranging audiences. Many viewers of both dramas were engaging with these historical events for the first time.

These early television series drew considerable attention, and they helped stimulate the emergence of new memory narratives about both the Holocaust and slavery. Novels such as William Styron's *Sophie's Choice* (1979) and Toni Morrison's *Beloved* (1987), as many have noted, effectively narrated the dilemmas for Jewish and black characters and thus introduced a critical turn and a key departure in how the past could be remembered, and more specifically narrated, for audiences who were not likely to have had a prior sense of their history as it was told in these public ways. What these two novels accomplished was to provide a way of framing the ethical paradoxes that a subjugated person faced and their working through of the moral conflicts of their action. Both novels became major motion pictures, once again drawing large audiences, in the US and beyond. Both built new public memories within which new subjectivities could be imagined. It was not just those who had been the actual victims of the historic state-sponsored atrocities who were to be remembered, but also the generations who came after them and who understood their group's identity and history as intimately bound by crimes too horrible to mention. Marianne Hirsch (2008) uses the term "generation of postmemory" to refer to people who did not directly experience the Holocaust but for whom the experience felt no less real. These groups could insert their public memory-based history into an international discourse that tried to name the after-effects. What happened in the last part of the twentieth century was the circulation of a lexicon beyond the specific community of Holocaust survivors – a lexicon for describing the emotional residue of horrendous crimes.

 Holocaust memory helped audiences imagine other histories in new ways. The articulation of Holocaust memory categories and vocabularies generated a way of thinking about self-making and interiority. It opened up possibilities for people or groups, particularly black Americans and other minority groups who were not typically granted an interiorized humanity or a recognizable way to speak about their suffering. What the 1990s discourse around memory achieved is an understanding of trauma, public responsibility, and moral sentiment that intervened in public discourse in new ways and inspired new publics. This was possible because of a multidirectional dialogue – and thus legibility – across memory projects.

One of the most influential contributors to such circulations has been Nobel Prize winning novelist and essayist Toni Morrison, who draws resonating parallels between the Jewish Holocaust and the Middle Passage. Morrison imagines her work as an intervention into public understandings of memory that move beyond a single community. Putting black American memory in self-conscious dialogue with other groups' experiences, including those of Holocaust survivors, Morrison's work is an exploration of the interiority of the traumatic experience. In her essay "Site of Memory," Morrison brings new nuances into the European discussion of memory. In contrast to Nora's use of the concept of "sites of memory" (e.g. Nora 1989), for Morrison this opens up a discussion of tensions and contradictions, akin to Tsing's "frictions." Rather than connoting a gap between state histories and subaltern memories, Morrison's sites of memory encompass both official and vernacular knowledge, as well as local and transnational struggles. For example, slave narratives (that is, personal experiences of the horrors of slavery found in the published accounts of enslaved people) make use of Enlightenment conventions of representation at the same time as they exceed them. Slave narratives build the rational subject position of the teller, yet they also show the limits of such subject positions. Morrison explains her desire to delve into such limits, arguing that slave narratives never disclose the full traumatic impact of slavery. In those very places where the violence of slavery threatens to undermine the rational subject position of the teller, it is curtained from view. "[O]ver and over,"

Morrison explains, "the writers pull the narrative up short with a phrase such as, 'but let us drop a veil over these proceedings too terrible to relate'" (1987a, 109–110). As a result, the narrators and their readers are protected from the troubling – yet also empowering – features of internal psychological dynamics, as these are shaped by trauma. "Most importantly – at least for me," Morrison continues, "There was no mention of their [the narrators'] interior life." This becomes the site of Morrison's own intervention. "For me – a writer in the last quarter of the twentieth century, not much more than a hundred years after Emancipation, a writer who is black and a woman … [m]y job becomes how to rip that veil drawn over 'proceedings too terrible to relate'" (1987a, 110). Morrison narrates trauma, with all of its consequences for the formation of identity. From the beginning, she recognizes this as a public historical task: the task of creating public memory.

Morrison explores trauma and the way it forms a zone of tension across state histories and subaltern memories. It is a palpable force in the present, she argues, even as it draws from the past. It can kill without physical contact and leave everyone staggering in what Morrison refers to as "rememory." Men and women try to rebuild their lives but never leave behind the damaging effects of slavery. On rememory, Marianne Hirsch adds: "Rememory is neither memory nor forgetting, but memory combined with (the threat of) repetition; it is neither noun nor verb, but both combined. Rememory is Morrison's attempt to re-conceive the memory of slavery, finding a way to re-member, and to do so *differently*, what an entire culture has been trying to repress" (1994, 94).

A critical text for black American memory, Morrison's novel *Beloved* is an exploration of the haunted contradictions of rememory. The characters cannot get over slavery even after its abolition, but continually work through the space of trauma. In this, the novel joins a transnational dialogue between the memory of slavery and the memory of the Holocaust. Note the dedication of *Beloved*: "To Sixty Million and More." This was much to the alarm of some, as Morrison's dedication recalls the figure of six million commonly associated with the number of Holocaust victims.[9] The novel's plot is inspired by a nineteenth-century newspaper article about an escaped slave woman who kills her young daughter to prevent her from being returned to slavery; this woman, Margaret Gardner, became the character Sethe in Morrison's fictional account. This character's founding trauma crushes any sense of innocent purpose and makes it clear that survival is a troubled, and yet a courageous goal. Morrison's characters overall have a deep and rich interior self, which entitles them to respect as ethical modern citizens.

---

9 For an extended discussion of the problems of the comparison between the Holocaust and slavery, see Zierler (2004).

Consider the parallels with the novel *Sophie's Choice* (1979), in which William Styron tells the story of a woman haunted by the choice she has been asked to make between her two children since she is not able to save them both from the maws of the Holocaust. Her subsequent insanity stands for that of her people; she, like Sethe, is the mother who cannot protect her children. Public memory emerges here, as in Morrison's novel, in the forming of icons of trauma, icons who are not just individual victims but ones who share in a much broader incapacity to continue as before. As intellectual and artistic space becomes occupied by such figures, memory does not dissipate but draws all sides – whites, blacks, Christians, Jews – into anguished dilemmas. This is not a glorification of victims, but an exploration of continuing contradictions *within* rememory.

In 2005, Morrison undertook a more explicit collaboration with a Jewish composer when she joined forces with Richard Danielpour to complete an operatic version of the story of Margaret Garner. Danielpour says of the project:

> More than anything else, Margaret Garner is an opera that reminds us that we all belong to the same human family, and it demonstrates what can happen when we forget this fundamental truth. While slavery has been outlawed in the United States since 1865, its lingering effects have proven over the years that the issues in our country concerning race, class, and the true meaning of freedom are in no way resolved. Visiting Washington DC today, one can see memorials to heroes from every war and cause, but there is not one memorial to the people who suffered under the institution of slavery. It is my hope that Margaret Garner will both memorialize and remind us of what we as a society are so easily inclined to forget. (Danielpour 2005)

Danielpour traces the idea for the collaboration to his earlier reading of a book of poetry by runaway slaves, which deeply inspired him. As in the cases discussed by Michael Rothberg, the collaboration between Morrison and Danielpour demonstrates how alliances and conversations across communities can inspire moments of mutual recognition and empathy, and propel both memory and solidarity.

Some interpreters understand Morrison as highlighting the dichotomy between elite and subaltern memory work (see e.g. Hartman 1994). As numerous critics have demonstrated, Morrison's work is subtle and calls up many readings (see Smith 2012). In my reading, Morrison's sites of memory are not an attempt to banish state histories in favor of the purity of grassroots memory. Instead, she explores the contaminated space where these categories overlap and shape each other, thus allowing trauma not to be a benediction but rather the continuing curse we all navigate to survive. In what follows, I present three illustrations of the productiveness of Morrison's understanding of 'site of memory.' In each of the following cultural performances, public memory work is split by internal struggles – the fallout of multiple positionings in regard to official histories – even as it asserts its difference.

Site of memory 1: a film revival

Julie Dash's *Daughters of the Dust* (1991) is one of several memory initiatives that, like *Beloved*, helped to inspire a new public. Over the twenty-five years that have passed since the film first opened in major movie theaters, the film's popularity has grown exponentially. When it first appeared, the film was greeted in many circles with ambivalence because the ways of knowing or remembering that it presented were not familiar to many viewers, not even to those with regional ties to the US South. Some residents from the area were unhappy with the film, fearing that the region's distinctive culture would once again make the Sea Islands appear too exotic. The film played only briefly. Yet, in 2004 *Daughters of the Dust* was inducted into the US National Registry of films. It is now often publicly screened in the US and elsewhere in the world. How has this film come to cross back and forth between state histories and subaltern memories?

From the first, the film opened up tensions between local and more distant audiences. *Daughters of the Dust* used a series of props to offer a sense of place. Newsprint wallpaper, a bottle tree, hands stained blue from indigo dye, an old semi-submerged figure from a slave ship, a weathered Koran left by the shore – all brought the materiality of memory to life. Local people had been taught that their culture was an impediment to progress. Nonlocal audiences were also put off. Many viewers, both black and white, found the cultural practices represented in the film difficult to understand and the characters' language incomprehensible.

In the years since its release in 1991, however, appreciation for the movie's significance in generating a sense of public awareness of Gullah Geechee culture has been evident in outpourings of support for it. The film has won a number of awards and is being shown widely. The film itself has gathered a past; its story of memories is itself collecting memories through engaging with the productive space between the official and the vernacular. Some of those at a conference I attended at the College of Charleston's Avery Research Center for African American History and Culture in 2011 to commemorate the anniversary of the film's release, claimed their appreciation of the film even when it was first released, but others admitted that when they first watched the film they could not understand what was happening or understand what the characters were saying. What they did appreciate, though, was the beauty of the place and the characters. Because several years later there was much more awareness of Gullah Geechee culture, these viewers could now better understand the profound contribution of Dash's work. What has emerged over the last two decades is a public culture in which memory, produced by black Americans and others, has become much more prevalent and part of a robust discourse, both local and transnational, both state-sponsored and grassroots.

As viewed today, Julie Dash's film mobilizes this wider trend by mining contradictions and tensions. On one level, the film is a simple depiction of the Gullah Geechee community. It presents artifacts and sensibilities that provide the sense of a day in the life of an island family as some of the members are about to depart for the US North and thus seek a future elsewhere. The film has other stakes, however: it depicts a future in the grip of Morrisonian rememory, in which the tensions of multiple positionings are the conditions for moving on. One of the characters is a specter yet to reach mortal status, called the Unborn Child. The Unborn Child was conceived by rape, and the quarrels about her rape-stained future pervade the film. The Unborn Child also witnesses other quarrels about strategies for survival vis-à-vis dominant institutions. It is she who not only gets a glimpse of the world as it is but who can also cast a future for herself *beyond* the world as it is. Through her projection into the future for herself, film viewers are brought into the possibilities of an emergent world. The Unborn Child, which stands for the emergent and the yet-to-come aspect of Dash's work, represents this space for imagining new publics, in all their contradictions.

Consider Dash's future cast in dialogue with Derrida's distinction between the future and *l'avenir* (interviewed in *Derrida*, 2002):

> The future is that which – tomorrow, later, next century – will be. There's a future, which is predictable, programmed, scheduled, and foreseeable. But there is a future, 'avenir' (to come) which refers to someone who comes whose arrival is totally unexpected. For me, that is the real future – that which is totally unpredictable. The Other, who comes without me being able to anticipate their arrival. So if there's a real future beyond this other known future, it's l'avenir in that it's the coming of the *Other* when I am completely unable to foresee their arrival.

Site of memory 2: the bench and the fort

As memories of slavery have become part of the US museum landscape, they have carried with them the tense interplay between official and vernacular, black and white, and multiple positionings. We see this in particular in commemorative activities 'added on' to state memorialization, such as a bench for contemplation of slave memories, in the shadow of a fort. The National Park Service administers both the bench and the fort. They are both elements in state memorialization. But they are crafted to evoke separate affect worlds, and in this crafted difference, in all its in-and-out engagements with state categories, we can see rememory – and its making of new publics.

The bench I visited, located on Sullivan's Island, in South Carolina, was installed in 2008 at the instigation of the Toni Morrison Society. The bench looks out on one of the ports of arrival of the ships that carried enslaved Africans to the US. The bench aims to sponsor contemplation on the heritage of slavery and its traumas. The idea for this commemoration came from a speech given by Morrison, who had said in 1988:

> There is no place you or I can go, to think about or not think about, to summon the presences of, or recollect the absences of, slaves; nothing that reminds us of the ones who made the journey and of those who did not make it. There is no suitable memorial or plaque or wreath or wall or park or skyscraper lobby. There's no 300-foot tower. There's no small bench by the road. There is not even a tree scored, an initial that I can visit or you can visit in Charleston or Savannah or New York or Providence, or better still, on the banks of the Mississippi. (Morrison 1989)[10]

In recent years, the National Park Service has extended the earlier story of the significance of the fort that looms over the bench, by including the story of the transatlantic slave trade. At the same time, the fort's main story and indeed attraction for most visitors is its military presence in wars, including the American Revolutionary War. It also served as a barrier against northern forces during the US Civil War, as South Carolina hoped to secede rather than give up slavery. The two commemorative histories are intertwined – yet separated by performative practices that evoke varied affects.

The installation of the bench transformed the site into a space of both celebration and mourning. A procession of three hundred people, including members of the Toni Morrison Society along with community members from Charleston, South Carolina, placed the bench. In their ceremony, they recalled that Sullivan's Island was the first site of medical inspection as ships approached Charleston. Many passengers had survived the long journey in deplorable conditions. Before the ships' arrival on the island, sick passengers would be dumped overboard so as not to raise suspicion about the health of others on board. If ship captains suspected or discovered illness among its human cargo, once the ship had docked those who were ill would remain on the quarantine island for several weeks. Some forty percent of the enslaved Africans brought to the US first travelled through Charleston. This encouraged some black Americans to refer to Sullivan's Island as the Ellis Island (the usual site for the arrival of European immigrants) of black Americans.

---

10 See also the website of the Toni Morrison Society, www.tonimorrisonsociety.org/bench.html (accessed 21 March 2014).

During the procession, Morrison explained, "It's never too late to honor the dead.... It's never too late to applaud the living who do them honor ... This is extremely moving to me" (quoted in Lee 2008). The prominent participants in the bench-placing ceremony wore white dresses and carried open yellow parasols as they made their way to commemorate and memorialize those who had arrived at this site before they were taken to the auction block. The day's high humidity and soaring temperatures gave a vivid impression of what it might have been like for the newly arrived who were carried in the hull of a ship and tied to one another during the long journey, filling in what history's facts failed to convey. Organizers poured libations to those who had come before. Morrison, along with Mrs. Tomalin Polite, who recently learned that she was a seventh-generation descendent of one of the enslaved families, cast a wreath of daisies in the water as a sign of respect. A local group of drummers, dressed in African-inspired attire, used their performance to culturally link Africa and the New World. Perhaps these details convey a sense of the ways the ceremony borrowed from many cultural traditions: enslaved Africans did not arrive in white dresses, but the white dresses honored them; 'African' libations and 'European' wreaths were equally necessary. Such cultural formality made the bench a space for experiencing both collective and individual grief.

In contrast, Fort Moultrie, which towers over the bench and its small plaque, impresses visitors with its grandeur – the grandeur of the state. It is a site for remembering the nation; and it claims to represent all. The fort's gift shop offers a panoply of multicultural items: souvenirs and books on colonial America, Native Americans, and black Americans line the shelves. Yet by representing everyone, no one is allowed to contemplate or mourn. That is the work of the bench outside.[11]

Much like the area designated for reflection in the National Holocaust Museum in Washington DC, the bench marks a place where historically significant events are not just commemorated but rather affectively remembered by the living. Yet these initiatives are not without their entanglements with the very state that created the conditions for trauma. The US federal government along with community leaders from many minority groups forms articulations that move back and forth between sometimes initially adverse agendas. In seeking public recognition, so-called grassroots efforts form alliances with federal agencies and private corporate donors that enable plans to move forward. It is sometimes possible to evade the state's gaze. The "Lest We Forget" Black Holocaust Museum in Philadelphia, for example, began in someone's home and has since collected materials from

---

11 For a comparative public memory project, see Wallace (2006).

black American history and heritage; but it has struggled to remain open. In contrast, the new National Museum of African American History and Culture, situated on the National Mall in Washington DC, is due for completion by 2015. This institution comes into being with the support of government and private donors. Like the Holocaust Museum, the staffing and maintenance of these museums require adherence to certain guidelines to make them both specific to a group's history and generalizable, so that they become public memory.[12] Memory projects come to life between the state and grassroots community efforts – between the fort and the bench.

Site of memory 3: the plantation tour

I turn now to my last ethnographic example, the commercial memory tour. The vitality of public memory – and its circulation between elites and ordinary people – is signaled by the significance and growing presence of 'memory tourism.' Much like tourists travelling to Auschwitz and Dachau, there are nowadays more and more visitors at sites of slavery memory. These sites allow the memory tourists to connect with the emotional life of the past. Culture and cultural tourism have become major economic enterprises. Thus, the intersection between memory and commercial circuits is globally important, encouraging further transnational connections.

One site of this growing industry, also in South Carolina, is the plantation tour. Southern plantations remain an important site of mainstream popular memory in the US. In recent years, however, a more diverse set of visitors – including more non-white tourists – is taking an interest in these tours. Public memories that have now become broadly circulating encourage visitors to ask tour guides about stories and experiences that had not previously been considered part of the tour, such as what it was like for a child to be a slave. Tour guides often feel committed to inserting their plantation into a story about the pleasures of southern regionalism, and in the past, plantation tours overwhelmingly assumed an Anglo-American audience. If enslaved people were discussed, even in the early 1990s, they were referred to in generic terms such as 'the help,' which erased their actual social status. Enslaved people were merely 'the workers.'

---

12 Performances such as those aimed towards public recognition at once challenge dominant narratives and incorporate official tropes. For an extended discussion of the politics of recognition, see Povinelli (2011).

It is becoming increasingly difficult for plantation tours to ignore contestations about the history of the US South. In the 1990s, for example, an extended battle ensued over the presence of the Confederate flag that – as the state flag – was flown over the South Carolina state capitol building. As the flag of the southern states, popularized during the US Civil War, it continues to connote for many a support for secession and for the institution of slavery and its aftermath. An ongoing point of contention, for those who do not see their alliances with the southern secessionists, is why a symbol that celebrates a regional past should continue to represent the state. Yet, for southerners who feel that the Confederate past *is* their past and find that it is increasingly being erased, an easy compromise is not evident. A tussle over varying versions of history is apparent: should tour guides tell of the vitality of the South, including the Confederacy, or of its terrors in the history of slavery? In such tussles, both versions of history gain force. Southern history has the force of regional and national allies; but slave history has the public force of transnational memory work. Even ordinary interactions between visitors and hosts on the plantation show these struggles in action, stretching concepts of history and memory. Tours, I argue, embody the contradictions between the varied points of insertion into official histories; such contradictions are part of the tourist performance. The 'memory project' of slavery emerges from such contradiction-filled performances.

During the mid-1990s, I first accompanied a group of black students and professors as they spent a week in the Sea Islands in order to learn about the history and culture of the region. One part of the weeklong experience brought us to a plantation that was, at that time, notorious for its attempts to bring back the old South. Images of plantation splendor no doubt filled the typical tourists' minds. That was not the case for this group: age and sentiments could not draw us to be nostalgic about this place. Making our way past the entrance, in the distance, a gate could be seen, behind which a modest colonial house came into view. We were directed to a parking area to the right of the house. A small patch of cotton on the side of the parking lot led a few students to try to see what it was like to pick. The hot sun further brought home the reality of having to work in such conditions. Even before our group arrived at the front door of the main house, the students had already started to imagine what it must have been like to have to work in the fields – fields that stretched far beyond where one could see. One student said: "Imagine if all you could see was nothing but a long field of cotton before you and no way out."

After several minutes of waiting, our Anglo-American tour guide arrived at the front door of the mansion, dressed in a hooped skirt, and resembling the central character Scarlett in the famous Margaret Mitchell novel (1936) and subsequent movie (1939), *Gone with the Wind*. We were told a few things about the history of the house itself and its place in the history of the area, but we were also very aware of its fictive life as this circulated in popular films. Once we were led to the main house, our anxieties immediately began to mount over the way in which the furniture and renovations done on the house were described in great detail, while little mention was made of the people who were involved in the house's upkeep and maintenance. As we walked from the parlor to the dining room, the tour guide continued to point out details about the furniture while giving all credit for its appearance to the owner of the house. Finally, a student pointedly asked, "Where did the slaves stay?" No comment: the tour guide continued with her script. Another student followed up: "Did the owner really put in that ceiling or did the slaves?" Again, no comment. A third student joined in: "Where did the slaves live?"

At first the guide seemed not to hear the questions. The students repeatedly asked, however, trying to interrupt her performance, and their questions proved more insistent than the guide's refusal to answer. Eventually, worn down by this persistence and apparently drawing the obvious conclusion that this group was not interested in the life of a plantation owner but rather in that of the captive laborers, the guide explained that she was not allowed to deviate from her script. At the very end she relented and asked if we had noticed a set of brick structures on the side of the oak-lined road leading to the main house as we drove in. This is where some of the slaves had lived, she said. This area had not been marked in any distinctive way; we had hardly noticed it.

After the house tour finally ended, our group hurriedly went to look on the side of the road and found a pile of rubble from brick buildings that appeared long abandoned. As we wandered around, noting the dirt and damp foundation, some fantasized aloud what it must have been like to live in such small quarters. The area was covered in dense vegetation, and the remains of only a few structures could still be seen. Still, most of us were affected by what we saw; students began to imagine what it must have been like to be enslaved. The ruins, particularly in their unrestored state, brought the past to life. The students were moved; some stepped inside and stood amidst the deteriorating walls, and thus tried to travel back to the era when their relatives lived.

Already their expectations were different from those of the preceding generation. It is likely that in contexts such as a plantation tour, earlier black tourists would not have assumed that their story would be included. To the post-civil rights generation, however, this exclusion was not acceptable. Their generation is firmly entrenched in the new public sphere, in which they expect to be treated as anyone else.

On a more recent visit, in June 2011, I could see that the cabins of the enslaved, once unidentifiable, had been restored. The main house still stands with antebellum period-attired tour guides poised to greet visitors on the porch, and one is immediately drawn into their performance space through their dress, styles of speech, and comportment. In contrast to my earlier visits, however, during which there was no black American history to comment on other than for its absence, tourists are now encouraged to visit the African American site. There is now an area called Slave Street, where eight cabins stand as markers of the black American history on the plantation. Each cabin tells the story of slavery; tourists progress from slave crafts (with a contemporary basket maker and a display of baskets) to a slave church and a room of artifacts. Then we reach the exhibit's moment of triumph: the election of President Obama! As a coda, the very last cabin is the site of the "Gullah Theater," reserved for a performance in which the audience learns about local Gullah language and culture and is invited to join the performers as they tell folktales in the Gullah tradition.

Clearly, in the time since my earliest visit, great efforts have been made to include the black American experience in the story of the plantation. Of course, what should be included in the account remains disputed. Thus, for example, one of the stories that is meant to appease both black and white tourists is the account of the 'task system.' The task system was a labor system in which slaves worked by the task and not the hour. The white tour guide explained: "Slaves didn't have it all that bad; when they finished they could work for themselves." As a more empathetic participant commented: "Who could work for themselves after working fourteen hours a day – especially in the heat and humidity of South Carolina? The fact that these were people in bondage and not in control of their lives seems hard [for some people] to accept."

In the years since my first visit to this and other plantations, the audiences that I have been a part of – whether black American or non-black American tourists – are less and less willing to simply accept the plantation owners' story as the whole story. They want, at the very least, a multi-perspective account. Black Americans expect some commentary on the conditions of the enslaved, including an account of the trauma of slavery. Moreover, visitors also expect to hear about other white experiences – for instance, the experiences of small farmers who lived without slaves. Visitors are forcing a change in tour guides' practices; the structure of the tour is changing. Performances of difference and refusal are increasingly expected as part of the tour; furthermore, tour guides often preempt such critical commentaries by offering their own official version of slave memory. This change draws directly from the rise of tourism as a lucrative economic venture and from the growing diversity of tourists. It also originates from the push of a public memory project that has crucially been strengthened by its transnational clout and by its resonance with other stories of suffering. This has not only helped slavery to become visible in the public arena, but also to draw the attention of a varied set of constituents.

Conclusion

Transnational dialogues bring memories to life – even if they are mobilized within the more limited contexts of national and regional debates. Intertwined discussions of the Holocaust and the Middle Passage have been formative for US public memory: they have brought us the ability to imagine the horrors of history through the continuing trauma of survivors, as well as a repertoire of communal memory practices with a healing potential. The limitations of some of these practices have been shown here, but also the possibilities they offer for creating new formations of political identity and action.

New publics are formed through the production and consumption of circulating memories, which catch viewers and consumers in unexpected ways, and hence open up possibilities for imagining a public sphere that is inclusive of people and groups who are not used to seeing themselves as active makers of culture. In this way, public memory projects become important sites for moving across and beyond national political spheres. The practices described in this essay involve multiple sources, both official and vernacular. For minority groups in the US, the state has at times played a critical role in generating legislation of inclusion, as is evident in the marking of the National Heritage Corridor along the southeastern coastal region of the US, the Gullah Geechee Heritage Corridor. Yet this Corridor also overlaps with the South Carolina National Heritage Corridor. These Corridors are conceived in contradiction. Together they simultaneously host memorialization of slave holding and of slavery's trauma. It is in the interplay between such multiple enactments that public memory projects – and new publics – come into being.

References

Agee, James and Walker Evans. *Cotton Tenants: Three Families*. 1936. Brooklyn: Melville House, 2013.

Anderson, Benedict. *Imagined Communities: Reflections on the Origin and Spread of Nationalism*. 1983. London: Verso, 1991.

Carney, Judith. *Black Rice*. Cambridge: MIT Press, 2001.

Chandler, Genevieve W. *Coming Through: Voices of a South Carolina Gullah Community from WPA Oral Histories*. Eds. Kincaid Mills, Genevieve C. Peterkin, and Aaron McCollough. Columbia: University of South Carolina Press, 2008.

Danielpour, Richard. "Composer Note." *Margaret Gardner*. By Richard Danielpour. Libretto by Toni Morrison. 2005.

Dash, Julie. *Daughters of the Dust: The Making of an African American Woman's Film*. New York: New Press, 1992.

Daughters of the Dust. Dir. Julie Dash. Kino International, 1991.

Demo, Anne and Vivian, Bradford, eds. *Rhetoric, Remembrance, and Visual Form: Sighting Memory*. New York: Routledge, 2012.

Derrida: The Film. Dir. Dick Kirby and Amy Ziering. Zeitgeist Films, 2002.

Dow Turner, Lorenzo. *Africanisms in Gullah Dialect*. Chicago: University of Chicago Press, 1949.

Fassin, Didier, and Richard Rechtman. *The Empire of Trauma: An Inquiry into the Condition of Victimhood*. Trans. Rachel Gomme. Princeton: Princeton UP, 2009.

Filene, Benjamin. *Romancing the Folk: Public Memory and American Roots Music*. Chapel Hill: University of North Carolina Press, 2000.

Georgia Writers' Project, Savannah Unit. *Drums and Shadows: Survival Studies among the Georgia Coastal Negroes*. 1940. Westport: Greenwood Press, 1973.

Gone with the Wind. Dir. Victor Fleming and George Cukor. Warner Brothers, 1939.

Habermas, Jürgen. *The Structural Transformation of the Public Sphere*. Trans. Burger Thomas with the assistance of Frederick Lawrence. Cambridge: MIT Press, 1989.

Haley, Alex. *Roots: The Story of an American Family*. New York: Bantam Books, 1976.

Hall, Stuart. "Cultural Studies: Two Paradigms." *Media, Culture, Society* 2.1 (1980a): 57–72.

Hall, Stuart. "Race, Articulation and Societies Structured in Dominance." *Sociological Theories: Race and Colonialism*. Paris: UNESCO, 1980b. 304–345.

Hartman, Geoffrey. "Public Memory and its Discontents." *Raritan* 13.4 (1994): 24–40.

Herskovits, Melville. *The Myth of the Negro Past*. Boston: Beacon Press, 1958.

Hirsch, Marianne. "Maternity and Rememory: Toni Morrison's *Beloved*." *Representations of Motherhood*. Eds. Donna Bassin, Margaret Honey, and Meryle Kaplan. New Haven: Yale UP, 2004. 92–110.

Hirsch, Marianne. "The Generation of Postmemory." *Poetics Today* 29.1 (2008): 103–128.

Holocaust: A Mini Series. Dir. Marvin Chomsky. Paramount, 1978.

Jones-Jackson, Patricia. *When Roots Die*. Athens: University of Georgia Press, 1997.

Joyner, Charles. *Down by the Riverside: A South Carolina Slave Community*, Champaign: University of Illinois Press, 1984.

Levy, Daniel and Natan Sznaider. *The Holocaust and Memory in the Global Age*. Trans. Assenka Oksiloff. Philadelphia: Temple UP, 2006.

Lee, Felicia R. "Bench of Memory at Slavery's Gateway." *New York Times* 28 July 2008. www.nytimes.com/2008/07/28/arts/design/28benc.html?pagewanted=all{&}_r=0 (accessed 21 March 2014).

MacDonald, David B. *Identity Politics in the Age of Genocide: The Holocaust and Historical Representation*. London: Routledge, 2007.

Mitchell, Margaret. *Gone with the Wind*. New York: MacMillan Books, 1936.

Morrison, Toni. "The Site of Memory." *Inventing the Truth: The Art and Craft of Memoir*. Ed. William Zinsser. Boston: Houghton Mifflin, 1987a. 101–124.

Morrison, Toni. *Beloved*. New York: Knopf, 1987b.

Morrison, Toni. "A Bench by the Road." *World: Journal of the Unitarian Universalist Association* 3:1 (January/February 1989): 4–5, 37–41. Available at: www.uuworld.org/ideas/articles/117810.shtml (accessed 21 March 2014).

Nora, Pierre. "Between Memory and History: *Les Lieux de Mémoire*." Trans. Marc Roudebush. *Representations* 26.1 (1989): 7–24.

Phillips, Kendall R. and G. Mitchell Reyes, ed. *Global Memoryscapes: Contesting Remembrance in a Transnational Age*. Tuscaloosa: University of Alabama Press, 2011.

Phillips, Kendall R. *Framing Public Memory*. Tuscaloosa: University of Alabama Press, 2004.

Povinelli, Elizabeth. *Economies of Abandonment: Social Belonging and Endurance in Late Liberalism*. Durham: Duke UP, 2011.

Rothberg, Michael. *Multidirectional Memory: Remembering the Holocaust in the Age of Decolonization*. Stanford: Stanford UP, 2009.

Roots: A Mini Series. Dir. Marvin Chomsky. Warner Brothers, 1977.

Smith, Valerie. *Writing the Moral Imagination*. Malden: Wiley Blackwell, 2012.

Stewart, Mart A. '*What Nature Suffers to Groe:' Life, Labor, and Landscape on the Georgia Coast, 1680–1920*. Athens: University of Georgia Press, 1996.

Styron, William. *Sophie's Choice*. New York: Random House, 1979.

Tsing, Anna Lowenhaupt. *Friction: An Ethnography of Global Connections*. Princeton: Princeton UP, 2005.

Wallace, Elizabeth Kowaleski. *The British Slave Trade and Public Memory*. New York: Columbia UP, 2006.

Warner, Michael. "Publics and Counterpublics." *Public Culture* 14.1 (2002): 49–90.

Zierler, Wendy. "'My Holocaust Is Not Your Holocaust:' 'Facing' Black and Jewish Experience in *The Pawnbroker, Higher Ground*, and *The Nature of Blood*." *Holocaust and Genocide Studies* 18.1 (2004): 46–67.

Elizabeth Edwards

Between the Local, National, and Transnational: Photographic Recording and Memorializing Desire

> Human memory, … albeit quite unconsciously, recollection and imagination will blend when an effort is made to construct a mental picture of the past. A pictorial record in such cases will serve the double purpose of checking vagaries of memory by reference to actual facts, and of recalling to mind, through the powers of suggestion, details that otherwise would be irreclaimable. (Gower et al. 1916, 4)

For the authors of *The Camera as Historian* (1916), a handbook for survey photographers, quoted above, there was no doubt that their endeavors to make a systematic photographic record that would be a "true pictorial history of the world" (Harrison 1893) involved the self-conscious production of memory texts.[1] The authors had been involved with the Photographic Survey and Record of Surrey, founded in 1903, cajoling and encouraging amateur photographers to make photographic records of the material remains of the past in the county of Surrey. These photographs, some 14,000 in all, made and collected over some 15 years, were deposited in the local library for the general good of the borough's populace.

The Surrey Survey was just one of many such endeavors to harness the energies of amateur photographers and their cameras to make records that would serve as a focus for historical information and for recollection of the past for both makers and consumers. In this essay, I shall argue that despite their apparent localism, the various photographic surveys constituted a transnational cultural moment that emerged, on the one hand, from a shared response to the dynamic interrelationship of the past, present and future and, on the other hand, from the efficacy of photography and archival systems in creating memory banks for the future.

1 I should like to thank the Institute of Advanced Study at the University of Durham, where I was fellow in early 2012 and where I developed this chapter. It is a wonderful environment and I am grateful to my colleagues there for their ceaselessly stimulating conversations. I owe great thanks to Annelies Cousserier (Leuven), Ewa Manikowska (Warsaw) and Estelle Sohier (Geneva) for sharing their work and interesting finds with me so generously, to Chiara De Cesari and Ann Rigney for encouraging me to write this essay and saving me from various infelicities, and to Divya Tolia-Kelly in Durham and the Social Anthropology Seminar at the University of Oxford for their very helpful comments as the argument developed.

While the concept of the transnational tends to assume a contemporary context, the "constellation of mutually conditioning factors and parallel processes" (Vertovec 2009, 23) that defines it can be demonstrated historically, as a number of scholars have argued, even if the precise configuration and flavor differ. The concept offers a new analytical framework for the long antecedents of contemporary studies in transnationalism (Grant et al. 2007, 2). However, most studies have focused on the nascent transnationalism of empires. Instead, I want to explore the impact of such an analytical framework nearer to home – indeed on projects aimed precisely at defining that European 'home' and which can be described as transnational through their shared aims, objectives, methods, networks and values.

Self-identified and self-defined projects of photographic survey were undertaken in many European countries between about 1885 and 1920 (the period of the first flush of survey activity), largely by amateur photographers and enthusiasts. There were movements in, for instance, Great Britain, Scandinavia, Switzerland, France, Poland, Italy and Germany, which, despite their apparent localism, emerge from this trans-European cultural moment of modernity, itself constitutive of the transnational. There were also projects in countries of settler colonialism and Empire. However, European survey projects are defined by their amateur base and must be distinguished from the surveys of overt state apparatuses, such as those in British India. Nonetheless, both types of survey emerged from the same cultural matrix of historical desire and technical possibility.

To an extent I am using 'the photographic survey movement' as a heuristic convenience to discuss a wide variety of memorializing desires manifested through organized photographic recording. But this movement must not be over-homogenized. While the various projects all self-identified as 'survey photography' and recognized the patterns of associations and influence that I am describing here, the amateur surveys cannot be reduced to an over-determining fantasy of archival control, although they did share the language of utopian possibility in some of their more expansive moments. With their serendipity and epistemic fissures, they are, beneath the rhetoric, structurally too diverse and fragile to carry such an analysis. What they do is demonstrate, however, a cultural moment in which photographic and memorializing desire intersected, and clustered around the material remains of the past and the perceived value of the latter to the future in a moment of aspiration and memorializing ambition. In particular, these projects are a useful prism through which to explore the perceived relationship between photography, memory and historical imagination because the photographs were intended by their makers precisely as a record of that disappearing past and a self-conscious articulation of a set of memorializing values.

What unites these diverse projects and gives them their transnational character are three sets of intersecting values. Firstly, there is the importance and validity of the photographic record as an instrument of memorializing practice. The use of the camera in this way meant espousing a specific transnational documenting impulse (Mittman and Wilder forthcoming). Secondly, there was a shared anxiety about, and valuation of, the impact of modernity on both cultural practices and the remains of the past through which identities might be negotiated. Finally, their aim was to establish archives for the public good, which would be accessible through libraries, museums or learned societies, and shown in exhibitions and in lantern lectures. Even though these processes were heavily mediated and selective, there was a sense of a utopian access to information, especially that of history, for the good of the civic body (see Edwards 2012, 137–144).

My starting point is the debate as it unfolded in Britain, because this has been the focus of my particular research (see Edwards 2012). What emerged strongly from that study, however, was the sense that the collective, and the communicative networks of photography, in both its aesthetic and documentary modes, cannot be contained simply within a national dimension. Not only were patterns of connection and aspiration transnational in nature, but some of the more expansive and vociferous advocates of survey photography also had all-encompassing, universalizing and encyclopedic ambitions for their medium. These ambitions were integrally linked to practices of memorialization and anticipated memory. As contemporary commentators noted, photographs would be "refreshing his [the viewer's] memory about things that he has wholly or half-forgotten, and would rejoice to be reminded of" for "such photographic records will before long become the one thing needful in connection with every country, society, or body having interest in its history, or other body having any interest in its history being handed down to posterity" (Sachse 1890, 653; Photography and History 1913).

So while the founding ideologies of such endeavors were determined and developed at a national level, responsive to specifics of national and nationalist agendas, at the same time there was a critical collective sense of the appropriateness of a photographic response to memorialization and a collective evaluation of techniques and strategies through which these might be achieved. As an amateur photographer involved with the Heimatschutz movement in Germany commented, "the pictorial arts are among the most powerful allies of Heimatschutz" (quoted in Rollins 1997, 174).

The potential of photographs, their flow through the networks of knowledge and political and cultural desire, made these processes both intensely local and intensely global. This was a shared methodology which also drew on transnational debates in photography about the merging of photographic technique, archival desire and memorializing practice, and about the very purposes of photography itself. The self-conscious desire to harness photography and its inscriptive qualities to a prosthetic archiving and memorializing practice, forms a value system and a cultural moment which in its perception was potentially truly transnational, even if in practice endeavors fell short of such an ideal. Photographic survey was one of a number of experiments with modern media and the possibility of memory (Amad 2010, 5). It arises out of a clearly identifiable cultural moment of historical imagination which was a response to the accelerating experience of modernity, industrial and urban change, and cultural disappearance. It is this matrix of values and the actions they initiated that I term 'memorializing desire,' an explanation for which lies in the flows, networks and connections of the photographic endeavor, and its application to an archive addressing a future that was anticipated as being both international and global.

Importantly though, photographic survey emerges not only from the way in which the modern imaginary relates to the past, but also from photographers' own sense of modernity. The photographic surveys depended on their values appealing to a large public of amateur photographers engaged with the expanding technology of photography. While these appeals were to the photograph as an objective record, they also addressed a more subjective sense of civic, national and even humanistic duty to record for the future. Whatever the individual and specific collective hopes for these projects might have been, they drew on a broad series of common and transnational desires, emerging from shared values about the importance of the past in the future, the desire to create records and the indisputable efficacy of photography in achieving those aims. However, as I shall argue, it was precisely the shift from transnational rhetoric and network to transnational practice that constituted a point of fracture for those endeavors.

Photography and the mediation of memory

The presence of photography has saturated consciousness of the past for over 150 years. Scholars as diverse as Siegfried Kracauer, Jacques Le Goff and Raphael Samuel have posited the advent of photography as the turning point in historical consciousness. However, much writing, especially that of Benjamin and Kracauer, has used photography as a metaphor and as site of a critique of the nature of history itself, rather than engaging with photographs as an embedded historiographical practice of memorializing translation (About and Chéroux 2001, 10).

Photography not merely added a new form of 'text' to memory practices but produced a reconfiguration that attends to the latter's properties at a fundamental level (Koshar 2000, 10). Photography "revolutionizes memory: it multiplies and democratizes it, gives it a precision and a truth never before attained in visual memory, and makes it possible to preserve the memory of time and of chronological evolution" (Le Goff 1992, 89). As such, photography constituted one of the "new connectors in temporal perspectives" that Paul Ricoeur notes, and accelerated the "primacy of the visual" which has marked memory construction from antiquity on (Ricoeur 1988, 116). Its impact on memory practice has been described by Scott McQuire as "photomnemonics," that is, "the impact of the camera cannot be limited to filling gaps in historical content. On the contrary, the profound technological mutation of the archive necessitates questioning the very concept of history, and exposing the collusion between representation and the time it has long presupposed" (McQuire 1998, 108).

While the impulse to make photographic records was a response to anxieties about progress, the fragility of experience and a loss of the past within both a national and a European modernity, it was, of course, linked to broader interests in and debates about the preservation of ancient monuments and the codification of national heritage as a memorializing practice. These interests themselves were not necessarily contained within national and political boundaries, but were part of a broader cultural moment and a sense of connected and emergent European heritage and its institutionalization (Swenson 2008). While the wider contexts of the concept of cultural heritage and patrimony have attracted a substantial literature in both their transnational and particularly national character (see for instance Altenburg et al. 2008; Hall 2011), the role of photography as definitional and consolidating of this cultural moment has received less attention. Rather the emphasis has been on the role of photographs within canonized national projects and attempts at institutionalization, which is perhaps also linked to the emergence and similar canonization of national historiographies of photography itself.

There are clear cultural and intellectual links between record photography and preservationist movements that defined national heritage, such as the Society for the Protection of Ancient Buildings in Britain. However, photographic projects did not necessarily map entirely on to infrastructures of national projects and their demographics in a direct or simple way. Particular national projects reflect a range of complex class and demographic questions, differing greatly in density, range, social make-up and efficacy. There was a downward social spread of photographic activity by 1900, linked to an expansion in the range of photographic technology and a reduction in costs, which extended the possibility of making historical statements. However, what was imaginable and achievable in terms of record photography was also shaped by local patterns of association, class, access to leisure and access to technology. For instance, survey projects in Poland were the work of small numbers of local social elites, whereas those in Britain had a much wider social base. Nonetheless, the idea of photographic recording drew an increasingly wider range of people into the self-conscious use of photography as an expression of collective historical imagination. These new networks of imagination and activity placed less reliance on professional and quasi-professional photographers than had been the case in, for instance, the 1850s when the French state-funded La Mission Héliographique recorded France's cultural patrimony, Charles Marville made photographs of a Paris threatened by Haussmann's remodeling of the city, and James Burgoyne recorded Birmingham for a similar purpose, or in the 1870s when the Society for Photographing the Relics of Old London produced portfolios of photographs by private subscription (Foote 1987; Boyer 2003; James 2004, 101). We are looking at practices of a different order, enabled by the expansion of photographic practice.

This expansion, however structured, was harnessed in the organization of photographic survey to a scientific model of amateur and provincial data production working with an interpreting center, which had pertained from the eighteenth century onwards. But it was also one that enabled amateurs to participate in the inscription of histories which defined who they were and where they belonged, and at the same time to contribute to an expanding transnational archival agenda.

The realization of memorializing desire can also be linked to shifting theories and evaluations of the constitution of memory itself. The photographic surveys and the promise of photography as a recording device were grounded in a positivist view of history. However, a defining characteristic of photography is its intervention in space and time, producing fragments of the experienced world translated into the photographic frame. Through this process photographs elevated, heightened and intensified the everyday fragment as a history of the present (Amad 2010, 4). While this works at many levels, the amassed fragments and memorializing bricolage inscribed in the photographs were woven into coherence in the archive. The archive was thus not only a metaphor for memory itself, but also a site of practices that determined the parameters of history and memory (Amad 2010, 8).

Practices of photography in general, and the survey movement in particular, resonate in this period with philosophical thinking on memory, in particular with that of Henri Bergson whose work placed memory in everyday experience and collective habit. While Bergson had an ambivalent attitude to the mechanical inscriptions of time and the externalizations that the archive represented, his privileging of time, of the everyday and of experience in the construction of memory accords with the inscriptive abundance of both photography and film.

His influence is most clearly established in his relationship with the wealthy French financier Albert Kahn who funded *Archives de la Planète*.[2] Although Kahn's

---

2 Perhaps the most successful advocate of the universal visual memory bank was the French financier Albert Kahn who, until his ruin in the crash of 1929, poured money into a project to

mammoth project is beyond the scope of this chapter, it was perhaps the apotheosis of universal and encyclopedic visualization and of the intended production of a global memory bank through record-making. While in his emphasis on the everyday, Kahn followed Bergson, his memorializing desires were linked also to an encyclopedic and inclusive impulse to record. This privileging of the everyday fragments of experience, and its ethnographic dimensions of the valorization of the 'traditional,' resonate through the memorializing desires of the amateur survey movement and were the basis of its claims to a collective memory function. As W. Jerome Harrison, who was instrumental in the development of the photographic survey movement in Britain, put it, linking the everyday, change and preservation:

> It is important that we should record the *life of the nation* – the trades, the dress, the occupations of the people, their habits and their amusements. We live in an era of unusually rapid change. The improved means of communication, the discoveries of modern science, and the spread of education all combine to abolish the differences of language, dress, and of manners. (Harrison 1906, 60)

This is not to argue that all survey photographers were responding directly to Bergson, although his work did reach an extensive and popular audience. Rather, such thinking marked the significance of the everyday and the ordinary as a space of memory production – one that could be translated into archival form through photographs.

Indeed, from the start the surveys were conceived as a form of externalized collective memory, in both its real and metaphorical roles – a 'holding' of the past in which photography, properly executed, monitored and archived, could become a memory bank which fulfilled the inscriptional and performative qualities of memory and hence of the cultural milieu. These debates encompass those on the quality of observation, scientific and mechanical objectivity, and material practice, those on style and aesthetics, and those on the social production of the bodies of amateur survey photographers themselves (Edwards 2009). As Celia Lury has argued, the making of both individuals and collectives is premised

---

document the world (Amad 2010). This is a project of a very different order. It depended on professional photographers and filmmakers, and even ethnographers, not the vagaries of amateur participation. It was simply an impulse to record. While the major part of Kahn's project was filmic rather than photographic, the early work of the project employed photographers resulting in, first, 4,000 stereoscopic records and then some 72,000 autochromes (Amad 2010, 6–7). Although Kahn's project had no ostensible sense of dynamic public utility, there was nonetheless a memorializing dimension to its desire for universal knowledge capture. The early and enthusiastic application of color technologies is also integral to this.

on sets of narrative techniques that endow and maintain the authority of a continuity of consciousness (1998, 7–8). Debates about the relationship between, on the one hand, visual knowledge as a memory form and, on the other, the archive as prosthetic memory shaped the practices of survey photographers.

In particular the heightening effect of photographs, in the way they bring objects and moments into visibility and focus attention, endowed them with the quality of a statement. In the process, a wide range of materials were imbued with an institutionalized memorializing significance.[3] Banal memory functions of everyday space and action become translated, even transfigured, into the space of the memory bank. Photographs consequently extended the repertoire of the historically significant by bringing it into focus: "beyond any interest which they may have from their own merits, these things have an interest as forming a link in our national art-history" (Harrison 1885, 364).

There were of course profound national and sub-national differences in the signifying intensities of photographs. The sense of national heritage and the density of connective tissue which it carried was rooted in different political imperatives (Swenson 2008, 85–86). Sometimes these processes worked in opposite directions. For instance, the production of photographs of cultural heritage was used in Italy to create a visual sense of unity after 1870s, whereas in Poland photographic surveys were used to delineate the specifically regional within the multinational dissipation of Polish heritage in the homogenizing discourses of the Russian, Prussian and Austro-Hungarian empires successively (Manikowska 2011a; Mattiello 2011).

The impulse to photographic survey was part of "accumulated and interwoven layers of local and distant linkages" (McMahon 2011, 74) through which identity and its associated memorializing practices were being constituted. It was part of an extension of the archival impulse embracing not just photography and film, but also ethnography and the collection of material culture. In particular, archaeology and ethnography underpinned much survey work. This is reflected in similarities in the evaluation of the 'significant.' Although the scale of particular projects varied, there was a similarity between them in scope, content and aspiration. A common purpose underlay the memorializing desiderata issued by a whole range of surveys, from such local endeavors as the Photographic Survey and Record of Surrey in England, to those of the British Association for the Advancement of Science (BAAS), or the Musée de Suisse des Photographies Documentaires, as they listed buildings, farming practices, ritual practices, ancient

---

3 In this period the professionalization of history was, especially in France and Germany, marginalizing 'the local' (Applegate 1999, 1160).

Fig. 1. Ostrykół, church interior. Adolf Bötticher, 1890–1896; reproduced with permission of Instytut Sztuki Polskiej Akademii Nauk, no. 60244.

artifacts, clothing and assorted folkways as key areas of recording. In particular, even if in realization it was limited, the importance of recording 'peasant,' 'folk,' 'rural lifeways' and 'customs' before they disappeared, was a central and recurring feature of the rhetoric of the photographic survey movement. For instance, in Germany, Poland and Hungary, ethnography in particular was linked to national identities. Ethnological knowledge translated into knowledge of the nation and its history, as peasant and rural custom stood for the grounding of identity in the very soil of the nation (Vermeulen and Alvarez Roldán 1995, 10).

Consequently, there were strong links between the making of the photographic record and the emergence of local ethnology museums in the former Prussia and Poland (for instance in Dresden and Danzig, see Joschke 2004, 64), just as there would be in Scandinavia a few decades later where photographic survey was systematized under the auspices of the Nordic Museum (Becker 1992). Even in Britain, where perhaps these linkages were less marked, there were strong conceptual and discursive links between the BAAS's Ethnographic Survey of the British Isles, launched in 1893, and local photographic surveys (Edwards 2009).[4] All were concerned with recording and tracing the long histories of place "in a world that stood on the threshold between the traditional and the modern, the local and the global" (Amad 2010, 8).

This broad view, articulated in different ways with different intensities, informs a wide range of salvage agendas in the late nineteenth and early twentieth centuries. One cannot, of course, be certain of the extent to which individual photographers were, or were not, aware of theories of memory or cultural evolution in any directly causal way. What is clear is the correlation between science, especially ethnography and anthropology, its poetic translation as salvage and preservation, and the values of the photographic survey and related movements such as architectural preservation, in a broad currency of ideas. They are patterned by shared epistemological assumptions around temporalities of salvage and preservation. This sense of urgency that "the matter is one that will not brook any undue delay ... as the evidence is slipping out of our grasp" (Brabrook 1893, 74), was a moment, as Nora puts it, of the "irrevocable break of peasant culture, that quintessential repository of collective memory" (Nora 1989, 7).

Racial mappings of Europe which, in many cases, were entangled with ethnographic description, were also deeply inflected with a discourse of origin and nation (McMahon 2011). While there are colonial implications here too of course, many surveys included both ethnographic and anthropometric dimensions, especially in what were perceived as the margins of Europe – the Balkans, northern Scandinavia, and in the British case, Ireland. Ireland was the only site where the physical anthropology parts of the BAAS' survey were fully realized photographically through the work of Alfred Cort Haddon and Charles Brown, where "mathematically and pictorially calibrated Irish types" were defined in areas "yet to be corrupted by Anglocentric modernity" (Carville 2011, 105–106).[5] As McMahon has argued, the delineation of European races, and indeed languages, was used "to scientifically legitimize nations as ancient families and naturalize their geopolitical maneuverings, ethnic power struggles and ideological responses to modern change" (2001, 71). But he also demonstrates the ways in which, like the endeavors of photographic survey, these concepts moved across national boundaries, defin-

---

4 This period also saw Henry Balfour's failed call for a museum of English folklife (Balfour 1909).
5 Modeled on Francis Galton's Anthropometric Laboratory, Haddon had established a similar facility in the Department of Anatomy at Trinity College, Dublin.

HEIMATSCHUTZ IM THURGAU   AUS WAAGENHAUSEN

Fig. 2. Heimatschutz postcard, Switzerland. E. G. Hausamann, c. 1920; author's collection.

ing what it was to be European. In a sense, the inscriptive quality of photographs and the indexical tracing of material traces constituted a way to hold the flux and ambiguity of histories.

In all these endeavors visual media, especially photography, was used not only to make records but as a means to disseminate the values of survey, themselves nested within the moral landscapes and vocabulary of nation. For instance, in Germany, the Heimatschutz movement, although more broadly grounded in landscape, a sense of 'home' and an aesthetics of nationhood (Knorpp 2009) than surveys focused largely on tangible heritage, understood photography and other visual forms as central to its agendas. Thus, Fritz Koch, a young lawyer from Thuringia, and a leading light in the movement, instigated a series of picture postcards, describing them as being of "extraordinary significance ... for the propaganda of the Heimatschutz" (quoted in Rollins 1997, 175).

Transnational connections and transnational visibilities

If photographic survey offered the potential for world history, constituted through the multiple ties and connections between people and institutions that characterize transnationalism, it is also necessary to look at the ways in which memorializing desires manifested themselves as a set of concrete transnational connections through networks of knowledge, practices of photographic exchange and exhibition. The survey movement might be characterized as what Anderson famously described as an "imagined" and "print" community: groups of people, not necessarily known to or communicating directly with one another, but bound by common values, modes of imagining and technical practices, articulated through print media (Anderson 1991).

This press did much to sustain the rhetoric through their expansive visions of photography. The existence and progress of photographic survey projects across the world was noted in the photographic press. The photographic achievements of the Archaeological Survey of India, despite its governmental status, were held up as an example to amateur photographers in Europe, and the journal *Photogram*, which carried a column and list entitled "Doomed or Threatened," also included threatened antiquities in other countries, including imperiled examples in Florence, Ratisbon and Paris. Exchanges of information and contacts were noted, for example the English survey movement was in contact with Léon Vidal in Paris; Boston Camera Club sent a set of lantern slides of their survey to the Liverpool Photographic Society; Giacomo Boni, who was undertaking surveys of Italian antiquities, corresponded with Philip Webb of the Society of the Preservation of Ancient Buildings who had links with the Survey of London; the National Photographic Record Association was in correspondence with Léon Vidal, with enthusiasts in Mysore State, India, and with a nascent project in Stockholm (Doomed or Threatened 1897; Pollock 2009; Mattiello 2011, 220, 226; Edwards 2012). These articulations constitute a shared consciousness, processes of cross-fertilization and a mode of reproduction that encompass a wide variety of groups, individuals and organizations, emerging from a "common consciousness and bundles of experiences which bind people into social forms and networks" (Vertovec 2009, 4–6, 27). There are many more examples of photographic interchange, but what they suggest is the dense web of interconnected concerns and values for which photography was the connective tissue.

While discourse here, as is so often the case, exceeds practice, there was nonetheless an expansive impulse to record. W. Jerome Harrison conceptualized photographic survey, both literally and metaphorically, as universal. Drawing on new wave theories of light, he suggested that light, as it reflected off the earth into the universe, might carry with it, in a quasi-photographic fashion – a sort of giant photographic plate at the end of the universe – a record of the planet's history in the greatest detail, constituting an all-embracing prosthetic memory bank in the sky of infinite and inclusive quality. It is worth quoting at length:

> It is a wonderful thought, that every action which has ever occurred on this sun-lit Earth of ours – or indeed, for that matter, anywhere within the illuminated universe – is recorded by the action of light, and is at this moment visible somewhere in space, if any eye could be there placed to receive the waves of light … speeding away from our orb, which would now be visible only as a star, we should pass in review the lives of our parents and ancestors. History would unfold itself to us. We should only have to continue the journey long enough

to see Waterloo and Trafalgar fought out before our eyes; we should learn the truth as to the vaunted beauty of Mary Queen of Scots; and the exact landing place of Julius Caesar on the shores of Britain would no longer be a mystery. If we had the curiosity to ascertain by ocular demonstration, the truth of Darwinian theory, a still more extended flight would disclose the missing links – if such existed – by which man passed from an arboreal fruit-eating ape-like creature to a reasoning omnivore. (Harrison 1886, 23)

The transnational quality of these expansive memorializing desires is borne out in two projects which attempted to translate the local into the transnational, global and universal, and realize the anticipated visual demands of an international future. Both failed in their different ways – they were wildly over-ambitious and unwieldy in relation to the human and financial resources available, and failed to account for the different densities of affective connections that drove the surveys in practice. However, they are nonetheless paradigmatic of the more encyclopedic aspirations for photographs that developed out of smaller projects.

Potential interconnectedness was given concrete form in the first instance at the Chicago World's Fair (1893). Here, at an auxiliary congress on photography organized by the Photographic Association of America, a meeting advocated that an "international bureau [be] established to record and exchange photographic negatives and prints" (Harrison 1893, 548). In this way, Harrison moved his national vision for photographic survey onto the global stage, calling for a systematic photographic record "of the face of the earth."

Premising his argument on the international project for the mapping of the heavens, inaugurated in the mid-1880s, he asked, "is not a photographic survey of *the face of the earth*, at least as important as that of the celestial sphere?" (Harrison 1893, 548, original emphasis). The aim should be "a true pictorial history of the present day." However, crucially he continues: "it seems a great pity that the results should be confined to the locality in which they are produced" (Harrison 1893, 548). Implied is that while these photographs had local or national significance, they also constituted a record and potential memory of human experience and human existence. Harrison goes on to position the flow of survey images clearly as a grounded transnational memory:

How many thousands there must be in the United States who would welcome the opportunity of examining the lists of British Photographs which would be furnished to their local institution ..., and of selecting therefrom pictures of the village, town and county from which they or their forefathers came; or of the places of which they read in history or their daily papers. And we in England would many of us gladly hail similar opportunities of obtaining pictures of that wide land where our relations dwell ... (Harrison 1893, 548)

The international committee included members from the United States, Canada, Japan, India and France. Significantly in this context several members of the committee had transnational connections as recent migrants: John Nicol, a Chicago-based pharmacist of Scottish origins had been connected with the Edinburgh Photographic Society and their nascent survey of the city, and John Carbutt, a Philadelphia photographer who had links with Sheffield where photographic survey had been discussed in 1889. In response to this call for photographic action, Léon Vidal held a meeting in Marseilles in 1894 under the auspices of the International Union of Photography to launch "a new international effort" to which "interested people from all parts of the world" were invited to "organize a universal museum of photographic documents" (Photographic Record 1906, 307–8). The following year, supported by French photographic innovator J. Fleury-Hermagis, Vidal founded the Musée des Photographies Documentaires in Paris, which by 1900 had over 20,000 negatives (Joschke 2004). A similar project called the Musée Suisse des Photographies Documentaires, was founded in Switzerland, under the presidency of Eugène Demole in 1901, and in the same year, the International Institute of Photographic Documents, modeled on Vidal's Paris project, was founded by Ernest de Potter in Brussels under the auspices of the International Institute of Bibliography (Cousserier 2010).

The International Institute of Photographic Documents provides a second instance of the intense transnational desire that I noted above. It is significant that it is closely linked from the beginning to the transnational management of knowledge, a point to which I shall return.[6] Instigated by a group of Brussels enthusiasts, notably de Potter, its roots were local but its ambitions became expansive. Again it was premised on photographs being an exchangeable form and on the universality of the language of knowledge. Like the British survey movement, it attempted to establish standards for photographic inscription and to provide a systematic rendering of the material traces of past. It saw its remit in terms not only of cultural heritage, but also of zoology, landscape and the conditions of modern life, as "a dream of an exhaustive inventory of the visible world" (Cousserier 2010).

Despite these projects and the universalizing aspiration for photography, the Chicago meeting progressed little beyond inspiring rhetoric, although the committee, by all accounts, "did good work in disseminating a knowledge of the survey movement" (Harrison 1906, 58). By 1902, in Paris Vidal was lamenting that "we yet lack an international organization for the production and preservation of record photographs ... The various photographic societies – English, French German Austrian etc. – should have excellent reasons to undertake the making of collections of photographs showing the state and progress of each country, but an

---

6 I am enormously grateful to Annelies Cousserier for generously sharing with me her unpublished PhD work on this archive.

obvious preliminary to organized international action is to arrange the conditions under which photographs are to be taken, and to formulate some system by which the contracting nation or association can exchange sets of prints" (Vidal 1902). The project in Brussels likewise failed to attract the support of photographers, many of whom preferred to put their efforts into the more local projects of cultural heritage from which universal aspirations had emerged (Cousserier 2010). But important for my argument is the fact, not that these projects were actually realized, but that they were considered desirable and achievable. They represent a moment of cultural aspiration around memory practice at its most expansive, and demonstrate the belief in the efficacy of photography to deliver these desires.

While the universal dreams of archival possibility collapsed under the weight of their own ambition, the transnational potential of photographic collaboration and its memorializing desire remained more strongly articulated at a local level. Survey endeavor with its multiple strands of convergence and coherence was conceptualized in terms of linked projects rather than as unified archive.

A particularly cogent demonstration of this occurred at the 1909 Dresden International Photographic Exhibition when individual survey endeavors were presented in a context of collective and interconnected action. This exhibition contained no less than 21 rooms of survey photography from across Europe and beyond. There were contributions from Austria, Russia and Germany, including a series of photographs of "Old Hamburg" and another series from Saxony itself that had been made in conjunction with Dresden's museum of ethnology. The United States, which had survey endeavors in Boston and Pennsylvania among other places, was instead represented through photographs of Native American people and their everyday life, an autochthonous deep past for the United States, provided by the Smithsonian Institution in Washington. There were also contributions from photographer and journalist Herbert G. Ponting who was working in Asia in this period,[7] and from the burgeoning local surveys in the UK – from Warwickshire, Surrey, London and the National Photographic Record Association, which had co-ordinated the British contribution. These survey contributions included photographs of the historical built environment, folk customs and folkways and "peasant types," notably those from Russia by the ethnographic pictorialist Sergei Lobovikov (Dresden Exhibition 1909, 514; Joschke 2004).

Such photographs were also shown at the great exhibitions and world's fairs, which frequently displayed survey photographs within national narratives. These exhibitions were more generally saturated with photographs, proclaiming and af-

---

7 Herbert Ponting is best known for his Arctic work as photographer and cinematographer on Captain Scott's Arctic exploration. He left before the second fatal winter of 1912/13.

firming the richness of raw materials and of modern industrial processes and in-frastructures. Countries such as Australia and Canada used these exhibitions as vehicles for encouraging migration and settlement, as they performed the bene-fits of their nascent countries photographically (Hoffenberg 2001, 162–163). The Chicago World's Fair of 1893 appears to have included some survey photography. Apparently a series from Glamorganshire was included in the Welsh representa-tion (Pollock 2009, 12). Photographs from the colonial government's Archaeolog-ical Survey of India and an extensive collection of Benjamin Stone's photographs of British folk customs and ancient sites were both exhibited at the St. Louis Expo-sition of 1904. The memorializing qualities of the latter were particularly noted: "every photograph in the collection throws a strong light upon some feature in the life of humanity, and is of deep interest in the only half-written, ill-understood history of institutions" (Parker 1904, 145). Survey photographs were also shown in relation to patriotic agendas, for instance photographs from the Warwickshire and Kent surveys that were shown in the context of an imperialist extravaganza, namely, the 1911 'Festival of Empire' in London.[8] But these images were shown across the world not merely as exercises in nostalgia, but also as examples of what could be achieved through photography in relation to a sense of history and mem-ory positioned within the contexts of progress-oriented events, with a strong em-phasis on industrial development, and indeed patriotic pride in the same (Zelljadt 2005, 307).

The massing of images at the Dresden Exhibition also suggests the way in which European memory was being constructed in relation to colonial experience. The height of the survey movement coincides exactly with the European moment of high imperialism and colonial consolidation. This saw a massive increase in the circulation of imperial and colonial discourse and its impact on concepts of the nation and national being. The significance of this is indicated by the extent to which 'overseas' photographic survey endeavors, whether elsewhere in Europe, in settler colonialism or in empires, were reported frequently within the photo-graphic press and noted at meetings of survey societies, and equally frequently conceptualized in shared terms, through networks of influence, interaction and exchange.

It could be argued that the surveys were only thinkable because of the all-embracing transnational presence of Empire, and that significantly, the surveys constituted a mapping of Empire at home, a clear delineation of a contained na-

---

8 There are indications that this patriotic extravaganza would probably have contained more survey photography had it not been postponed on the death of King Edward VII in 1910. In the interim the National Photographic Record Association was disbanded.

tional heritage and sense of home to be preserved against both the racial and cultural presages of empire (Edwards 2012, 153–159). Not only was this the case in the broadest and obvious sense of the relationship between photography and colonial expansion in geo-political and economic terms. Metropolitan/colonial relations were themselves expressed through the transnational networks of photography which cohered it as a medium of both aesthetic and documenting practice. At Harrison's meeting in Chicago, there was constant reference to the successful survey work of both the Ethnographic and Archaeological Surveys of India which were working at this date (Guha 2010). Harrison was keen to expand the surveys to the colonies more generally (Harrison 1906, 63), and his committee included Bombay photographer Sharpurjee N Bhedwar.[9]

While a sense of the colonial formed the substratum through which folk life in Europe was understood (Amad 2010, 266), one should not assume an overly direct causal relationship between the two, because the idea of photographic survey cuts across colonial power and colonial experience. This was not only in the differing shapes, ethos and densities of European colonialism. Some countries where there were forms of photographic survey, for instance Finland[10] and Poland, were themselves subject to colonial relationships, in which photographs were part of a counter-narrative. Nonetheless these histories and memorializing desires engendered within the colonial were integrated into the demonstration of the value and efficacy of photographic survey as a global memory system. Photographs were seen as enabling these relations, "for all photographers are brothers" through which the "light science … tends to bring its fellow-workers together in no ordinary degree" (Harrison 1893, 549), so that survey would "link together the photographers of the entire civilized world by an extension of the 'survey' idea …." Through this it "was hoped that every country would have a photographic survey with local and national depots 'containing both negatives and prints relating to the whole country' and facilities for exchange and purchase of prints" (Harrison 1906, 58).

If all these projects had similar objectives, to make encyclopedic inventories as "the illustration of human activity in all its manifestations" (Gower et al. 1916, 30), more particularly, they were paradigmatic of the expanded historical and memorializing desires that I have noted. If in practice these projects were unsuccessful, they remain significant for the way in which they illustrate a belief in the transnational exchangeability of photography through both visual translation

---

9 I am grateful to John Falconer of the British Library for supplying me with more detail on Sharpurjee N. Bhedwar.
10 For instance I. K. Ihna's photographs of the landscape of the Finnish national epic, the Kalevala of the 1890s.

and material forms. All were premised on the possibility of recording, collecting and ordering photographs in a quasi-bibliographic manner, whereby a record of current experience could be articulated. They speak to the interconnectedness of histories and illustrate a common form of apprehension.

The archive and the prosthetic memory bank

Informing all survey activities, whatever their individual scales, was the idea of public access and public utility, through which photographs could affect their memory work. From its inception the movement strove to create an externalized or prosthetic 'collective memory' bank, a holding of the past both metaphorically and literally through the prosthetic eye of the camera itself.

This process was enabled through the confluence and repetition of values, desires and techniques that were able to transcend the local, regional and national, as the particular was universalized within that broader cultural moment of modernity and photographic potential which vastly widened the possibilities for making historical and memory statements. It was, as Celia Lury has described such prosthetics, "an artificial expansion of capability, resulting in transferable potential" (Lury 1998, 18), as the photographs in archives themselves shifted their conceptualization from simply servicing local or national needs (as cultural patrimony, for instance) to an expansive vision of a global dimension to the past (Herzfeld 2003, 2–3).

This constituted a crucial shift from the act of recognition and recollection translated into photographs to a sense of efficacy premised on the mechanics of the camera as it intersected with the mechanics of archival arrangement, management and exchangeability. These projects have been characterized in Foucauldian terms as the management of disciplinary knowledge and as a gathering of signs in the production of knowledge (Foucault 1995; Derrida 1996, 3; Tagg 2009). It was a heterotopia of "indefinitely accumulating time, accumulating everything, resonating with the will to 'enclose in one place all times, all epochs, all forms, all tastes'" (Preziosi 1989, xvi quoting Foucault). The photographic archive also represented knowledge that was popularly perceived as having the affective qualities of memory since "such a record survey collection, if carefully and systematically brought together, cannot fail to be of the greatest value and interest both to the present and to future generations" (Proposed National 1897, 6).

The photographs that made up the archive emerge, as we saw in the Dresden example, from very different styles, contexts and patterns of association, from amateur practice through to aesthetic pictorial photography, commercial practices to the effectively photo-journalistic. What is significant is the way in which they became absorbed into the broader rhetoric and records of the world (Joschke 2004; Edwards 2009). Their 'objective' quality was stressed in the language used. The photographs were seldom described as 'photographs,' but rather as 'records' or 'documents.' Intellectual and memorializing unity was privileged over variations of style and content, emerging from a common conception of the work to which photographs could be put and the kind of information that was required. This was integrally related to the mechanical archival management of photographs. It is significant that photographic survey was formulated as a transnational force at a moment which also saw the emergence of international and universal systems of bibliographic classification for rendering knowledge. These systems provided a framework for the control of photographic meaning, as photographs were integrated into these systems, at both local and transnational levels.

The involvement of lawyer and bibliographer Paul Otlet in the Brussels project is particularly significant because it marked a shift in scale as regards the utopian potential of photography and its archive. Otlet was interested in the synthesis and transferability of knowledge. He had developed the Universal Decimal Classification at his Office International de Bibliographie in 1905, and worked with de Potter on a standardization of photographic description which was presented a year later at the Congrès International de la Documentation Photographie (Cousserier 2010).

If Brussels' International Institute of Photographic Documents was a manifestation of Paul Otlet's bibliographic standardization, even local endeavors were increasingly absorbed into library classification systems that contained the messiness of photographic inscription and knowledge. It is significant that *The Camera as Historian* both devoted some 54 of its 250 pages to a locally developed system drawn from the structure of Otlet's Universal Classification and included an illustration of the International Institute of Photographic Documents. This local classification was in all likelihood the work of one of the authors, Croydon borough librarian Stanley Jast who had a deep knowledge and experience of the potential for the expansion of knowledge through library reform, especially the application of modern systems of classification and open access. In particular, Jast, a theosophist, was guided by a belief in the interconnectedness of the 'human race' at a metaphysical level. The flow of knowledge, and thus memory, contained in documents such as photographs, and the role of libraries within that system, was for Jast part of that global interconnectedness (Black 2007, 180–181).

Although in practice there is little evidence that the classification was used in its pure form, survey photographs in libraries were increasingly absorbed into universal systems of knowledge management that, in their turn, became tools of memory management as they framed ways into photographs, setting up 'preferred readings' and marginalizing others. However, in terms of memory practices, as Roland Barthes argued (1984), photographs always exceed their intentions, and are infinitely recodable, capable of being absorbed into multiple histories against the taxonomic grain. It was this point of fracture in the archive that opened the space for recollection. Indeed, these projects were in some ways the forerunners of post-WWI global archiving projects such as Paul Otlet's significantly named *Mundaneum*, designed, but never built, for Geneva by Le Corbusier (Amad 2010, 102). Otlet was also associated with the Scottish sociologist, geographer and urban planner Patrick Geddes whose work was influential on the latter part of the amateur survey movement in Britain (Rayward 2007, 3; Edwards 2012, 246–247). There are many other examples one could cite. What I am arguing is that a conceptual interconnectedness together with social networks enabled the articulation of the memorializing desire of the photographic survey, even if in its transnational dimension it was inevitably flawed. The transnational foundered on tensions between the localized desire of amateur photographers and the rhetoric of a world archive. As *The Camera as Historian* put it tactfully, such collections "can never attain the completeness of local surveys" (Gower et al. 1916, 30). It was the global system of knowledge management that made the photographic memory bank thinkable, but the affective qualities of recollection that worked against it.

It has been argued that the surveys and their absorption into a broadly-defined memory practice is merely an aspect of the "world-as–exhibition" articulated through scopic regimes of truth and an appropriative ocularcentrism (Pollock 2009, 8). While there are undoubtedly elements of this at work (especially in the universal projects in Paris and Brussels), there is something more complex going on. At one level, this process indeed constitutes the transfer from head to archival artifact, from recollection to storage, and from individual to collective, in the way that Le Goff, Nora and Assmann have argued (1992; 1989; 2011). However, in these manifestations of historical activity, practices of recollection and the framing of the archive cannot necessarily be neatly compartmentalized. While at one level archives indeed became centralized and artifactual, their creators trusted that the appeal of the photographs would remain in people's heads and hearts – making for better citizens. Again while there were local variations in both the shape of this aspiration and its socio-political construction, this memorializing activity was driven by the "ideal of the active citizen," in which voluntary action and self-improvement led directly to political life advancing an open, prosperous and modern society (Harrison 2003, 87–88).

Thus, as a memorializing practice, the significance and power of the photographs was located successively in their making, their storage and their consumption as forms of recollection. Making the archive was itself understood as educational, and it engaged photographers in the very process of recollecting, thinking about the past and positioning themselves in relation to it; the act of photography involved a recognition of the mnemonic significance of a subject. These hopes of the affective quality of the archive blur Assmann's distinction between recollection and archival semanticization (2011). For photographic survey translated recollection into archivable form which, through the immediacy of the photographic image, permitted recollection in the future and thus re-internalization in the future.[11] Recollection was thus located both in the moment of photographic recognition and at the moment of apprehension in the archive.

The point of rupture was not, therefore, the removal from the heart to the archive. Instead, the point of alienation occurred with the systematization of the photographs within global knowledge. While the possibility of photographic survey as memorializing practice emerged from transnational moments of cultural anxiety and desire, coupled to a belief in photographic efficacy, there were practical and emotional barriers to the universalist and indeed utopian vision of photographic utility. Photography remained tensioned between the local, the national and the transnational.

Closing thoughts

Photography was seen, in the late nineteenth and early twentieth centuries, as a transnational practice linked to a range of supra-national values which defined Europe and by implication much of the world's relation with the past. I have argued that whatever the immediate constitution of photographic surveys, their success or failure, and their various forms and densities, they were all inflected with the possibility of a transnational dynamic, through the networks, connections and indeed aspirations which shaped them. These emerged from a moment of specific transnational historical consciousness and imagination in relation to modernity and the values of the past. They are part of a broad cultural matrix which saw the salvage and archiving of the past as an act of cultural memory in the face of presumed disappearance. This moment was one of transnational intensity, expressed through ethnography, photography, film, museum collecting, the codification of cultural heritage and a range of popular preservationist movements. These strands might be locally expressed, but their intellectual framing is far from local. They operated on a dialectic of scale which encompassed national, regional

---

11 For a discussion of the material and semanticizing practices of the British photographic survey, see Edwards (2012, 114–120).

and local contexts, framed through shared meanings and values through which collective practice was both legitimized and motivated (Vertovec 2009, 43–44).

To think about the endeavors of survey photography in the context of transnational memory practices opens up "broader analytical possibilities for understanding the complex linkages, networks and actors" (Hofmeyr 2006, 1444) on which it depended. These processes defined photographic survey as the product of a specific but fluid matrix of transnational values, aspirations, and archival apparatuses which was manifested locally at a specific historical moment. These endeavors were held together by a specific vision of photographs as records, by a community of practice and its "ability to link the civilized world" (Harrison 1893), by Otlet's bibliographic utopia, and by Jast's universalist humanist belief in the emancipating power of knowledge, including visual knowledge. It was a memory practice that self-consciously looked both back to the past and forward to the future. Yet, what limited the reach of these projects and constituted a point of fracture was a shift in the conceptualization and application of the photographs from a quasi-utopian ideal of democratic access, to tools of recollection (however mediated they might have been), to a utopian mechanical archival management of total knowledge which overstretched the connective tissue of transnational endeavor.

Further, the particular brand of cosmopolitanism that had informed the sense of world history and memorializing exchange, and which had marked the photographic surveys, was obliterated by the experience of WWI. Ethnographic delineations[12] and practices of photographic survey retreated into more overtly nationalist agendas (Beck 2007, 286) despite the wider political constitution of peace leagues and a restorative political internationalism after WWI. However, despite their general drift into invisibility, the burgeoning of contemporary scholarship on photographic surveys, on the visualizing practices of world description, and the visual deposits of a wide range of nationalistic and preservationist desires points to the significance of the after-lives of these projects and their expansive agendas.

They are now being drawn back into active engagement in the contexts of renewed tensions between national and transnational memory in contemporary Europe. In face of the reassertion of national identities and national hegemonies, these photographs are being put to work in contemporary geo-politics where transnational capital has perhaps been weakened, not by the spread of global media and supranational structures, but by the resurgence of fragmenting nar-

---

12 The rise of modern social anthropology, with its increasing focus on the delineation of the anthropological object as non-European, also removed the theoretical dynamic of European ethnography, marginalizing it from the increasingly international character of academic anthropology (Vermeulen and Alvarez Roldán 1995).

ratives of the particular. The form of the photograph – infinitely recodable, intervening in space and time – serves such narratives with ease. Such photographs are being used, for instance to define a newly invigorated expression of Polish cultural heritage in the post-Soviet era (Manikowska 2011b). At a microlevel photographs are being absorbed into the personal histories of local historians and family historians, reflecting a desire to belong, to have roots, and identity within the larger narratives of history. This in turn reflects a cultural moment in which memorializing desire is simultaneously atomized and transnational.

References

About, Ilsen and Clément Chéroux. "L'histoire par la photographie." *Études photographiques* 10 (2001): 8–33.

Altenburg, Detlef, Lothar Ehrlich, and Jürgen John, eds. *Im Herzen Europas: Nationale Identitäten und Erinnerungskulturen.* Cologne: Böhlau, 2008.

Amad, Paula. *Counter-Archive: Film, the Everyday, and Albert Kahn's Archives de la Planète.* New York: Columbia UP, 2010.

Anderson, Benedict. *Imagined Communities: Reflections on the Origin and Spread of Nationalism.* 1983. London: Verso, 1991.

Applegate, Celia. "A Europe of Regions: Reflections on the Historiography of Sub-National Places in Modern Times." *American Historical Review.* 104.4 (1999): 1157–1182.

Assmann, Aleida. *Cultural Memory and Western Civilization: Functions, Media, Archives.* Cambridge: Cambridge UP, 2011.

Balfour, Henry. "Presidential Address – Call for a National Folk Museum." *Museums Journal 9* (1909): 5–18.

Barthes, Roland. *Camera Lucida.* Trans. R. Howard. London: Fontana, 1984.

Beck, Ulrich. "The Cosmopolitan Condition: Why Methodological Nationalism Fails." *Theory, Culture, Society* 24 (2007): 286–290.

Becker, Karin. "Picturing Our Past: An Archive Constructs a National Culture." *Journal of American Folklore* 105 (1992): 3–18.

Black, Alistair. "Networking Knowledge before the Information Society: The Manchester Central Library (1934) and the Metaphysical-Professional Philosophy of L. S. Jast." *European Modernism and the Information Society.* Ed. W. Boyd Rayward. Aldershot: Ashgate, 2007. 165–184.

Boyer, M. Christine. "*La Mission Héliographique*: Architectural Photography, Collective Memory and the Patrimony of France, 1851." *Picturing Place: Photography and the Geographical Imagination.* Eds. Joan M. Schwartz and James R. Ryan. London: I. B. Tauris, 2003. 21–54.

Brabrook, Edward. "On the Organization of Local Anthropological Research." *Journal of the Anthropological Institute* 22 (1893): 262–274.

Carville, Justin. *Photography and Ireland.* London: Reaktion, 2011.

Cousserier, Annelies. "Archive to Educate: The Musée de Photographie Documentaire and the Institut International de Photographie in Brussels, 1901–1913." Unpublished conference paper, Photography Next, Nordiska museet, Stockholm, February 2010.

Derrida, Jacques. *Archive Fever*. Trans. Eric Prenowitz. Chicago: University of Chicago Press, 1996.

"Doomed or Threatened." *Photogram* (1897): xxvi, 329.

"Dresden Exhibition." *British Journal of Photography* 2 July 1909: 514.

Edwards, Elizabeth. "Photography and the Material Performance of the Past." *History and Theory* 48.4 (2009): 130–150.

Edwards, Elizabeth. "Salvage Ethnography at Home: Photographing the English." *Photography, Anthropology and History*. Eds. Christopher Morton and Elizabeth Edwards. Aldershot: Ashgate, 2010. 67–88.

Edwards, Elizabeth. *The Camera as Historian: Amateur Photographers and Historical Imagination 1885–1918*. Durham: Duke UP, 2012.

Foote, Kenneth E. "Relics of London: Photographs of a Changing Victorian City." *History of Photography* 11.2 (1987): 133–153.

Foucault, Michel. *The Archaeology of Knowledge*. Trans. Alan Sheridan. London, Routledge, 1995.

Gower H. D., Louis Stanley Jast and William W. Topley. *The Camera as Historian: A Handbook to Photographic Record Work for Those who Use a Camera for Survey and Record Societies*. London: Sampson Low, Marston and Co., 1916.

Grant, Kevin, Philippa Levine and Frank Trentman, eds. *Beyond Sovereignty: Britain, Empire and Transnationalism, c. 1880–1950*. Basingstoke: Palgrave Macmillan, 2007.

Guha, Sudeshna, *Marshall Albums: Photography and Archaeology*. New Delhi: Mapin Publishing/Alkazi Collection, 2010.

Hall, Melanie, ed. *Towards World Heritage: International Origins of the Preservation Movement 1870–1930*. Farnham: Ashgate, 2011.

Harrison, Brian. "Civil Society by Accident: Paradoxes of Voluntarism and Pluralism in the Nineteenth and Twentieth Centuries." *Civil Society in British History: Ideas, Identities, Institutions*. Ed. Jose Harris. Oxford: Oxford UP, 2003.

Harrison, W. Jerome. "Work for Amateur Photographers." *Amateur Photographer* 13 March 1885: 364.

Harrison, W. Jerome. "Light as a Recording Agent of the Past." *Photographic News* 8 January 1886: 23.

Harrison, W. Jerome. "The Desirability of an International Bureau." *British Journal of Photography* 25 August 1893: 548–549.

Harrison, W. Jerome. "The Desirability of Promoting County Photographic Surveys." *Reports of the 76th BAAS Meeting*, York (1906): 58–67.

Herzfeld, Michael. *The Body Impolitic: Artisans and Artifice in the Global Hierarchy*. Chicago: University of Chicago Press, 2003.

Hoffenberg, Peter. *An Empire on Display: English, Indian, and Australian Exhibitions from the Crystal Palace to the Great War*. Berkeley: University of California Press, 2001.

Hofmeyr, Isabel, in "AHR Conversation: On Transnational History." Christopher A. Bayley et al. *American Historical Review* 111.5 (2006): 1440–1464.

James, Peter. "Birmingham, Photography and Change." *Remaking Birmingham: The Visual Culture of Urban Regeneration*. Ed. Liam Kennedy. London: Routledge, 2004.

Joschke, Christian. "Aux origines des usages sociaux de la photographie: La photographie amateur en Allemagne entre 1890 et 1910." *Actes de la recherche en sciences sociales* 4.154 (2004): 53–65.

Knorpp, Barbara. "Heimat Museums and Notions of Home." *Journal of Museum Ethnography* 22 (2009): 9–21.

Koshar, Rudy. *From Monuments to Traces: Artifacts of German Memory 1870–1990*. Berkeley: University of California Press, 2000.

Le Goff, Jacques. *History and Memory*. Trans. Steven Rendall and Elizabeth Calman. New York: Columbia UP, 1992.

Lury, Celia. *Prosthetic Culture: Photography, Memory and Identity*. London: Routledge, 1998.

Manikowska, Ewa. "Building the Cultural Heritage of a Nation: The Photo Archive of the Society for the Protection of Ancient Monuments at the Twilight of the Russian Empire." *Photo Archives and the Photographic Memory of Art History*. Ed. Costanza Caraffa. Berlin: Deutscher Kunstverlag, 2011a. 279–288.

Manikowska, Ewa. "Turning Local into Universal: Museums, Photography and the Discovery of Poland's Cultural Patrimony (1918–1939)." Unpublished conference paper. Photo Archives IV: The Photographic Archive and the Idea of Nation, Kunsthistorisches Institut in Florenz, October 2011b.

Mattiello, Andrea. "Giacomo Boni: A Photographic Memory for the People. Documenting Architecture through Photographic Surveys in Post-Unification Italy." *Photo Archives and the Photographic Memory of Art History*. Ed. Costanza Caraffa. Berlin: Deutscher Kunstverlag 2011. 217–226.

McMahon, Richard. "Networks, Narratives and Territory in Anthropological Race Classification: Towards a More Comprehensive Historical Geography of Europe's Culture." *History of the Human Sciences* 24.1 (2011): 70–94.

McQuire, Scott. *Visions of Modernity: Representation, Memory, Time and Space in the Age of the Camera*. London: Sage, 1998.

Mittman, Gregg and Kelley Wilder, eds. *Documenting the World: Film, Photography, and the Scientific Record*. Chicago: University of Chicago Press (forthcoming).

Nora, Pierre. "Between Memory and History: *Les Lieux de Mémoire*." Trans. Marc Roudebush. *Representations* 26.1 (1989): 7–24.

Parker, George F. "History by Camera." *The Century Magazine* 68 (May 1904): 136–145.

"Photographic Record Work: New Efforts." *Photogram Magazine* (January 1906): 307–308.

"Photography and History." *Eastern Daily Press* 2 December 1913.

Pollock, Verna Louise. "Dislocated Narratives and Sites of Memory: Amateur Photographic Surveys in Britain 1889–1897." *Visual Culture in Britain* 10.1 (2009): 1–26.

Preziosi, Donald. *Rethinking Art History: Meditations on a Coy Science*. New Haven: Yale UP, 1989.

"Proposed National Photographic Record and Survey." *The Times* London 14 April 1897: 6.

Rayward, W. Boyd. "Introduction." *European Modernism and the Information Society*. Ed. W. Boyd Rayward. Aldershot: Ashgate, 2007.

Ricoeur, Paul. *Time and Narrative*. Vol. 3. Trans. Kathleen Blamey and David Pellauer. Chicago: University of Chicago Press, 1988.

Rollins, William H. *A Greener Vision of Home: Cultural Politics and Environmental Reform in the German Heimatschutz Movement 1904–1918*. Ann Arbor: University of Michigan Press, 1997.

Sachse, Julian. "The Camera as Historian of the Future." *Photographic News* 22 August 1890: 653–654.

Swenson, Astrid. "Zwischen Region, Nation und Internationalismus: Kulturerbekonzepte um die Jahrhundertwende in Frankreich, Deutschland und England." *Im Herzen Europas:*

Nationale Identitäten und Erinnerungskulturen. Ed. Detlef Altenburg, Lothar Ehrlich and Jürgen John. Cologne: Böhlau, 2008. 81–103.

Tagg, John. *The Disciplinary Frame: Photographic Truths and the Capture of Meaning*. Minneapolis: University of Minnesota Press, 2009.

Vermeulen, Han F. and Arturo Alvarez Roldán, eds. *Fieldwork and Footnotes: Studies in the History of European Anthropology*. London: Routledge, 1995.

Vertovec, Steven. *Transnationalism*. London: Routledge, 2009.

Vidal, Léon. "News from France: Record Photography." *Amateur Photographer* 18 August 1902: 165.

Zelljadt, Katja. "Presenting and Consuming the Past: Old Berlin at the Industrial Exhibition of 1896." *Journal of Urban History* 31.3 (2005): 306–333.

Slawomir Kapralski
Memory, Identity, and Roma Transnational Nationalism

Roma (Gypsies),[1] the largest European minority, form a diasporic population of about 15 million people worldwide. During World War II, Roma were persecuted on racist grounds by the Nazis, their allies and collaborators, a genocidal continuation of hundreds of years of oppression in Europe. The Roma of Germany, Austria, the Czech Lands, the Netherlands, and, to a certain extent, Poland, the Baltic states and the satellite Croatian fascist state perished in death camps, while large numbers of Roma from German-occupied Poland, the Soviet Union and Serbia were murdered in summary executions. The situation of Roma in the countries that were allies of Nazi German varied: from Bulgaria, where Roma had been relatively safe, to Vichy France, where Roma had been put into internment camps, to Romania, where part of the Roma population was deported to places of settlement and died there of hunger and disease.

Today Roma can be characterized as a transnational community, or rather as an assembly of such communities, "structured by individuals or groups settled in different national societies who share some common reference – national, ethnic, religious, linguistic – and define their common interest beyond boundaries" (Kastoryano 2007, 159). The "common reference" mentioned in the definition constitutes, however, one of the most controversial issues within Romani Studies; namely, the problem of Romani identity or identities. Following Manuel Castells (1997, 6), I will understand identity as the "process of construction of meaning

---

1 In this text I am using the term 'Roma' in its political meaning, advocated by the activists of the Romani political movement, which is an umbrella term describing all communities otherwise known (in English) as 'Gypsies,' regardless whether or not their own ethnonym is 'Roma' (in the 'ethnic' meaning). Those who call themselves 'Roma' usually live or originated in Eastern Europe and are divided into numerous groups such as, for example, Kalderaša, Lovara, Čurara, Erlii, Bugurdži or Polska Roma. Those who do not describe themselves as Roma live mostly in Western Europe. These are Sinti, who live in Germany, Austria and Northern Italy, Manoushes, who live in France and are closely related to Sinti, Spanish Cale who do not object to being called Gitanos and often use the latter word to describe themselves, and various groups living in the UK, who use the word 'Gypsy' as an acceptable self-description. Needless to say, they all are 'Roma' in terms of historical origins, certain cultural and linguistic features as well as contemporary social position, but they often appreciate their internal differentiation.

on the basis of a cultural attribute, or related set of cultural attributes, that is/are given priority over other sources of meaning." I would claim, however, that the attribute in question does not necessarily have to be cultural and may take different forms, for instance social, economic or political, although its representation must of course be given in a symbolic discourse that belongs to culture broadly understood. Taking Castells' definition as a starting point, we may speak of Romani identities in two main dimensions: on the one hand, the attribute or attributes that make Roma a distinct group; on the other hand, the social practices, oriented towards such attribute(s), that regulate how members of a particular Roma group actually make sense of their collective existence.

More traditionally oriented scholarship has essentialized the cultural features attributed to Roma and assumed that they have a strong ethnic-cultural identity grounded in common ancestry, language, customs or mores, feelings of solidarity and respect for internal hierarchies, lifestyle, or even external appearance. Those attributes are, according to essentialism, reproduced in the everyday life of Roma communities (their practices) in such a way that we may speak of 'Roma identity' as a stable phenomenon that does not change in time.

In recent decades, the essentialist standpoint has been challenged by the constructivists or relationists who have claimed that (1) there is no single Roma identity; (2) Romani identities are social rather than cultural; (3) they are products both of the relations between Roma and the non-Romani environment and of the purposeful activities of the Romani political movement. Wim Willems, the leading representative of this approach, claims that 'Gypsies' is a collective term for diverse groups, the unity of which has been created from the outside by persecutions and labeling and from the inside by Roma interest groups. "What we know about the ... history of Gypsies," Willems writes

> obliges caution when considering the proposition that they make up a single people. What I mean to say here is that not everyone to whom the label of 'Gypsy' has been applied ... leads an itinerant way of life, speaks Romani ..., stands out through bodily characteristics from others in their surroundings, is conscious of being subject to strict, group specific mores, or shares an awareness of common roots. This is not to contend, however, that Gypsies do not exist. The history of the persecution of persons and groups so labeled ... is already in itself sufficient to establish the reality of their existence beyond denial. Interest groups ... also testify to the feeling that there is a need for group self-presentation along ethnic lines. It is merely that this has probably not always been true and it seems that the idea that all ethnic Gypsy groups belong to one people obscures, rather than clarifies, their complex history. (Willems 1997, 6–7)

If we follow Willems' approach, however, we would have to admit that 'being Rom' is defined in part by the interest groups within the Romani movement and that these definitions (1) often take ethnic-cultural form; (2) claim a form of basic Romani unity in spite of the empirical differences between particular communities; (3) are often presented in a processual manner, with reference to history. The first aspect of Romani self-definition means that we need to rethink the concept of ethnicity and instead of taking it as an independent variable we should rather think of it as a correlate of political actions taken to secure the existence of Roma and to provide them with recognition. These activities also aim at an at least partial unification of diverse Roma communities and provide them with the rhetoric and symbolism of such projected unity (Mayall 2004, 207).

The historical dimension of identity emphasized by Romani activists presupposes an ability to construct an "appropriated representation of a life leading up to the present, that is, a life history fashioned in the act of self-definition" (Friedman 1994, 117). It also presupposes a future-oriented project and a vision of the desired shape of Roma communities: in Castell's terminology a "project identity," a process in which "social actors, on the basis of whichever cultural materials are available to them, build a new identity that redefines their position in society" (Castells 1997, 8).

Different versions of such a project identity have recently become a part of Romani transnational nationalism which, in general terms, can be understood as a "nationalism that is expressed and developed beyond and outside the borders of a single state and its territory, and that ... creates new expressions of belonging and a political engagement that reflects the nationalization of communitarian sentiments" (Kastoryano 2007, 160). This is the dimension of identity in which memory plays an enormous role, serving, to use David McCrone's expression, "to evoke a future imaginable throughout the past" (McCrone 1998, 52).

Identity, understood as an imagined link between a group's past, present and future, is related to memory in a mutually determining way: "the core meaning of any individual or group identity," writes John R. Gillis (1994, 3), "is sustained by remembering, and what is remembered is defined by the assumed identity." Following Maurice Halbwachs' work filtered through Jan Assmann's conceptual propositions (Halbwachs 1992; Assmann 2011), I will understand social or collective memory as a probability that individuals who belong to a given group will remember/forget in a similar way the events that constitute the group's history. Such probability depends on the existing frames of remembrance and structures of communication, which increase the chance of similarity in remembrance/forgetting and are instrumental in producing two main forms of collective memory: cultural and communicative. The first of these is produced by specialized memory experts (priests, artists, writers, educators) and contained in the institutionalized frameworks of rituals, myths, material artifacts with their symbolic meaning, educational systems and official festivals. The second is a living memory rooted in biographical experience and passed on in the course of informal interactions between, usually closely related, members of a particular social unit.

Frames of remembrance are resources, institutionalized and shared by members of a given group, which contain ideas, images and feelings about the past (Irwin-Zarecka 1994). They are mostly responsible for producing the cultural memory of a group: "the manner in which a group or a society can guarantee the continuity of its culture and its identity over several generations" (Kitzmann et al. 2005, 17). Structures of communication decide which aspects of the group's past and which frames of remembrance are important for its members (Lebow 2006) and are always embedded in power relations.[2] "[A] past time lived in relation to other people" (Misztal 2003, 6), is always "embedded in complex class, gender and power relations that determine what is remembered (or forgotten), by whom, and for what end" (Gillis 1994, 3). This means that social memory is always the product of negotiation (Sennett 1998), something that is particularly important for dispersed groups like the Roma who strive in this process not only to construct their project identity but also their corresponding community of memory.

The concept of project identity indeed corresponds well with a process we witness among Roma and that has been called by one of its actors, Nicolae Gheorghe, an ethnogenesis (Gheorghe 1997, 157). The Roma ethnogenesis, which according to Gheorghe is similar to nation-building, consists of attempts to improve the social standing of the Roma by moving them from a position of inferiority to "some kind of respectability with a sort of equality with other social groups in the hierarchy of social stratification on the basis of a revised perception of their identity" (158). Correspondingly, it is also a project to develop a cultural identity, "to transform a stigmatized identity into something different – to move from Gypsies to Roma" (159). In other words, we may say that Romani ethnogenesis is an attempt

---

2 By 'structures of communication,' I understand technological, social and political settings of the communicative interactions such as the access to the technical means of communication, division of labor, social hierarchies, distribution of power, density of contacts, relation between the public and private spheres, conventionally or politically determined level of freedom of expression, and eventually the whole situation of particular groups – all that decides how and what their members are talking about in a given moment. A special role is played in this context by media of various kinds. Generally, mass media, especially in their more traditional form, mediate between dominant forms of cultural memory and communicative memory, shaping the latter in terms of the former. With the advent of the new electronic media, however, communicative memory becomes relatively independent of the dominant discourse which is particularly important for marginalized groups. In addition, it offers them a chance to strengthen the position of their own cultural memories. The rapid development of Romani internet resources in the last decade testifies to that (see Reading 2011).

to achieve the recognized status of an ethno-national, non-territorial and transnational group (Gheorghe 1991, 831).

Such an attempt seems to be more realistic in times when "many disadvantaged tribal or ethnic peoples and groups – lacking a homeland and/or independent statehood, some of whose members are dispersed across many countries – have been simultaneously engaged in using global forums as one key vehicle for seeking worldwide support while maintaining concrete cultural and kinship ties across several countries built around primordial identities" (Kennedy and Roudometof 2002, 16). The first part of this quotation illustrates very well the activities of Romani leaders who are campaigning internationally for recognition by transnational institutions such as the European Union or the UN. One leader has asserted that "we can build up an ethnic dynamic and a new image by reference to and in interaction with non-national institutions or supra-national institutions" (Gheorghe 1997, 161). While Roma do maintain "concrete cultural and kinship ties" across boundaries, their identity is not primordial but is instead "forged" in the dynamic of the Romani ethnic-national movement and in the interactions with the world of supra-national institutions (161).

Campaigning for identity and its recognition sustains, selects, and constructs memories of marginalized groups. Multiculturalism in contemporary democratic societies means, among other things, the "idea that various disadvantaged groups in society have equally valid views of history as that of the established culture of the majority" (Kitzmann et al. 2005, 16). As a result, "most ethnic groups and minorities today strive to rehabilitate their past and their culture of memory and therefore welcome their ethnic identity" (16). This is the case for contemporary Roma who in the older literature were often presented as "people without history" who live in an "eternal present" and have no tradition of commemoration (Yoors 1967; Cohn 1973; Ficowski 1989). As I have argued elsewhere (Kapralski 2007, 2008, 2012, 2013), this orientalizing picture of the Roma was largely the result of a process of "differential deprivation of history" (Bauman 1992), "othering" them by placing them in an "allochronic discourse" (Fabian 1983) through the "erasure of interconnection" (Wolf 1982), and "silencing" their past (Trouillot 1995) or projecting on them the repressed dreams of Western modernity (Trumpener 1992). It must be said, however, that although Roma remember their past (Mróz 2000; Gay y Blasco 2001, 2004; Filhol 2003; Stewart 2004), they do so in a way that is accessible to a community that until recently did not control the mainstream frames of remembrance, including history-writing. This situation is changing but nevertheless the rehabilitation of Romani culture(s) of memory often takes the form of an "invention of tradition" (Hobsbawm 1983) or "authentication" of the past (Smith 1998). This latter term is of particular importance for the present argument. To authenticate the past means "to select from all that has gone before that which is distinctive, unique ... and thereby to mark out a unique shared destiny" (43). Although this point has been made with reference to nation-making in general, it seems particularly applicable to the network of dispersed communities constituting Roma.

Such processes are possible in contemporary society because, according to Delanty and O'Mahony (2002), globalization radically transforms the "world of nations" as inherited from classical modernity and has two important consequences: (1) the decoupling of nation and state, and (2) the decoupling of citizenship and nationality. The first process means the "dis-embedding of the political project of the state from the cultural project of nationhood" which opens up opportunities for new nations and new ideas of nationhood that may now be developed in "a highly complex interlocking network of relations that is spread over national, subnational and the transnational levels" (170). The second process involves a growing importance of transnational politics, in which "citizenship is no longer exclusively defined by nationality," and the growing role of transnational actors and processes, as a result of which "participation in political community no longer occurs exclusively on the national level" (174–175).

Decoupling of nation and state: transnational prospects for Roma nationalism

For groups like the Roma the new constellation of contemporary nationhood means that the claims of their elites to be recognized as a certain kind of nation, which date back to the beginnings of the nineteenth century[3] and have been advocated persistently since the 1970s, do not look as unrealistic as they did within the nineteenth-century nationalist paradigm. The lack of a territory, the lack of a state or at least an elected representation that would be commonly and internally recognized, the lack of a common culture which would involve the sense of a shared past and historical destiny and which would serve as a set of criteria for inclusion and exclusion – these are the obstacles traditionally faced by Ro-

---

3 One can mention here a number of Romani national organizations established between 1925 and 1939, for example in the Soviet Union, Romania and Greece, the beginnings of the pan-European Romani movement (the conference "United Gypsies of Europe" held in 1933 in Bucharest), and the appeals of Romani leaders to politicians to grant Roma a piece of land to establish their state (Acton 1974; Crowe 1996; Hancock 2002).

mani activists in their attempts to imagine their people in terms of a nation in the Westphalian tradition (Rorke 2007; McGarry 2008, 454).

Today, however, stateless people who lack a homeland and a homogeneous culture may construct themselves as distinct collectivities more easily since territory, statehood and cultural homogeneity are no longer considered necessary preconditions of nationhood. They can also claim recognition and support for their identity projects in the global network of transnational institutions, while their activities are supported by new means of communication, international migration and reconfigurations[4] of the links between migrants' countries of residence and those of origins (Kastoryano 2007, 160).

This process affects the dispersed assembly of Roma groups that now resembles, according to Gabriel Sheffer (2003, 139), the "incipient diasporas" emerging from processes of migration. Generally, globalization and transnationalization make the Roma of today less 'different' in the perception of the mainstream majority than those of yesterday. They have largely remained the same in a world in which many other collective agents, including those that used to serve as the yardstick for the idea of nationhood, have become decomposed and deterritorialized. For the Roma, decomposition and deterritorialization have always been a part of their history and hence of their identity. Moreover, whereas in the past Roma had difficulties maintaining contacts across borders and did not have much sense of collectively belonging to a larger transnational unit, this too has changed, largely because of the work of the new elites.

The Roma may therefore serve as proof that the detachment of nation from territory is possible; they "define themselves as a group whose entire national consciousness has been formed in the absence of territory and who today claim the right to nonterritorial self-determination and to recognition in the international system ... They call themselves a nation without a state or without a territory. Their claim overlaps with those of immigrant populations and political refugees, referring to human rights, to the fight against racism and discrimination, and to integration ... in the country of immigration" (Kastoryano 2007, 167).

In spite of such optimistic pronouncements, Roma still face problems in relation to their 'sense of belonging' and even the Romani elites are divided regarding self-definition in national terms (whatever actual content such definition may

---

4 This means that for contemporary migrants the receiving countries are no longer the only framework in which they can create their new lifeworlds as in the classic essay by Alfred Schutz (1976). Global flows of people and the new networks of communication create hybrid zones of encounter in which migrants live simultaneously in their old and new worlds, moving between them and forming relations between them according to their needs (Appadurai 1996).

have), not to mention the 'grassroots' (Marushiakova and Popov 2004). This is largely due to the fact that, as Manuel Castells observes, a nation is not merely the result of manipulation by elites but is based on experiences, histories, projects and narratives that are shared by people who are otherwise divided by gender, class, ethnicity and territory (Castells 1997, 29). In other words, the transnational project of the Romani elites would need to be supported by already existing bonds, or ones forged out of pre-existing elements, to become a viable and more or less commonly accepted identity for the Romani diaspora.

This 'sense of belonging' or 'communal identity' represents a variation on the old national code which, in the circumstances created by the process of globalization, "has been opened up to new codifications of belonging" and to "new interpretations arising from cultural opportunities for new demands for self-determination" (Delanty and O'Mahony 2002, 171). As a result, Roma elites may now use a wider spectrum of cultural models that do not have to be very deeply rooted in traditional practices of Roma communities. The Roma case thus exemplifies the fact that identities (including ethnic ones) "can be conspicuously devoid of solid cultural content" (Fitzgerald 1992, 116) and that in the case of both ethnicity and national identity "claims about ancestry and culture may ... be as much a matter of fiction and myth as a matter of fact" (Fenton and May 2002, 2). As Michel-Rolph Trouillot has argued, however, "not any fiction can pass for history: the materiality of the socio-historical process ... sets the stage for the future historical narratives ..." (Trouillot 1995, 29). In Anthony Smith's approach, the area for construction depends on how "full" or how "empty" is the history of a group (Smith 1986, 177), or, to use Trouillot's terminology, how dense is this history regarding the traces left by the past and their material representations, which then serve as frames of remembrance that sustain identities.

This means that the *transnational* status of Romani identity is ambiguous: on the one hand, globalization is leading to the decomposition of modern nations, which offers a chance for previously suppressed identities to be re-constructed within a transnational framework. To be successful, however, such re-construction must build upon the existing identities of diasporic groups so as to "resonate" (Schöpflin 1997) with their cultural, religious or political content. Fortunately enough for the Roma elites that carry out such processes of re-construction, the importance of the cultural substance of an identity is nowadays diminishing and the history of Romani communities, due to the already outlined strategies of "differential deprivation of history" (Bauman 1992) or "erasure of interconnection" (Wolf 1982), is relatively empty. This gives the elites a degree of freedom in developing their transnational identity constructs, but is in fact a mixed blessing because those constructs may not be easily integrated within the symbolic systems of particular communities and may not contribute significantly to their own frames of remembrance, as provided by oral tradition, folklore or social institutions.[5]

Decoupling of citizenship and nationality: in search of a narrative

According to Delanty and O'Mahony, "globalized citizenship" can be understood as participation in a political community which focuses on issues defined as globally important (2002, 175). One such issue, although not listed as an example by the authors mentioned, is in my opinion the globalized memory of the Holocaust as the transforming event that changed the world and our perception of ourselves, perhaps the only one which resonates in the global network of contemporary communities of memory.[6]

This idea of 'citizenship' as participation in a globalized, Holocaust-based community of memory can be exemplified by Diana Pinto's emotional appeal at a conference on Jewish-Polish relations in June 1995 in Krakow. In the context of the return of intolerance and xenophobia in Europe, she argued, Auschwitz should acquire a new, more European meaning. In particular, the countries of Eastern Europe, aspiring to be included in the European structures, should make this site of memory the center of reflection on a heterogeneous, pluralist and multicultural Europe, once incarnated by the Jews in spite of age-old antisemitism (Pinto 1996, 176).[7]

This question has been widely debated recently (Pakier and Stråth 2010) and such debates indicate the "globalization of the Holocaust discourse" (Huyssen

---

5 It is important to note that having an 'empty' history does not mean that a group does not have its own frames of remembrance and thus does not remember its past. It does mean, however, that it may be difficult to construct the identity of such a group around the memory of events that are important in the mainstream historical narrative.

6 The concept of the Holocaust as a transforming event has been developed within post-Holocaust theology (see Katz et al. 2007, especially Part 3) and then applied in secular, existential and universal contexts (see, for example, Milchman and Rosenberg 1998; Wyschogrod 1985; LaCapra 1998). In the field of memory studies, Levy and Sznaider (2002) have argued that the memory of the Holocaust becomes a cosmopolitan one, reconfiguring the national cultures of memory, similarly to Huyssen (2000) who approached the Holocaust as a globalized paradigm for historical trauma. Van Baar (2011), on the other hand, points out some of the problems that the globalization of Holocaust memory creates for the groups that, like Roma, define themselves as the Holocaust's victims.

7 See also a similar but less optimistic claim by Andrea Tyndall (2004).

2000), which means that the Holocaust becomes a universal pattern for any historical trauma, applicable to various instances of genocide. Some Romani activists benefit from the globalization of the Holocaust discourse, by using it as a 'master narrative' of a pan-Romani identity, claiming recognition for Romani suffering in the past, and de-legitimizing present-day acts of anti-Romani violence as a continuation of Nazi persecution. In this way, Huub van Baar (2011, 272) writes, "Romani groups are mobilizing memory as a strategy to inscribe Romani histories in the European memorial landscapes and to claim a place in national and European histories and memories." Other Romani intellectuals and groups, however, do not feel comfortable with participation in the globalized Holocaust discourse, which in their opinion may misrepresent Romani suffering in a cultural code tailored for someone else (300–301).

Despite such reservations, references to the Romani suffering during WWII have figured in several important declarations of identity issued by international Romani organizations, especially by the International Romani Union or the Central Council of German Sinti and Roma. Their leaders are aware that identity is a question of empowerment and that the past is a resource for the production and legitimization of identity constructs. Those who control the past – by controlling access to the means of production of history, by censoring representations of the past, or by selecting frames of remembrance that increase the probability that certain memories will emerge and endure – also control identity. This means that the identity of disfranchised and disempowered groups remains repressed, their histories unrecognized as belonging to "History" with a capital "H" (Achim 2004, 1). Accordingly, struggles for empowerment will also take the form of wresting their past from those who control historical discourses.

The official standpoint of the International Romani Union (IRU), as formulated by two Romani activists, Andrzej Mirga and Nicolae Gheorghe, is that the Roma

are a legitimate part of European culture and society and ... by virtue of their unique history and problems they deserve special treatment within a European framework. The IRU advocates recognition of the Roma as a nation and is dedicated to building unity around its symbol, a standardized Romani language. The IRU demands the creation of a special status for the Roma and Sinti as a non-territorial (multistate-based or transnational) minority in Europe, in order to protect a people who experienced a holocaust during World War II and violence, pogroms, and genocide in the present era. (Mirga and Gheorghe 1997, 22)

We have here a clear reference to the "unique history" of the Roma, as well as the firm conviction that this history is an integral part of the history of Europe. One has to stress that in the vision of Romani history presented by the IRU, and supported by many Romani activists, the fact that the ancestors of today's Roma come from India receives little or no attention. Although the Indian heritage may be attractive in pointing to the roots of today's Roma in an ancient civilization, it is also seen as potentially dangerous as a "discursive exclusion" from those social and political contexts in which contemporary Roma live (Simhandl 2006).

The main event of Romani history that is mentioned in the IRU standpoint is "a holocaust during World War II" – not capitalized for diplomatic reasons: some Romani activists are careful not to agonize relations with those who believe that the Holocaust was uniquely Jewish. At the same time, Roma suffering in the time of the Holocaust has been related to present-day acts of anti-Romani violence with the clear intention of condemning the latter by linking them to persecution by the Nazis. In presenting Romani transnational identity, Mirga and Gheorghe write:

> Romani political elites were never driven to demand their own territory and state. Thus, to legitimize their claim, they advanced other elements of the concept of nation – the common roots of the Romani people, their common historical experiences and perspectives, and the commonality of culture, language and social standing. The experience of the Porrajmos – the Romani holocaust during World War II – played an important role in providing the Romani diaspora with its sense of nationhood. (Mirga and Gheorghe 1997, 18)

In this standpoint, the 'sense of belonging' has been conceptualized around 'classical' national features – cultural and social, along with a reference to the past ("experiences") and to the future ("perspectives") of the Roma. The "Romani holocaust" (again not capitalized) is listed as the only event that influenced Romani "diasporic nationhood." It is important to note that Mirga and Gheorghe use the term "Porrajmos" which is a neologism introduced by another Romani activist, Ian Hancock (1996),[8] and rejected by most Romani intellectuals as having a sexual connotation which is inappropriate in this context (see e.g. Tcherenkov and Laederich 2004). Their use of this concept, however, indicates a growing need on the part of Romani intellectuals to have their own vision of history, a frame of remembrance that would be controlled by them and expressed in their own language so that Romani historical experience would be independent of the historiography of others.[9]

The "Declaration of Roma Nation" issued in 2001 by the International Romani Union reads:

> We, a Nation of which over half a million persons were exterminated in a forgotten Holocaust, a Nation of individuals too often discriminated, marginalized, victim of intolerance

---

8 Hancock (2010) claims he has heard the word used by Roma themselves to describe their fate.
9 An illustration of an elaborated vision of Romani history, divided into periods named in Romani language, can be found in another work by Ian Hancock (2002).

and persecution, we have a dream, and we are engaged in fulfilling it. We are a Nation, we share the same tradition, the same culture, the same origin, the same language; we are a Nation. We have never looked for creating a Roma State. And we do not want a State today, when the new society and the new economy are concretely and progressively crossing-over the importance and the adequacy of the State. (IRU 2001)

In this document, significantly, we find a reference to the number of Roma victims[10] of the Holocaust (this time capitalized), associated with the ongoing victimization of Roma in the course of history and linked to the classical inventory of homogenizing nation-making factors (tradition, culture, origin, and language). Nevertheless, the Declaration of the Roma Nation also firmly stresses, with reference to the contemporary process of globalization, that having one's own state is not the purpose of the Romani movement.[11] Moreover, it is this "historic refusal of searching for a state" that the Roma, as a "transnational Nation" that "needs a transnational rule of law," offer to the global society (IRU 2001).

Scholars are divided on whether political declarations such as those presented above, or the scholarly work of Romani intellectuals like Ian Hancock, have any real impact on the Romani identities or communities of memory as they function in everyday life. According to Roni Stauber and Raphael Vago (2007), for example, the Romani Holocaust is already the main element of Roma national identity and the central point of their historical memory: "The Romani search for identity ... entails an assertive stand on the uniqueness of their people, on the one hand, and emphasis on their suffering ... – conveyed through commemoration of the martyrdom of the 'Romani Holocaust' ..., the principal axis of memory – on the other" (Stauber and Vago 2007, 130). Elena Marushiakova and Vesselin Popov (2004), in contrast, claim that although the concept of the Romani Holocaust is already a part of European public discourse, within the Roma world it only figures among the elites, with a limited impact at grassroots level. The elites who develop the remembrance of the Holocaust are simultaneously those who aspire to the creation of Romani nationhood, and the vision of history they advocate legitimizes both their position as elite and their political programs. The Romani "grassroots," according to Marushiakova and Popov, are indifferent to the elite-

---

10 The figure of 500,000 is conjectural only but since it is used in the political context by Roma and non-Roma alike, it has acquired a kind of 'official' character. The number of Romani victims that can be documented at the moment is ca. 200,000, the real figure (definitely much higher) will probably never be known due to the specificity of the persecution of the Roma and related lack of written sources (see Kenrick 2010).

11 Such claims have sometimes been made of course, but it is debatable whether they have been made seriously.

supported "national history" based on the memory of the Romani Holocaust, as a rule do not identify with it, and search instead for the particular histories of their own sub-groups.[12]

While Stauber and Vago are too optimistic regarding the status of Holocaust memories as the main factor of Romani identity, in my view, Marushiakova and Popov underestimate the importance of such memories and the chances for Romani nationhood. Where the former exaggerate the unity of the Roma, the latter exaggerate their fragmentation. Using the conceptual distinctions introduced earlier, I will try to resolve this contradiction by arguing that Stauber and Vago are right when it comes to the frames of remembrance constructed by the Romani intellectuals and activists. Due to their activities, the remembrance of the Roma genocide has indeed been granted the status of cultural memory within the Romani transnational diaspora and may serve, at least potentially, as a common frame of reference for various constructions of Romani identity in which the Roma can be conceptualized as the people whose existence was threatened during the Holocaust. Marushiakova and Popov, however, are right when it comes to communicative memory: not all Romani groups are equally interested in activating Holocaust-related segments of pan-Romani cultural memory in their everyday communicative practices. Many groups do not particularly focus on that aspect of their past, do not commemorate it explicitly and when such commemorations are staged, they are elite events with limited impact on popular discourses.

Partisans of the Romani transnational nation are nevertheless trying to successfully sell their idea to the masses by first creating a rhetorical discourse,

---

12 There are several approaches to the internal differentiation of Roma. One of them (Tcherenkov and Laederich 2004) divides Roma into "metagroups" (the main criterion is linguistic similarity) such as Vlax, Balkan, Carpathian and Nordic. Within a "metagroup" a further distinction is then made between groups; the Vlax metagroup, for example, includes the Kalderaša, Lovara, Čurara, Mačvaja or Gurbeti. Groups are then further divided into smaller units (big lineages – clusters of clans that refer to common origins – or groups associated with a given territory) called "nacija" (also written as "natsia"): the "nacijas" of the Kalderaša include, for example, the Vungrika, Grekuria and Moldovaja or Serbijaja. The nacijas are then divided into clans called "vica" (the clans of the Vungrika, for instance, are the Joneštji, Badoni and Čajkoni or Parakoni), which are then further divided into sub-clans called "vica i cigni" (the Petreštji constitutes a sub-clan of the Joneštji clan, for example). In addition to this, there are units that cut across the top-down structure described above, namely, "kumpanjas" (also known as kîrdo) that sometimes consist of people from different clans or nacijas, who organize for economic purposes. Marushiakova and Popov claim that Roma are not interested in the history of the 'Roma,' or even in the history of their own group, but instead focus on the level of nacijas, vicas, or kumpanjas.

polemically directed at alternative visions of identity (at the particularism of a group like the German Sinti, or the assimilationist tendencies of some groups in Slovakia), and then turning their vision of the Romani nation and its history into a taken-for-granted popular discourse, "a largely uncontrollable rhetorical field inside which all political actors themselves have to operate" (Fentress and Wickham 1992, 129). The success of such transformation largely depends on the commonality of the symbolic universe in which both elite and masses operate. It is, however, also conditioned by a number of social, economic and political factors. Roma activists, together with external experts, are therefore developing various initiatives aimed at creating such a universe. They include educational programs (like the Dik i Na Bistar – Look and Don't Forget program organized in 2013 in Krakow and Auschwitz by Ternype: International Roma Youth Network), websites (www.romasinti.eu), museum exhibitions (like the one in Heidelberg and at Auschwitz-Birkenau), exhibitions of Romani artists like Ceija Stojka or Omara Olah who portray in their work the experience of the Holocaust, and a growing number of Romani newspapers and works of literature.

Two factors in particular that contribute to the success of such initiatives need to be mentioned here. First, the success of the Holocaust memory as a building block of Roma transnational identity will largely depend on the existence of an intermediary category connecting cultural and communicative memories. According to Wulf Kansteiner, collective memory can be conceptualized "as the result of the interaction among three types of historical factors: the intellectual and cultural traditions that frame all our representations of the past, the memory makers who selectively adopt and manipulate these traditions, and the memory consumers who use, ignore, or transform such artifacts according to their own interests" (Kansteiner 2002, 180). The frames are already there and have been constructed with the help of the globalized Holocaust discourse. The group of memory makers – the transnational Romani leaders and intellectuals – has already been constituted and actively propagates the memory of the Roma genocide to support the Romani political, social, and economic agenda. The consumers of memory, who originally tended to ignore the efforts of memory makers, have been gradually changing their attitudes. This was due to the actions of a group of middle-rank Romani activists, which developed in the second half of the 1990s, whose members perform the role of "memory retailers" (Kapralski 2012), translating the ideas of memory makers into concepts and activities the grassroots are familiar with, for example through the organization of local commemorative events, or educational trips to the Auschwitz-Birkenau Museum. It is thanks to that group of activists, the existence of which calls for a modification of Kansteiner's model, that the memory of the Holocaust has started to resonate within local Romani communities of memory (Kapralski et al. 2011).

The second factor that helps to transform cultural memory into a communicative one[13] is a wide transnational network of commemorative practices in which the painful past is re-presented. This network operates on several levels. The first involves simple transborder communication between different Romani groups which mutually import experiences and approaches towards the past. This process can be illustrated by the "commemorative collaboration" between German and Polish Romani organizations leading to the campaign for the growing visibility of Roma suffering within an international commemorative context. Annual commemorations of the murder of Roma at Auschwitz, jointly organized by the Zentralrat Deutscher Sinti und Roma and the Association of Roma People in Poland, exemplify this kind of transnational collaboration (Kapralski 2012).

The second level of transnationalization of Romani remembrance consists of the growing exposure of the Roma to the global Holocaust discourse and, correspondingly, the growing desire on the part of Roma for visibility in the transnational memorial sites related to the Holocaust. One can mention here the intellectual efforts of activists to include the Roma as legitimate victims of the Holocaust, the campaign of Romani leaders to be represented in the United States Holocaust Memorial Museum, the development of the Roma section of the Auschwitz-Birkenau Museum, and the campaign for a Berlin Memorial for the Murdered Sinti and Roma as a part of the memoryscape of the new Berlin (Zimmermann 2007; Sodaro 2008; van Baar 2011; Blumer 2013).

The third level of transnationalization is shaped by different forms of collaboration between Roma and non-Roma resulting in various forms of hybrid, invented or authenticated traditions. This can be illustrated by the "Caravan Memorial," the annual commemorative ritual of the Roma from Southern Poland, developed by local Romani leaders and non-Roma curators of a local museum, with the participation of a wide international network of Roma and non-Roma scholars, NGO activists, journalists and educators (Kapralski 2004). Such commemorative rituals supply Romani history with a form. As Trouillot (1995, 116) more generally claims, such rituals "help to create, modify, or sanction the public meanings attached to historical events deemed worthy of mass celebration." They also have an educational function: again in Trouillot's words, they "package history for public consumption" and produce the feeling of solidity and concreteness of the past as given in its particular image (116).

---

13 Contrary to Assmann (2011) who posits that the two kinds of memory exist separately and that if there is any connection, it involves merely the transformation of communicative memory into cultural memory, I believe that collective remembrance is a top-down process in which those who have power aim at making the content of cultural memory an object of everyday communication. This aim proves successful especially in the nation-building process.

Finally, the international network of Romani NGOs provides a further frame-work for commemorative practices. Thus the OSCE's Contact Point for Roma and Sinti Issues was recently involved in the commemoration of the Roma Genocide and, supported by the UN, put pressure on the Polish Government to officially decree a National Day of Remembrance of the Romani fate during WWII. Such a day was eventually proclaimed in 2011 by the Polish Parliament, and presented, moreover, as an activity within the Polish presidency of the EU, which adds an ad-ditional transnational dimension to Romani commemorative practices (Kapralski 2012).

We may therefore conclude that the transnationalization of Romani remem-brance has been leading to the transformation of Romani cultures of memory. Roma are better educated and organized, there is a growing awareness among them that the struggle to improve their life will take place largely on non-Romani territory and with the use of methods peculiar to the non-Romani world. Con-sequently, we may observe the process of political organization of the Roma, an important part of which is the construction of a new collective identity with a transnational character, transcending the existing divisions between Romani groups and referring, among other things, to the concept of a community of fate and to more or less clear visions of Romani history. Within this process we can observe a growing interest on the part of Roma in their past, involving various acts of commemoration and a gradual process of coming together of cultural and communicative memories.

Prospects for Roma transnational memories

Being denied access to the production of history (in the sense of making his-tory and writing history) means social subjugation and cultural dispossession. In terms of identity it means, according to Friedman (1994, 117), that the "people without history ... are the people who have been prevented from identifying them-selves for others." This situation can be described in terms of Jürgen Habermas's (1984) theory as "distorted communication" or, in the words of Axel Honneth (1996), as "denial of recognition," which may be understood as a refusal to com-municate as equal partners that involves a "cynical dismissal of other people's constructions of their pasts ..." (Friedman 1994, 144). Romani leaders under-stand that and, in the last twenty years, have produced a number of discourses and practices aimed at communicating Romani identities to gain recognition for the Roma and their history.

Communication through the use of media (as opposed to its traditional forms) is perhaps the crucial concept for the modern understanding of society, power and identity (see Anderson 1991). In the Westphalian world of nation-states, characterized by the attempt to internally homogenize its units, communication understood as the ability to address each other across the boundary of difference and geographical distance is a necessary precondition of nationhood. The post-Westphalian, transnational world radically changes the meaning and crucial characteristics of communication.[14] According to Nancy Fraser (2007, 60), in the transnational world, communication partners form "a collection of dispersed interlocutors, who do not constitute a demos." Modern media operate "across vast reaches of the globe, in a transnational community of risk" which is characterized neither by strong solidarity nor by clear identities. Contemporary acts of communication take place largely in "deterritorialized cyberspace," utilize a "nexus of disjoint and overlapping visual cultures" and their addressee is an "amorphous mix of public and private transnational powers that is neither easily identifiable nor rendered accountable."

The transnational world is a world of cultural heterogeneity, which is possible, according to Friedman (1994, 142), thanks to the disappearance of the mechanisms of power that have formerly maintained the "political hegemony over time." As a result, a multiplicity of cultural identities "is expressed in the proliferation of histories" (142). This means for Friedman that the once dominant Western modernist narrative of identity and history no longer controls or represses "alternative, ethnic and subnational identities" together with their representations of the past. Of course transnational identities may well be added to the list assembled by Friedman who concludes that the "dehegemonization of the Western-dominated world is simultaneously its dehomogenization" (1994, 117).

For the Roma, (trans)nationalization has two outcomes that contradict one another. It is a bitter paradox that, just when the transformation of power relations has allowed the Roma to transnationally express their nationhood, and when they have developed elites who know how to do that, the national idea has faded and even the prefix "trans" cannot really make it more appealing. Now that the Roma are able to develop transnational ties and organizational structures, it may well turn out that they remain inefficient, and that Romani history and memory, duly written and carefully institutionalized in various forms of remembrance, will disappear among so many other histories and memories, melting in multicultural indifference.

---

14 Or, alternatively, the new mediated modes of communication are changing the Westphalian world.

According to some of its critics the Romani political movement is insufficiently transnational and relies too much on an inadequate, old-fashioned national idea, copying nineteenth-century nationalism in its worst, Eastern European version, instead of exploring the new opportunities offered by the process of globalization (see Guy 2002, Acton 2006). In the cosmopolitan, free market of identities, an identity advocated by the Romani political movement, based on an authoritative, official and homogeneous version of Romani history, may not necessarily be appealing, even for those who potentially belong to its target group.

Among its most recent critics one can also find younger-generation Romani intellectuals who, having been influenced by some postmodern conceptions of identity, accuse their political leaders of imposing upon the multiplicity of Romani groups a single and ready-made construct. They prefer instead to play with several, mostly hybrid identities existing on various levels of the social universe and involving different degrees of distance on the part of their users (see Belton 2010; Kwiek 2010; and, particularly, Le Bas 2010).

Studies of social memory indicate, however, that institutional homogenization (e.g. by introducing a common representation of history) does not mean the cultural homogenization of all the groups participating in the institutionalized representations of the past and in commemorative rituals. Cultural representations of the past (rituals of remembrance, museums, cemeteries, monuments etc.) may still be partly successful "in providing many people with a sense of common identity no matter how dispersed they may be by class, region, gender, religion, or race" (Gillis 1994, 14).

In addition, if we take into account the process of "synchronization" of cultural and communicative social memories, mentioned above, we may be able to say that Roma will probably remain a highly diversified network of groups with their identities fragmented "due to differences in ... geography, income, occupation, language, religion, and familial and clan ties" (McGarry 2008, 450), but that they will nevertheless be undergoing to some extent a process of political and cultural unification. The future identities of Roma will probably form a dynamic continuum between a global historical narrative and local communities of memory. As a result, Roma may be united in commemoration but divided in communicative memory, which, one can say, is quite typical of transnational communities.

References

Achim, Viorel. *The Roma in Romanian History.* Budapest: CEU Press, 2004.

Acton, Thomas. "Romani Politics, Scholarship, and the Discourse of Nation-Building." *Gypsies and the Problem of Identities: Contextual, Constructed and Contested.* Eds. Adrian Marsh and Elin Strand. Istanbul: Swedish Research Institute, 2006. 27–38.

Acton, Thomas. *Gypsy Politics and Social Change.* London: Routledge & Kegan Paul, 1974.

Anderson, Benedict. *Imagined Communities: Reflections on the Origins and Spread of Nationalism.* 1983. London: Verso, 1991.

Appadurai, Arjun. *Modernity at Large: Cultural Dimensions of Globalization.* Minneapolis: University of Minnesota Press, 1996.

Assmann, Jan. *Cultural Memory and Early Civilization: Writing, Remembrance, and Political Imagination,* Cambridge: Cambridge UP, 2011.

Bauman, Zygmunt. *Mortality, Immortality and Other Life Strategies.* Cambridge: Polity Press, 1992.

Belton, Brian A. "Knowing Gypsies." *All Change! Romani Studies through Romani Eyes.* Eds. Damian Le Bas and Thomas Acton. Hatfield: University of Hertfordshire Press, 2010. 39–48.

Blumer, Nadine. "Disentangling the Hierarchy of Victimhood: Commemorating Sinti and Roma and Jews in Germany's National Narrative." *The Nazi Genocide of the Roma: Reassessment and Commemoration.* Ed. Anton Weiss-Wendt. Oxford: Berghahn Books, 2013. 205–228.

Castells, Manuel. *The Information Age: Economy, Society and Culture.* Vol. 2: *The Power of Identity.* Oxford: Blackwell, 1997.

Cohn, Werner. *The Gypsies.* Reading: Addison-Wesley, 1973.

Crowe, David M. *A History of the Gypsies of Eastern Europe and Russia.* New York: St. Martin's Press, 1996.

Delanty, Gerard and Patrick O'Mahony. *Nationalism and Social Theory: Modernity and the Recalcitrance of the Nation.* London: Sage, 2002.

Fabian, Johannes. *Time and the Other: How Anthropology Makes its Object.* New York: Columbia UP, 1983.

Fenton, Steve and Stephen May. "Ethnicity, Nation and 'Race': Connections and Disjunctures." *Ethnonational Identities.* Eds. Steve Fenton and Stephen May. Basingstoke: Palgrave Macmillan, 2002. 1–20.

Fentress, James and Chris Wickham. *Social Memory.* Oxford: Blackwell, 1992.

Ficowski, Jerzy. *The Gypsies in Poland: History and Customs.* Warsaw: Interpress, 1989.

Filhol, Emmanuel. "The Internment of Gypsies in France (1940–1946): A Hidden Memory." *Ethnic Identities in Dynamic Perspective: Proceedings of the 2002 Annual Meeting of the Gypsy Lore Society.* Eds. Sheila Salo and Csaba Pronai. Budapest: Gondolat, 2003. 11–17.

Fitzgerald, Thomas K. "Media, Ethnicity and Identity." *Culture and Power: A Media, Culture, and Society Reader.* Eds. Paddy Scannell, Philip Schlesinger and Colin Sparks. London: Sage, 1992. 112–136.

Fraser, Nancy. "Transnationalizing the Public Sphere: On the Legitimacy and Efficacy of Public Opinion in a PostWestphalian World." *Identities, Affiliations, and Allegiances.* Eds. Seyla Benhabib, Ian Shapiro and Danilo Petranović. Cambridge: Cambridge UP, 2007. 45–66.

Friedman, Jonathan. *Cultural Identity and Global Process.* London: Sage, 1994.

Gay y Blasco, Paloma. "Evangelical Transformations of Forgetting and Remembering: The Politics of Gitano Life." *Memory, Politics and Religion: The Past Meets the Present in Europe.* Eds. Francis Pine, Deema Kaneff and Haldis Haukanes. Münster: Lit Verlag, 2004. 255–272.

Gay y Blasco, Paloma. "'We Don't Know Our Descent': How the Gitanos of Jarana Manage the Past." *The Journal of the Royal Anthropological Institute* 7.4 (2001): 631–647.

Gheorghe, Nicolae. "The Social Construction of Romani Identity." *Gypsy Politics and Traveller Identity.* Ed. Thomas Acton. Hatfield: University of Hertfordshire Press, 1997. 153–172.

Gheorghe, Nicolae. "Roma-Gypsy Ethnicity in Eastern Europe." *Social Research* 58.4 (1991): 829–844.

Gillis, John R. "Memory and Identity: The History of a Relationship." *Commemorations: The Politics of National Identity.* Ed. John R. Gillis. Princeton: Princeton UP, 1994. 3–26.

Guy, Will. "Late Arrivals at the Nationalist Games: Romani Mobilisation in the Czech Lands and Slovakia." *Ethnonational Identities.* Eds. Steve Fenton and Stephen May. Basingstoke: Palgrave Macmillan, 2002. 48–83.

Habermas, Jürgen. *The Theory of Communicative Action.* Vol. 2: *Lifeworld and System: A Critique of Functionalist Reason.* Boston: Beacon Press, 1984.

Halbwachs, Maurice. *On Collective Memory.* Ed. Lewis A. Coser. Chicago: Chicago UP, 1992.

Hancock, Ian. "On the Interpretation of a Word: *Porrajmos* as Holocaust." *The Holocaust in History and Memory* 3 (2010): 19–23.

Hancock, Ian. *We Are the Romani People: Ame sam e Rromane dzene.* Hatfield: University of Hertfordshire Press, 2002.

Hancock, Ian. "Responses to Porrajmos: The Romani Holocaust." *Is the Holocaust Unique?* Ed. Alan S. Rosenbaum. Boulder: The Westview Press, 1996. 39–64.

Hobsbawm, Eric J. "Introduction: Inventing Traditions." *The Invention of Tradition.* Eds. Eric J. Hobsbawm and Terence Ranger. Cambridge: Cambridge UP, 1983. 1–14.

Honneth, Axel. *The Struggle for Recognition: The Moral Grammar of Social Conflicts.* Cambridge: Polity Press, 1996.

Huyssen, Andreas. "Present Pasts: Media, Politics, Amnesia." *Public Culture* 12.1 (2000): 21–38.

IRU (International Romani Union). 2001. "Declaration of a Roma Nation." www.hartford-hwp.com/archives/60/132.html (accessed 3 March 2011).

Irwin-Zarecka, Iwona. *Frames of Remembrance: The Dynamics of Collective Memory.* New New Brunswick: Transaction Publishers, 1994.

Kansteiner, Wulf. "Finding Meaning in Memory: A Methodological Critique of Collective Memory Studies." *History and Theory* 41.2 (2002): 179–197.

Kapralski, Slawomir. "Rituals of Memory in Constructing Eastern European Roma Identity." *The Role of the Romanies: Images and Self-Images of Romanies/'Gypsies' in European Cultures.* Eds. Nicholas Saul and Susan Tebbutt. Liverpool: Liverpool UP, 2004. 208–225.

Kapralski, Slawomir. "The Holocaust in the Memory of the Roma: From Trauma to Imagined Community?" *Constructing and Sharing Memory: Community Informatics, Identity and Empowerment.* Eds. Larry Stillman and Graeme Johanson. Newcastle: Cambridge Scholars Publishing, 2007. 114–123.

Kapralski, Slawomir. "The Voices of a Mute Memory: The Holocaust and the Identity of Eastern European Romanies." *Der nationalsozialistische Genozid an den Roma Osteuropas: Geschichte und künstlerische Verarbeitung.* Eds. Felicitas Fischer von Weikersthal,

Christoph Garstka, Urs Heftrich and Heinz D. Löwe. Cologne: Böhlau Verlag, 2008. 93–114.

Kapralski, Slawomir. *Naród z popiołów. Pamięć zagłady a tożsamość Romów* [A Nation from the Ashes: Memory of Genocide and Roma Identity]. Warsaw: Scholar, 2012.

Kapralski, Slawomir. "The Aftermath of the Roma Holocaust: From Implicit Memories to Commemoration." *The Nazi Genocide of the Roma: Reassessment and Commemoration.* Ed. Anton Weiss-Wendt. Oxford: Berghahn Books, 2013. 229–251.

Kapralski, Slawomir, Marta Martyniak, Joanna Talewicz-Kwiatkowska. *Roma in Auschwitz.* Oświęcim: Auschwitz-Birkenau State Museum, 2011.

Kastoryano, Riva. "Transnational Nationalism: Redefining Nation and Territory." *Identities, Affiliations, and Allegiances.* Eds. Seyla Benhabib, Ian Shapiro and Danilo Petranović. Cambridge: Cambridge UP, 2007. 159–178.

Katz, Steven T., Shlomo Biderman and Gershon Greenberg, eds. *Wrestling with God: Jewish Theological Responses during and after the Holocaust.* Oxford: Oxford UP, 2007.

Kennedy, Paul and Victor Roudometof. "Transnationalism in a Global Age." *Communities across Borders: New Immigrants and Transnational Cultures.* Eds. Paul Kennedy and Victor Roudometof. London: Routledge, 2002. 1–27.

Kenrick, Donald. "The Genocide of the Gypsies: What We Now Know and What We Still Don't Know." *The Holocaust in History and Memory* 3 (2010): 25–29.

Kitzmann, Andreas, Conny Mithander and John Sundholm. "Introduction." *Memory Work: The Theory and Practice of Memory.* Eds. Andreas Kitzmann, Conny Mithander and John Sundholm. Frankfurt am Main: Peter Lang, 2005. 9–24.

Kwiek, Gregor D. "Afterword: Rom, Roma, Romani, Kale, Gypsies, Travellers, and Sinti … Pick a Name and Stick with It, Already." *All Change! Romani Studies through Romani Eyes.* Eds. Damian Le Bas and Thomas Acton. Hatfield: University of Hertfordshire Press, 2010. 79–89.

LaCapra, Dominick. *History and Memory after Auschwitz.* Ithaca: Cornell UP, 1998.

Le Bas, Damian. "The Possible Implications of Diasporic Consciousness for Romani Identity." *All Change! Romani Studies Through Romani Eyes.* Eds. Damian Le Bas and Thomas Acton. Hatfield: University of Hertfordshire Press, 2010. 61–70.

Lebow, Richard N. "The Memory of Politics in Postwar Europe." *The Politics of Memory in Postwar Europe.* Eds. Richard N. Lebow, Wulf Kansteiner and Claudio Fogu. Durham: Duke UP, 2006. 1–39.

Levy, Daniel and Natan Sznaider. "Memory Unbound: The Holocaust and the Formation of Cosmopolitan Memory." *European Journal of Social Theory* 5.1 (2002): 87–106.

Marushiakova, Elena and Vesselin Popov. "The Roma – a Nation without a State? Historical Background and Contemporary Tendencies." *Segmentation und Komplementarität: Organisatorische, ökonomische und kulturelle Aspekte der Interaktion von Nomaden und Sesshaften.* Ed. Bernhard Streck. Halle: Orientwissenschaftliche Hefte, 2004. 71–100.

Mayall, David. *Gypsy Identities 1500–2000: From Egipcyans and Moon-men to the Ethnic Romany.* London: Routledge, 2004.

McCrone, David. *The Sociology of Nationalism: Tomorrow's Ancestors.* London: Routledge, 1998.

McGarry, Aidan. "Ethnic Group Identity and the Roma Social Movement: Transnational Organizing Structures of Representation." *Nationalities Papers* 36.3 (2008): 449–470.

Milchman, Alan and Alan Rosenberg. "Postmodernism and the Holocaust." *Postmodernism and the Holocaust*. Eds. A. Milchman and A. Rosenberg. Amsterdam: Editions Rodopi, 1998. 1–22.

Mirga, Andrzej and Gheorghe, Nicolae. *The Roma in the Twenty-First Century: A Policy Paper.* Princeton: Project on Ethnic Relations, 1997.

Misztal, Barbara A. *Theories of Social Remembering*. Maidenhead: Open University Press, 2003.

Mróz, Lech. "Niepamięć nie jest zapominaniem: Cyganie-Romowie a Holokaust" [Non-Memory is Not Forgetting: Gypsy-Roma and the Holocaust]. *Przegląd Socjologiczny* XLIX 2 (2000).

Pakier, Małgorzata and Bo Stråth. "A European Memory?" *A European Memory? Contested Histories and Politics of Remembrance*. Eds. Małgorzata Pakier and Bo Stråth. Oxford: Berghahn, 2010. 1–24.

Pinto, Diana. "Pięćdziesiąt lat po Zagładzie: konieczność budowania nowej pamięci polsko-żydowskiej" [Fifty Years after Shoah: The Necessity of Building New Polish-Jewish Memory]. *Pamięć żydowska, pamięć polska* [Jewish Memory, Polish Memory]. Krakow: Instytut Francuski w Krakowie and C&D International Editors, 1996. 165–199.

Reading, Anna. "Globalisation and Digital Memory: Globital Memory's Six Dynamics." *On Media Memory: Collective Memory in a New Media Age*. Eds. Motti Neiger, Oren Meyers and Eyal Zandberg. Basingstoke: Palgrave Macmillan, 2011. 241–252.

Rorke, Bernard. "No Longer and Not Yet: Between Exclusion and Emancipation." *Roma Diplomacy*. Eds. Valeriu Nicolae and Hanah Slavik. New York: International Debate Education Association, 2007. 87–102.

Schöpflin, George. "The Functions of Myth and a Taxonomy of Myths." *Myths and Nationhood*. Eds. Geoffrey Hosking and George Schöpflin. London: Hurst & Company, 1997. 19–35.

Schutz, Alfred. "The Stranger: An Essay in Social Psychology." *Alfred Schutz, Collected Papers*. Vol. 2. The Hague: Martinus Nijhoff, 1976. 91–105.

Sennett, Richard. "Disturbing Memories." *Memory*. Eds. Patricia Fara and Karalyn Patterson. Cambridge: Cambridge UP, 1998. 10–26.

Sheffer, Gabriel. *Diaspora Politics: At Home Abroad*. Cambridge: Cambridge UP, 2003.

Simhandl Katrin. "'Western Gypsies and Travellers' – 'Eastern Roma:' The Creation of Political Objects by the Institutions of the European Union." *Nations and Nationalism* 12. 1 (2006): 97–115.

Smith, Anthony D. *Nationalism and Modernism: A Critical Survey of Recent Theories of Nations and Nationalism*. London: Routledge, 1998.

Smith, Anthony D. *The Ethnic Origins of Nations*. Oxford: Blackwell, 1986.

Sodaro, Amy. "Whose Holocaust? The Struggle for Romany Inclusion in the United States Holocaust Memorial Museum." *International Journal of the Inclusive Museum* 1.4 (2008): 27–36.

Stauber, Roni and Raphael Vago. "The Politics of Memory: Jews and Roma Commemorate their Persecution." *The Roma: A Minority in Europe: Historical, Political and Social Perspectives*. Eds. Roni Stauberand Raphael Vago. Budapest: CEU Press, 2007. 117–134.

Stewart, Michael. "Remembering without Commemoration: The Mnemonics and Politics of Holocaust Memories among European Roma." *Journal of the Royal Anthropological Institute* 10.3 (2004): 561–582.

Tcherenkov, Lev and Stephane Laederich. *The Roma*. Vol. 1: *History, Language, and Groups*. Basel: Schwabe Verlag, 2004.

Trouillot, Michel-Rolph. *Silencing the Past: Power and the Production of History*. Boston: Beacon Press, 1995.

Trumpener, Katie. "The Time of the Gypsies: A 'People without History' in the Narratives of the West." *Critical Inquiry* 18.4 (1992): 843–884.

Tyndall, Andrea. "Memory, Authenticity and Replication of the Shoah in Museums: Defensive Tools of the Nation." *Re-presenting the Shoah for the Twenty-First Century*. Ed. Ronit Lentin. Oxford: Berghahn Books, 2004. 111–126.

Van Baar, Huub. *The European Roma: Minority Representation, Memory, and the Limits of Transnational Governmentality*. Phd dissertation. Amsterdam: Universiteit van Amsterdam, 2011.

Willems, Wim. *In Search of the True Gypsy: From Enlightenment to Final Solution*. Portland: Frank Cass Publisher, 1997.

Wolf, Eric R. *Europe and the People without History*. Berkeley: University of California Press, 1982.

Wyschogrod, Edith. *Spirit in Ashes: Hegel, Heidegger, and Man-Made Mass Death*. New Haven: Yale UP, 1985.

Yoors, Jan. *The Gypsies*. New York: Simon and Schuster, 1967.

Zimmermann, Michael. "The Berlin Memorial for the Murdered Sinti and Roma: Problems and Points for Discussion." *Romani Studies* 17.1 (2007): 1–30.

Christina Schwenkel
Imaging Humanity: Socialist Film and Transnational Memories of the War in Vietnam

In Hải Ninh's wartime feature film, *Em Bé Hà Nội* (Little Girl of Hanoi, 1974), Ngọc Hà, played by the ten-year-old first-time actor Lan Hương, frantically runs through the streets of war-torn Hanoi looking for her soldier father in the aftermath of the 1972 Christmas bombing that killed her mother and younger sister. Filmed on site amidst the actual rubble and embers of the still-smoldering city, *Em Bé Hà Nội* conveys both the scope of urban devastation and the profound sense of loss – of life, family, home, and community – as seen and experienced through the eyes of a traumatized young girl. Ngọc Hà returns from the countryside where she had been evacuated to find sections of her city and her street of Khâm Thiên lying in ruins. With the help of a neighbor, she locates the site of what was once her house and is now a bomb crater, and scavenges through the wreckage for traces of her family's material history. The film alternates between Ngọc Hà's memories of a secure, joyful past and a tragically altered present, and her flashbacks evoke an image of a cultured family and the comfortable socialist lifestyle they once enjoyed: from family outings and weekend rides on the merry-go-round at Lenin Park to playful moments in their modest home, laughing together and singing in tune with Ngọc Hà's violin. As the embodiment of innocence wrenched from the dream-world of her childhood, Ngọc Hà's character comes to symbolize the pure essence of humanity, a figure with whom the viewer cannot help but identify. As the search for her father continues, Ngọc Hà comes face to face with a group of captured US pilots who are being led through the street past the fires and the wreckage that their bombs have inflicted upon the population. Her dark eyes stare down the injured pilots as they limp past in succession, and their own gaze moves nervously from the angry bystanders who threaten to beat them for the deaths of their loved ones, to the little girl who stands before them holding a tattered and burnt schoolbook in her hands, a sign of the family and childhood she has lost and, more broadly, of the civilization the pilots have attempted to destroy.

Em Bé Hà Nội was shot in black-and-white, in a documentary style combining archival footage – such as aerial views of the extensive destruction of northern Vietnam – with panned, close-up shots of the ruins that constitute the backdrop of the set. The film unfolds amidst the urban chaos that followed the bombing, and, as such, offers rare and compelling insights into life in wartime Hanoi, even if the individual scenes were staged and enacted. It incorporates, for example, the alarm system used to alert residents of approaching B52s, and it demonstrates the escape systems that were in place – the maze of trenches and concrete tubes, or single person bunkers, placed around the city, in which residents descended quickly to protect themselves during raids. Such images were also common fare in international socialist documentaries and newscasts made during the war and served to constitute a unique socialist iconography based on recurring images, figures, and themes, including that of the innocent child and the vanquished and vulnerable pilot as exemplified in *Em Bé Hà Nội*. As M. Anne Pitcher and Kelly Askew have observed, socialist countries "shared a discourse and iconography of socialism that was grounded in certain universal themes" (2006, 10–11) – themes that were highly gendered, racially inflected, and historically contingent. In this chapter, I examine this shared discourse and iconography across a number of socialist films produced between 1965 and 1979 by East German and Cuban filmmakers, to ask: What kinds of images of self and other emerge in socialist documentaries about the war? And how did such images express particular ideas about life and what it means to be human? During the American War, socialist filmmakers produced a large collection of documentary films of the bombing of northern Vietnamese cities and villages that are little known or acknowledged in the West. I consider how these powerful cinematic representations produced a postnational scopic regime of memory, which mobilized "affective communities" (Gandhi 2006) and a vision of global humanity rooted in ideologically persuasive notions of international solidarity, socialist friendship, and anti-imperialist unity. I focus on two seemingly contradictory figurations of humanity that are recurrent in these films – the child and the POW, as representative of self and other – in order to trace how particular understandings of the human condition gave shape to a cosmopolitan socialist memory that continues to shape transnational memory practices today.

Almost four decades after the 'liberation' of Saigon, there remains little analysis of socialist representations of the "American War" and the memory cultures they have come to constitute.[1] Scholarship on visual culture and the "Vietnam War," on the other hand, has been more abundant, although it has privileged the role that US cultural production and "technologies of memory" have played in shaping a contested public sphere of remembrance in the United States (Sturken

---

[1] For exceptions, see Alter (1997) on film; Taylor (2004) on art; and Schwenkel (2008, 2009b) on photojournalism.

1997).[2] How this iconography has circulated beyond US borders to incorporate much of the capitalist world in a global imaginary and memory of Vietnam and the Vietnamese as a devastated country and people has been largely overlooked (but see Alneng 2002; and Schwenkel 2006). More recent work has attempted to decenter the nation-state as the dominant analytic for examining historical memory of the war by focusing on exilic (Roth 2001) and travelling (Schwenkel 2009a) memories, and their oft-fraught encounters in transnational spaces of commemoration.

In this essay, I draw attention to the unique visual record of the war produced through socialist collaborations between international filmmakers and Vietnamese cultural producers and institutions. I have chosen to focus on documentaries made on site during the 1960s and 1970s, rather than co-produced feature films from the 1980s, such as *Tọa độ chết – Координаты смерти* (Co-ordinates of Death, 1985) or *Dschungelzeit – Những Mảnh Đời Rừng* (Time in the Jungle, 1987), though I acknowledge that these films, too – the former about the wartime visit of a US actress to northern Vietnam and the latter about German defectors from the French Legionnaires to support the Vietnamese revolution – are important in the formation of cosmopolitan socialist memory. I also choose to focus on East German and, to a lesser extent, Cuban documentaries on account of my own linguistic abilities and – more importantly – because of the revival of interest that these films have enjoyed in recent years. Some of the documentaries discussed below have been re-released on DVD, and others are available for online viewing. This is not to say that GDR[3] and Cuban films are indistinguishable or that they express a uniform global socialist aesthetic and praxis. Rather, differing national, cultural, and historical contexts gave shape to vastly different film industries. The tense post-revolution relationship between the United States and Cuba figures prominently in Cuban documentaries of the war, especially in the poetic montages of Santiago Álvarez. In East Germany, the well-funded state film studio, DEFA, produced a larger group of filmmakers who traveled to and filmed in Vietnam. Although an underlying paternalism is sometimes palpable in the GDR documentaries and expressions of solidarity, filmmakers of both countries saw themselves as active participants in the global anti-colonial and anti-imperial struggle, and as such, their films similarly reflect a deep capacity for human empathy and the desire to represent and reaffirm the dignity of the Vietnamese.

---

2 This scholarship has spanned more than three decades and shows little sign of abating. See, for example, Louvre and Walsh (1988); Jeffords (1989); Rowe and Berg (1991); Sturken (1997); Dittmar and Michaud (2000); Hoskins (2004); Martini (2007); and Hagopian (2009).
3 German Democratic Republic or East Germany.

Fig. 1. "Invincible Vietnam;" GDR postage stamps, 1966 and 1968; public domain.

In what follows, I argue that these short films and documentaries, which were disseminated across the socialist world, yet remained largely unknown in the West, have forged a competing global historical memory of the war that is likewise gendered and racialized, though for different effect and purpose. For example, in contrast to recurring images in US media and popular culture of Vietnamese women as passive and helpless victims of US military violence, socialist representations regularly portrayed women as assertive, rational, and compassionate actors in war. In both cases the female body stood in for the Vietnamese nation: in the former, the violated female body alluded to US might and triumph (or, to more critical readers, the war as debacle), while in the latter case, images of young, gun-toting women, often in the act of apprehending American pilots, emerged as an international socialist symbol of Vietnamese resilience and defeat of US imperialism (Figure 1). An examination of East German and Cuban filmmaking as formative of a cosmopolitan memory that, on the one hand transcended the nation-state to co-constitute global socialist memory of the war, and on the other, reaffirmed national perspectives and distinctions (such as "Cuban" and "GDR" cinema), reveals the unique ways in which socialist visual cultures of war imaged humanist values and particular notions of universal humanity through cultural encounters between self and other.

Visions of humanity and transnational memories of Vietnam

Western media images of the war in Vietnam have played a central role in shaping popular cultural memory, arguably more than those of any other US military

Fig. 2. "Abu Ghraib 'Nam';" Dennis Draughon, *Scranton Times*, 12 May 2004; courtesy of Dennis Draughon.

occupation. The prolonged and in-depth media coverage of graphic violence and mutilation in Vietnam contrasts sharply with the largely absent bodies and perfunctory reporting of later wars and invasions, particularly the surreal representations of Operation Desert Storm, which led Jean Baudrillard (1995) to claim that the Gulf War "had not taken place" (see also Feldman 1994; Hoskins 2004). In the United States, iconic bodies associated with extreme acts of violence – the napalmed body of Phan Thị Kim Phúc, the self-immolated body of Thích Quảng Đức, the tortured body of John McCain – continue to shape popular memory and global imaginaries of the war, even as these images are appropriated and inserted into new contexts to highlight contemporary political and military debates. In 2006, for example, John McCain's flight suit in the 'Hanoi Hilton' prison-turned-museum became the object of a treasure hunt on the reality show *Amazing Race*, and in May 2004, Dennis Draughon's political cartoon, "Abu Ghraib 'Nam'," which depicts Phan Thị Kim Phúc linked via electrical wires to the hooded Abu Ghraib figure looming behind her, circulated in the *Scranton Times* and on the Internet (Figure 2).[4] The alternative music scene has also incorporated iconic images into their marketing strategies to disseminate anti-war messages, as well as to promote the sale of albums (see for example the use of the image of the burning body of Thích Quảng Đức by rapcore band *Rage against the Machine*). From the Finnish glam band *Hanoi Rocks* to the surf-punk music of California's *Agent Orange*, 'Vietnam' has come to stand for a set of globally constructed and frequently conflicted ideas, images, memories and meanings, which are commodified and highly politicized, and used in myriad ways to advance leftist causes on the one hand, and more conservative worldviews and political agendas, on the other.

---

4 For an analysis of the *Amazing Race* episode as linked to Vietnamese museum representations and John McCain's torture claims, see Schwenkel (2009c). For an analysis of Draughon's cartoon, see Hariman and Lucaites (2007). The image can also be viewed online at editorialcartoonists. com/cartoon/display.cfm/10557/ (accessed 19 March 2014).

One of the most controversial and iconic figures of the war that continues to play an important role in conservative political circles in the United States is that of the prisoner of war, or POW. Discursive and visual representations of POWs have long occupied a central place in US historical memory and social imagination of 'Nam,' right up to and including the 2008 presidential campaign of John McCain. As Thomas M. Hawley (2005) has argued, the absent bodies of US troops deemed missing in action (MIA) in Southeast Asia – and presumed by many of their families to have been held prisoners long after the conflict ended[5] – have been enduring signifiers of both communist deceit and US defeat. Images and narratives of captivity have long gripped global consumers of US popular culture, including in popular Hollywood films such as *Deer Hunter* (1978), *Rambo: First Blood, Part 2* (1985), and *Uncommon Valor* (1983). According to Edwin Martini (2007), the POW figure has been key to postwar imaginaries of Vietnam as an enduring aggressor rather than victim, and to the continuation of war by cultural, economic, and political means. At the center of these representations has been the broken body of the white male soldier-turned-tortured prisoner. Beginning in the late 1960s, emotionally charged reports of POW abuse served as proof of the inhumanity and callousness of the enemy, turning the POW into a powerful political symbol whose wounded and scarred body provided irrefutable proof that US presence in Vietnam was indeed warranted (Gruner 1993, 19).

The figure of the POW also became a recurring motif in socialist films, but for differing motives and to a contrary effect. Socialist representations of captured US pilots served to convey to international audiences the *humanist* practices of the Vietnamese in the face of unprovoked enemy assault. Female soldiers and medical practitioners, for example, were frequently shown as "gentle warriors" and humanitarians caring for wounded POWs who were rescued from angry crowds by benevolent bystanders after their aircraft had been shot down (Schwenkel 2009c).[6] In certain ways, these celebratory representations of humane rescue and maternal care, which were crucial to sustaining Vietnamese morale and to mobilizing the support of the socialist international community, resonated with images in US cultural memory of the 'Vietnam vet' who suffered yet another emasculating defeat upon his return to the United States to face a critical, and at times hostile

---

5 On the ways in which 'live sightings' in the postwar years captivated US social imagination and shaped government policy toward a reunified Vietnam, see Franklin (1993).
6 I borrow the term "gentle warriors" from Heather Marie Stur (2011). Such representations were part and parcel of a Cold War battle over images: photographs of Vietnamese maternal caregivers were not unlike those of US troops as "gentle warriors" who provided aid and paternal protection to southern Vietnamese populations, especially orphans, in order to present the United States and its democratizing mission as "the humane option to oppressive communism" (Stur 2011, 143).

public, and a difficult social and economic reintegration (Jeffords 1989). As I argue below, ironically enough, these socialist representational practices worked to reconfigure the subjectivity and humanity of POWs in ways that blurred the line between perpetrator and victimhood, and allowed for more ambiguous and at times empathetic images of the enemy Other to emerge.

East German and Cuban documentaries of the war frequently took as their main subject the protracted bombing of northern Vietnam. In combination with print media, a powerful repertoire of iconic images, figures, and symbols soon took shape. Even films that focused on other topics commonly drew upon this iconography. Santiago Álvarez's documentary, *79 Primaveras* (79 Springtimes, 1969), on the life and death of Hồ Chí Minh, for example, begins with a close-up of a lotus flower – a Buddhist symbol of purity and humanity that in Vietnam is also commonly used to represent the nation. Black-and-white, time-lapse photography captures the lotus blossom as it opens to the sun. Its flower and petals then morph into the tail fins of aerial bombs falling vertically in slow motion before exploding on the ground. In many documentaries, including *Eintritt kostenlos* (Free Admission, 1976) and *Abril de Viet Nam en el año del gato* (April in Vietnam in the Year of the Cat, 1975), as well as in the GDR weekly television newscast *Der Augenzeuge* (The Witness), long shots of mass destruction were commonly juxtaposed with stock images of exploding US bombers – balls of fire plunging to the earth, signifying penetrability of the US military and its modern technology. In *79 Primaveras*, the transition between each major stage in the political life of Hồ Chí Minh (such as from the French War to the American War) is marked by aerial footage of bomb cargoes being released and falling from the sky, followed by long shots of the blooming of springtime flowers. At the end of the film, with Hồ Chí Minh's famous words – "We will build a new homeland twice as beautiful" – Álvarez returns to the time-lapse image of the lotus blossom growing out of the mud to transform into a beautiful flower – a symbol of the Vietnamese nation rising from the wreckage of war.

That socialist documentaries focused on the bombing of northern Vietnam was mainly a consequence of global geopolitics. The Cold War had temporarily divided the country into the US-backed Republic of Vietnam (RVN) in the south and the socialist Democratic Republic (DRV) in the north. International journalists and filmmakers who worked south of the seventeenth parallel were typically from the West and western-friendly countries, while photographers and filmmakers from socialist countries worked primarily in the DRV, and a few in the south with the National Liberation Front.[7] Visual records of the war were thus largely

---

7 There were of course some exceptions. Photographers with communist sympathies, such as Wilfred Burchett from Australia, were also welcomed to practice their trade in the DRV.

shaped by a politics of access that reflected the very different experiences of warfare across the two regimes: cameramen and women in the RVN focused more on combat and military operations, while those in the DRV were able to film during and after the air strikes. As the filmmakers travelled through the provinces with much difficulty and uncertainty (because of the threat of raids), they filmed where few or no other cameras were present. At times, filmmakers such as Santiago Álvarez, in *Hanoi, Martes* 13 (Hanoi, Tuesday the 13th, 1967), even experienced the assaults along with local residents (Chanan 2004, 229), thus contributing to a strong sense of solidarity that formed the basis of an emerging cosmopolitan socialist cinematic memory.

Unlike photojournalism in the West, there were no ideological presumptions of 'objectivity' at work here. Socialist filmmakers did not claim political neutrality, but openly advocated support for, and solidarity with, the revolutions unfolding in Third World countries. Perhaps the most well-known of socialist documentarians, Walter Heynowski and Gerhard Sheumann, or H&S as they were collectively called, emphasized that they were "political artists" who endeavored to capture and convey harsh realities through the camera (Michel 1979, 4).[8] H&S saw filmmaking as a form of active social and political engagement, and they expressed their convictions through an experiential style that combined montage and portraiture with reportage and satire, a technique that was also similar for Santiago Álvarez. Across the socialist world, documentary film was considered a "weapon" (*Waffe*) in the class struggle, and in the context of war, it became a valuable tool in the fight against imperialism, one that could also contribute to promoting and maintaining peace (Tràn 1987, 34).

What did the war look like through the socialist camera lens? Elsewhere, I have argued that Vietnamese photojournalists immersed themselves in the everyday lives of their photographic subjects, at times spending years working and living in a particular community, and thus produced a deeply ethnographic, visual record of the war which captured not only death and destruction, but also the daily rhythms of routine life – the joys, sorrows, desires, and despair (Schwenkel 2008; 2009b). This is also reflected in the words of one Vietnamese filmmaker, commenting on the use of violence in western war films: "Representing the atrocities of war is certainly necessary. But perhaps it is even more necessary to have films that explore the love and compassion that exist between people, ethnic groups, and countries" (Tràn 1987, 35). East German and Cuban filmmakers did not live in Vietnamese villages for extended periods, but they, too, focused on

---

8 H&S produced around 70 documentaries, 14 of which were on Vietnam. Their own "Studio H&S" was fully autonomous from 1969–1982 (Steinmetz 2004, 366).

documenting the impact of the war on local residents as they attempted to go about their everyday lives under constant threat of aerial attack. Here, however, their messages point more explicitly to the productivity and functionality of a de-railed but not destroyed socialist system. In *Hanoi, Martes 13*, the camera lingers on the industrious activities that Vietnamese habitually engage in on a seemingly normal day: fishing, preparing food, eating, transplanting rice, riding a bicycle, sewing in a state factory, studying, plowing the fields – all of which are disrupted when the B52s are heard overhead. "Hatred into energy" [*El odio en energia*] the narrator proclaims, as the film cuts to a group of women working diligently to fill in the resulting bomb craters, while men hurriedly lay new train tracks in an attempt to resume the work of socialist nation-building. In Peter Ulbrich's *Ihr fragt, wie wir leben* (You Ask How We Live, 1967), the plenitude of socialism is contrasted with the destruction of war: "Look at our large and prosperous home-land," the Vietnamese narrator commands as the camera pans over the vast rice fields of the province of Nghệ An. "We are not poor," she continues to the tune of the popular folk song, *Trống Cơm* (Rice Drum) while the camera shifts its focus to the region's industry. "We have built factories that have made us richer. We have increased productivity. Does this look like poverty?" In the capital city, Hanoians, too, enjoy the wealth of socialism in *Hanoi, Martes* 13, much like Ngọc Hà in *Em Bé Hà Nội*. In this unscripted documentary of daily life on the streets, women browse the merchandise in the city's central market while men drink coffee at Hoàn Kiếm Lake. Lovers hold hands and dancers perform. A local photographer positions a group of dapper college students in front of a historical temple. It appears to be a normal Tuesday afternoon on 13 December 1966, until the alarms sound and residents run for cover, donning their protective straw hats and jumping into trenches and concrete cylinders.

Socialist documentaries thus became an important political tool for filmmak-ers to respond to what they saw as the gross injustice of the war in Vietnam and to articulate their anti-imperialist positions. They did so in ways that, unlike in the West, did not rely on images of suffering as a dominant visual trope to represent the humanity of the Vietnamese people (Schwenkel 2008), but were also Oriental-ist in their emphasis on the peaceful and timeless nature of Vietnamese peasant society on its path toward socialist development. Similar to contemporary human rights media (see especially Malkki 1996; Allen 2009), the images produced by socialist filmmakers conveyed an abstract global humanity, though in this case they also generated empathy and a sense of solidarity by highlighting the agency, determination, and ingenuity of a socialist 'brother' nation under threat from a more powerful enemy. Film consequently emerged as an ethical, humanist prac-tice thought to transcend racial and historical difference, as well as the liberal individual self as the basis for political action and social change (Marcuse 1965).

Thus, in *400 c.c.*, by H&S (1966), the clenched fists of GDR blood donors signal solidarity in conflict (the fist as an illustration of the determination to fight) alongside the biomedical requirement to maintain the flow of blood. Here, science and politics intersect through the circulation of blood to homogenize and unify a collective political force (Todorov 1995, 49). Set to an original *a capella* composition, the film suggests that blood donations to Vietnam transformed socialist friends into biological kin: "Wir sind Blutverwandte geworden" (We became blood relatives), H&S claim. More than a decade later in *Die fernen Freunde nah* (A Visit from Vietnamese Friends, 1979), viewers learn with surprise that East German blood sent to Vietnam had been used to save US pilots, not wounded Vietnamese. H&S maintained this secret for several years before revealing it on film. As the camera closes in on the pained face of an American prisoner undergoing surgery – inviting emotional participation as his heavy eyes stare deep into the camera – they conclude that such acts should be understood as having been consistent with the values of socialist humanism and its recognition of the rights and humanity of POWs.

In the next sections I turn to examine in greater depth two iconic figures of humanity in transnational socialist memory of the war: the figure of the child as a symbol of innocence and global humanity that represents the universal socialist self, and the figure of the POW as an image of guilt and radical Otherness that is ultimately rendered human and familiar.

Imaging innocence: the figure of the child in socialist memory of the war

There is perhaps no other global figure that has come to represent the tragedies and injustices of war around the world as consistently as that of the child. As Liisa Malkki has argued, affectively powerful images of suffering children, believed to embody pure innocence and common humanity, tend to elicit strong feelings of compassion in individuals, and also appeal to a shared sense of human suffering across race, nation, and culture (2010, 64–65). During the Cold War, the figure of the white, middle-class child at risk and in need of protection became a powerful image in the United States that was used to justify expansion of its nuclear defense system (Stephens 1997). Like in the West, the use of children and the theme of childhood in socialist media was also an important representational practice and form of social commentary on the human condition, and on the brutality and irrationality of the war in Vietnam. In socialist documentaries, it is through the eyes of the child that one is able to see the war and grasp the impact of protracted US bombing on family and nation. This convention was employed, for example, in the film *Em Bé Hà Nội* in the figure of Ngọc Hà, whose controlled gaze at the POWs while standing amidst the rubble of her demolished street startled the American pilots as they looked back uneasily at the child, into the face of innocent humanity. As I demonstrate below, as figures of international solidarity and global socialist humanity, children – and their disrupted childhoods – came to stand in for the moral goodness of socialism and the interrupted project of socialist nation-building.

One of the archetypal figurations of the child found in socialist films is that of the innocent victim. In *79 Primaveras*, Santiago Álvarez cuts from film footage of Hồ Chí Minh playing with children in the presidential gardens – a common image circulated in the DRV to show the president as a paternal figure caring for the future of the nation – to scenes of the death and deformity of Vietnamese children in the aftermath of air strikes. The images are uncharacteristically graphic for socialist media, and while the montage of death and mutilation conveys the magnitude of the violence of bombardment, this cinematic technique serves to dissociate the individual child from the social and geographical context of his or her casualty. Malkki, in particular, has been critical of such image-making practices in liberal humanitarian interventions, which "strip children of their personhood" and their individual histories to constitute a depoliticized and ahistorical image of the "generic" child as innocent and suffering victim (2010, 65–6). However, as Levy and Sznaider have argued, it is precisely this decontextualization that has allowed for abstracted "violations of humanity" to be appropriated as a form of cosmopolitan memory that "functions as a prerequisite for the spread of human rights as a universally recognized idiom" (2010, 15).

East German films, in particular, attempted to counter this tendency toward "anonymous corporeality" (Malkki 1996, 389) through the conventional use of witness testimony, allowing for concrete persons with specific histories and kinship identities to emerge from the pool of generic humanity. In *Denkt an mein Land* (Remember My Country, 1965), Peter Ulbrich introduces Lâm Ngọc, mayor of Nghĩa Hội commune in the province of Nghệ An, who, standing in front of their demolished home, cradles his infant son Trung. Listening to the first-person narrative voice of Lâm Ngọc, as told through the German translator, the viewer learns that Trung is the only remaining child of nine after an air raid on this rural community killed the rest of the family. As the camera slowly pans through the material remains of the home-turned-ruins, we hear Lâm Ngọc's thoughts and hopes – his desire to rebuild and secure a better future for Trung, now his only child and remaining family member. As Malkki has observed, the figure of the child in the arms of a protecting adult is a conventional symbol of hope for the future. In his father's embrace, staring directly into the camera, Trung represents "the principle of hope on which many futuristic utopias depend, and also a universalizing (but not universal) standard of a certain basic purity" (2010, 77). *Denkt an mein Land* is essentially a eulogy to Lâm Ngọc's deceased family and to the other child victims of US bombing campaigns.[9] It ends with a series of close-up shots of the smiling faces of girls and boys from Nghệ An, anonymous children that represent the socialist future of Vietnam, as Lâm Ngọc's voice implores: "Remember Trung, the last of nine. Remember Vietnam's children. I want them to live. Why else would I have survived? Remember my country, Vietnam."

In socialist films, children are not only depicted as innocent and unknowing victims of unjust violence and warfare, but also as actors involved in important survival and resistance activities. This victim-actor duality suggests another domain of the figure of the child in socialist humanism that departs from the mode of depiction in liberal human rights practices. Scholars have noted how liberal humanist discourse typically portrays children as either vulnerable and passive, or put "at risk" by having too much agency (Stephens 1995) – two kinds of representations that are more oppositional than they are complementary. When portrayed as "the moral conscience of the world," Malkki suggests, "it is nearly impossible for actual children to act in the world as political, historical subjects" (2010, 79). They are therefore typically seen as the beneficiaries of actions, particularly adult actions, but not as actors themselves (Stephens 1996, 76).

By contrast, in socialist documentaries the figure of the child is often endowed with agency and subjectivity in relation to the work of national defense and socialist nation-building. In *Hanoi, Martes 13*, for example, children weave thick straw hats to protect their heads from shrapnel; in *Ihr fragt, wie wir leben* children are hard at study in evacuated schools in the forest, far from their families. "They [Americans] don't want Vietnam's children to laugh," the narrator proclaims, "but we're ready for them." "Learning and fighting go together," we are later told. As the bombers approach and the teacher bangs the drum to sound the alarm, the children quickly don their protective headgear and jump into the trenches they have dug under their desks. Leaving their schoolbooks behind, they run zigzag through fortified ditches and descend underground into shelters that they have helped to build. Scenes of studious children continuing their education in "jungle schools" (*Dschungel-Schulen*) are also present in *Denkt an mein Land* and *Report für Katrin* (Report for Katrin, 1970). After the bombing has subsided, the documentary *Ihr fragt, wie wir Leben* reveals, young pioneers return to their community to join in the effort to rebuild their destroyed schools. The camera slowly surveys the

---

9 In *Die Söhne der Thai* (Sons of the Thai, 1973), Gitta Nickel – the only female documentarian to work in Vietnam to my knowledge – also employs witness testimony to give voice and representation to aging Mr. Kim, who reflects on the deaths of his sons in the war.

destruction inside Thiệu Vận elementary school in Thanh Hóa province, pausing for a moment on the scattered papers, lone sandal, toppled globe, and broken abacus that lie on the floor. The youth volunteers search through the wreckage, looking for salvageable desks, chairs, and other equipment they can take back to and use in the forest. "We will rebuild deep in the jungle," the narrator declares, conveying the pupils' resolve.

Beyond the dual signification of children as victim and actor, socialist documentaries also employ the figure of the child to represent international solidarity, an almost spiritual principle that, like Renan's modern nation, is "constituted by the feeling of the sacrifices that one has made in the past and of those that one is prepared to make in the future" (1990, 19). The Vietnamese child is poised to transcend racial, historical, and geopolitical difference in order to signify the universal socialist self. The child of Vietnam is kin to every socialist man and woman, united symbolically through blood (i.e. transfusions) and the psychic bonds of a shared struggle against imperialism. East German filmmakers, in particular, played extensively with the metaphor of socialist kinship in their films, usually through editing techniques of cutting back and forth between German and Vietnamese childhoods to convey a sense of similitude and siblinghood. In the opening scene of *Ihr fragt, wie wir leben* – a "film for children" – a group of jubilant Vietnamese girls and boys are shown laughing and playing together in the park. The camera then cuts to East German children who are similarly enjoying playtime with games like "Ring around the Rosie." These two scenes serve to universalize a particular experience of socialist childhood as linked to the fulfillment of material, recreational and emotional needs through shared forms of play. But notions of play and their symbolic associations with safety and protection, Stephens has observed, are "difficult to maintain in the straitened circumstances of children in various sorts of 'war zones' around the world" (1995, 34). Back in Vietnam, a montage of images shows children full of life and then, tragically, dead. "Look at how Vietnamese children live, what they have to endure," the narrator demands. "They have learned to hate the war."

Report für Katrin similarly develops the motif of the universal socialist child that transcends nation, race, and culture to unite the communist world into a single family of humanity. The documentary follows Thomas Billhardt, an East German photographer well known for his powerful and intimate portraits of the war, both as he experiences the birth of his second child, Katrin, and as he prepares for his return to Hanoi. The juxtaposition of images and reflections on his personal and professional life serves to draw a parallel between the children of East Germany and those of Vietnam, while universalizing particular sentiments of parenthood. The documentary travels between East Germany and Vietnam, at first suggesting similitude in meaning and experience. In the hospital, Billhardt excitedly embraces his daughter for the first time. He is then shown in the airport in Berlin on his way to Hanoi as he reminisces about the "beautiful children of Vietnam with their beautiful eyes." In the next shot we see a group of Vietnamese schoolboys laughing and playing, before cutting to another shot of his newborn. Here, however, the images begin to diverge and the normalcy of Vietnamese childhood is disrupted with footage of "defenseless" (*schutzlos*) children in thickly woven grass hats in Hanoi standing next to concrete cylinders, into which they climb to shield themselves during an air raid. We then return once more to East Berlin, this time in a car with Billhardt and his wife who are bringing their baby home from the hospital. When the camera cuts back to Vietnam, we see a woman who has also recently given birth at a hospital in Hanoi. She embraces her newborn with pride; we then see Billhardt's wife in the car doing the same. The uniformity of experience is again unsettled as we find ourselves back at the hospital in Hanoi, watching as the alarms sound and nurses work quickly to evacuate the newborns, passing them to their mothers who have descended underground into a bomb shelter. Back in the GDR, Billhardt brings his daughter into their apartment and introduces her to his toddler son. Their comfortable lifestyle in socialist public housing is contrasted with a demolished village close to the seventeenth parallel, where no house remains standing after an air assault. The camera lingers on the now-homeless children who play among the ruins on the edge of a bomb crater, their socialist childhoods and futures now shattered.

In East German films, the disrupted childhoods of Vietnam's youth became a site of affective community intervention and the work of international solidarity. The normalcy of play and the desire for children to enjoy peace and the fruits of socialism are themes that echo across many of the documentaries, from *Em Bé Hà Nội* to *Abril de Viet Nam en el año del gato*. It is in the East German documentaries, however, a country that was in a stronger position to 'help' Vietnam, that humanitarian aid and action took shape, motivated by a concern for lost childhoods. On film, acts of socialist friendship and affective solidarity were performed at gifting ceremonies in Vietnam with blood and monetary donations made by visiting GDR delegations, as well as in the presentation of toys and stuffed animals to the children of Vietnam. In *Die fernen Freunde nah*, a postwar H&S film, the work of international solidarity is manifest through the figure of the traumatized child. One year earlier, the documentary, *Am Wassergraben* (At the Ditch, 1978), had introduced the East German population to a young boy from Mỹ Lai village, Đỗ Hòa, who had been rescued from a dyke during the massacre that took the lives of his family. In 1979, a delegation from Vietnam that included Hòa travelled to the GDR for the premiere of a film on the revolution in the Mekong Delta called *Die eiserne Festung* (The Iron Fortress, 1977). The delegation's visit is documented in *Die fernen Freunde nah*. In it, Hòa is given a hero's welcome upon his arrival in the GDR, much to his bewilderment. He is presented with gifts and given standing ovations at each of his appearances. He is taken under the wing of the youth pioneers who bring him to parks, school, festivals, and carnivals. They warmly absorb him into their playgroups, and introduce him to German foods, games, music, and rides in amusement parks. Through such activities, Hòa is able to relish the wholesome fun of genuine childhood and enjoy the material comforts of undeterred socialist development. Yet his presumed interests and needs as a child are defined according to universalized GDR standards. At the end of his visit, Hòa receives more gifts so that his East German "family" will always remain in his memory, just as his village, Mỹ Lai, remains in theirs. The camera then follows Hòa as he climbs the stairs to board his plane and return to Vietnam. At the top of the stairway, he pauses, and then turns one last time to the crowd to smile and wave goodbye, his childhood lost to the war now restored.

Imaging guilt: socialist memory of American POWs

In contrast to the image of the innocent child who embodies pure humanity and unifies the socialist world into a postnational family, the image of the POW served to reaffirm Otherness and fundamental difference. In socialist media, the figure of the American prisoner of war was pervasive. Daily headlines in the Vietnamese press kept a tally of downed US aircraft, at times accompanied by an image of an exploded plane hurtling toward the ground in a ball of flames.[10] The enemy pilot (*giặc lái*) was seen as a threat to be neutralized, and his capture was likewise celebrated with statistics on the number of men in captivity. The discursive and representational shift from aircraft to pilot – from machines to bodies – provided readers with a human face for the abstract "American imperialist" (*đế quốc Mỹ*). Unlike in the south, the US military did not have a presence in northern Vietnam, so the enemy had remained largely faceless and, consequently, became the subject of much myth-making, with poems and cartoons alluding to their large and fearsome bodies, and their greed and evil intent. In newspapers, small headshots of captured POWs – arranged in rows, and identified by name and rank – provided readers with a first-hand, close-up view of the imprisoned men. In the images, few of the pilots look directly at the camera, and many hang their heads as if conveying a sense of shame for their deeds. Presented as individuated portraits, the men

---

10 For example, on 8 June 1972, *Nhân Dân* [The People] announced that "Hà Nội, Hải Phòng and Hà Tây Shot Down 3 US Planes (2 F-4s and 1 A7)." In bold, black letters the byline read: "TOTAL is 3640 US Aircraft Destroyed to Date."

Fig. 3. "Little Guerilla;" Phan Thoan, 1965; reproduced with permission of the Vietnam News Agency.

Fig. 4. "No Words;" *Văn Hóa Miền Bắc* [Journal of Northern Culture]. Đỗ Đức, 1968; public domain.

are rendered powerless and isolated, disconnected from their technology and collectivity. Their withdrawn and at times bandaged faces hint at defeat and despair, while the black borders around each photograph suggested containment of the enemy and the threat to the nation.

The capture and care of US pilots who ejected from their jets and plummeted into rice fields provided a means to showcase Vietnam's socialist humanity and moral legitimacy to the rest of the world. In the communist bloc, gendered and racialized images of strong white men surrendering to petite native women profoundly shaped socialist public memory and dominant media practices. All of the documentaries discussed in this chapter incorporate an image or a scene – sometimes recreated – of a young Vietnamese woman apprehending a US pilot. The iconic power of such images derived largely from attention to and fascination with difference and incongruity – of woman against man, of the weak and innocent prevailing over the stronger and more powerful, and of Third World socialism defeating First World imperialism. In one of the most well-known photographs in socialist memory of the war, a young, female, barefoot militia member, Nguyễn Thị Kim Lai, leads captured US pilot William Robinson in what is the present-day province of Hà Tĩnh. The set of contrasts embodied in the picture taken by Phan Thoan in 1965 reified an image of a feminized, diminutive, yet determined nation up against – and ultimately defeating – a much larger, technologically superior, and now emasculated enemy Other (Figure 3). During the war, these sorts of representations were reproduced in a variety of media, including political posters and cartoons in newspapers and journals, often playing up the humiliation of American defeat and the inevitability of Vietnamese victory (Figure 4).

In contradiction to memory in the West, in global socialist memory, once in captivity, POWs were not tortured or regarded unconditionally as the abhorred enemy, but were often treated as human beings with dignity and respect. The image of socialist humanism presented here was also highly gendered – with women acting as maternal caregivers and even saviors, tending to the wounds of the pilots, providing them with food and water, and at times even protecting them from angry villagers who sought to beat them (Schwenkel 2009b). Such acts, including the use of donated East German blood to nurse the pilots back to health, required cultural recognition and representation of the fundamental humanity of the POW. This was accomplished by reinscribing the POW as both perpetrator *and* victim, as one who instigated 'crimes' (*tội ác*) against the Vietnamese people, yet did so as a mere tool of US imperialism. In the communist world, the POW thus became the emblematic figure of both guilt and victimhood. In what follows, I examine this ambiguity and the techniques for imaging humanity in the East German documentary mini-series directed by H&S, *Piloten im Pyjama* (Pilots in Pajamas, 1968).

The ambiguous figure of the perpetrator in *Pilots in Pajamas*

In contrast to seeing the war through the eyes of an innocent child, in *Pilots in Pajamas* audiences are shown the war from the viewpoint of the perpetrator. At first, this approach seems to de-center victimhood as the dominant trope and representation of war and suffering. However, like the child who is shown as both victim and agent, the figure of the POW also embodies a complex duality, eliciting both anger and empathy on account of the camera techniques employed by H&S. Filmed in 1968, during Operation Rolling Thunder, *Pilots in Pajamas* was a collaborative production between Vietnam and East Germany that was shot on site in Hỏa Lò prison, or the Hanoi Hilton, with the "support of prison officials and the people of Hanoi." Each of the four-part series begins with this reminder. Through close-up, talking-head shots of ten American "air pirates" (*Luftpiraten*)[11] with nervous hands, sweating brows, and vacant darting eyes, *Pilots in Pajamas* is a psychological exploration of the guilty mind, and it attempts to capture on film

---

11 *Luftpiraten* was commonly used in the East German press during the war and appears to be a direct German translation of the Vietnamese term, *giặc lái* – enemy pilot; with *giặc* often translated as 'invader' or 'pirate.' In *Abril de Viet Nam en el año del gato*, Santiago Álvarez refers to the pilots as "air executioners" (*ejecutor aire*) and "modern-day cowboys" who kill people they consider to be of an inferior race.

and convey to viewers the broken spirits of the pilots and their conflicted emotional states of shame, regret, and fear. The individual interviews with American POWs that constitute the focus of the documentary are recorded on site in a room with a single chair surrounded by a team of technicians and equipment. The documentary often cuts, however, to footage from the war (some of which is reenacted), including the arrest of downed pilots, the evacuation of schoolchildren during air raids, the urban and environmental devastation of aerial assaults, and subsequent cleanup and recovery efforts. For the viewer, this visual repertoire of stock images from socialist mass media has the effect of providing a broader context for the offenses that the POWs have committed and a reminder of the reasons for their imprisonment.

The male interviewer remains absent and anonymous throughout the miniseries, each of which runs for one hour. As his deep omnipresent voice poses the same set of questions for each POW, the camera remains focused on their individual faces, recording their bodily affect and the emotions behind each facial expression. The POWs appear nervous and low-spirited; they come across as men to be pitied, more than feared and despised. They are cautious and seemingly unsure about the filmmakers' intent. In one segment, when handed their pistol and asked why they had surrendered and not fired to avoid arrest (in violation of the US Military Code of Conduct that calls for resistance by any means, the interviewer points out), the startled pilots – one after the next – are visibly distressed and refuse to hold the gun, possibly fearing a setup. To get inside their heads and divulge their state of mind while carrying out "crimes against humanity," the filmmakers ask the pilots about their targets, their aircraft, number of missions, and technical expertise. They inquire as to why the pilots decided to join the military in the first place, and probe the POWs about their religious beliefs and their families – a difficult subject for the men, as their pained expressions reveal. H&S are particularly interested in how the prisoners have come to view and understand the Vietnamese people since their captivity, and how they have benefited from socialist humanitarian values and practices. The pilots are encouraged to share the stories of their arrests, their treatment in prison, and the medical attention they received, and to reflect on how such actions contradicted their anticommunist training. One POW responds with surprise that they had not been killed, and suggests such an outcome if the tables had turned and the United States had been bombed. Another refers to his treatment as "fair," to which the narrator replies:

> Lieutenant, you are experiencing in practice an example of socialist humanity … [P]eople here are capable of differentiating between real criminals who hold the decisive positions in government, and their tools who carry out their plans. You are enjoying more or less the

advantages of this socialist concept which does not absolve you of guilt or minimize your actions, but does differentiate in each case between the initiators of a policy and their mere lackeys.

With these words, H&S reveal the "banality of evil" as one of the underlying themes of the series.[12] Contrary to popular assumptions, the POWs were not murderous brutes, but mundane, if not morally flawed, men who accepted uncritically the basic premises of the war state and the division of military labor.

Not surprisingly, US officials disparaged the film, calling it "East German propaganda." Yet, as Nora Alter has argued, despite obvious ideological and political inclinations, the tactical way in which the film crew directed the questions largely allowed the POWs to "speak for themselves" in order to "expose more or less [their] unconscious and ideological contradictions, motivations, and legitimations" (1997, 54). The result is an ambiguous figuration of the US POW that communicates a contradictory message to viewers, at once highly critical and yet strangely empathetic. Through their personal stories and struggles to endure imprisonment in the DRV, the figure of the perpetrator emerges as a broken and tormented human being, neutralized and – like the Vietnamese – victimized by the US military. The radical Otherness of the pilots is thus reduced to common vulnerabilities that mark the human condition and are shared across the spectrum of humanity.

In Part 1 of *Pilots in Pajamas*, entitled "Yes Sir," viewers are introduced to the ten POWs imprisoned at the Hanoi Hilton who agreed to talk with H&S (only two refused, they claim). After reciting their names, ranks, and military identification numbers, they are asked to recall the actions and deliberations that led to the split decision to eject from their aircraft and parachute into enemy territory. What were your first thoughts when you hit the ground? What did you expect would happen to you? Who did you first see? What happened next? "I was handled well," one POW replied flatly. "I thought the villagers would shoot me, and was shocked that they didn't," another answered. Yet another man responded that, to his surprise, it was a woman who had arrested him. He smirks uncomfortably. The film then cuts to a scene of a white, injured American pilot surrendering to a Vietnamese woman. Like the photograph of Nguyễn Thị Kim Lai apprehending William Robinson, corporeal difference and radical Otherness are emphasized. The camera lingers on the scene and follows the pair along a path through the rice fields: a confused and apprehensive US pilot limping in front of a female youth volunteer who assertively

---

12 It is perhaps not a coincidence that Hannah Arendt (1963) coined this phrase only five years earlier in her controversial work, *Eichmann in Jerusalem*.

nudges him along with her rifle. Such scenes form a common motif in the *Pilots in Pajamas* series. H&S appear particularly drawn to the gendered dynamics of such stories, so much that the interviewer returns to this memory to ask the pilot if the gender of his captor influenced his decision *not* to use his weapon as stipulated in the Code of Conduct: "Was it an act of chivalry that led you to not defend yourself against a woman?" The pilot smirks again. He plays with the towel in his hand and answers that he did not have time to shoot and that it would have been useless anyway, shifting the focus away from the role that gender played in his capture.

For H&S, gender difference and other contrasts embodied in these iconic representations are acutely significant and rich in symbolic meaning. The poor, native, technologically inferior female stands in for both the Vietnamese nation and for socialism; her capture of the enemy Other suggests the triumph of socialist humanity and moral integrity over capitalist malevolence. Like the figure of the child, the Vietnamese woman is also figured as "an embodiment of basic human goodness" (Malkki 2010, 60), who is more likely to care for others than to kill them. H&S temper the image of the assertive militarized female with footage of women engaged in affective labor, such as nursing the wounds of confused and injured prisoners and offering them basic provisions. The pilots also note these benevolent acts (and, predictably, do not mention the abuse and mistreatment to which they had also been subjected). "We are well taken care of," they repeat, presenting to viewers a romanticized image of a hospitable rather than hostile nation, where natives are gentle, peace-loving and forgiving, and treat invaders like guests rather than adversaries.[13] H&S refer to such conduct as embodying the core tenets and values of socialist humanism. Some of the pilots nod in agreement. They had been trained to despise communists and to expect cruel torture and a painful death if captured, we are told. "You have been taught that communists are lesser human beings?" the interviewer asks at one point. A pilot concurs: "Yes, most in the United States have this anticommunist concept."

Pilots in Pajamas presents a seemingly empathetic portrait of the American POWs incarcerated in the Hanoi Hilton. The use of "imaginative empathy" as a cinematic device to frame cosmopolitan memory encourages viewers to identify with and "recognize the Other's human complexity" (Gavriely-Nuri and Lachover 2012, 58). In their efforts to explore the psychological depths of the pilots' inhumane acts, H&S end up reaffirming the very humanity of the men. They are presented as ordinary and essentially decent human beings: they are cooperative,

---

13 In the French-produced film, *Prisoners in the Hanoi-Hilton* (1992), General Nguyễn Văn Phương refers to the pilots as "uninvited guests" who were well-educated and psychologically prepared to drop bombs "without knowing what was happening below." The film centers on interviews with former POWs as they view socialist footage of their imprisonment for the first time.

polite and respectful of the film crew (answering questions with "Yes, sir"); they are homesick and miss their families; and – most interesting to H&S – they are full of contradictions and moral uncertainty. This ambiguous figuration draws upon the socialist distinction that H&S raised between governments that initiate wars and the people ordered to fight them. The POW is thus cast in a dual role as both perpetrator and victim of US imperialism, fundamentally "Other" in his guilt, and yet seemingly familiar in his victimhood. In Part 2, "Hilton Hanoi," H&S attempt to complicate notions of guilt and accountability, a subject they continue to explore in Part 3, "The Job." Are the soldiers culpable, H&S ask, or are they mere lackeys in a larger imperial agenda that cares little for those who carry out the work of empire? The POWs contemplate their roles in the devastation they have wrought upon the country and begin to break down on camera. "Do you think of your own children when you see the deaths of Vietnamese children?" the narrator asks. One man nods his head. "Do Vietnamese children have less human value than American children?" No, he quietly answers. As the pilots reflect on their struggles to cope with the death and destruction they have caused, they stumble and begin to reverse their positions. They were "just carrying out a job," but it is a job that carries a heavy emotional burden. "We were only following orders," one POW rationalizes. In their attempt to grasp the complexities of war and the beliefs and convictions of those who carry it out, H&S recast the POWs as unlikely victims – not of Vietnamese brutality as portrayed in the West, but of the machinations of an imperial war waged against an innocent nation. In recognizing this duality and ambiguity, the Vietnamese people, the film suggests, are able to treat the pilots humanely, rather than seek revenge. In turn, the pilots are shown as gradually coming to terms with the very humanity of their enemy, who have proven through their non-retaliatory acts that they are not "lesser human beings" as the pilots had been taught.

Conclusion: toward a cosmopolitan post/socialist memory of Vietnam

In their influential article, Daniel Levy and Natan Sznaider identify the process whereby lived experiences and memories of violence and trauma are incorporated into a global discourse as "cosmopolitan." Cosmopolitan memory, they argue, transcends ethnic and national boundaries to recognize the history and humanity of the Other (2002, 88). It does not supplant national memory so much as reconfigure it, expanding the horizons to become a more complex entity that fosters universal humanist values (Gavriely-Nuri and Lachover 2012, 54). Similarly, the above case studies of GDR and Cuban films reveal a specific Cold War scopic regime of cosmopolitan memory that took shape in what was then a bifurcated world. Memories of the violence in Vietnam were multidirectional (Rothberg 2009) and traveled widely within the socialist bloc; local Vietnamese experiences were taken up as global socialist concerns, and were subsequently localized in other communities to produce new affective solidarities. In the process, these memories were appropriated and embedded in new national contexts, and put to different use transnationally. While it can be argued that socialist cinematic memory of the war was already extra-territorial, even before contemporary capitalist globalization, GDR and Cuban films on Vietnam were also intended to showcase national achievements. Álvarez drew upon his country's own political history and rich literary tradition of poetry as the basis for his cinematic technique and the content of his documentaries. In the GDR, films on Vietnam were as much about the state's efforts to carve out a place of power in the Eastern Bloc, as they were expressions of genuine solidarity. Documentaries showed GDR aid to and citizens' support of Vietnam, reaffirming economic and technological superiority. Thus, the subject of *400 c.c.* was more the benevolence and moral rectitude of the German people who donated blood and applied modern science to the cause of anti-imperialism than it was about the war. In both cases, the *cosmopolitanization* of cinematic memory was nation-specific as well as nation-transcending (Levy and Sznaider 2002, 92), and came to define "Cuban" and "East German" cinema and memory of Vietnam as much as it defined "Vietnam" to a global audience.

To be sure, memory of the war in Vietnam has never been strictly confined to the nation, nor 'owned' by Vietnam; it has always been global, mobile, and mediated. In the capitalist West, the Vietnam War also played out on a global stage to produce another regime of transnational memory that was dominated by US media. One could argue, then, that socialist international memory of Vietnam was but one form of cosmopolitan memory culture during the Cold War, one that circulated almost exclusively beyond the 'Iron Curtain' and often conflicted with memory in the West. This is not to argue that socialist memory was more inclusive or radical in its critique. On the contrary, while it affirmed certain humanist tenets, it deviated from others; for example, it showed no willingness to critically reflect on and redress wartime injustices committed by the DRV. Nonetheless, even though the memory of POW maltreatment was forgotten and excluded from *Pilots in Pajamas*, it did provide a comparatively humanist representation of the prisoners to underscore both the tragedy and complexity of war. In addition, like in contemporary global rights discourses, the figure of the child in socialist film also came to stand in for a universal humanity, though here the children of socialism were typically less abstracted than in liberal media, and shown with more agency and personhood.

The end of the Cold War brought new opportunities for socialist memory. Rather than disappear, cultural productions of the war traveled in new directions and across once-forbidden terrains to give shape to an emerging cosmopolitan post-Cold War memory. Today, socialist films and documentaries have found new markets of distribution and consumption, endowing such work with additional historical (and also economic) value and meaning. The cross-fertilization of memories that rarely intersected before the collapse of the Soviet Union has now rekindled critical debate and dialogue about the war. Thomas Billhardt's work caught the eye of filmmakers from western Germany who, in *Eislimonade für Hong Li* (Ice Lemonade for Hong Li, 2000), document the photographer's return to Hanoi in 1999 to reunite with the subjects of his photographs. In an interview, Hải Ninh, the director of *Em Bé Hà Nội*, discusses the renewed life and expanding market for his commemorative film in the United States and Japan (Thu 2007). Likewise, GDR filmmakers have enjoyed a revival of interest in their films in the United States and have been invited to speak to American audiences. Even *Pilots in Pajamas* became popular in the weeks leading up to the 2008 Obama-McCain election as US television networks and press agencies rushed to publish stories on American POWs in Vietnam.[14]

What have been the consequences of these now intersecting and co-constitutive memory cultures? Have they produced a more inclusive and accommodating postnational memory of the war? Or have they reinscribed ideological and historical difference along former Cold War lines? The resurgence of John McCain's torture claims during his presidential campaign, and the national outrage it provoked in Vietnam, demonstrates that cosmopolitan memory is still fraught with tension and conflict. Yet, as Levy and Sznaider have argued, "these transnational memory cultures … have the potential to become the cultural foundation for global human rights politics" (2002, 88). This can be seen in the POW torture vs. compassionate care debate, which provoked a critical discussion of the humane treatment of prisoners, with McCain himself – drawing on his own experiences – publically condemning CIA "enhanced interrogation techniques" as torture. Cosmopolitan post-Cold War memory may be far from 'democratic' in the fullest sense of the term, as notable silences and conflicting accounts of the past remain. Yet, given that all memories are situated and all truths are but partial, it is perhaps less important to identify which memory and figuration of humanity is the most legitimate, than to recognize the force of the debate and the existence of shared values which most people agree are important to follow and defend.

---

14 ABC News, for example, rush ordered the series from the library at University of California, Riverside, one of the few institutions in the United States to house the four-part documentary.

References

79 Primaveras [79 Springtimes]. Dir. Santiago Álvarez. Instituto Cubano del Arte e Industrias Cinematográficos, 1969.

400 c.c. Dirs. Walter Heynowski and Gerhard Scheumann. Studio H&S Berlin (GDR), 1966.

Abril de Viet Nam en el año del gato [April in Vietnam in the Year of the Cat]. Dir. Santiago Álvarez. Instituto Cubano del Arte e Industrias Cinematográficos, 1975.

Am Wassergraben [At the Ditch]. Dirs. Walter Heynowski and Gerhard Scheumann. Studio H&S Berlin (GDR), 1978.

Allen, Lori A. "Martyr Bodies in the Media: Human Rights, Aesthetics, and the Politics of Immediation in the Palestinian Intifada." *American Ethnologist* 36.1 (2009): 161–180.

Alneng, Victor. "'What the Fuck is a Vietnam?' Touristic Phantasms and the Popcolonization of (the) Vietnam (War)." *Critique of Anthropology* 22.4 (2002): 495–523.

Alter, Nora M. "Excessive Pre/Requisites: Vietnam through the East German Lens." *Cultural Critique* 35.1 (1997): 39–79.

Arendt, Hannah. *Eichmann in Jerusalem: A Report on the Banality of Evil.* New York: Viking Press, 1963.

Baudrillard. Jean. *The Gulf War Did Not Take Place.* Bloomington: Indiana UP, 1995.

Chanan, Michael. *Cuban Cinema.* Minneapolis: University of Minnesota Press, 2004.

Deer Hunter. Dir. Michael Cimino. Universal Pictures, 1978.

Denkt an mein Land [Remember My Country]. Dir. Peter Ulbrich. DEFA-Studio für Dokumentarfilme (GDR), 1965.

Die eiserne Festung [The Iron Fortress]. Dirs. Walter Heynowski and Gerhard Scheumann. Studio H&S Berlin (GDR), 1977.

Die fernen Freunde nah [A Visit from Vietnamese Friends]. Dirs. Walter Heynowski and Gerhard Scheumann. Studio H&S Berlin (GDR), 1979.

Die Söhne der Thai [Sons of the Thai]. Dir. Gitta Nickel. DEFA-Studio für Dokumentarfilme (GDR), 1973.

Dittmar, Linda and Gene Michaud, eds. *From Hanoi to Hollywood: The Vietnam War in American Film.* London: Rutgers, 2000.

Dschungelzeit – Những Mảnh Đời Rừng [Time in the Jungle]. Dirs. Jörg Foth and Trần Vũ. DEFA-Studio für Spielfilme with Hãng Phim Truyện Việt Nam, 1987.

Eintritt kostenlos [Free Admission]. Dirs. Walter Heynowski and Gerhard Scheumann. Studio H&S Berlin (GDR), 1976.

Eislimonade für Hong Li [Ice Lemonade for Hong Li]. Dirs. Dietmar Ratsch and Arek Gielnik. Filmakademie Ludwigsburg/Filmpool, 2000.

Em Bé Hà Nội [Little Girl of Hanoi]. Dir. Hải Ninh. Hãng Phim Truyện Việt Nam, 1974.

Feldman, Allen. "On Cultural Anesthesia: From Desert Storm to Rodney King." *American Ethnologist* 21.2 (1994): 404–418.

Franklin, H. Bruce. *M.I.A. or Mythmaking in America: How and Why Belief in Live POWs Has Possessed a Nation.* New Brunswick: Rutgers UP, 1993.

Gandhi, Leela. *Affective Communities: Anticolonial Thought, Fin-de-Siècle Radicalism, and the Politics of Friendship.* Durham: Duke UP, 2006.

Gavriely-Nuri, Dalia and Einat Lachover. "Reframing the Past as a Cosmopolitan Memory: Obituaries in the Israeli Daily." *Communication Theory* 22.1 (2012): 48–65.

Gruner, Elliott. *Prisoners of Culture: Representing the Vietnam POW*. New Brunswick: Rutgers UP, 1993.

Hagopian, Patrick. *The Vietnam War in American Memory: Veterans, Memorials, and the Politics of Healing*. Boston: University of Massachusetts Press, 2009.

Hanoi, Martes 13 [Hanoi, Tuesday the 13th]. Dir. Santiago Álvarez. Instituto Cubano del Arte e Industrias Cinematográficos, 1967.

Hariman, Robert and John Louis Lucaites. *No Caption Needed: Iconic Photographs, Public Culture, and Liberal Democracy*. Chicago: University of Chicago Press, 2007.

Hawley, Thomas M. *The Remains of War: Bodies, Politics, and the Search for American Soldiers Unaccounted for in Southeast Asia*. Durham: Duke UP, 2005.

Hoskins, Andrew. *Televising War: From Vietnam to Iraq*. New York: Continuum, 2004.

Ihr fragt, wie wir leben [You Ask How We Live]. Dir. Peter Ulbrich. DEFA-Studio für Dokumentarfilme (GDR), 1967.

Jeffords, Susan. *The Remasculinization of America: Gender and the Vietnam War*. Bloomington: Indiana UP, 1989.

Levy Daniel and Natan Sznaider. "Memory Unbound: The Holocaust and the Formation of Cosmopolitan Memory." *European Journal of Social Theory* 5.1 (2002): 87–106.

Levy Daniel and Natan Sznaider. *Human Rights and Memory*. University Park: Penn State UP, 2010.

Louvre, Alf and Jeffrey Walsh, eds. *Tell Me Lies About Vietnam: Cultural Battles for the Meaning of the War*. Philadelphia: Open UP, 1988.

Malkki, Liisa. "Speechless Emissaries: Refugees, Humanitarianism, and Dehistoricization." *Cultural Anthropology* 11.3 (1996): 377–404.

Malkki, Liisa. "Children, Humanity, and the Infantilization of Peace." *In the Name of Humanity: The Government of Threat and Care*. Eds. Ilana Feldman and Miriam Ticktin. Durham: Duke UP, 2010. 58–85.

Marcuse, Herbert. "Socialist Humanism?" In *Socialist Humanism: An International Symposium*. Ed. Erich Fromm. New York: Anchor Books, 1965. 106–117.

Martini, Edwin A. *Invisible Enemies: The American War on Vietnam, 1975–2000*. Amherst: University of Massachusetts Press, 2007.

Michel, Robert. *Studio H&S: Die Filme 1965–1978*. Berlin: VOB, 1979.

Nichols, Bill. *Representing Reality: Issues and Concepts in Documentary*. Bloomington: Indiana UP, 1991.

Piloten im Pyjama [Pilots in Pajamas]. Dirs. Walter Heynowski and Gerhard Scheumann. Studio H&S Berlin (GDR), 1968.

Pitcher, M. Anne and Kelly Askew. "African Socialisms and Postsocialisms." *Africa* 76.1 (2006): 1–14.

Prisoners in the Hanoi-Hilton. Dir. Bill Kurtis. Daniel Roussel Productions, 1992.

Rambo: First Blood Part 2. Dir. George P. Cosmatos. Tristar Pictures, 1985.

Report für Katrin [Report for Katrin]. Dir. Harry Hornig. DEFA-Studio für Dokumentarfilme (GDR), 1970.

Renan, Ernest. "What is a Nation?" 1882. *Nation and Narration*. Ed. Homi K. Bhabha. New York: Routledge, 1990. 8–22.

Roth, Moira. "Obdurate History: Dinh Q. Lê, the Vietnam War, Photography, and Memory." *Art Journal* 60.2 (2001): 38–53.

Rothberg, Michael. *Multidirectional Memory: Remembering the Holocaust in the Age of Decolonization*. Stanford: Stanford UP, 2009.

Rowe, John Carlos and Rick Berg, eds. *The Vietnam War and American Culture*. New York: Columbia UP, 1991.

Schwenkel, Christina. "Recombinant History: Transnational Practices of Memory and Knowledge Production in Contemporary Vietnam." *Cultural Anthropology* 21.1 (2006): 3–30.

Schwenkel, Christina. "Exhibiting War, Reconciling Pasts: Journalistic Modes of Representation and Transnational Commemoration in Contemporary Vietnam." *Journal of Vietnamese Studies* 3.1 (2008): 36–77.

Schwenkel, Christina. *The American War in Contemporary Vietnam: Transnational Remembrance and Representation*. Bloomington: Indiana UP, 2009a.

Schwenkel, Christina. "'The Camera was Our Weapon': News Production and Representation of War in Vietnam." *The Anthropology of News and Journalism: Global Perspectives*. Ed. Elizabeth Bird. Bloomington: Indiana UP, 2009b. 86–99.

Schwenkel Christina. "From John McCain to Abu Ghraib: Tortured Bodies and Historical Unaccountability of US Empire in Vietnam." *American Anthropologist* 111.1 (2009c): 30–42.

Stephens, Sharon. "Introduction: Children and the Politics of Culture in 'Late Capitalism'." *Children and the Politics of Culture*. Ed. Sharon Stephens. Princeton: Princeton UP, 1995. 3–48.

Stephens, Sharon. "Reflections on Environmental Justice: Children as Victims and Actors." *Social Justice* 23.4 (1996): 62–86.

Stephens, Sharon. "Nationalism, Nuclear Policy, and Children in Cold War America." *Childhood* 4.1 (1997): 103–123.

Steinmetz, Rüdiger. "Heynowski & Scheumann: The GDR's Leading Documentary Film Team." *Historical Journal of Film, Radio and Television* 24.3 (2004): 366–378.

Stur, Heather Marie. *Beyond Combat: Women and Gender in the Vietnam War Era*. Cambridge: Cambridge UP, 2011.

Sturken, Marita. *Tangled Memories: The Vietnam War, the AIDS Epidemic, and the Politics of Remembering*. Berkeley: University of California Press, 1997.

Taylor, Nora. *Painters in Hanoi: An Ethnography of Vietnamese Art*. Honolulu: University of Hawaii Press, 2004.

Thu, Nguyên. "Đạo diễn Hải Ninh nhớ "Em bé Hà Nội" [Director Hải Ninh Remembers "Little Girl of Hanoi."]. *Dân Trí*, 18 March 2007.

Tọa độ chết – Координаты смерти [Coordinates of Death]. Dirs. Samvel Gasparov and Nguyễn Xuân Chân. Gorky Film Studio with Hãng Phim Truyện Việt Nam, 1985.

Todorov, Vladislav. *Red Square, Black Square: Organon for Revolutionary Imagination*. Albany: SUNY Press, 1995.

Trần Kim Thành. "Hội thảo Điện ảnh Quốc tế về Chiến tranh – Hoà bình" [International Film Conference on War and Peace]. *Nghệ thuật Điện ảnh* [Cinematic Arts] 1.57 (1987): 33–35.

Uncommon Valor. Dir. Ted Kotcheff. Paramount Pictures, 1983.

Part III: **Scales**

Chiara De Cesari
World Heritage and the Nation-State: A View from Palestine

The universalizing project of World Heritage aims to transcend the heritage logic of the nation-state, particularly so after its more recent reforms that emphasize the role of the grassroots and of cultural diversity.[1] The objective of this UNESCO program is to identify, help preserve, and promote sites and monuments deemed to be of universal significance – i.e. relevant beyond the borders of the states within which they are located – which are to constitute the elements of a shared memory of humanity able to foster a global sense of human commonality and intellectual solidarity.[2] In opposition to UNESCO's self-image, in this essay I show how World Heritage not only builds upon the tradition of national heritages but in fact reproduces, amplifies, and expands this tradition's logic and infrastructure, not always but often at the expense of the grassroots. Moreover, I highlight the unsuspected entanglement of World Heritage and national sovereignty, and the paradoxical ways in which the transnational memory articulated by the World Heritage discourse tends to reinscribe sites into a national logic and spatial imagination.

To this end, I explore World Heritage through a double ethnographic and textual lens. I begin discussing the pragmatics of World Heritage at work in Palestine/Israel, a locale which might seem peculiar but will help illuminate several structural features and gaps of this discourse. I then proceed to analyze the key policies that regulate UNESCO's heritage work. These include the 1972 World Heritage Convention but also more recent reforms that attempt to address the Eurocentric biases of the chief representational device of World Heritage, the World Heritage List (hereafter, 'the List'). I will argue that World Heritage has

---

[1] Earlier versions of this essay appeared as "World Heritage and Mosaic Universalim: A View from Palestine," *Journal of Social Archaeology* 10.3 (2010): 299–324, and as blogpost on the *Leiden-Stanford Heritage Network*, 6 December 2011, available at www.networkedheritage.org/2011/12/06/world-heritage-and-national-sovereignty-on-palestine{%}E2{%}80{%}99s-unesco-bid/ (accessed 21 March 2014). I would like to thank the *Journal of Social Archaeology* for granting permission to re-use parts of my old essay.

[2] Disentangling memory and heritage tends to be a fruitless endeavor (Wilson 2009, 378) for much more can be extrapolated from their productive intersections. However, for the sake of clarity, I usually distinguish heritage as a specific, materially-mediated, rather institutionalized and hegemonic form of memory.

been shaped by contemporary political discourses centered on the negotiation and management of cultural diversity, from assimilation to multiculturalism. Building on theories of the politics of recognition, I will examine the ways in which UNESCO's multicultural policies tend to reproduce Eurocentric patterns and hierarchies between reified heritages and cultures. Finally, I will consider how the structural relationship between World Heritage and the nation-state, inscribed as it is in UNESCO's constitution and its documents, can prevent broader democratic participation in the heritage process.

The battle for World Heritage in Palestine

On 31 October 2011, UNESCO's general conference voted to admit Palestine as a member state by a large majority. One hundred and seventy countries voted in favor, 14 voted against (including the US, Israel, Germany, Canada, and Australia) and 52 abstained. Soon afterwards, the US and Israel, who had strongly opposed this move, announced their 'retaliation' against both UNESCO and Palestine. The US immediately halted its UNESCO contributions, throwing the organization into chaos and forcing a revision of its overall budget.[3] Israel, on the other hand, not only withheld its UNESCO contribution but immediately punished the Palestinian Authority (PA), announcing the construction of 2,000 more housing units in its West Bank and East Jerusalem settlements, as well as halting the transfer of the tax revenues it collects (being in control of all West Bank external borders) on behalf of the PA. What was the reason for these ostensibly disproportionate reactions? On paper, the main consequence of UNESCO's recognition of Palestine as a member state consisted in its opening up the possibility for Palestinians to request their most significant heritage sites to be considered for inscription on the World Heritage List. In the following, I argue that the clash over Palestinian UNESCO membership tells us something about the multifaceted relationship between World Heritage and national sovereignty.

"The State of Palestine finally exists:" this was the incipit of Lebanon's *Daily Star* editorial the day after the general conference vote, rightly emphasizing the symbolic politics of the Palestinian move (It's about Time 2011). The article was referring to a particular kind of 'existence,' for few believed that the UNESCO mem-

---

3 Note that the US contributed at that time ca. 22% of UNESCO's budget, and that this contribution was supposedly considered a strategic asset in the context of the new multilateral policies of the Obama administration reversing a decades long American hostility toward the UN cultural body.

bership was going to change much in terms of realities on the ground. Indeed, membership itself did not change the essentially patchworked and very limited sovereignty of the PA. This interim governing body was created by the Oslo Accords in the 1990s to administer the areas of the West Bank and Gaza from which Israel had withdrawn. Due to the failure of the so-called peace process, however, the PA never developed into an independent, viable state. In this context, the UNESCO bid was part of a wider Palestinian campaign to obtain full international recognition as a state within the UN system, of which the overwhelming vote of the General Assembly in November 2012 to recognize Palestine within the 1967 borders as a non-member state with observer status probably represents the most significant moment. For Israel, the campaign constitutes a rejection of the path of negotiation. However, for Palestinians, it is precisely a response to the failure of over 20 years of US-brokered negotiations with Israel. This time span has seen the population of the Israeli colonies built inside the Palestinian territories occupied in 1967 double (they now number well over 500,000 people), and the settlements, which are illegal under international law and constitute in the eyes of many the main obstacle on the way to achieving a two-state solution to the Israeli-Palestinian conflict, are greatly expanding.[4] As a response to this Israeli policy of creating facts on the ground, the Palestinian leadership decided to move its battle to the UN, considered to be a more impartial setting, calling for a larger involvement of the international community as a whole. It also decided to move the battle to the symbolic level, by seeking formal, international recognition of sovereignty before effective control of the territories. This is a strategy I have called elsewhere *anticipatory representation*, to refer to the calling into being, through national representation, of national institutions that do not yet fully exist (De Cesari 2012).

Apparently, then, Palestinian UNESCO membership has nothing to do with real sovereignty on the ground. While this opens up accession to a number of other UN bodies, it is fundamentally a symbolic victory – the culmination of a long history of international recognitions of Palestinian national rights grounded in the fundamental commitment of the UN to the right of nations to self-determination. Yet several Palestinian commentators, including Nabil Shaath, a senior Fatah figure long in charge of foreign relations, have emphasized the importance of UNESCO membership because it will "further empower us [Palestinians] to protect our cultural, historical, and religious sites from Israel's continuous illegal exploitation and attack" (Shaath 2011). Indeed, World Heritage status might give

---

4 For background and statistics related to the settlements, see the website of the Foundation for Middle East Peace at www.fmep.org/settlement_info/settlement-info-and-tables/stats-data/comprehensive-settlement-population-1972-2006 (accessed 25 March 2014).

Palestinians more control over parts of their land and a new weapon in their battle against the occupation.

In line with the international image it wants to promote of itself, the Palestinian Authority decided to put forward Bethlehem's Church of the Nativity as the first site to be nominated for the World Heritage List; the Church as "birthplace of Jesus" was then inscribed in 2012. This decision, however, was not at all without opponents within Palestine. Local organizations and NGOs had preferred the early candidacy of other Palestinian heritage sites, which are currently under intense pressure from the occupation and need urgent protection. One such case is the Old City of Hebron, an important historic city partly occupied by Israeli settlers. Yet, the nomination file that caused the most frictions between the PA and local organizations is the proposal to inscribe on the World Heritage List the cultural landscape of Battir near Bethlehem,[5] which, after long delays, the Authority ended up submitting under an emergency procedure only right before the closing annual deadline in January 2014. The PA had stopped Battir's nomination procedure also because of informal agreements with the US and Israel in the attempt to get back to the negotiating table.[6]

Battir is a West Bank village that has remarkably managed to preserve a unique evolving landscape and irrigated farming system dating back to the Roman period. This cultural landscape and the village's inhabitants are threatened by the construction of the so-called separation wall, which Israel is building allegedly to separate Israelis from Palestinians. In reality, however, it runs for the most part deep into the West Bank, and has thus been the object of worldwide criticism as, among other things, a disguised form of territorial annexation.[7] The wall, as it is currently planned, would not only cause grave damage to the heritage of Battir, but also mean the loss of large tracts of land for the Palestinian villagers, who appealed to the Israeli High Court of Justice to stop its construction.[8]

---

5 I have discussed the story of Battir and World Heritage in Palestine during multiple interviews and conversations with UNESCO personnel and local organizations, particularly in January 2012 and November 2013; see also Lazaroff (2014) and Ravid (2014).

6 For background to these informal agreements, see the entries in the previous footnote as well as www.palestinemonitor.org/details.php?id=hxk79ma4466y6bjq4eqcl (accessed 11 March 2014).

7 The fact that the wall is not being built along the Green Line, i.e. the internationally recognized border between Israel and the West Bank, constituted the main reason why it was deemed illegal under international law, according to the advisory opinion given in 2004 by the International Court of Justice, the principal judicial organ of the UN, see www.btselem.org/topic/separation_barrier (accessed 11 March 2014).

8 For a list of background documents related to the High Court's Battir petitions, see the website of the Friends of the Earth Middle East foeme.org/www/?module=events{&}record_id=121 (accessed 11 March 2014).

While they had long awaited the PA's decision to submit Battir's nomination, the villagers found a number of unlikely allies in court: not only Israeli environmentalists but even the Israeli Nature and Parks Authority itself.[9] While this book is going into print, both decisions on Battir – by the World Heritage Committee and by the High Court – are still pending. But there is no doubt that the achievement of World Heritage status would have a key impact on the judicial procedure. At that point it will become clear that while World Heritage weaves the story of a heritage site into a transnational memory narrative that ostensibly cuts across and overcomes the borders of the state in which it is located, in fact it is helping to refigure state sovereignty in unexpected ways.

A World Heritage in the making

Until the 1990s, the occupied status of the Palestinian territories had made the inscription of West Bank and Gaza sites on the World Heritage List technically impossible. Indeed, only officially recognized states parties to UNESCO and the World Heritage Convention can initiate the procedure for sites located in their territories. The Old City of Jerusalem – annexed illegally by Israel post-1967 – was the only one in the area to have been inscribed on the List, following a contested Jordanian nomination in the 1980s. However, with the Oslo Accords and the establishment of a 'proto-state' in the form of the PA, the road to World Heritage status seemed closer, and a UNESCO office opened in Ramallah in 1997. Due to Israel's opposition, and its frequent accusations of "politicization" aimed at UNESCO, the Palestinian UNESCO office's mandate did not include East Jerusalem, where heritage initiatives are limited and usually managed from the organization's Paris headquarters: for Palestinians and other critics this is a clear symptom of the limits of UNESCO's enforcement power and of its ultimate weakness in front of powerful nation-states (see Dumper and Larkin 2012). After the Israeli reoccupation of the major Palestinian cities in 2002 and the ensuing widespread destruction of cultural properties – with snipers targeting Bethlehem's Nativity Church becoming the iconic image of such destruction – UNESCO decided to empower the

---

9 The Israeli High Court case of Battir is peculiar in other ways. Indeed, here petitioners do not "seek to improve the wall along the least invasive path, but, rather, for the first time in this forum, to claim for its impossibility *tout court*;" moreover, "the case is not brought about on behalf of human rights at all (claims on behalf of these rights stopped having any meaning in this area), but rather in the name of the rights of the environment, of nature and of heritage" (www.forensic-architecture.org/investigations/the-landscape-of-battir-vs-the-state-of-israel-2/, accessed 11 March 2014).

cultural desk of its Ramallah office as well as the Palestinian Department of Antiquities and Cultural Heritage (DACH). It therefore made funds available to compile a so-called "tentative list" to pave the way for the protection of selected Palestinian heritage sites. There was controversy over what the Palestinian tentative list was to be called, due to Israel's sensitivity on the issue (the non-specific phrasing "Inventory of ... Heritage Sites of Potential Outstanding Universal Value in Palestine" was ultimately decided on instead), and this is itself a barometer of how UN jargon has the potential to invest actors with the mantle of sovereignty. However, despite their tentative list being completed in 2005 (DACH 2005), Palestinians could not submit nominations for years, until they achieved UNESCO membership.

Since the early 2000s, UNESCO has been very active in Palestine – mostly in the West Bank, since Gaza and Jerusalem are rather out of reach – with the express objective of helping to save a transnational heritage of tremendous relevance. While conducting fieldwork in the West Bank to study the politics of Palestinian heritage and memory, I have followed the work of UNESCO from the mid-2000s onwards. One of the agency's projects that I have monitored quite consistently across the years is the so-called "cultural routes project," which I will offer here as an example of World Heritage in the making. Cultural routes and cultural landscapes represent two relatively new categories of cultural property that entered the World Heritage vocabulary in the 1990s, as part of a broader UNESCO move towards multicultural policies. As multicultural property, testimony to former globalizations and the proper heritage for our interconnected times, cultural routes seemed ideal for Palestine. Not only for being true to the rich interconnected past of a region known as the crossroads of civilisations but also, in particular, because this concept promises a heritage of peace, a symbolic overcoming of ethno-national and religious boundaries. In the words of its Palestinian promoters, the concept is an opening of new "horizons" of interactions and a "reinforcing [of] mutual cooperation and understanding among regions of the Mediterranean."[10] An interdisciplinary task force had been set up by various PA ministries in cooperation with UNESCO Ramallah to work out a vision and a multi-sited pilot project targeting heritage rehabilitation and tourism development along a route yet to be defined. This was a very promising project in spite of the virtual absence of Palestinian civil society, which is usually very active in heritage matters (De Cesari 2010). Yet, uncannily, cultural routes have run into borders, checkpoints and walls, as well as the problem of state sovereignty.

---

10 My notes from the introduction to the cultural routes task force meeting, Ramallah, 2 March 2006.

Two contested matters dominated the cultural routes task force meetings I attended in the period 2005–2006. The first subject of contention concerned the focus of the project, that is, whether to make religion, and especially Christianity, the main theme of Palestinian cultural routes. The heightened christianization of the Holy Land heritage is a phenomenon that concerns not only Jordan (Maffi 2009), but Israel too, and that can be partly explained by escalating commodification and the key role played by Christian pilgrims in the regional economies (see Scham 2009). Yet it is also one of the legacies of a deeply-rooted history of colonial heritage privileging biblical and Christian sites as well as pre-Islamic archaeology. This legacy, in addition to the influential cultural role played by Palestinian Christians, shaped the Palestinian tentative list and the PA heritage politics.[11] Indeed, as mentioned earlier, Bethlehem was the first site to be nominated to the World Heritage List, against the will of multiple interest groups in Palestine. Having sites on the List constitutes an important trapping and symbol of nation-statehood, and guarantees a place within global taxonomies of cultural value (see Herzfeld 2004, 2005). These sites articulate a particular idea, very condensed, of the state they represent, and function as a nation-branding device. As Lynn Meskell has argued (2014), World Heritage comes with a highly prized "sign value" (237) attached to it, also because sites on the List "operate as transactional devices whereby cultural, and thus political, recognition both masks and enables a multifarious network of economic values" (224). It is in this highly politicized 'statist' global context that the representational politics of the PA has to be understood.

The second matter of contention among the members of the task force was the question whether or not to accept the realities of the 'walled' geography of Palestine. This clash culminated in another contested choice regarding the location of the route and the sites involved, namely, the exclusion of Jerusalem. How can tourists explore a landscape criss-crossed by an eight-meter high concrete wall and multiple other kinds of visible and invisible barriers? Realism and feasibility were the keywords of UNESCO's position. The organization favored a no-nonsense, pragmatic strategy aimed at "getting things done," and centered on two ideas: feasibility and the involvement of the private sector (the representatives of which, incidentally, almost never attended the meetings, thus showing their then limited hopes for the development of tourism). Attending to feasibility meant working on accessible and effectively PA-controlled segments of the

---

11 Among the first ten properties listed in the Palestinian tentative list, eight have a biblical connection and five of those have a strongly Christian significance, while the other two figure prominently in the history of Ancient Near Eastern Archaeology, see DACH (2005).

original trajectory between the northern West Bank and Gaza, the Israeli part being clearly unfeasible from the start. Concretely, prioritizing feasibility meant focusing only on Bethlehem and Jericho. The PA Antiquity Department's position, however, emphasized the principled territorial integrity of the West Bank, and their refusal to "work according to the occupation" by letting it determine the trajectories of cultural routes, especially in a future-oriented perspective. Between UNESCO's *Realpolitik* and the PA's acting *as if* Palestine were a sovereign state, fragmentation soon emerged as the main feature of Palestinian cultural routes, with a northern segment around several biblical archaeological sites and a central one around Bethlehem and Jericho, but without including "unfeasible" East Jerusalem. On the project map of the Jericho-Bethlehem trail Jerusalem had been simply cut out, reduced to an empty spot: cultural routes certainly do not cross checkpoints. Eventually, the project sank in the wake of the Western embargo that paralyzed the PA after Hamas' electoral victory in 2006.

Even though cultural routes represent a highly promising concept, particularly for imagining transnational memories, this heritage category is not used as much as it could and should be in our globalized world. What is the problem with UNESCO's multicultural policies? The Palestinian stories I have just discussed present a set of possible answers to this question. World Heritage is deeply tied to nation-state sovereignty, and it is nation-states (and nation-state authorized experts) that are constituted as the proper actors on the World Heritage stage. This is also why Israeli authorities are sensitive in this regard, and the titles given to technical reports are important. Constitutionally transnational, cultural routes defy this logic.

The idea of World Heritage

I would now like to consider UNESCO's rich textual production, which provides the vocabulary and grammar of the transnational heritage language. This language has deep roots in nationalist thought and practices (Abu El-Haj 2001; Handler 1985; Herzfeld 1991; Meskell 1998). At the intersection of nationalism and colonialism, a concept of heritage as the shared past of the nation-state developed in the course of the nineteenth and the twentieth centuries, along with the infrastructure required to manage it (see e.g. Choay 2001); and ever since it has had an important nation-building function (Anderson 1991). As part of the development of international institutions for the maintenance of peace, the idea of 'humanity's heritage' began to take shape in the interwar period, but was only to emerge fully after WWII (Labadi 2007b, esp. 26). Shaped by increasing concerns for the

disruptive effects of modernization, world heritage signified at that time international intellectual cooperation, the worldwide diffusion of knowledge and ('high')
culture, and the education of the 'masses' – all integral aspects of UNESCO's efforts in the cultivation of the "intellectual and moral solidarity of mankind" as the
key to building peace "in the minds of men," as stated in UNESCO's Constitution
(UNESCO 1945).

Prefigured in the 1954 Hague Convention (the Convention for the Protection
of Cultural Property in the Event of Armed Conflict) and first realized in a series
of international monument rescue initiatives led by UNESCO in the 1960s, World
Heritage was officially born with the Convention Concerning the Protection of the
World Cultural and Natural Heritage, adopted by the UNESCO General Conference
in 1972 (UNESCO 1972). The World Heritage Convention (WHC) states that some
cultural and natural heritage of "outstanding universal value" – this is a key concept – represents a "unique and irreplaceable property," which, "whilst fully respecting the sovereignty of the States on whose territory [the property] ... is situated," is to be considered "part of the world heritage of mankind" and "for whose
protection it is the duty of the international community as a whole to co-operate"
(Introduction and Article 6.1). The convention is the main legally-binding instrument for the conservation of world heritage for the sake of future generations. It
fundamentally defines what constitutes heritage of outstanding universal value,
which principles should be applied in its conservation, and who is authorized to
engage in this process. Furthermore, the Convention established the infrastructure necessary for its own implementation, including the constitution of the intergovernmental World Heritage Committee, in charge of producing and keeping up
to date the World Heritage List. The Convention's bylaws, the *Operational Guidelines for the Implementation of the World Heritage List*, have been periodically revised since then.

Several scholars, including UNESCO experts, have produced critical accounts
of the Convention, in particular of its Eurocentric approach to heritage conservation which produced a List, a representation of humanity's heritage, that is dominated by European monumental properties (e.g. Byrne 1991; Cleere 2001; Meskell
2002; Labadi 2007a). Critical heritage scholars have denounced World Heritage as
a "case of Western imperialism" (Byrne 1991, 272) because Western languages, values, and practices of the past, genealogically related to nationalist and capitalist
projects (Gamboni 2001), are subtly imposed at a global level as standard practices. World Heritage is rooted in the European heritage discourse and the science
of conservation, which, since the nineteenth century, has understood heritage as
a fetishized object of knowledge and aesthetic pleasure, endowed with historic,
artistic, and economic value at the expense of other values. Traditional understandings of what constitutes a historic monument and cultural property frame

heritage as a thing to be conserved "as found," and value authenticity of fabric (however this is defined) over, for instance, use and social significance (Smith 2006; Byrne 2009). Such a framing of heritage values and the selection criteria deriving from it produces an emphasis on certain kinds of heritage and therefore their concentration in specific areas of the world.

Use, re-use, and the preservation of the living significance of a place – principles of other, less materialistic modes of conservation (Byrne 1995) which are also key to Palestinian heritage organizations – are antithetical to a central idea of the European science of conservation, which focuses on physical authenticity. While the UNESCO notion of authenticity has been updated (UNESCO 1994b), conservation still privileges physical authenticity. In this way, it wrenches heritage objects from the everyday and the habitual to recontextualize them 'under the glass case;' structurally, the preferred function of significant sites is tourist display (Kirshenblatt-Gimblett 1998; 2006), rather than preservation for local communities. Therefore, and in spite of mounting calls to open up heritage to community participation, the world-heritagization of sites tends to hinder use, and in fact produces heightened surveillance, if not the outright freezing of habitual activities – as well as, often, gentrification (see e.g. Bissel 2005; Collins 2008). Often too, world-heritagization involves the bureaucratization and heavy regulation of life around the sites in question. These adverse effects of heritagization thus complicate the laudable mission that World Heritage tries to live up to.

The 'cultural property' language produces heritage not simply as a thing, but as a thing to be owned by specific actors, individuals or collectives like nations (see also Carman 2005; Rowlands 2002). According to Richard Handler (1985), it is nationalism (aided by anthropological knowledge) that discursively frames heritage and culture as properties, as that which a nation must *possess* in order to exist as such, because "we are a nation because we have a culture" (210). Property, in Western legal discourse, refers to "the (exclusive) right to the possession, use, or disposal of a thing,"[12] and implies the right to exclude others from the same. Heritagization crucially defines the legitimate stakeholders. Laurajane Smith has argued that the "Authorized Heritage Discourse" (2006), as she calls it, strictly circumscribes not only what heritage is and how to deal with it, but also who can execute it – namely, experts. She goes on to contend that this discourse reinforces national narratives and national identities. I argue more specifically that by establishing the nation-state as the main heritage stakeholder, the 1972 Convention in fact authorizes not only experts but also the nation-state and its representatives as the proper subjects of World Heritage. Other interested parties are

---

12 *Oxford English Dictionary*, s.v. "property" 4, www.oed.com (accessed 25 March 2014).

not only excluded by default, but silenced in the process. The UNESCO-sponsored Palestinian cultural routes task force I discussed above is a good example of the alliance between UNESCO and 'state' apparatuses to the disadvantage of, for instance, the local civil society. Although Palestinian local committees and NGOs play a key role in the preservation of the Palestinian past, they were left out of the meetings.

The reasons for the pre-eminence of the nation-state in the mechanism of World Heritage are manifold, and go beyond the nationalizing legacy of the heritage discourse. This pre-eminence is chiefly the product of the very structure of UNESCO as an intergovernmental agency. UNESCO has a specific mandate to work with governmental bodies, also because it believes it is right to promote institution-building in those contexts where state infrastructures are very weak. The idea grounding these policies is that there is no effective heritage protection without working national frameworks and policies, and that NGOs and grassroots organizations cannot be substitutes for a state because their action is limited temporally and spatially: this was the gist of UNESCO's defensive argument against Palestinian NGOs' critiques of their alliance with the PA 'state' agency.

Imagining transnational memories: from 'mankind' to multiculturalism

What imaginaries of the world are articulated in the different manifestations of the List? I argue that we can trace a shift in the ways in which World Heritage has represented transnational memory and the world through it. The early discourse of World Heritage voices the post-WWII hopes for solidarity and peace based on a new sense of human commonality and universal values. There is a parallelism between the early discourse of World Heritage and a political discourse which developed at the turn of the century but was still salient in the 1960s and 1970s: the melting pot. As a model of integration within the nation-state, the popular image of the melting pot, associated with the once hegemonic sociological theory of assimilation, was predicated upon the ideal of a blending of the diverse groups and communities living on the state's territory into a new, but homogeneous societal entity (see Hirschman 1983). In a popular textbook written by Robert Park, the founder of the modern sociology of race and ethnicity, assimilation is defined as "a process of interpenetration and fusion in which persons and groups acquire the memories, sentiments, and attitudes of other persons or groups, and, by sharing their experience and history, are incorporated with them in a common cultural life" (Park and Burgess 1969, 360, quoted in Hirschman 1983, 400). Developing solidarity and a common cultural life by sharing experience and history is also the cornerstone of UNESCO's project of building a common heritage of humanity. Yet, in both cases, the egalitarian imaginary of the crucible and the blend masked what was actually a process of cultural absorption on the part of dominant groups vis-à-vis weaker ones (see Gordon 1964). A form of what sociologists called "Anglo-conformity" and cultural assimilation can be detected in the ways in which the transnational language of heritage adopted a Eurocentric approach to the past, silencing 'other' heritages, as has been discussed in the previous section.

The 1990s marked a shift in UNESCO's discursive framing of culture. Although a concern for cultural diversity was already a fundamental part of its Constitution, it is only in the last decades that cultural matters have been couched in the specific language of multiculturalism, linking cultures in the plural with community development and democracy (for a discussion of the historical changes in UNESCO's approach to cultural diversity, see Stenou 2003; 2007). Epitomized by the report *Our Creative Diversity* (WCCD 1995), which laid the foundations for the 2001 UNESCO Universal Declaration on Cultural Diversity (UNESCO, 2001), this discursive move was arguably nourished by a broader political development: the shift from a politics of redistribution to a politics of recognition.

According to Minoo Moallem and Iain Boal, multiculturalism represents a "corrective" discourse to the crisis of liberal institutions, "an attempt by the liberal ideological apparatus to overcome the inadequacy of its existing institutions for the protection of freedom and cultural difference" (1999, 244–245). In other words, critics of liberalism view (mainstream) multiculturalism as the institutional response, articulated in a set of policies, to the growing visibility and political significance of a diverse array of social movements mobilized under identity banners such as gender, sexuality, 'race,' and ethnicity, which range from the women's movement to minority struggles and indigenous peoples' movements. Emphasizing cultural domination and social misrecognition as forms of oppression, what characterizes these movements is that they foreground claims for the recognition of cultural difference and group identity over claims for socio-economic redistribution: here culture is explicitly politicized (e.g. Taylor 1994; Kymlicka 1995; Fraser 1997; 2000). At the level of popular imaginaries, the language of recognition evokes an image of cultural difference that is the opposite of the melting pot: the mosaic. As a model, both of and for society, with a long history in the USA and Canada, institutional multiculturalism is predicated upon a mosaic of different cultures and ethnicities cohabiting the same space but retaining their distinctiveness.

Inhabiting a critical position from within, political philosopher Nancy Fraser has alerted us to the potential dangers of this change in the political master grammar, in that it not only risks concealing social politics and the key question of growing economic inequalities, but also producing essentialized, fixed, and monologic cultures and identities (see also Benhabib 2002; Povinelli 2002). She identifies two fundamental problems in the politics of recognition:

> We are facing, then, a new constellation in the grammar of political claims-making – and one that is disturbing on two counts. First, this move from redistribution to recognition is occurring despite – or because of – an acceleration of economic globalization, at a time when an aggressively expanding capitalism is radically exacerbating economic inequality. In this context, questions of recognition are serving less to supplement, complicate and enrich redistributive struggles than to marginalize, eclipse and displace them. I shall call this *the problem of displacement*. Second, today's recognition struggles are occurring at a moment of hugely increasing transcultural interaction and communication, when accelerated migration and global media flows are hybridizing and pluralizing cultural forms. Yet the routes such struggles take often serve not to promote respectful interaction within increasingly multicultural contexts, but to drastically simplify and reify group identities. They tend, rather, to encourage separatism, intolerance and chauvinism, patriarchalism and authoritarianism. I shall call this *the problem of reification*. (Fraser 2000, 108)

Multiculturalism is neither a unified ideology nor a highly homogeneous discourse (Vertovec and Wessendorf 2010), and several scholars understand it as being open to multiple significations, and as a terrain of struggle, a battlefield. They distinguish between a cooptive liberal or mainstream multiculturalism and a more radical, engaged, and relational "polycentric multiculturalism" (Shohat and Stam 1994) that seeks to displace Eurocentrism. The main differences between the two interpretations of multiculturalism revolve around the critical nodes identified by Fraser: the eclipse of social politics and reification of culture. Polycentric multiculturalism, indeed, "demands change not just in images but in power relations" (Shohat and Stam 1994, 48), but also envisions culture and identity as products of relational, dialogic practice. In other words, while radical multiculturalism is transformative and generative from the margins, mainstream multiculturalism is affirmative, if not cosmetic, in that it does not disturb the underlying framework that generates inequalities and misrecognitions (see also Fraser 1997).

Post-9/11 and particularly in recent years, multiculturalism has come under intense criticism, most prominently on the part of the British, German, and French political leaders in 2010–2011, as an allegedly 'failed' and divisive experiment and as a threat to national cohesion which must be replaced by a return to the integration model (see Vertovec and Wessendorf 2010). Multiculturalism's death has been proclaimed from many sides. Supporters have thus come to its defense. For some, it is questionable whether multicultural policies have ever "amounted to more than piecemeal affairs" (Lentin and Titley 2011; see also Valenta 2011) while other people see "descriptive multiculturalism," as David Theo Goldberg (2004) calls it, or the reality of multiculture (Gilroy 2004), as a fact of our globalized lives that policy makers cannot but recognize. Most forcefully – and crucially for my own argument – Tariq Modood has argued that multiculturalism is itself a mode of integration within the nation-state, an argument for pluralizing national identities, and thus not at all incompatible with or antithetical to the national principle (Modood 2012; 2013).

UNESCO is a crucial site for the production of the discourse of multiculturalism, owing to its prioritization of the promotion of cultural pluralism as leading to tolerance, dialogue, and creativity. UNESCO's multicultural turn was grounded in a revision of its notion of culture, which took place in the context of shifting, more culturalist development discourses, and a new sense of the entanglement of culture and democracy, as embodied by subaltern and minority struggles for cultural self-determination (see Stenou 2007). No longer chiefly understood as 'high culture' and as universal knowledge to be spread throughout the world, culture is understood in this newer vision in an anthropological, holistic sense as the totality of the cultural practices of a people; and a people is no longer the equivalent of a nation. Yet, in spite of the emancipatory potential of this approach, the problem of reification continues to haunt it. UNESCO's discourse of culture is not homogeneous and monologic, of course, but it is nonetheless indebted to old essentialized anthropological concepts that leave only marginal space for contestations, hybridities, and change (Eriksen 2001).

The report *Our Creative Diversity* (WCCD 1995) is a case in point. Sometimes equated to biodiversity, here culture encompasses the entire range of spiritual, material and intellectual values that typify a particular group or society (see the quote from Marshall Sahlins that opens the report, WCCD 1995, 21). Culture is difference, and cultural difference is visualized as a mosaic (e.g. 7). In this vision, culture is close to the idea of tradition, unique to and distinctive of a group, continuous through time and bound in space. It is represented as a treasure, homogeneously shared by the people to whom it *belongs*, while also in danger of getting lost, as if it were the solid ground of identity that must be 'strengthened.' The end effect is the heritagization of culture that is evident, for instance, in the first article of the UNESCO Declaration on Cultural Diversity (UNESCO 2001), which defines cultural diversity as the common heritage of humanity. Through such discursive practices, the complex, the contested, and the relational are displaced by hegemonic images of cultures as separate entities, as cultural property that can be itemized on a list.

The idea of the world as a mosaic of different cultures – at least partly coinciding with nations– has shaped World Heritage practices since the 1990s, particularly new attempts by UNESCO to achieve its goal of universality without imposing uniformity. (Indeed, in manifold contexts well beyond UNESCO, postcolonial heritage has been increasingly couched in recent decades in the language of recognition and multiculturalism (Rowlands 2002; Weiss 2007), and claimed as part of human rights.) The growing concerns, inside and outside UNESCO, about the evident imbalances of the List in terms of regions, types of properties, and periods represented, and about its focus on 'great' European monuments and 'great' civilizations have provoked a rethinking of approaches to accommodate cultural diversity and less Eurocentric understandings of heritage values (Cleere 2001). This rethinking materialized in the so-called Global Strategy for a Representative, Balanced and Credible World Heritage List launched in 1994 and revised in the years that followed (UNESCO 1994a; see also Labadi 2005).

The goal was that the List "should present an overview of the great diversity of the different cultures which make up mankind, including of course 'living' cultures;" in order to provide a "truly global and complete vision of [the] world," the answer to the concerns about the List's Eurocentrism was to "include ... other cultures" within the new multicultural vision of World Heritage as a mosaic with several missing pieces (Ensuring a Representative List 1994, 4–5). The Global Strategy implies a shift in focus from 'uniqueness' and aesthetic and historic value, to representativeness and anthropological value or social significance: it discovers the intangible qualities of heritage (UNESCO 1994a). Since the inauguration of the Strategy, the criteria for inclusion on the List have been modified to make space for new themes and new types of property (such as cultural landscapes and cultural routes) with revised, less materialist notions of authenticity (UNESCO 1994b), in an attempt to fill in the gaps in the representativeness of the list and to redress its imbalances. Furthermore, under the Strategy, UNESCO encourages underrepresented and non-represented countries to become members and submit nominations, while states parties which are already well-represented on the List are encouraged to slow down the frequency of new nominations (see UNESCO 2008).

Almost fifteen years after the launch of the Global Strategy, a report analyzing the implementation of the World Heritage Convention (Labadi 2007b; see also Labadi 2007a) found out that its objectives had not been met, and over half of the properties on the List were still located in Europe and North America in spite of near universal membership. Like the politics of recognition, new multicultural heritage policies suffer from both the problem of reification and the problem of displacement described above, as well as from the tendency to reproduce hierarchies between cultures. Minoo Moallem and Iain Boal have noted that liberal multiculturalism often conforms to "a politics of inclusion based on the model of a solid core surrounded by a periphery of the marginalized and the minorities" (1999, 253). A study of nomination dossiers between 1977 and 2002 indicates that, in spite of the Global Strategy, there has been no substantial change in the kinds of values given prominence by state parties. The values mentioned most often in the dossiers are the ones associated with Eurocentric heritage approaches: historical, aesthetic, and architectural significance, together with a site's connection to men from the middle and upper classes (Labadi 2007a, 158). Women, the lower socio-economic classes and indigenous people, together with local communities, are still being marginalized by the World Heritage process. Tentative lists and nominations tend to conform to hegemonic national (or colonial) representations that acquire transnational qualities by being very similar across the world: linear, homogeneous, and heroic narratives of grandeur engraved in stone (Labadi 2007a, esp.161). In other words, World Heritage has so far produced a "vision of world cultures" that, far from being "truly global and complete," is not only biased in terms of represented regions but also not representative of single nations.

To explain the ineffectiveness of the Global Strategy, Sophia Labadi, the author of the nomination dossiers study, points the finger at states parties' lack of knowledge of the system and, more incisively in my opinion, at a crucial lack of democratic participation in terms of the active involvement of states parties in the work of the World Heritage Committee and of the grassroots in the World Heritage process (Labadi 2007a, 159–60). Following mounting criticism, the revised *Operational Guidelines* (UNESCO 2008, 7) have also included among five strategic objectives the enhancement of the role of local communities in the implementation of the Convention. Yet this objective is hard to achieve because of the way the system works. Pushing Labadi's reasoning a bit further, I would argue that the lack of participatory democracy in World Heritage is structural. It is tied, on the one hand, to the powerful alliance between World Heritage as an intergovernmental project and the institutions of the nation-state, and on the other, to the "rule of experts" (Mitchell 2002; Smith 2006) produced by the World Heritage process.

My analysis is shaped by the ways in which World Heritage operates in Palestine, which, some could argue, is not a suitable yardstick of general trends because of its exceptional political situation. On the contrary, I think there are some important global lessons to learn from the ethnographic material I have presented precisely because of Palestine's paradoxical 'quasi-state' status. States and experts are the two subjects of the World Heritage discourse because there is no nomination or site management without state supervision and expert knowledge of the transnational heritage language, while consultation of the grassroots can be easily ignored (see also Askew 2010; Meskell 2013).[13] World Heritage cannot as yet function without working state infrastructures. Therefore, when those are

---

13 Here my analysis is indebted to Foucauldian critiques of development, a discursive formation that is intertwined with and replicated by heritage. In particular, I have been inspired by Jim Ferguson's (1994) analysis of development as producing the expansion of bureaucratic state power and the depoliticization of poverty through the use of a technocratic language.

absent or weak a whole arsenal of personnel, training workshops, and capacity-building initiatives must be set in place to obviate the problem. Underrepresentation, as in the case of the Arab states (Labadi 2007b, 149), is often a problem of the lack of state infrastructures capable, for instance, of producing and maintaining a national inventory of heritage sites that can provide the basis for a tentative list; in other words, a problem arises when so-called weak states do not "know" (Scott 1998) and thus do not control their territory. Under- and non-represented states lack the financial resources and institutional capacity to produce tentative lists and nomination dossiers, not to mention to conserve their heritage, and frequently cannot ask for UNESCO international assistance because of their arrears to the World Heritage Fund. This also shows how the institutional discourse of multiculturalism in heritage and the language of recognition mask, or in Fraser's terminology, *displace* underlying radical socio-economic inequalities that prevent the realization of multiculturalism's stated democratic and pluralistic goals, in particular that of establishing a well-balanced List.

In the Palestinian case, uproar over the destruction of world-famous monuments in 2002 forced the World Heritage Committee to intervene and disburse funds for the institutional development of the Palestinian Authority's Department of Antiquities and for the preparation of the tentative list. UNESCO's intervention has definitively empowered the 'state' heritage department and broadened its reach throughout the territories. Palestinian civil society heritage practitioners, who, as I mentioned earlier, are at the forefront of a movement to protect the local vernacular heritage, use a kinship metaphor to describe this alliance between UNESCO and the PA. During a conference on heritage conservation in Palestine that brought together many of the actors involved in the field, the department of antiquities, heritage NGOs, UNESCO, and several key donors, this alliance was jokingly referred to as a 'marriage' that could only receive a limited blessing from civil society organizations, for it tends to exclude them, while effecting stricter regulation of their activities. UNESCO's reply to the marriage joke was always the same: "My hands are tied ... UNESCO is an intergovernmental organization. I cannot marry you [civil society heritage organizations], even though I would prefer to marry you rather than the department of antiquities."[14] In other words, UNESCO is mandated to work with state institutions, which, while obviously beneficial to institutional development and capacity building at the national level, creates fric-

---

14 My notes from the third day of the Conference on Cultural Heritage in Palestine, Jericho, 22 February 2006.

tion with grassroots organizations and often hinders community participation beyond a token acknowledgement of its importance.

Nancy Fraser and Ella Shohat, as I discussed above, have shown that institutional multiculturalism tends to affirm, rather than transform, underlying, inequality-producing structures, particularly through a mechanism of displacement. Similarly, UNESCO's multiculturalism has neutralized pushes for more democratic and inclusive World Heritage practices by *displacing* the problem of participation onto a new list. Instead of changing the World Heritage system, UNESCO's recognition of the significance of heritage's intangible dimension and the crucial role of civil society in heritage management has led to the development and adoption of a new legal instrument, the 2003 Convention for the Safeguarding of the Intangible Cultural Heritage (UNESCO 2003), with its attendant "Representative List." While the model is still the WHC, crucial differences between the preservation of tangible cultural heritage and the safeguarding of intangible heritage concern on the one hand the new role of local communities and tradition-bearers, and on the other, the rejection of the criterion of "outstanding universal value" in favor of representativity (Aikawa-Faure 2009; for a general interdisciplinary discussion of the newer convention, see Smith and Akagawa 2009).

Meanwhile, the Convention on the Protection and Promotion of the Diversity of Cultural Expressions (UNESCO 2005) is the latest among UNESCO's standard-setting instruments. Unlike the two heritage conventions, this one primarily protects the products of individual or collective creativity as "published or conveyed by modern carriers of culture" (Stenou 2007, 134). Displaced onto multiple lists, institutional multiculturalism tends to produce a structural hierarchy between different but equally essentialized cultural forms, and between a heritage of universal significance and a heritage that is safeguarded for the "fear of losing diversity" (Aikawa-Faure 2009, 40). The addition of the new convention for the protection of 'modern' cultural expression further conveys a Manichean representation of world cultures as substantially divided between dead heritage (in its twin aspects of universal civilizational monuments and dying marginalized traditions) and 'contemporary' creativity. In this cosmology, intangible heritage, rather than being an aspect of all kinds of heritages and cultures, is reified into another itemized list and devalued in relation to more 'universal,' timeless and/or modern cultural forms.[15] Neither universal nor truly 'of the present,' certain forms of cultural production are relegated to an uncertain limbo thanks to the denial of their coeval-

---

15 For another critique of the ways in which the introduction of intangible heritage did and did not change World Heritage, see Schmitt (2008); Harrison (2013).

ness (see Fabian 2007, 106) – itself a form of misrecognition – operationalized by the postcolonial taxonomy of UNESCO's cultural conventions.

Conclusions

In this essay, I have moved from telling the story of World Heritage in Palestine/Israel to an analysis of the transnational heritage discourse. I have argued that the project to reform World Heritage, stimulated by critiques of the Eurocentrism of the List, has adopted a multicultural frame, inspired in particular by what scholars call mosaic or liberal multiculturalism. According to critics, this way of seeing and managing cultural difference tends to effect a reification of dynamic cultural processes; it recreates borders in unlikely places. Moreover, instead of transforming dominant structures and practices from the margins, this multiculturalism not only risks solidifying differences, but also the asymmetries between them. Clearly, the case of UNESCO shows the predicaments of "a comprehensive universalism that contains challenges to its validity by becoming more internally diverse" (MacKenzie 2009, 348 discussing Butler 1995). Yet, these critiques should not be taken as a repudiation of multiculturalism, which has indeed further expanded and diversified World Heritage. As Judith Butler (1996) has argued, the quality of being "that which is yet to be achieved" (52) might well be a key feature of the universal itself for "the universal begins to become articulated precisely through challenges to its existing formulations" (48). Furthermore, "the contingent and cultural character of existing conventions governing the scope of universality does not deny the usefulness or importance of the ... *universal*. It simply means that the claim of universality has not been fully or finally made" (46, original emphasis). Critiques and contestations, tensions and contradictions are crucial to the very making of the universal as an ongoing process.

Like the unresolved tension between a strong commitment to universalism and inclusiveness and the persistence of Eurocentric and imperial legacies, the friction between transnational and national rationalities has also marked the discourse and work of World Heritage since the beginning. Undeniably, a host of UNESCO's practices simultaneously inscribe heritage sites into a double logic and spatial horizon. While promoting a transnational memory, the World Heritage List, the main product of UNESCO's heritage activities, is still subdivided into separate national listings. A national logic is inscribed into UNESCO's very constitution since this organization, like the UN, is an intergovernmental body made up of, rather than transcending, nation-states; ultimately, it is "pacting" among powerful states the force that propels its decision-making process (see Meskell 2014). Because of UNESCO's specific mandate to work with national institutions, all World Heritage activities necessarily pass through the agencies of member states, which are thus empowered (and sometimes even created anew) in the process. Thus, World Heritage paradoxically furthers the reach and scope of the nation-state.

The case of Palestine that I have discussed shows the multilayered articulations of such a troubled relationship. The exceptional character of Palestine, an occupied nation endowed with symbolic (through the UNESCO and UN decisions), as opposed to real sovereignty, made it possible for Palestinians to navigate this paradox to support their national rights and gain a little more control over their heritage. At the same time UNESCO is still prey to the will of powerful states, such as the US, particularly through the withdrawal or release of key funding for the agency. Finally, the ways in which the heritage of humanity reinforces the nation-state and provides it with symbolic paraphernalia often comes at the expense of the grassroots.

References

Abu El-Haj, Nadia. *Facts on the Ground: Archaeological Practice and Territorial Self-Fashioning in Israeli Society*. Chicago: University of Chicago Press, 2001.

Aikawa-Faure, Noriko. "From the Proclamation of Masterpieces to the Convention for the Safeguarding of Intangible Heritage." *Intangible Heritage*. Eds. Laurajane Smith and Natsuko Akagawa. New York: Routledge, 2009. 13–44.

Anderson, Benedict. *Imagined Communities: Reflections on the Origins and Spread of Nationalism*. 1983. London: Verso, 1991.

Askew, Marc. "The Magic List of Global Status: UNESCO, World Heritage and the Agendas of States." *Heritage and Globalisation*. Eds. Sophia Labadi and Colin Long. London: Routledge, 2010. 19–44.

Benhabib, Seyla. *The Claims of Culture*. Princeton: Princeton UP, 2002.

Bissel, William. "Engaging Colonial Nostalgia." *Cultural Anthropology* 20.2 (2005): 215–248.

Butler, Judith. "Contingent Foundations: Feminism and the Question of 'Postmodernism.'" *Feminist Contentions: A Philosophical Exchange*. Eds. Seyla Benhabib, Judith Butler, Drucilla Cornell, and Nancy Fraser. New York: Routledge, 1995. 35–57.

Butler, Judith. "Universality in Culture." *For Love of Country: Debating the Limits of Patriotism*. Martha C. Nussbaum with respondents, ed. by Joshua Cohen. Boston: Beacon Press, 1996. 45–52.

Byrne, Denis. "Western Hegemony in Archaeological Heritage Management." *History and Anthropology* 5 (1991): 269–276.

Byrne, Denis. "Buddhist Stupa and Thai Social Practice." *World Archaeology* 27.2 (1995): 266–281.

Byrne, Denis. "A Critique of Unfeeling Heritage." *Intangible Heritage*. Eds. Laurajane Smith and Natsuko Akagawa. New York: Routledge, 2009. 229–252.

Carman, John. *Against Cultural Property: Archaeology, Heritage and Ownership*. London: Duckworth, 2005.

Choay, Françoise. *The Invention of the Historic Monument*. Cambridge: Cambridge UP, 2001.

Cleere, Henry. "The Uneasy Bedfellows: Universality and Cultural Heritage." *Destruction and Conservation of Cultural Property*. Eds. Robert Layton, Peter Stone and Julian Thomas. London and New York: Routledge, 2001. 22–29.

Collins, John. "'But What if I Should Need to Defecate in your Neighborhood, Madame?' Empire, Redemption, and the 'Tradition of the Oppressed' in a Brazilian World Heritage Site." *Cultural Anthropology* 23.2 (2008): 279–328.

Cowan, Jane, Marie-Bénédicte Dembour and Richard Wilson. "Introduction." *Culture and Rights*. Cambridge: Cambridge UP, 2001. 1–26.

Department of Antiquities and Cultural Heritage (DACH) Inventory of Cultural and Natural Heritage Sites of Potential Outstanding Universal Value in Palestine. Ramallah: DACH, 2005.

De Cesari, Chiara. "Creative Heritage: Palestinian Heritage NGOs and Defiant Arts of Government." *American Anthropologist* 112.4 (2010): 625–637.

De Cesari, Chiara. "Anticipatory Representation: Building the Palestinian Nation(-State) through Artistic Performance." *Studies in Ethnicity and Nationalism* 12.1 (2012): 82–100.

Dumper, Michael and Craig Larkin. "The Politics of Heritage and the Limitations of International Agency in Contested Cities: A Study of the Role of UNESCO in Jerusalem's Old City." *Review of International Studies* 38 (2012): 25–52.

"Ensuring a Representative List: Towards a Global Strategy." *World Heritage Newsletter* 6 (November 1994): 4–5.

Eriksen, Thomas Hylland. "Between Universalism and Relativism: A Critique of the UNESCO Concept of Culture." *Culture and Rights*. Eds. Jane Cowan, Marie-Bénédicte Dembour and Richard Wilson. Cambridge: Cambridge UP, 2001. 127–148.

Fabian, Johannes. *Memory Against Culture: Arguments and Reminders*. Durham: Duke UP, 2007.

Ferguson, James. *The Anti-Politics Machine: 'Development', Depoliticization, and Bureaucratic Power in Lesotho*. Minneapolis: University of Minnesota Press, 1994.

Fraser, Nancy. "From Redistribution to Recognition? Dilemmas of Justice in a 'Postsocialist' Age." *Justice Interruptus: Critical Reflections on the "Postsocialist" Condition*. New York: Routledge, 1997. 11–39.

Fraser, Nancy. "Rethinking Recognition." *New Left Review* 3 (2000): 107–120.

Gamboni, Dario. "World Heritage: Shield or Target?" *The Getty Conservation Institute Newsletter* 16.2 (2001): 5–11.

Gilroy, Paul. *After Empire: Multiculture or Postcolonial Melancholia*. London: Routledge, 2004.

Goldberg, David Theo. "The Spaces of Multiculturalism." *openDemocracy* 15 September 2004. www.opendemocracy.net/arts-multiculturalism/article_2097.jsp (accessed 21 March 2014).

Gordon, Milton. *Assimilation in American Life*. New York: Oxford UP, 1964.

Handler, Richard. "On Having a Culture: Nationalism and the Preservation of Quebec's Patrimony." *Objects and Others: Essays on Museums and Material Culture*. Ed. George Stocking. Madison: University of Wisconsin Press, 1985. 192–217.

Handler, Richard. "Cultural Property and Culture Theory." *Journal of Social Archaeology* 3.3 (2003): 353–65.

Harrison, Rodney. *Heritage: Critical Approaches*. London: Routledge, 2013.

Herzfeld, Michael. *A Place in History: Social and Monumental Time in a Cretan Town*. Princeton: Princeton UP, 1991.

Herzfeld, Michael. *The Body Impolitic: Artisans and Artifice in the Global Hierarchy of Value*. Chicago: University of Chicago Press, 2004.

Herzfeld, Michael. "Political Optics and the Occlusion of Intimate Knowledge." *American Anthropologist* 107.3 (2005): 369–376.

Hirschmann, Charles. "America's Melting Pot Reconsidered." *Annual Review of Sociology* 9 (1983): 397–423.

"It's about Time." *The Daily Star* 1 November 2011: 7. www.dailystar.com.lb/Article.aspx?id= 152731{#}axzz2vBnzljhV (accessed 6 March 2014).

Kirshenblatt-Gimblett, Barbara. *Destination Culture: Tourism, Museums, and Heritage*. Berkeley: University of California Press, 1998.

Kirshenblatt-Gimblett, Barbara. "World Heritage and Cultural Economics." *Museum Frictions: Public Cultures/Global Transformations*. Eds. Ivan Karp, Corinne Kratz, Lynn Szwaja, Tomás Ybarra-Frausto, Gustavo Buntinax, Barbara Kirschenblatt-Gimblett, and Ciraj Rassool. Durham: Duke UP, 2006. 161–202.

Kymlicka, Will. *Multicultural Citizenship: A Liberal Theory of Minority Rights*. Oxford: Oxford UP, 1995.

Labadi, Sophia. "A Review of the Global Strategy for a Balanced, Representative and Credible World Heritage List 1994–2004." *Conservation and Management of Archaeological Sites* 7.2 (2005): 89–102.

Labadi, Sophia. "Representations of the Nation and Cultural Diversity in Discourses on World Heritage." *Journal of Social Archaeology* 7.2 (2007a): 147–170.

Labadi, Sophia, ed. *World Heritage: Challenges for the Millennium*. Paris: UNESCO World Heritage Centre, 2007b.

Lazaroff, Tovah. "UNESCO to Weigh Listing Battir as World Heritage Site in 'Palestine.'" *Jerusalem Post* 16 February 2014. www.jpost.com/Middle-East/UNESCO-to-weigh-listing-Battir-as-World-Heritage-site-in-Palestine-341530 (accessed 21 March 2014).

Lentin, Alana and Gavan Titley. *The Crises of Multiculturalism: Racism in a Neoliberal Age*. London: Zed Books, 2011.

MacKenzie, Julie. "Refiguring Universalism." *Australian Feminist Studies* 24.61 (2009): 343–358.

Maffi, Irene. "The Emergence of Cultural Heritage in Jordan: The Itinerary of a Colonial Invention." *Journal of Social Archaeology* 9.1 (2009): 5–34.

Meskell, Lynn, ed. *Archaeology under Fire: Nationalism, Politics and Heritage in the Eastern Mediterranean and Middle East*. London: Routledge, 1998.

Meskell, Lynn. "Negative Heritage and Past Mastering in Archaeology." *Anthropological Quarterly* 75.3 (2002): 557–574.

Meskell, Lynn. "UNESCO and the Fate of the World Heritage Indigenous Peoples Council of Experts (WHIPCOE)." *International Journal of Cultural Property* 20.2 (2013): 155–174.

Meskell, Lynn. "States of Conservation: Protection, Politics, and 'Pacting' within UNESCO's World Heritage Committee." *Anthropological Quarterly* 87.1 (2014): 217–244.

Mitchell, Timothy. *Rule of Experts: Egypt, Techno-Politics, Modernity*. Berkeley: University of California Press, 2002.

Moallem, Minoo and Iain Boal. "Multicultural Nationalism and the Poetics of Inauguration." *Between Woman and Nation*. Eds. Caren Kaplan, Norma Alarcón, and Minoo Moallem. Durham: Duke UP, 1999. 243–263.

Modood, Tariq. "Multiculturalism and the Nation." *openDemocracy* 20 December 2012. www. opendemocracy.net/ourkingdom/tariq-modood/multiculturalism-and-nation (accessed 21 March 2014).

Modood, Tariq. *Multiculturalism*. 2nd ed. Cambridge: Polity, 2013.

Park, Robert and Ernest Burgess. *Introduction to the Science of Sociology*. Chicago: University of Chicago Press, 1969.

Povinelli, Elizabeth. *The Cunning of Recognition: Indigenous Alterities and the Making of Australian Multiculturalism*. Durham: Duke UP, 2002.

Prott, Lyndel. "Understanding One Another on Cultural Rights." *Cultural Rights and Wrongs*. Ed. Halina Niéc. Paris: UNESCO, 1998. 161–175.

Ravid, Barak. "Palestinians Renew Call for UN World Heritage Status for West Bank Village." *Haaretz* 13 February 2014. www.haaretz.com/news/diplomacy-defense/.premium-1.574171 (accessed 5 March 2014).

Rowlands, Michael. "Heritage and Cultural Property." *The Material Culture Reader*. Ed. Victor Buchli. Oxford: Berg, 2002. 105–133.

Shaath, Nabil. "Palestine on the World Map." *This Week in Palestine* 163 (November 2011). www.thisweekinpalestine.com/details.php?id=3549{&}ed=200{&}edid=200 (accessed 25 March 2014).

Scham, Sandra. "Diplomacy and Desired Pasts." *Journal of Social Archaeology* 9.2 (2009): 163–199.

Schmitt, Thomas. "The UNESCO Concept of Safeguarding Intangible Cultural Heritage: Its Background and *Marrakchi* Roots." *International Journal of Heritage Studies* 14.2 (2008): 95–111.

Scott, James. *Seeing Like a State*. New Haven: Yale UP, 1998.

Shohat, Ella and Robert Stam. *Unthinking Eurocentrism: Multiculturalism and the Media*. London: Routledge, 1994.

Smith, Laurajane. *Uses of Heritage*. London: Routledge, 2006.

Smith, Laurajane and Natsuko Akagawa, eds. *Intangible Heritage*. New York: Routledge, 2009.

Stam, Robert and Ella Shohat. "De-Eurocentrizing Cultural Studies: Some Proposals." *Internationalizing Cultural Studies: An Anthology*. Eds. Ackbar Abbas and John Nguyet Erni. Oxford: Blackwell, 2005. 481–498.

Stenou, Katerina. "UNESCO and the Question of Cultural Diversity: Review and Strategies, 1946–2007." Paris: UNESCO, 2007. unesdoc.unesco.org/images/0015/001543/154341mo. pdf (accessed March 2014).

Stenou, Katerina. "UNESCO and the Issue of Cultural Diversity: Review and Strategy, 1946–2003." Paris: UNESCO, 2003. unesdoc.unesco.org/images/0013/001302/130209mo.pdf (accessed March 2014).

Taylor, Charles. "The Politics of Recognition." *Multiculturalism: Examining the Politics of Recognition*. Ed. Amy Gutmann. Princeton: Princeton UP, 1994. 25–73.

UNESCO. *Constitution*. UNESCO, 1945. unesdoc.unesco.org/images/0013/001337/133729e. pdf{#}page=7 (accessed 21 March 2014).

UNESCO. *Convention Concerning the Protection of the World Cultural and Natural Heritage*. UNESCO, 1972. whc.unesco.org/archive/convention-en.pdf (accessed 21 March 2014).

UNESCO. Expert Meeting on the 'Global Strategy' and Thematic Studies for a Representative World Heritage List (20–22 June 1994). World Heritage Committee – 18th Session (12–17 December 1994). WHC-94/CONF.003/INF.6. Paris: UNESCO, 1994a. whc.unesco.org/ archive/global94.htm (accessed 21 March 2014).

UNESCO. Nara Document on Authenticity. Experts Meeting, 1–6 November 1994. World Heritage Committee – 18th Session (12–17 December 1994). WHC-94/CONF.003/INF.008. Paris: UNESCO, 1994b. whc.unesco.org/archive/nara94.htm (accessed 21 March 2014).

UNESCO. *Universal Declaration on Cultural Diversity*. UNESCO, 2001. unesdoc.unesco.org/images/0012/001271/127160m.pdf (accessed 21 March 2014).

UNESCO. *Convention for the Safeguarding of the Intangible Cultural Heritage*. UNESCO, 2003. unesdoc.unesco.org/images/0013/001325/132540e.pdf (accessed 21 March 2014).

UNESCO. *Convention on the Protection and Promotion of the Diversity of Cultural Expressions*. UNESCO, 2005. unesdoc.unesco.org/images/0014/001429/142919e.pdf (accessed 21 March 2014).

UNESCO. *Operational Guidelines for the Implementation of the World Heritage Convention*. Intergovernmental Committee for the Protection of the World Cultural and Natural Heritage WHC-08/01. Paris: UNESCO, 2008. whc.unesco.org/en/guidelines (accessed 21 March 2014).

Valenta, Markha. "Multiculturalism and the Politics of Bad Memories." *openDemocracy* 20 March 2011. www.opendemocracy.net/markha-valenta/multiculturalism-and-politics-of-bad-memories (accessed 21 March 2014).

Vertovec, Steven and Susanne Wessendorf. "Introduction." *The Multicultural Backlash: European Discourses, Policies and Practices*. Eds. Steven Vertovec and Susanne Wessendorf. London: Routledge, 2010. 1–31.

Weiss, Lindsay. "Heritage-Making and Political Identity." *Journal of Social Archaeology* 7.3 (2007): 413–431.

Wilson, Ross. "History, Memory and Heritage." *International Journal of Heritage Studies* 15.4 (2009): 374–378.

World Commission on Culture and Development (WCCD). *Our Creative Diversity*. Paris: UNESCO, 1995. unesdoc.unesco.org/images/0010/001016/101651e.pdf (accessed 21 March 2014).

Stephan Feuchtwang
Haunting Memory: The Extension of Kinship Beyond the Nation

> There is for all of us a twilight zone of time, stretching back for a generation or two before we were born, which never quite belongs to the rest of history. Our elders have talked their memories into our memories until we come to possess some sense of a continuity exceeding and traversing our own individual being … (Conor Cruise O'Brien in Tóibín 2012)

The memory evoked in the passage quoted above is what I propose calling 'haunting memory.' This is what we are induced to remember as our own memory even though it is the story of our intimate forebears extending and haunting our recollection. In what follows, I develop this concept and, in doing so, offer a critique of discussions of cultural memory which seem premised on a fundamental opposition between intimate (usually family) relations and larger social formations. In particular, I shall challenge the distinction between *milieux de mémoire* and *lieux de mémoire* advanced by Pierre Nora, and his claim that in the last two hundred years we have witnessed the emergence of a new kind of society in which collective memory is ceasing to exist, having been replaced by a state-driven cultivation of a network of memory sites.

I want to stress instead the co-existence, within contemporary society, of different if not incompatible collective memories that often involve linkages of transnational sites of memory. In the current condition of people-states, a co-ercive and persuasive politics elicits the idea of a 'people' through mediated mobilizations of communities of descent (ethnicity and race), tradition (including regional), language and faith, even though each and any of them extends spatially in ways that do not coincide with the others. I want to point out that there is another kind of memory, focusing on families and the intimate sphere, that transgresses or extends across national borders.

These intimate transmissions become part of the memory of the bearer even when they were not part of personal experiences (other than those of their telling). I shall remark on how some of them are recorded in personal archives, as well as how these archives relate to more public archives. Most of what is remembered personally is not transmitted and most of what is transmitted to children disappears. But my main contention is that some of what is transmitted through kinship and the most intimate relations of adulthood can be pinned down and reinforced in personal archives, rituals and other kinds of commemoration that are alternative to those of the nation state.

Starting again from scratch: the formation of memory by the interpenetration of selves

This could be the moment to assert against Pierre Nora that religious and familial *milieux de mémoire* coexist with *lieux de mémoire* and that history does not, as he argued, condemn them to death. But in one respect I agree with him – that in Europe 'memory' as a philosophical and psychological object emerged at the same time as did critical history, in the last half of the nineteenth century (Nora 1989, 15). The emergence of the human sciences framed, and was framed by, the problematic of the collective and the individual. So memory became an object of the psychology of human individuals seen as subjects of collective institutions and cultures. By the last quarter of the twentieth century, an anthropology critical of the Eurocentrism of its own masters and those of psychology has established a new basis from which to start thinking about memory and its transmission. It has much to say about the intimately social formation of memory. So it is to this cognitive anthropology that I now turn. I shall then argue against Nora that this use of psychology in anthropology does not foreclose familial *milieux de mémoire*, despite the prevalence of people's stories and their *lieux de mémoire*. On the contrary, cognitive anthropology is no longer based on a single unilinear history of progress into modern psychology and its institutions.

Memory is necessarily reducible to an individual human being's cognitive and emotional functions. But humans learn from early infancy by putting themselves in the place of others, other humans and other things or animals, to see themselves as intentional beings perceived by other intentional beings. This is the basis of human sociality and also of the construction of human senses of the world. Let me elaborate by reference to Maurice Bloch, *Anthropology and the Cognitive Challenge* (2012), which further illustrates what he (2007 and 2011) called the "interpenetration of selves." His main argument is that for humans, as for all social animals, there is a blurring or indistinctness of the unit of life. The evolved organism is both the individual and its interaction with and mutual dependence on others. For humans more than for any other primate, this social extension of the self involves sharing intentionality, acting in terms of a capacity to read the beliefs of others and to accept the content of others' minds by deferring to their competences and communicating with and about them. Kinship systems are, in Bloch's view, a particular and distinct representation, historically formed in specific ways in different societies, of the general fact that we go into each others' bodies, not just through acts of communication and deferral, but through sex and birth. Feeding and communicating with ancestors is an extension of this representation, imputing continued intentionality to the dead, who are important and trusted elders. Participation in rituals addressing ancestors is a conscious submission to the instructions of dead elders.

What then does the interpenetration of selves do in the formation of memory? The concepts and schemata that cognition is based on are practical knowledge, enabling very fast, moment-to-moment appraisal and action, which is not narrative and is not available to consciousness. Bloch (2012) reports on research showing that cognitive concepts and schemata are based on sense data and storage, probably in a three-dimensional network of connections among the brain's neurons. As sense data they can barely be described as memory, except that they leave neural traces. But in addition, concepts and schemata must also be accessible to mini-narrative statements in the course of learning (for instance, in an apprenticeship which is mainly learning by doing). Such statements *are* recalled and they trigger practical schemata. Schemata are constantly modified in the stream of moments of experiential learning, not just by observation and mimicry but also by occasional narrative statements.

Similarly unavailable to consciousness is the necessary sense of self, the idea that one's individual being is constant over time, and that other beings are too. This is unconscious representation, the self of autobiographical memory. But on top of autobiographical memory a selection of episodes (rarely longer than a few hours) are usually available for recall. Like the mini-narratives of habit learning, episodes are formed in social interaction at the time of storage. Selection depends on emotional intensity at the time of their being recalled.

All recallable memory is based on snippets of narration that at a further remove can be pieced together as a chronology of the autobiographical self. Meta-autobiographical memory, the narration, at any given time, of continuity (not just constancy) of the self over time, is formed by semantic memory, the layer of facts and concepts learned in both formal and informal contexts. The retelling of a learned story or the learning of ways to tell a story, so that different stories are legible or comprehensible as variants of a common story, could be described as learning state ideology, or hegemony, including variants on an identifying history of a 'people.' But my main point about the formation of meta-autobiographical memory is that it is formed in relations of intimacy that make it qualitatively more vivid than any other cultural transmission. For this reason, I propose to call it *haunting memory*. It is formed in intimate interaction with others upon whom we are dependent or who, later in life, are dependent on us in especially intimate ways. These others enter into us, and in the course of a lifetime we may formulate a memory of them as specific internalized objects (images), just as they do of us, and these memories are constituent parts of our growing selves. Among cultural schemata, those that govern the most intimate and dependent relations, namely those of childhood or, in the other direction, the care of children, are relations of kinship, friendship or teaching. In other words, we can posit that the most emotively laden parts of our meta-autobiographic selves are the images of those from whom we first learned to be a self and, subsequently, of those with whom we modified our selves.

Consider again a human child, after it has lived for a few months, entertaining the dawning recognition of another person, inevitably a nurturer, and of being recognized by them. This period of the growth of recognition of self and other has been commented on in different ways by psychologies other than the experimental and cognitive. For Freud, it is in the game played as a rhythm of 'gone,' 'back' (*fort, da*) by an infant standing in its cot, imagining an absent mother leaving and coming back. For Lacan it is the mirror phase, where the child sees its image, as a self that is an other and of the self as the object of the other's 'desire' (a broad sense of desire, including intention and projection). For cognitive psychologists it is the dawning in the infant of a theory of mind or of intentionality, a perception of others as beings with intentions towards third persons and toward the infant as a third person, crucially including the premise of the infant's own intentionality. This internalization of others in the very formation of self, which includes objects and beings other than humans, with intentionality imputed to them, is imagined most vividly with reference to those with whom we share food, suffering, our names, and indeed transmitted and shared memories.

Now that I have arrived at this internalization of other intentionalities, let me briefly turn to Marshall Sahlins' (2012) answer to the question 'what is kinship?' His answer is "mutuality of being." Kinship involves being joined by love, fear, intense ambivalence and an obligation governed by an ontology – different in different cultures – of consubstantiality and the facts, as well as the ideas, of birth, sex, marriage and death. Sahlins' main stress, like that of Halbwachs, is on the cultural or social formation of kinship. My main stress, instead, is on the shared personality produced in the most intense experiences of childhood learning. Though they are of course governed by ideas of kinship, they also produce variations upon those ideas and even more so differentiations from the most general conceptions of the social.

Intimate shared personhood involves a cumulative process of parental care in which memory is essential for the later recall of acts of compassion – or its denial – in the cycle of nurturance, parental for children, children for the elderly. This then is the most vivid part of the piecing together of the episodes and mini-narratives of habit into shared memory, into memory of reciprocal obligation, along with the shared substances and feelings of mutual being.

From childhood to adulthood to ancestor-hood

Most of memory and what is recalled from it disappears. This is not surprising for two reasons. Firstly, most memory is inaccessible to recall with only a small portion of what *is* recalled being transmitted and learned. Secondly, what is recalled includes obligations or other even less tolerable things such as stories of intense suffering that children prefer not to know or hear. But some of it is retained and transmitted and some of that is recorded and kept, for instance, in stories told about photographs in an album.

Children are not, for the most part, interested enough to sustain more than momentary openness to what their elders can tell them about themselves, while of course they are open to the endless telling of stories and myths of a more general character, even those that contain warnings and threats. They learn these general stories at home or in local rituals and, in the process, they grow to recognize themselves in them to the extent that they identify with the collective – imagined communities of all kinds – about which these stories are told. In any one so-called 'cultural' setting, however, the same person will have heard and learned many different ways of telling these stories. When Maurice Bloch returned one rainy day to the people he had worked with over a period of more than 40 years, the Zafimaniry of Madagascar, he heard what was for him a new account of the 1947 French retaliation for the anti-colonial revolt in the village of his adoptive family. In this, many villagers had been killed, and the rest had fled into the hills. The new account he heard on this occasion was entirely different from the more ritualized account he had heard before. It was a much more eventful, descriptive, journalistic story. Later, on yet another visit, he was given a similarly journalistic account but this time by a large group of his adoptive family, including children. Both were triggered by their physical location, a hut high above the village in a forest to which the family had fled in 1947. What was notable was that the story was told not just by the older man whose experience it had been, but by his children, who had not experienced anything but the telling of it; yet they all used the inclusive 'we' as the subjects of the events. Besides the ritualistic and the journalistic accounts of recent events, Bloch mentions another kind of storytelling among the Zafimaniry, one that is prefaced by the teller as 'lies' and is the stuff of animal spirits and humans, stories told to scare and amuse. Zafimaniry children, like children elsewhere, encountered various types and genres of storytelling (Bloch 1998, Ch. 7 and 8).

Bloch has very interesting things to add about how eventful stories may come to resemble meta-autobiographical memory. First, the narrative needs a trigger, such as a point in the landscape. Second, it is not so much the narrative, the bare story, that is remembered, but vividly imagined bits of it that themselves trigger the rest of the narrative. Through inference from them, the rest is imagined. Third, the narrative could be invented but is checked and corrected by the first transmitter of the story. Fourth, these images can be searched just as the images of the experiences of autobiographical memory can be searched by the mind of the person recalling them.

Bloch does not say why some stories become like meta-autobiographical memories while others are less well imagined. But it should not be surprising that what sparks his suggestion that some stories become like meta-autobiographical memory is the eventful story. The more ritualized story and the scary mythic stories may be part of the cultural memory of a community of tellers and hearers, including those based on kinship ties. But the eventful story conveys a much closer mutual identification because it is about a recent past that is not patterned according to an accepted order (the ritualized story of the same occurrence). Nor is it in a metaphorical and contiguous relation to another space and time from the present in which it is told (the myth). More to the point of what I am arguing is that the event is not only about an 'I' who lived through it, but that the meta-autobiographical self is in a family of listeners, a 'we' of primary inclusion of those to whom it is transmitted (including Maurice Bloch as adoptive son in the example given above). The fact that the same event can be told in two different ways, one more ritualized than the other, shows how the most intimate sharing of memory can be included in a more general imagined community, one that also includes myths and fairy tales. All of these together can evoke a shared community of kinship that is itself differentiated from the imagined community of a nation-state.

Stories of mutual being are usually told in later life when the elders sense their own mortality and want to pass on their sense of obligation toward previous generations or to tell of their own sufferings and debts; when they become anxious about their own survival after death as they become ancestors to their descendents, and when children are adult enough both to hear their stories and care for them. Even if their stories do not become part of their hearers' autobiographical selves, their hearers are already primed to be haunted by them because they have already internalized them.

Both kinds of story, the more general, cultural memory, and the haunting memory, are recalled, told and learned in local cultural styles or genres and their contents are determined according to the desires and wishes of the teller. Acquired genres of storytelling can turn the familial into a version of a more generalized historical mode told in the third person, though often with an exclusive implied 'us,' and in the opposite direction turn history into familial mode using the first person. Stories are therefore quite varied even as they are recognizable, by which I mean they are narratives with which and through which tellers and hearers identify with each other in more or less intensely imagined ways, with the most intense feelings being fear, apprehension, resentment, anger or love.

To illustrate the idea of haunting memory and to show its extension beyond two generations I turn first to an example of oral transmission and then to one of documentary, archival transmission. In each case, we see intimate, family memory interact with national narratives and national sites of memory. But at the same time they transgress state and national boundaries.

Extensions of haunting memory: the Sora

The first case relates to a shamanic people, the Sora, who live in contemporary India and whose lives have been studied by Piers Vitebsky (1993), who stayed with them in 1976–1977 and 1979, with return visits in later years including a much later visit (Vitebsky 2008). The Sora live high in forested hills in an area on the border between the states of Orissa and Andhra Pradesh on India's eastern seaboard. They live by shifting cultivation, selling some of their produce in local markets. Some of them worked, as they still do today, as migrant laborers. They are incorporated into the Indian nation as a 'scheduled tribe' (*adivasi*) and, belonging to this population category, they are both dominated by and dependent on the Indian state, from which they retreat into their out-of-the-way places (see Tsing 1993), the land of their ancestors. Similarly, they are attracted to and repelled by the market towns where they buy craft and manufactured products, taking them into their own material culture.

Every day in a Sora village at the time of his first study in the 1970s, Vitebsky could hear the sounds of a conversation with an ancestor through a shaman. Shamans are people with a special gift of trance who, through dreams, become aware of a connection to a spirit mediator who escorts them to the Underworld and eventually to a spirit-world marriage partner – the latter being the spirit son or daughter of the living shaman to whom the new shaman is apprenticed and who is usually a patrilineal relative (Vitebsky 1993, 19–20). Eventually the master shaman dies and becomes another spirit mediator. A Sora shaman is either the more revered funeral shaman, usually a woman, or a diviner, more often a man. Shamans are both incarnators and dramatists (250). Until the disappearance of the tradition, funeral shamans conducted and channeled "dialogues with the dead," the title of Vitebsky's book. Through them the living conversed with the dead and heard from them new information, somehow instigated by the dialogue, which also included the dead conversing among themselves each through a shaman turning away from the living and facing the other shamans (18).

According to Vitebsky, remaining faithful to what he learned in the seventies from the Sora and their shamans, the dead exist in the landscape and in the flesh of rememberers who are related by kinship. Like the old, the dead are extensions of the intimate relations learned in childhood through the framework of kinship. The landscape is event-laden, full of places of danger where people have fallen ill or had an accident, or places where someone died. These memories of experiences are assimilated to categories of symptoms that are also causes, called *sonum*, which are never just of the experience itself. They are a reminder of a claim upon living relatives by a dead person who has made them ill or caused an accident similar to one suffered by the dead person (89). *Sonum* are thus extended in scale to a cosmology of Sun, Earth, Leopard and a limited number of other cosmological categories (260–263). Every death and all the immediate dead are *sonum*, threatening their nearest relatives, against which threat sacrifices are made in healing rites.

In the course of a cycle of funeral rituals over three years, followed by a further period after which the name of the ancestor was finally passed on to a newborn, the dead underwent a cleansing from this ambivalent link to experience in which their past was an illness or some other misfortune in the present of one of their kin. They eventually became simply ancestors residing in an Earth site of their kin, on land that is their property. Thus they were cleansed of immediate, communicative memory in Jan Assmann's (2006) sense and could eventually be forgotten, after dying a second death in the Underworld (Vitebsky 1993, 219). But by then they were perpetuated in an ancestral line and their names embedded in a landscape. The Sora would seem to have ritualized communicative memory into what I have called haunting memory by extending it into a cosmology of *sonum* and ancestors.

Vitebsky theorizes shamanically enabled conversation as trans-sentience, crossing between and going beyond experiential memories. Among the Sora the equivalent of a time beyond experience is the idea of completed ancestor-hood, including the land whose use is inherited in the same way as ancestors are inherited in a line of kinship. It is extension beyond birth, life and death, in which molding and forging is both birth and threat to life. The contrast with a monotheistic or secular view of the dead is not quite as blunt as it might appear at first sight, because we can say in general that the living are also fictions, in the sense of being construed and reconstructed at junctures of their lives both by themselves and by others.

In the course of time, Sora cosmology incorporated elements of the larger Indian nation and its key category of caste. Necessary but dangerous work, like forging and molding, or the work of the dirty Sun, became associated with low-caste smiths, while ancestor-hood culminated in the clean Earth, seen as their own, not Indian. Sora have incorporated threats from the Indian state and its dominant ideology into these cosmological senses of their ancestry in which they think of themselves as of Earth and as warrior caste Ancestors, while the Sun is of the unclean Gansi blacksmith caste. Underworld husbands of funeral shamans became another incorporation, as they were considered to be high caste. In other words, we see here an example of how co-extending cultural memories make it impossible to define delimiting boundaries between cultures, even while identities are formed by differentiation from others who are strangers. Through her Underworld marriage, the funeral shaman became a half-stranger in the Sora midst. This bringing in of the outside turned oppressive strangers into allies against other threats. Through dialogues with their dead the Sora thus took strangers into a cosmology that is on a scale that passes through their own ancestry to a greater sense of the world, greater in scale than the India in which they live. It transgresses the nation and its policed community of belonging by insisting on kinship and by the cosmology that encompasses kinship, providing a different narrative than the state's historical narrative, even while including elements of that narrative (for example, the Hindu caste system) into its own.

In his later visit, Vitebsky (2008) found that there were no longer any practicing shamans. The young had converted to Baptist Christianity. They had repudiated the dialogue with their parents and ancestors. There had long been a Baptist mission in what Vitebsky calls a "frontier" town between the Hindu nation and the Sora hills, but between the 1970s and the 1990s aggressive road-building and constructions of primary schools, the physical and ideological apparatuses of nation-building, involved the young in trading, schooling and bureaucracy at a great pace. It left them in a state of shame about their sparsely clad, hard hillside agriculture and the shamanic ways of their mothers and fathers. Baptist Christianity had now become a way of avoiding complete Hinduization. The sense of superiority in their shamanic dialogues and a land marked by the ancestors had given way to two alternatives of repudiating all that. For Hindus, the Sora were credited with a prehistory of one or more of the key Hindu spirits, in a national historical narrative that turned Sora into a *lieu de mémoire*. On the other hand, Baptist Christianity now served as a new way to achieve and maintain their distinctiveness. Both narratives repudiated shamanic dialogues with ancestors. But this is not a story of the inevitable. The maintenance of an ancestral cosmology and landscape in the face of Indian nation-formation could not be sustained in this instance; yet, other Austronesian peoples in India and throughout Southeast Asia (for instance in Taiwan, see Yang 2005), did indeed maintain their memories and traditions, even when they combined them with Christianity.

I have discussed the Sora as an example of an extension of intimate, haunting memory into a cosmology, because Vitebsky's ethnography emphasizes a characteristic that I want to continue exploring in my next example: that of prolonged answerability between the dead and the living.

Extensions of haunting memory: a Jewish family in Berlin

My second illustration of haunting memory comes from my own work with a Russian Jewish family in Berlin.[1] This is the Berlin of unified Germany. Compared to the Sora, the contrast is great, with a much more text-based system of learning, remarkable in this instance for a concerted effort by the state, not just through schools but also through memorials, museums and the law, to bring its population to know and reject Nazism, and to recognize its Jewish past (Feuchtwang 2011, Ch. 8). An important way in which Jews in contemporary Germany, nearly all of them post-war immigrants, are included in the unified nation is through the institution of city Communities (*Gemeinde*), self-governing but tax-financed organizations of Jewish rite, schooling and culture. The head of the family, Baruch, to whom I now turn, was a stalwart of the Berlin Community when I met him in 2002.

In the family of Baruch and his wife Julia, a key part of their personal archive is a text he wrote about his internal dialogues with his immediate patrilineal ancestors, his father and grandfather, and through them a line reaching back to King Solomon's goldsmith. Of course, this is not a story he learned through German schools or any German history or memorial site. It is, however, a story that is recognizable to other Jews and, through their incorporation as German communities, assimilated as a subculture of Germany. Even so, the imagined community that his extension beyond his meta-autobiographical self creates and invokes, takes him and his family well beyond Germany.

---

1 For the context of this family, see Feuchtwang (2011); for another example of a Berlin Russian Jewish family, see Feuchtwang (2005).

Their record of the family includes a landscape of burials that are also of great significance to Baruch's discovery of a Jewish commitment and Julia's discovery of her Jewish matriline. The text, to which he gave the title *Die Stimmen* (The Voices), was in the words of his son Solomon a work of history and the replacement for a greater archive:

> Once your parents have died, history disappears with them. For my father too this is a new theme, whereas it wasn't for twenty years ... It is not easy to hold on to this kind of information these days when we are overwhelmed with different kinds of information. There was a large family archive in Leningrad but it was annihilated (*vernichtet*) during the war. So my father took a major step.

These remarks fit well with Pierre Nora's 'prosthesis memory' (1989, 14), inaugurated by the cult of history and sites of memory. This makes the extensions of Baruch's German family different from those of the Sora. Nevertheless Baruch's extensions also take us beyond the nation despite their incorporation into a nation.

The Voices is both a record of communicative memory and a history extending that memory backwards, namely haunting memory. The voices in question are those of ancestors and living people heard during moments of crisis in the inner ears of Baruch, his father Israel and his father's father Solomon-Chaim. *The Voices* announces itself in its first sentences as a fiction, in the sense of a fabrication or a fable that carries out the biographical and pious (*fromm*) duty (*Pflicht*), directed by an illustrious patrilineal covenant, linked to Noah's covenant with God. In this covenant, humanity, not a people, was the subject. For readers and for those like you who are reading *about* it, the story is a personal vision of humanity, the Jewish humanism of a man in Berlin, and therefore it is a historical document. But for Baruch *The Voices* is a partial consummation of a meta-autobiographical self, fulfilling an obligation to be handed down the male line to his son. The ancestors he has created as heroes are also the voices to whom he is answerable and among whom he has included himself as his own hero. Positioning the narrator where the author can be seen makes *The Voices* more than a genealogy, because it places its author as an 'I,' not simply as one name among others. But starting from this 'I' it extends itself through ancestral biographies. At the same time it elaborates and commits to paper something that everyone does ordinarily. We all imagine our life being told, even as we live it, by recollecting others whose lives are intensely meaningful and who judge us. We are answerable to them, and they are proximate tellers of our meta-autobiographical story.

Writing the book came after a series of crucial decisions, which are events in his and Julia's life, told to his son Solomon, who like his father has the self-professed character, as they both told me, of one who must declare his life to be the result of decisions. For both of them, the ultimate decision is to choose what kind of human being you are, striving to be a decent and generous human being (a *Mensch*). On the way came some other personal decisions. The first of them for Baruch was the decision in 1975 to marry Julia, with whom he had fallen in love when he met her in his home city of Moscow, where she was a foreign university student of Slavonic studies. At the time of their decision she was already pregnant by him, and with marriage they also decided to bring up their child as Jewish.

Julia is less rationalizing. Despite her strictly Christian upbringing, she had made a gradual approach toward Judaism from hints and intuitions, until two of her great aunts informed her that her mother's mother was Jewish, but had been brought up as a Christian. It was only in 1990 that she and Baruch found her grave, in Saxony. But her decision to become Jewish meant defying her mother and sister, who insisted that she remains Christian. Her becoming Jewish meant they excluded her from her heritage as they asserted themselves to be the only heirs to her grandmother. She could not even inherit access to her grandmother's diary.

Baruch said to me that he had decided to be Jewish. First, however, he had "to make a decision to make this decision," as he put it, and in doing so go beyond the negative definition of Jewishness with which he was labeled in the Soviet Union. This could happen only after a period of confusion and shame, his state of mind at the time he met Julia. She "put me on my feet … After emigration [to Germany in 1975] it became a conscious work. I came to an insight that I must define myself religiously to become a *Mensch*." He then described his examination of all major religions in the history of religion with Julia's help, examining in each case their concepts of God, *Mensch*, World, Action and Faith, before deciding positively that Judaism had the best answers.

The haunting memory of kinship that the union of Baruch and Julia brought together includes the following archival treasures that could also be called sites of memory, but now with reference to a community of kin, not of a single nation: a gravestone in the Jewish section of an East Prussian graveyard that names Julia's maternal great grandmother, but without the inscription of a Hebrew blessing; a Torah roll of a Russian rabbi and scholar, Baruch's paternal great grandfather which is, with *The Voices*, a remainder and substitute for the 'annihilated' family archive in Leningrad/St Petersburg. Two further treasures must be added. One is a mass grave in Byelorussia, in Israel's (Baruch's father's) birthplace where Israel's first wife (before he married Baruch's mother) and son are buried along with many other paternal relatives after their slaughter by Nazi invaders.

The other is in Israel. When Baruch's father was fatally ill in Moscow, Baruch had succeeded after great difficulty in returning to Moscow in time to see him. On his deathbed in 1976, father Israel asked to be cremated and for Baruch to take his ashes from Moscow to be buried in the land of Israel. After overcoming great religio-bureaucratic difficulties when he got there with his father's ashes, he and a Moscow friend planted a cypress tree by the grave. Back in Germany it took him fifteen more difficult years to be in a position in which he could finance a trip to revisit his father's grave. The roots of the tree had caused upheaval and the tree itself had been split by lightening. He repaired the grave and left the scarred cypress, in his words, "as a memorial."

These memorial treasures constitute the personal historical archive that allows this small family and their internalized objects to extend beyond themselves, to each other, as well as to their parents and grandparents. They constitute the myths they live by, in the fiction of their lives which they tell of themselves as if in a narrative told by another. The treasures are objects that Baruch and Julia, principally, have created and to which they have made themselves answerable. In the process of creating or finding them they have recreated themselves as the persons they sincerely professed to be in our[2] interviews with them. In this social creativity they emphasize not only certain relations at the expense of others, Julia's Jewish matriline at the expense of her mother and sister, Baruch's relation with Julia and their son at the expense of his daughter Ursula and two other children, none of whom had become Jewish, and the countless ancestors he left out of *The Voices*; in Julia's case she also deliberately removed or re-signified what she had learned as a Protestant child.

The Voices is a recovery from great loss. There was the destruction of the family archive in the siege of Leningrad and the slaughter in Byelorussia. Yet even this stands for losses on a larger scale, those by which three nations are defined in their historiographies, school histories and commemorations: Russia/Soviet Union/Russia; Prussia/Germany/Third Reich/East and West/Germany; and the people of the covenants of Noah, Abraham, and Moses with a single and only God that Zionism turned into the nation of Israel. The stories of this Berlin family do not add up, however, nor do they scale up to these nation-stories. The emphasis, in Baruch's and Julia's own terms, is on loyalties to old friends in Moscow, one pair of whom are the parents of Solomon's wife, co-grandparents with Baruch and Julia. Another emphasis is on the Jewish community in Berlin and thence to the Jews of Germany, and thence to Israel and its claims on the Jewish diaspora. Their command to remember is for Jews to glorify a human as well as a Jewish covenant with their God, an identity that already creates a tension with the Jewishness promoted by the state of Israel. Here, in Germany, Baruch and Julia emphasize

---

2 My research colleague Tsypylma Darieva and myself. All quotes in this section come from my conversations with the quoted people, which took place in 2002.

their own understanding of the first covenant, a humanism of transcendental rationality (of being a *Mensch*) as an answer to the philosophical question 'How should I live?'

As interpenetrated selves, the voices that Baruch wrote about are not the only voices he must entertain; they must also include Julia's, for instance. Julia's voices in her turn undoubtedly include both those of the mother who rejected her and the grandmother who supported her. Solomon without doubt has others within him, in addition to those of his parents. I make no claims to know about any more than what they presented to us. Baruch's self-presentations were almost certainly idealizations. They can be summarized as constituting his ideal of a rationally choosing integrated self. More intimate knowledge would no doubt reveal undermining and shifting voices of kinship, of friendship, of denials and the results of hostile encounters that last in the mind, such as those he experienced in Moscow. They too are transmitted, or at least they were to us to a small extent. Idealized and negative, they are alike in being distinct and multiple. Yet their ambivalence is contained in the one, rather powerful person of Baruch. They make up his self-portrait at a certain time and place, his time with Julia since moving to Berlin.

When Baruch and Julia die, only what has been internalized in Solomon's, and differently in Ursula's communicative memory, will survive as an internal dialogue. But their archive and the coordinates of their haunting memory will extend to something that includes but goes well beyond Germany, to Russia and to Israel. It would be hard to say whether that belonging is congruent – that is to say of a kind and assimilable – with the historical narrative that is taught in the schools of any of these states. Baruch, Julia and Solomon contribute to each of the nation-stories their own understanding, of Russia as the land of an intelligentsia of dissidents, of Germany as the seat of a Nazi past that devastated Eastern Europe as well as Germany, of Israel as a refuge. As a family, though, they extend their story beyond all of these; their archive with its ruptures – ruptures that they have personally suffered through their kin – is not a prosthesis for a national memory, but for another, reproductive and reparative temporality.

Conclusion

From these illustrations, extremely different from one another, we can see that haunting memory leads in several directions, away from a narrow focus on the state as the social milieu of memory. Both of my cases distinguish the vivid voices of the recent dead, in external or internal dialogue with the living, rooted in the longer ancestral archive of the land(s) to which they refer as their homes. The Sora familial extensions led to a cosmology (now in their background, because they are fast becoming Christian). Baruch's humanist Judaism is shared by other Jews, but certainly not by the majority in Russia or Germany, or in Israel dominated by a Jewish nationalist ideology of a promised land for a chosen people. They do not defy state, faith or cultural memories; they simply add up to something else, in another temporality, that of familial reproduction. The extension of haunting memory is to a sense of community with others, visions of a world well beyond that of the people of a nation. They are visions of a trans-sentient formation (the interpenetration of selves) that has been extended. In Bakhtin's term, the extension is transgredient (intimate answerability writ large) in a way that simply does not coincide with the nation. For the community that shares such a vision of answerability, its rituals and memorial treasures will be familiar to others, to other Sora or, in Baruch's and Julia's case, familiar to other Jews. They diverge from the national cultural memory not as a reinterpretation but as something else, as another cultural memory or as familial sites of memory. Instead of assuming the family into the basic institution of a nation or of a faith as those nations' and faiths' ideologies always claim, I suggest that mutual being and interpenetrating meta-autobiographical memories can and do take their own paths of archiving, transmission and the formation of distinctive cultural memories.

References

Assmann, Jan. *Religion and Cultural Memory*. Stanford: Stanford UP, 2006.

Bloch, Maurice. *Anthropology and the Cognitive Challenge*. Cambridge: Cambridge UP, 2012.

Bloch, Maurice. "The Blob." *Anthropology of this Century* 1 (May 2011). aotcpress.com/articles/blob/ (accessed 21 March 2014).

Bloch, Maurice. "Durkheimian Anthropology and Religion: Going In and Out of Each Other's Bodies." *Religion, Anthropology, and Cognitive Science*. Eds. Harvey Whitehouse and James Laidlaw. Durham: Carolina Academic Press, 2007. 63–80.

Bloch, Maurice. *How We Think They Think: Anthropological Approaches to Cognition, Memory and Literacy*. Boulder: Westview Press, 1998.

Feuchtwang, Stephan. "Mythical Moments in National and Other Family Histories." *History Workshop Journal* 59.1 (2005): 251–265.

Feuchtwang, Stephan. *After the Event; The Transmission of Grievous Loss in Germany, Taiwan and China*. Oxford: Berghahn Books, 2011.

Halbwachs, Maurice. *On Collective Memory*. Trans. Lewis A. Coser. Chicago: University of Chicago Press, 1992.

Holquist, Michael and Vadim Liapunov, eds. *Art and Answerability: Early Philosophical Essays by M. M. Bakhtin*. Austin: University of Texas Press, 1990.

Nora, Pierre. "Between Memory and History: *Les Lieux de Mémoire*." Trans. Marc Roudebush. *Representations* 26.1 (1989): 7–24.

Nora, Pierre. *Rethinking France: Les Lieux de mémoire*. Ed. David P. Jordan. Trans. Mary Seidman Trouille. Chicago: University of Chicago Press, 2001.

Sahlins, Marshall. "What Kinship is." Parts 1 and 2. *Journal of the Royal Anthropological Institute* 17.1 and 2 (2012): 227–242.

Tóibín, Colm. "Writers and Their Families." *Guardian* 17 February 2012. www.theguardian.com/books/2012/feb/17/colm-toibin-how-i-killed-my-mother (accessed 21 March 2014).

Tsing, Anna. *In the Realm of the Diamond Queen: Marginality in an Out-of-the-Way Place*. Princeton: Princeton UP, 1993.

Vitebsky, Piers. *Dialogues with the Dead: The Discussion of Mortality Among the Sora of Eastern India*. Cambridge: Cambridge UP, 1993.

Vitebsky, Piers. "Loving and Forgetting: Moments of Inarticulacy in Tribal India." *Journal of the Royal Anthropological Institute* 24.2 (2008): 243–261.

Yang, Shuyuan. "Imagining the State: An Ethnographic Study." *Ethnography* 6.4 (2005): 487–516.

Susan Legêne and Martijn Eickhoff
Postwar Europe and the Colonial Past in Photographs

"Oh dear, let us not *also* include the War in the Pacific ..." This was the first re-action to our proposal to present a paper on WWII in the final conference of the research program photoCLEC. This program was charged with investigating the meaning of colonial photograph collections in contemporary Norway, the UK and the Netherlands.[1] As historians of Dutch colonialism, we saw a logical place for WWII in the study of photographic collections as colonial legacies. In Dutch historical discourse, colonialism and the war simply cannot be separated (Captain 2002; Scagliola 2002; Wiebenga 2012) since Indonesian Independence was de-clared only two days after the Japanese surrender on 15 August 1945. The Nether-lands did not accept this unilateral decision, and many people in the Netherlands today still know from first-hand experience how overseas the war's ending turned into a new period of violence and insecurity for civilians, also called the *bersiap* period. In recent exhibitions and documentary films the sequence of colonialism, war and the struggle for decolonization has been remembered through oral testi-monies, archival documents and historical photographs and films.[2] Any research into the colonial past in the Netherlands inevitably also touches upon the War in the Pacific. In the first instance, however, this seemed less evident in Norway or the UK.

---

1 Research for this article is based on the HERA project "Photographs, Colonial Legacy and Muse-ums in Contemporary European Culture" (photoCLEC), with Elizabeth Edwards (De Montfort Uni-versity Leicester) as program leader. See also photoclec.dmu.ac.uk (accessed 21 March 2014). The final conference took place at the Pitt Rivers Museum in Oxford, 12–13 January 2012. We thank the photoCLEC teams in the UK, Norway and the Netherlands for the inspiring and at times thought-provoking collaboration. Some of the arguments in this article with respect to museum policies and practices have been elaborated for an invited keynote lecture at the ICMAH/COMCOL Annual Conference 2012, Cape Town, 8 November 2012. The authors also thank Harco Gijsbers and René Kok of the NIOD-visual archive for their support and advice.
2 Recent examples are the documentary *Water van goud* (Water of Gold) made by Jos Janssen and Martin van den Oever and shown in the 'veteran cabin' in Museum Bronbeek in 2011; the docu-mentary *Merdeka! De oorlog na de oorlog, standplaats Castricum* (Merdeka! The War after the War, in Castricum) made by Pauline van Vliet and shown in the Strandvondstenmuseum Castricum in the summer of 2012.

The initial misunderstanding regarding the connection between colonialism and the WWII made us aware that we live today with different *national* histories of *European* imperialism. This chapter approaches photographs from the WWII as sources to understand this nationalization of empire. It argues that *postwar* – to quote the title of Tony Judt's famous grand narrative of European history after 1945 (Judt 2005) – the transnationalism that characterized European imperialism disappeared from national historiography and memory cultures, thus turning citizenship into an exclusive national phenomenon as well. Beginning with a brief excursus on the events in Surabaya in 1945 in which both the British and the Dutch were involved, we will then discuss how pictures of decolonization included in the main Dutch WWII archive show this historiographic nationalization of European imperialism. It is important to adopt a transnational perspective connecting WWII and decolonization in order to develop a better understanding of Europe's common history of colonialism.

Remembering Surabaya 1945

Filmmaker Peter Hoogendijk's mother Thera André was a teenager in Surabaya when young Indonesian nationalists (*Pemuda*) and Dutch civilians who had just been liberated from the Japanese internment camps confronted each other in the 'flag incident' at the *Hotel Oranje* on 19 September 1945, a few weeks after the Indonesian Declaration of Independence. After the Dutch had raised the Red-White-Blue national flag, this was brought down by the Pemuda who tore the blue bar, and raised the flag again, now as the Indonesian Red-White (*Merah Putih*) flag. This was the start of heavy fighting, in the course of which the British Brigadier Aubertin W. S. Mallaby of the 49th infantry brigade of the 23rd Indian Division, who was in the process of negotiating a ceasefire on 30 October 1945, was killed when his car became stuck in the hostile masses on the streets. In the ensuing Battle of Surabaya, which lasted from 10 November until early December 1945, at least 6,000 persons died – most of them Indonesians, but also hundreds of Indian soldiers. Dutch and Asian-Dutch civilians were hunted by the nationalists; many were murdered or died in the fighting or during the evacuation. Another 200,000 inhabitants of Surabaya fled the city. Thera André was evacuated and came to the Netherlands. The Battle of Surabaya was a disastrous episode in a complicated global history. In Indonesia, 10 November is a public holiday to commemorate the heroes of the national revolution; in the Netherlands these events are not widely known (see also Frederick 1989).

In 2007, Peter Hoogendijk made a documentary movie in which he reconstructs the events, together with his mother. To the DVD-edition of this documentary movie *Soerabaja/Surabaya* (2007) he added the uncut interview with the two sons of Brigadier Mallaby: Sir Christopher Mallaby, a former diplomat, and Antony Mallaby, a former major in the army. They had been six and nine years old when their father died. In Hoogendijk's film they tell his story in minute detail, each adding to the other's narration. While speaking about the events that led to the killing of their father, Antony Mallaby becomes very emotional. As if to explain himself, he suddenly states: "Getting caught up in somebody else's quarrel is of course the very worst thing that can happen to you." He goes on to say that the fighting turned into "a dreadful waste of human resources and human lives," obviously also including the death of his own father. In response to Hoogendijk's inquiry about the meaning of "somebody else's quarrel," Mallaby, still upset, replies that this was a quarrel "between the Dutch and the Indonesians, not our quarrel / nor between the Indian army and the Indonesians." At this point, Sir Christopher Mallaby takes over and explains in a somewhat patronizing mode – as if also to comfort his brother – how difficult it is to be caught up in problems that were "not your ultimate responsibility." Hoogendijk then asks him why the British nevertheless took this role, and the diplomat answers, now somewhat agitated as well: "*Some*body had to do it." Further, he emphasizes that it was also a matter of teaching the Pemudas a lesson: "Mountbatten said, you don't bump off the senior officer and think that you can get away with it, especially if you are an illegal regime." Mallaby thus redirects the account of the events and their personal sorrow as sons, to the formal position and military rank of his father and the events of history.[3] In historiography those events have been interpreted as "a tragedy in a power vacuum" (Tønnesson 1995, 121, 141–142; see also Frederick 1989).

It was precisely this interview that triggered our interest in the nationalization of narratives about the colonial past in the course of decolonization. Antony Mallaby voiced a fully understandable distance from what he and his brother saw as Dutch/Indonesian decolonization troubles. His reflections reside in personal sorrow and anger, age making him and his brother more vulnerable to the sad memories of the past. Yet we might also understand their reactions as more than personal emotions. We can see them as testimony to a dominant British historical framing of the history of decolonization, from which the imagined imperial futures of 1945 and pride in the common cause that the Allied Forces were serving

---

3 Peter Hoogendijk, *Soerabaya/Surabaya*, interview with Mallaby's sons; quotes between 27 min. 29 seconds and 30 min. 17 seconds. The DVD states that Mallaby's sons express their personal view, not officially authorized opinions.

in South-East Asia have disappeared. The trauma of the lost father then attaches itself to the trauma of decolonization as seen from a British perspective.

However, at a viewing of this interview fragment at the January 2012 photo-CLEC final conference in Oxford, the British participants were not as moved as we were (and somehow still are) each time we watch it. They seemed somewhat amused by the distinguished upper class style of the two brothers and their roles and interaction in the interview. This difference in perception made us realize again how any discussion on decolonization is value-loaded. Photographs are relational objects (Edwards 2006). As framed representations of past events, and as pictures framed in national collections, they may help us explain such different perceptions.

Fig. 1. Photograph by Peter Hoogendijk of his desk, including the famous photograph of Mallaby's car as a postcard from Hotel Majapahit in Surabaya; on the wall a copy of a posthumous portrait of brigadier A. S. Mallaby, to the left the cover of his 2007 documentary film; reproduced courtesy of Peter Hoogendijk.

When asked what was the most important historical photograph of the Surabaya events, and where he had found it, documentary maker Peter Hoogendijk chose the destroyed car in the streets of Surabaya, in which the British Brigadier Mallaby had been killed on 30 October 1945 (Figure 1). The photograph belongs to the collection of the Imperial War Museum in London and is dated November 1945 (IWM SE-5865; worldwide available now through Wikimedia Commons). It was, according to the documentation, taken by Sergeant D. Davis and/or Sergeant D. MacTavish (No. 9. Army Film and Photographic Unit).[4] Since these were British photographers, in the image the British are present through their absence; the army photographer documented the spot where Mallaby died. The military vehicles in the background and – visible only by zooming in on the digitized online image – the two Indian soldiers at the road block suggest that the situation is under control, whereas the undamaged sign celebrating Indonesian independence underlines the fact that the English did not interfere in the ideological battle which the Dutch did not yet (and in many respects still do not) understand as a battle that had already been lost in 1942.

Peter Hoogendijk's own copy, which is visible in Figure 1, is from a postcard bought at the Hotel Majapahit, the current name of the Hotel Oranje where the Flag Incident had incited the violent fights that would lead to the Battle of Surabaya.[5] From a Dutch perspective the image of Mallaby's destroyed Lincoln sedan reads as a clash between the irregular violence against Westerners that characterized the first months after the Indonesian unilateral declaration of Independence, and the pre-war modern urban late colonial Dutch order with its roads, street signs and street lighting. Insiders will recognize at the other side of the street the 'Gedung Cerutu' (cigar building) and the 'Internatio'-building situated at the Willemsplein (now Jl. Taman Jayengrono). In Indonesia, where the Battle of Surabaya is annually commemorated, Mallaby's car is the iconic image of that 'dreadful struggle for Surabaya' (pertempuran Surabaya yang bahsyat) as the back of the postcard reads. William Frederick characterizes the photograph – which was made the next day, according to his Indonesian informants who thus claim their agency in this image, by an Indonesian press photographer – as "a fine, evocative portrait" of the burned-out car, and "a mute testimony" against a backdrop of colonial architecture. It had been taken after "... the city returned to a resemblance of a clear-sky normality yet trembled with a sense of expectancy" (Frederick 1989, 264).[6]

This photograph thus refers to a contested transnational history, relevant to Indonesia, the UK, India, Japan and the Netherlands. It is an iconic picture with various historical developments and conflicting views on decolonization converging in its image. It is a postcard for tourists and re-emerges in many references to

---

4 Wikimedia commons. en.wikipedia.org/File:IWM-SE-5865-Brigadier-Mallaby-burnt-car -194511.jpg (accessed 6 January 2012).
5 The Hotel Oranje became Hotel Yamato during the Japanese occupation and is now Hotel Majapahit. The Flag Incident is commemorated with a plaque on the building.
6 Mallaby's death in this car is also described in Sutomo (1951, 123–128), however, without the photograph.

the Battle of Surabaya. Besides, it has become an iconic picture appealing to other contexts of (civil) war in an urban setting (Aasman 2010, 184).

Transnational histories in national historiography

The entanglements of colonialism, WWII and decolonization are interpreted differently in different European postcolonial contexts on the basis of diverging national historiographies, as we also experienced in the photoCLEC collaboration on Norway, the UK and the Netherlands. In Norway European colonialism is a part of national history, since Norwegians were involved overseas in the colonial superstructures of various European countries and in the internal colonization of Sámi people in the North (Tygesen and Wæhle 2006; Lien 2011). 'Decolonization,' however, seems not relevant to Norwegian historiography. In the Anglo-American literature, the War in the Pacific is generally associated with almost four years of warfare against the Japanese Southern Army, on the water, in the air, over land, by the South West Pacific Area Allied Forces under General Douglas MacArthur, and the British South-East Asian Command SEAC with its Indian Army troops led by Lord Louis Mountbatten (Tønnesson 1995, 117; Best et al. 2008, 196–199; Shipway 2008, 101 and passim). Against this background, the specific history of decolonization in Indonesia which dominates Dutch historiography and memory practices, features in the UK as just one aspect of a global Commonwealth history that also involves changing political relationships with Australia and New Zealand, Singapore, India, Malaya/Malaysia, Burma and many more countries in the British, French (Indochina), American (the Philippines) colonial realms, and the Chinese or Soviet sphere of influence. This British Empire history is not necessarily associated with England's 'finest hour' at the outbreak of WWII in Europe, nor with the decolonization which came after the war (Mead 2012).

Such differences with respect to decolonization histories and WWII also play out in different historical relationships to the founding of the United Nations. After Roosevelt and Churchill's Atlantic Charter of 14 August 1941, both the Norwegian and the Netherlands governments-in-exile were among the 26 countries that on 1 and 2 January 1942 signed the Declaration by United Nations and thus acknowledged "the right of all peoples to choose the form of government under which they will live."[7] In Dutch historiography, the signing of this Declaration by United Nations is hardly mentioned, and then certainly not connected to Dutch colonial

---

[7] A few months after signing the Declaration, Pangeran Adipati Soejono became the first and only Indonesian member ever of a Dutch Government (from 9 June 1942 until his death on 5 Janu-

history and decolonization, even though in 1945 the first article of the Indonesian Constitution would be a direct quote from this declaration.[8] After 1945 the Netherlands made a kind of 'false start' by its refusal to accept Indonesian Independence. Between 1947 and 1949 this even resulted in six Resolutions on Indonesia by that very Security Council (Shipway 2008, 106).[9] As in the case of the Battle of Surabaya, this is another example of how in the Netherlands the dominant understanding of Dutch/Indonesian history as a national history blocks a broader perspective on the postwar history of decolonization.

Counter to these national historiographies of decolonization, photograph collections bear witness to the many transnational moments of nineteenth- and early twentieth-century European colonialism. As argued on the photoCLEC website,[10] the images contained in such collections and their histories of acquisition show how imperialism referred to a common cause, which was culturally internalized throughout Europe (see also MacKenzie 2011). Burbank and Cooper argue that it was not nationalism, but thinking like an empire *in* Europe *beyond* the European continent that was inherent to European state formation (Burbank and Cooper 2010). In line with this, while discussing German involvement in colonialism after the loss of the German colonies in 1918, Bernhard Gissibl states that the "visual language of colonialism was exchangeable unless nationalized by contextualizing information" (Gissibl 2011, 180). This visual language was directly related to and an expression of historical practice that was not bound by the national borders of European nation-states. Although the Weimar Republic was no colonial power, Germans, like the Norwegians and other Europeans, stayed involved in transnational colonial processes, for instance through the expansion of colonial markets, the consumption of colonial products, settlement overseas or missionary activities (Gissibl 2011).

As a corpus, photograph collections exceed the narrative templates of national historiographies. Both image-wise and as printed objects with specific biographies and provenance, in many instances they refer to colonialism's transna-

---

ary 1943). The Dutch Government in exile did not follow up on his political views with respect to Indonesia's future (Shipway 2008, 87; Best 2008, 103; Giebels 1999, 320–322).

8 The preamble of the 1945 Indonesian Constitution opens with: "With independence being the right of every nation, colonialism must be eliminated from the face of the earth as it is contrary to the dictates of human nature and justice;" see web.parliament.go.th/parcy/sapa_db/cons_doc/constitutions/data/Indonesia/Indonesian{%}20Constitution.htm (accessed 1 December 2012). Hellema does not even mention the Dutch ratification of this Declaration by the United Nations (2006: 108–121; 133–139).

9 The Indonesian Republic and the Netherlands were assisted by a United Nations Good Offices Committee, see Security Council Resolutions 27, 31, 36, 63, 64, 67.

10 www.photoclec.dmu.ac.uk (accessed 21 March 2014).

tional dynamics: those situations where colonial powers collaborated overseas in order to balance their interests in Europe. We can read in the images how such transnationalism overseas concerned the organization of colonial labor and colonial armies; the missionary societies that sent their people all over the world; the shipping companies and other enterprises that foreshadowed the emergence of multinational economic cooperation connected to steel, coal and steam. Photographs also document how transnationalism was inherent in academic practices from geographical explorations and ethnography to cultural and physical anthropology that placed the overseas societies into a 'timeless present,' fixed in museum collections and displays. And finally, and this is our focus here, photograph collections visualize the political aspirations, war, peace and forced or voluntary migration associated with the transnational dynamics inherent to decolonization.[11]

Decolonization not only enlarged but also fundamentally changed the nature of the colonial photograph collections. In the case of the Netherlands and the Netherlands East Indies, pictures relating to the colonial past to a large extent were brought to the Netherlands in the very process of decolonization between 1945 and 1958. They came with the so-called repatriates (Europeans and people of Asian-Dutch descent who were leaving their country of birth), with demobilized soldiers of the colonial Royal Netherlands East Indies Army who did not opt for inclusion in the Indonesian Republican Army, soldiers demobilized from the Royal Netherlands Army, jobless Dutch civil servants, the company staff of nationalized Dutch or multinational enterprises and plantations, and with other groups who were forced to leave Indonesia or chose to do so. In the course of time, these immigrants or their children donated the photographs to various Dutch cultural institutions, both old ones like the former Colonial Museum (now Tropenmuseum), and newly-established ones like the NIOD (Willems 2001; Seriese 2011; Pattynama 2012; Van Dijk et al. 2012). With their donations to the colonial archive, people inserted their overseas histories of the Netherlands Indies into Dutch histories of the colonial past.

---

11 See the photoCLEC website at photoclec.dmu.ac.uk, and the special issue of *Photography and Culture* (Volume 5.3, 2012) with Sigrid Lien, Elizabeth Edwards and Susan Legêne as guest editors. See also Van Dijk et al. (2012); MacKenzie (2011).

The NIOD archive

We will approach this question of national perceptions of the end of European imperialism with the photograph collections of the *NIOD, the Netherlands Institute for War, Holocaust and Genocide Studies* in Amsterdam. This historical institute was founded in May 1945, directly after the end of WWII in Europe, and was given the name 'Rijksinstituut voor Oorlogsdocumentatie' (State Institute for War Documentation). As a state institution, it was charged with the task of 'documenting' the recent 'Dutch' experiences of war, occupation, collaboration, persecution and resistance. In February 1946 an 'Indies' department was added, based in what many Dutchmen still called Batavia (present-day Jakarta). It focused on the Japanese occupation of the Dutch East Indies and gradually also on what would follow, the *bersiap* period. In 1949, after the recognition of Indonesian Independence by the Dutch, the staff and the collection of this Indies department was moved to the Netherlands. Here, the collection grew considerably. The more than 10,000 'Indies' photographs were stored as part of the NIOD Visual Archive which nowadays includes more than 150,000 pictures. In 2000 this collection was digitalized and made available through the website *Beeldbank WO2 (Image Repository WWII)*.[12] Since 2008 this website provides access to the WWII-related photo collections of several Dutch institutions (Cohen 2007; Gruythuysen 2009).

In our discussion of the NIOD's pictures acquired since 1945, we want to emphasize the meaning of their provenance – the different pathways to their acquisition.[13] Pictures were collected in the context of decolonization, but also during the restoration of lawful order in the Netherlands itself, leading, for example, to the confiscation of the image collection of the photo press agency "Fotobureau Hollandia" that had collaborated with the Germans. Individual Dutch professionals and amateurs also added their personal photo albums. These scattered collecting practices gradually converged with the historical research done at the institute. Until the start of the twenty-first century, historical research focused exclusively on what was understood as 'Dutch' history at the time (Kok and Somers 2011; Van Dartel 2012). As such, the NIOD provides an outstanding example of the development of a dominant national framework applied to the transnational history

---

12 www.niod.nl/en/imagebase-ww2 (accessed 21 March 2014).
13 As we will see below, the reverse side of each picture and other contextual information provide ample information about its biography. In the process of archiving, NIOD has arranged the printed photographs according to subject, location or theme. Whereas this added a layer of information, it also obscured historical connections related to the maker of the photograph, the sequence of their making or their order, for example, within the initial archive of German friendly press agencies in the Netherlands (Bool 1991, 25; Edwards 2001; Stoler 2009).

of decolonization, as we will show with photographs related to the UK and the Netherlands.

Institutionally, the NIOD photograph collection has no direct roots in the empire. In Dutch *national* historiography, the end of WWII marks a turning point, and this is where the NIOD starts – whereas in Dutch *colonial* historiography its outbreak marks the beginning of the end, and this is where the colonial photograph collections end. To many people, memories of war, memories of decolonization and memories of migration are almost inseparably entwined, but they cannot easily be addressed at the same time. The stereo-sound of these two narratives creates a 'phase difference.' This difference might be connected to the "power vacuum" in the Empire's last transnational moments: the ending of the war. Out of this vacuum, as for instance in Surabaya 1945, the past would become nationalized. This nationalization of the colonial past has "virtually banished" imperial history to the margins of national historiography, according to Aldrich and Wards, emphasizing parallel histories of empire, with little consideration for the "contested relationship between empire and nation-state" (Aldrich and Wards 2010, 260; see also Legêne 2010, 13, 22).[14] This nationalization of Europe's imperial past was preceded by fundamental changes in the perception of Empire – the way European powers had 'thought' like an empire – that came with the outbreak of WWII.[15]

Martin Shipway argues that the Nazi-German invasion of other European countries and the arrival of governments-in-exile in London changed thinking about the purpose of Empire; in these times of national crisis, instead of being developed by them, colonies were initially supposed to bring support to their mother countries. Soon, the UN Declaration further changed the perception of 'imperial futures,' and ideas emerged about federative political bonds between

---

14 H. L. Wesseling's handbook on Europe's colonialism in the nineteenth century (2003, English Edition 2004) is a case in point. The careful description of the expansionist policies and colonial strategies of the major European colonial powers embedded in the balance of power politics of the European Concert system, is organized within a framework of nation-states that, as such, is not problematized. With its focus on the colonialism of the maritime empires, it also suggests a divide between Eastern and Western Europe, as would dominate historiography after WWII (Cooper 2005, 171; Leonhard and Von Hirschhausen 2011, 15; MacKenzie 2011). Leonhard and Von Hirschhausen, who aim to contribute to "writing Europe's history no longer as the sum of isolated national narratives, but as a complex interplay of imperial and national inventions and challenges, experiences and agencies" broaden the comparative frame by discussing Russia, the Habsburg Empire, the Ottoman and the British Empire up to 1914 (2011, 18).

15 This expression "thinking like an Empire" refers to Frederick Cooper's concept of imperial imagination, developed in discussion with Anderson's famous notion of "imagined communities," which is closely related to modern nation-state formation (Cooper 2005; Burbank and Cooper 2010; Leonhard and Hirschhausen 2011; MacKenzie 2011).

the European nation-state and independent or autonomous former colonies. Subsequently, however, it became clear that nationalists and their supporters in the colonies also changed their perception of Empire. To these former colonial subjects who were now fully involved in the various fronts of warfare, decolonization to obtain full sovereignty became the only way out of Empire, with the nation-state as the only political option to frame this ambition (Shipway 2008, 62, 235).[16]

Fig. 2. Celebration of Churchill's anniversary, Paramaribo, November 1940; photograph reproduced courtesy of NIOD; Father Simons (Album 5391).

---

16 Cooper (2005, 240) states: "If one tells the story as a movement from empire to nation-state … the tale gives too much weight to the concept of the nation-state, obscuring the fact that it shared imaginative space not only with empire, in its various manifestations, but with other forms of territory-crossing political imagination." We disagree with Chris Lorenz that concepts of historical identity related to ethnicity/race, class, religion, gender and the emergence of master narratives about the nation, can be discussed as both analytical categories and categories of practice, without discussing Europe's European and national colonial histories (see Lorenz 2008, 29–30, 32). Even nations that were not expansionist colonial powers like Norway did develop these concepts with reference to colonial practices.

A visual illustration of such changes in the imperial imagination both in the mother countries and in the overseas colonies can be found in a photograph from the NIOD collection showing people in the Dutch colony of Suriname celebrating Churchill's anniversary on 30 November 1940 (in R. D. Simons, Album 5391, NIOD collection, see Figure 2). The photograph (photographer unknown) belongs to an album on "Suriname during the War Time" compiled by R. D. Simons, Inspector of Education, to document those years with newspaper clippings, notes and some photographs. After WWII, Simons would play an active role in discussions on a more autonomous position of Suriname in the Kingdom of the Netherlands (Van Kempen 2003, 569–570). The photograph and the context of the album invite us to expand Shipway's analysis that it was the relationship between the colony and the mother country which initially changed after the outbreak of WWII. On the photograph, the Surinamese people celebrate Churchill's anniversary as an expression of their commitment not so much to the Netherlands, but to the allied struggle against the Nazi occupation in Europe at large. In the colony the war activated multiple historical bonds with Europe, as in this case its bonds with the UK through the history of the Hindustani indentured laborers. "God Blessings strengthen you leading tenacious struggle for Justice and Liberty to speedy victory," wrote Alfred Morpurgo of the journal *De Surinamer* in a telegram to Churchill (R. D. Simons Album 5391, NIOD collection). Fighting fascism and restoring order in Europe with the help of the supportive colonies overseas vitalized links between the colony and Europe at large. Soon, this would shift to the aspiration of an independent national future, which is exactly the discourse the collector of the Churchill photograph, R. D. Simons, was involved in.

In the case of Suriname and the UK, the acknowledgement of historical connections disappeared after WWII; in historiography the Dutch/Surinamese historical axis became dominant again. Meanwhile, following Indonesian Independence, empire ('Tropical Netherlands') turned into a national memory of a colonial past. According to Frederick Cooper, this 'memory' can be an integral part of empire, understood as "a political unit that is large, expansionist (or with memories of an expansionist past), and which reproduces differentiation and inequality among people it incorporates" (Cooper 2005, 27; see also Burbank and Cooper 2010). This 'definition' of past empires still makes sense with respect to for instance the contemporary UK and the Commonwealth, to France, Turkey, the former Soviet Union and contemporary Russia, or to China, where vestiges of the imperial past play a role in contemporary global political power relations. In the case of the Netherlands, however, the nation that remembers or commemorates is definitely not the Empire that it once was. Here, imperial history has become a national history that ended with decolonization, in 1949 with respect to Indonesia, in 1975 to Suriname. The memories of the Dutch expansionist past, for instance, hardly include Indonesian history after 1945. When the master of ceremonies at the 2012 annual national commemoration of Peace in the Pacific held at the Indies Monument in the Hague on 15 August, welcomed the hundreds of people, among whom the Dutch prime minister and delegates from the embassies of UK, New Zealand, Australia, USA and Indonesia, he stated that we had gathered to commemorate the ending of the war between the Netherlands and Japan.

Photography and remembering WWII in the NIOD archive

An iconic photograph in the NIOD collection that expresses this complex relationship between war and the end of Empire, is the press photograph showing soldiers of the Netherlands East Indies colonial army (Figure 3, photograph 48731). The soldiers are returning, on 1 March 1942 from a battle in South Sumatra, on the very first day of the Japanese invasion. At the reverse, its caption explains that these are soldiers of various ethnic descent (Javanese, Menadonese, Amboinese, Indo-Dutch and Dutch); that they were very motivated to fight against the Japanese armies; and that they were well equipped with modern weapons (although somebody, at some moment in the social life of this photograph, crossed out that latter

Fig. 3. Soldiers return from battle, 1 March 1942; photograph reproduced courtesy of NIOD (photograph 48731).

remark). *However* – the caption continues – the soldiers had not been able to withstand the Japanese.[17]

The caption turns this group of soldiers into a multi-ethnic armed 'Night Watch' team, mobilized to defend the status quo, implying a rightful order to be defended against a foreign invader.[18] As such, this iconic photograph opens the first section of the NIOD 'Big 40–45 Book' (*Het Grote 40–45 Boek*) published in 2011, which also includes the photograph of Churchill's Surinamese anniversary (Kok and Somers 2011, 10–11, 70–71). This book, which is really very big (250 × 320 mm; almost 4 kg), offers a grand visual narrative of WWII of which the Asia-Pacific War is an integral part. However, its focus is a history of the Netherlands, where, as the title of the book confirms, WWII indeed started in 1940 and ended in 1945. Moreover, the book hardly acknowledges the complex nature of the photographs as historical sources. The introduction states as its double aim to visualize how during the war society and peoples' life underwent dramatic and irrevocable changes, as well as to represent the *memory* of these years in photographs (Kok and Somers 2011, 9). It thus claims that the images visualize a 'reality,' published to represent living memories. This implies a static, fixed, relationship between image, history and memory; the photographs are believed to depict what happened and this is remembered. But in this way, as Roland Barthes has argued, photographs can actually block memory, and quickly become a counter-memory (Barthes 2000, 91; De Cesari 2012).

The Big 40–45 Book blocks memory through its construction of a dominant historicizing discourse, in which Dutch themes (and iconic photographs) from WWII combined with photographs from elsewhere are linked to a universal history through a generalization (or "anthropologization") of war time memories.[19]

---

17 In Dutch this reads (including the text that has been crossed out): "Op 1 Maart 1942 keerden te Batavia troepen terug van het Koninklijk Nederlandsch Indische Leger, welke in Zuid-Sumatra de Japanse invasie troepen hadden bestreden. Alhoewel ~~bewapend met moderne wapens en~~ bezield met goeden moed, moesten zij voor den overmacht wijken. Hier op de voorste rij een Javaansche, een Menadoneesche, en een Amboneesche soldaat. Op de tweede rij een Indo-Europeesche en een Hollandsche soldaat."

18 We interpret the photograph as a Night Watch, referring to Rembrandt's famous painting in the Rijksmuseum in Amsterdam. The iconic meaning of the Night Watch is confirmed in Anthony Short's invocation of images of decolonization in Southeast Asia. To "visualize the essential or idealized Dutch picture" he chose "*The Night Watch*, with a mixture of white and brown faces, bourgeois to a man, representing all the solid burgher virtues and joined in a common defense of the status quo." He mentions the Volksraad as the example, and states that the Dutch "had certainly learned nothing. They had forgotten nothing and were probably afraid of everything that even hinted at independence" (Short 1995, 21–22).

19 This is done by using ten war-related themes to structure the book (war, daily life, collaboration, civil victims, victory, defeat, resistance and terror, prosecution, children of wartime, lead-

Visually, the Asia-Pacific War is thus also integrated in *The Big 40–45 Book* but Empire and its ending is not a theme. The photographs of European children in an internment camp taken shortly after the Japanese capitulation, for instance, are placed in a chapter on 'War children' all around the world (Kok and Somers 2011, 338–339). Presented in the comparative frame of suffering by children, the photographs from ex-internment camps in Indonesia miss the point of being photographs of a specific situation, to which we will return below.

The effect of the blocking of memory through visual overkill with a universalizing message is strengthened by the limited amount of contextual information given concerning the making of the photographs, their framing and "social life" as printed objects in NIOD's own archive. In the case of the Churchill photograph, *The Big 40–45 Book* does not refer to the context of the album in which its collector, R. D. Simons, had gathered all kinds of clippings, photographs and notes on the events in Suriname during the war. To understand the photograph with the soldiers of the Netherlands East Indies colonial army (see Figure 3), it is not only the original caption with its crossed-out reference to their modern weapons which is relevant, the same goes for the question of how the photograph arrived at NIOD. In this case the stamps and other remarks suggest that it did not travel during the war but arrived after decolonization. Other photographs reached the Netherlands for instance via the Netherlands Information Bureau in New York, or via Tokyo and Berlin.

In the *Big 40–45 Book* this provenance, and thus the making and the framing of the photographs seems irrelevant to the narrative in which they are now put to work. Whether the person who shot the picture was a 'friend' or an 'enemy,' how and when the photograph arrived in the NIOD archive and together with what other pictures, seems not relevant to the memory work the book is supposed to sustain. This approach to visual sources does not just block memory but also prevents a historical discussion of what happened and who "must account for it."[20] We also need it to understand whether and how photographs contribute to the historiography of colonialism's transnational moments 'before' the nationalization of Europe's pasts of empire.[21] The next section will explore this, starting from

---

ers). For the concept of "anthropologization" in relation to war memory, see Welzer and Lenz (2007, 32).

20 See also Asma Abbas' critique "that the kinds of garrulity that do fill our ears about Auschwitz, may be seeking to drown the conversation – not of some ethical-existential-speculative nature but of a substantially political one – of who *must account for it*" (Abbas 2010, 89–90 [italics in original]). In our view, the indifference of the NIOD *Big 40–45 Book* towards who made the photographs in which context and with what aim is quite shocking (see Kok and Somers 2011).
21 See in this context also Kok et al. (2009).

the NIOD file 'Singapore,' which will bring us back to Indonesia in 1945 and the relationship between Allied warfare and decolonization.

Imperial defeats and the end(s) of empire

A search with the keywords 'Singapore' and 'overgave' (surrender) in the Dutch WWII online image bank, managed by the NIOD, yields 25 photographs from its own collection of which six explicitly relate to the surrender of 1942. One of them is a press photograph of General Lieutenant Arthur Percival, Commander of the British Commonwealth Forces during the Battle of Singapore, seen from the back at the surrender ceremony on 14 February 1942. In front of him and facing the camera, sits the Imperial Japanese Army general Tomoyuki Yamashita (photograph 55962, see Figure 4). Martin Shipway quotes Churchill, who called the sinking of the two British battleships in December 1941 and the following fall of Singapore the "worst disaster and largest capitulation in British history;" these were "imperial defeats" that in themselves were not caused by failing colonial rule (Shipway 2008, 69). As imperial defeat, the fall of Singapore marked the end of colonialism (Best et al. 2008, 102).

The 'back' of the photograph of Percival (which actually should also be included in the databank) is of equal importance to our reading of the picture as the front (Figure 5). The rubber stamps tell us that a Japanese press officer took the photograph. From Tokyo it was sent to Berlin, from there to the occupied Netherlands, with a caption in German explaining the event and a red stamp indicating that this photograph had been approved for publication by the German censor in the Netherlands. It was distributed in the Netherlands by the photo press agency Hollandia mentioned before. After the confiscation of the Hollandia collection for the NIOD documentation, this specific photograph got its 'final' stamp, which catalogued it as part of the 'Indies collection.'

This information on the reverse, expressed in a series of stamps and texts, turns the static picture which shows imperial defeat into a history of how this event became included in Dutch colonial history via Germany. Investigating this photograph beyond its sheer image turns it into an image-object that confronts us with many different connotations of European and Japanese imperial ambitions, framed within the opposing experiences and perceptions of occupation, collaboration, liberation and self-determination that were part of patriotic, colonial and anti-colonial rhetoric. As such it is also linked to the central notions in the Atlantic Charter mentioned earlier (Foray 2012).

Fig. 4. Press photograph of General Lieutenant Arthur Percival, Commander of the British Commonwealth Forces during the Battle of Singapore, seen from the back at the surrender ceremony, 14 February 1942; reproduced courtesy of NIOD (photograph 55962).

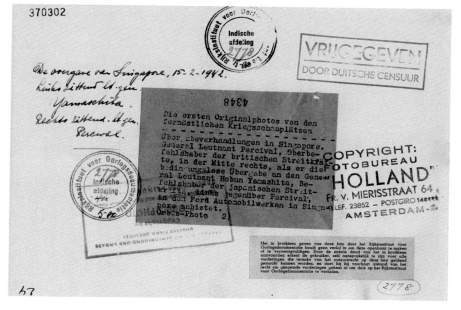

Fig. 5. Reverse of the press photograph of the surrender in Singapore on 14 February 1942; reproduced courtesy of NIOD (photograph 55962).

Other NIOD photographs of Singapore refer to Admiral Lord Louis Mountbatten, chief commander in South East Asia. The photographs with Mountbatten did not arrive in the Netherlands via the Tokyo/Berlin axis, but followed the route of the Allied liberation forces, and arrived in Amsterdam via Melbourne. We see Mountbatten at the surrender by the Imperial Japanese Army in 1945 (photograph 40739); or we see him addressing Dutch Prisoners of War in the Changi camp in Singapore, after the surrender of Japan (photograph 33218). The archive also has a photograph of Lady Mountbatten, visiting the wounded and sick in the Changi POW camp (photograph 33219), which she did in Java as well, shortly before the outbreak of the Battle of Surabaya.[22]

The most direct reference to the connection between WWII and decolonization history as a transnational history – which also links the Singapore file to the Battle of Surabaya – is the photographed newspaper clipping on Gandhi with Lady and Lord Mountbatten in 1947, kept in the same NIOD archive. Mountbatten is now the viceroy of India, working towards independence. The newspaper article gives a very angry analysis of Mountbatten's interference in Dutch affairs in the Netherlands East Indies. It quotes the *Times*, which is supposed to have stated at that time "that historians will not succeed in describing English behavior in the Netherlands East Indies as decent" (photograph 57884).

At this stage in our research we can only speculate about the impact of both the Japanese and the Allied photographs on the contemporary Dutch; it is unlikely that in 1942 many Dutch readers would have seen this picture of Percival's surrender. Their hope for the liberation of their own country had been directed at the Allied Forces, and especially at Churchill's England, as we also saw in the Surinamese birthday party for Churchill. After the British lost Singapore, it took only a few weeks before the Japanese invaded the Netherlands East Indies. Did the Dutch regard the surrender of Singapore as the beginning of the end of Dutch colonialism in Indonesia? The German propaganda weekly *Deutsche Wochenzeitung für die Niederlande* did present these events as "Das Ende des kolonialen Zeitalters" (The end of the colonial era) (Politische Umschau 1942). However, the caption to the photograph of the soldiers returning from the lost battle against the Japanese discussed earlier, suggests that the Dutch did not believe so.

In 1942, both in the occupied Netherlands and overseas, many Dutch people imagined solidarity between the Indonesians and the Dutch; as soon as the war would be over, they anticipated a return to 'normal;' that is to say, a return to colonial times (Captain 2002; Legêne 2004). Maybe this was also what the photogra-

---

22 The photograph of her visit to the women's camp Lampersari does not show her in person, only the explanation on the back of the photograph reveals that she must have been there at that very moment. Photograph 204975, collection Museon – beeldbank WO2.

Fig. 6. "Japanese guards at a prisoner camp;" photograph of the Camp Makassar in Jakarta/Batavia after the Japanese capitulation in 1945; reproduced courtesy of NIOD (photograph 61577 – 52084).

pher intended to record when in 1945 he took the image of people at the open fence of the liberated internment camp "Makassar" in Batavia/Jakarta. We see Japanese guardians, and a young Dutch girl surrounded by Indonesians (Figure 6). This photograph is another iconic photograph from the NIOD archive, published in various contexts. It refers to the *bersiap* time, remembered among Dutch and Indo-Dutch 'repatriates' in the Netherlands as a time of capitulation that did not bring liberation. The colonial 'normality' to which they had longed would never return. The original caption to the photograph suggests the uncertainty of the photographer about the events, depicting the unusual scene of Japanese soldiers who had turned from guardians into guards. At the back we read: "Jappanse [sic] bewaking voor een gevangenenkamp" (Japanese guards at a prisoner camp). The full photograph also depicts the fence, which is still prominent in ex-prisoners' memories (Captain 2002). During the internment period, outside the fence, Batavia had become Jakarta. Did the ex-prisoners in the camp expect that, with the opening of the fence, Japanese-baptized 'Jakarta' would turn into 'Batavia' again? What had they told their children? In its later use, by cropping the picture, not the Japanese but the girl has become the subject of the now iconic photograph.[23]

---

23 When in 1999 the NIOD used the image with the girl in the white dress centre stage for an exhibition on how Dutchmen, Japanese and Indonesians remembered the Japanese occupation, at least seven Dutch ladies recognized themselves in her and contacted the institute (Raben 1999).

That the British doubted a return to the pre-war colonial order is evident from the caption of the last Indonesian photograph in the NIOD collection that we will discuss here: a British photograph from the Battle of Surabaya (49249). It reveals how in November 1945 the end of the war and the end of Dutch colonialism had already become entwined for the British (Figure 7). The English text on the reverse side echoes the words of Mallaby's son more than six decades later:

> The tangled situation in Java has made much fighting necessary in recent weeks. The mission of the British in the first instance was to enter Java to disarm the Japs and evacuate Allied Prisoners of War and Internees. That the Indonesians desire their independence is a matter between themselves and the Dutch. Unfortunately, instead of allowing the question to be discussed round the conference table, Indonesian Extremists, aided by Jap renegades, have chosen to plunge the country into chaos and conflict. Meanwhile, until a settlement is reached, British Forces continue in the attempt to restore order and keep refugees from harm. A road block, erected by Indonesian Extremists, is torn down by Indian troops.

In this photograph, through the caption given to it, we find the nationalization of colonial history in the power vacuum that accompanied the ending of the War in the Pacific. The imperial defeat of 1942, and the Japanese capitulation of 1945, were followed by a fragmentation of the history of decolonization into different national histories.

Fig. 7. "A road block, erected by Indonesian Extremists, is torn down by Indian troops;" photograph reproduced courtesy of NIOD (photograph 49249).

Conclusion: decolonization and the hyper-reality of Europe

With the British photograph of Mallaby's car as a counterpart, we discussed just five out of hundreds of photographs from the NIOD archives relevant to different national histories of decolonization and war while also referring to transnational events and processes. We wanted to indicate that these specific connotations of the transnational events they depict are not shared in British, Indian, Indonesian, Japanese, Surinamese or Dutch historiography, because the nationalization of the history of the European Empires has fragmented the understanding of the pictures as sites of intersecting histories (Edwards 2001, 83). In the friction between war and decolonization, channeled through the frames of nation-states, Europe lost an important integrative mechanism which was based in imperial dominance overseas, and had been inherent to colonialism up to the end of the 1930s. Postcolonial scholars like Chakrabarty have rightly argued that Europe needs to be "provincialized" (Chakrabarty 2000). Europe should no longer be perceived as a kind of center-staged hyper-reality to which the nation-states of the former colonial world more or less relate themselves culturally, politically and above all historically. We agree with him. However, provincializing Europe needs a fuller picture of Europe's hyper-reality that acknowledges Europe's internal asymmetries and historical racist structures (Fanon 1986, 86–93; Gilroy 2001; Buettner 2011, 262–263), its transnational colonial past and the 'location' of its internalized imperialism (MacKenzie 2011). Understanding the historiographic nationalization of the colonial past in a certain part of postwar Europe is part of this.

By its very nature, decolonization was transnational, but Europe lacks a shared understanding of this aspect of the history of European nation-state formation – a history that is not only important for the process of European integration, but also for our understanding of the excluding mechanisms with respect to citizenship in Europe (Balibar 2004). In order to understand the agency at stake in the transition time of decolonization, we need to radically break with the ethnographic museum tradition from the time of Empire, which contributed to an internalized imperial culture. Photographs taken in these transition times are pivotal in this respect, as we showed with a selection from the WWII Dutch photographic archive of the NIOD. Suddenly, soldiers from Java, Menado or Ambon no longer represent ethnic types, but historical persons, who together with others, just lost a battle important to the Netherlands. The social biographies of these photographs, but also the images as such, tell transnational histories that not only connect the end of war to decolonization, but in connection to the ethnographic photograph collections of the colonial past also help to consider how Nazi-German expansion might have been connected to Europe's imperial past.

A critical approach to the work of cultural institutions in the construction of national narratives of Europe's imperial past is itself an aspect of decolonization (Aldrich and Wards 2010, 269), and brings issues of citizenship to the fore. Étienne Balibar has explained how analyzing legal citizenship at moments it is put to the test, teaches us much about the strength and weaknesses of the various layers of citizenship that work in the legal, cultural and socio-economic spheres (Balibar 2004, 76). The outbreak and end of WWII were moments of transformation and, from many perspectives, provided an ultimate test for the strength and weakness of citizenship, both with respect to the imperial citizens of Europe and to Europe's colonial subjects overseas. Visualizing these developments through the analysis of colonial photograph collections is topical, since the photographs insert into contemporary European history the histories of postcolonial immigrants and repatriated people from all over the world before they came to Europe. These new or returning citizens entered Europe with entitlements to a specific passport in a postwar order that turned into a Cold War order of nations and of antagonistic East/West blocks. The photographs, if understood within transnational frames beyond the national background of the institutions where they are kept, may enable us to better see how this created mechanisms of inclusion and exclusion, by constructing multiple parallel national histories, both in Europe and in the new postcolonial states, with their own interpretation of its visual manifestations.

It is striking that Tony Judt's *Postwar, A History of Europe since 1945* (2005) which emphasizes the European dimensions of WWII and the tremendous impact of the "shadow of Auschwitz" in postwar European history, hardly discusses the decolonization process that happened in the first two decades after 1945. This grand narrative of European history thus suggests that decolonization happened 'elsewhere,' and not also in Europe. While choosing a longer time perspective starting from the end of WWI, Mazower's *Dark Continent, Europe's Twentieth Century* (1998) discusses the impact of colonialism on the mounting ideological and political tensions in Europe before WWII, and adds a special focus on nationalism and ethnic minorities.[24] However, in *Dark Continent* Mazower does not discuss the impact of decolonization on Europe either. It confirms the fact that colonialism, decolonization and postcolonial migration are underexposed as constitutive elements in contemporary European history. Photographs can contribute to a different understanding of the inherent transnational character of Europe and its

---

[24] This is also one of the themes for comparative analysis in Leonhard and Von Hirschhausen (2011), which stops in 1914.

empires before WWII and decolonization, which has disappeared from the grand narratives of postwar Europe.

References

Aasman, Susan. "'Hard times come again no more': De verbeelding van de hedendaagse economische crisis en het culturele geheugen op internet." *Groniek* 187 (2010): 171–186.

Abbas, Asma. *Liberalism and Human Suffering: Materialist Reflections on Politics, Ethics and Aesthetics.* New York: Palgrave MacMillan, 2010.

Aldrich, Robert, and Stuart Wards. "Ends of Empire: Decolonizing the Nation in British and French Historiography." *Nationalizing the Past: Historians as Nation Builders in Modern Europe.* Eds. Stefan Berger and Chris Lorenz. Basingstoke: Palgrave Macmillan, 2010. 259–281.

Balibar, Étienne. *We, the People of Europe? Reflections on Transnational Citizenship.* Trans. James Swenson. Princeton: Princeton UP, 2004.

Barthes, Roland. *Camera Lucida: Reflections on Photography.* Trans. Richard Howard. London: Vintage, 2000.

Berger, Stephan, and Chris Lorenz, eds. *Nationalizing the Past: Historians as Nation Builders in Modern Europe.* Basingstoke: Palgrave Macmillan, 2010.

Best, Anthony, Jussi M. Hanhimäki, Joseph A. Maiolo, and Kirsten E. Schulze. *International History of the Twentieth Century and Beyond.* London: Routledge, 2008.

Bool, Flip. "Een foto zegt meer dan duizend woorden." *Groniek* 111 (1991): 23–26.

Buettner, Elizabeth. "Ethnicity." *A Concise Companion to History.* Ed. Ulinka Rublack. Oxford: Oxford UP, 2011. 247–268.

Burbank, Jane and Frederick Cooper. *Empires in World History: Power and the Politics of Difference.* Princeton: Princeton UP, 2010.

Captain, Esther. *Achter het kawat was Nederland: Indische oorlogservaringen en – herinneringen 1942–1995.* Kampen: Uitgeverij Kok, 2002.

Chakrabarty, Dipesh. *Provincializing Europe: Postcolonial Thought and Historical Difference.* Princeton: Princeton UP, 2000.

Cohen, Jaap, *Het bewaren van de oorlog: de roerige beginperiode van het Rijksinstituut voor Oorlogsdocumentatie 1945–60.* Amsterdam: Boom, 2007.

Cooper, Frederick. *Colonialism in Question: Theory, Knowledge, History.* Berkeley: University of California Press, 2005.

De Cesari, Chiara. "One Photograph: Colonialism Contained." *Photography & Culture* 5.3 (2012): 343–346.

Edwards, Elizabeth. *Raw Histories: Photographs, Anthropology and Museums.* Oxford: Berg, 2001.

Edwards, Elizabeth. "Photographs and the Sound of History." *Visual Anthropology Review* 21.1–2 (2006): 27–46.

Fanon, Frantz. *Black Skin, White Masks.* Trans. Charles Lam Markmann. London: Pluto Press, 1986.

Foray, Jennifer L. *Visions of Empire in the Nazi-Occupied Netherlands.* Cambridge: Cambridge UP, 2012.

Frederick, William H., *Visions and Heat: The Making of the Indonesian Revolution*. Athens: Ohio UP, 1989.

Giebels, Lambert. *Soekarno, Nederlands onderdaan: een biografie 1901–1950*. Amsterdam: Bert Bakker, 1999.

Gilroy, Paul. *Between Camps: Nations, Cultures and the Allure of Race*. London: Penguin Press, 2001.

Gissibl, Bernhard. "Imagination and Beyond: Cultures and Geographies of Imperialism in Germany, 1848–1918." *European Empires and the People: Popular Responses to Imperialism in France, Britain, the Netherlands, Belgium and Italy*. Ed. John M. MacKenzie. Manchester: Manchester UP, 2011. 158–194.

Gruythuysen, Michiel. *In de tussenruimte: het Nederlands Instituut voor Oorlogsdocumentatie en de erfenis van het Indisch verleden*. Amsterdam: NIOD, 2009.

Hall, Catherine and Sonya O. Rose, eds. *At Home with the Empire: Metropolitan Culture and the Imperial World*. Cambridge: Cambridge UP, 2006.

Hellema, Duco. *Buitenlandse politiek van Nederland: de Nederlandse rol in de wereldpolitiek*. Utrecht: Spectrum, 2006.

Judt, Tony. *Postwar: A History of Europe since 1945*. London: Penguin, 2005.

Kok, René and Erik Somers. *Het Grote 40–45 Boek*. Zutphen and Amsterdam: Uitgeverij Waanders/NIOD, 2011.

Kok, René, Erik Somers and Louis Zweers. *Koloniale oorlog 1945–1949: van Indië naar Indonesië*. Amsterdam: Carrera, 2009.

Legêne, Susan. "Photographic Playing Cards and the Colonial Metaphor: Teaching the Dutch Colonial Culture." *Photographs Objects Histories: On the Materiality of Images*. Eds. Elizabeth Edwards and Janice Hart. London: Routledge, 2004. 100–118.

Legêne, Susan. *Spiegelreflex: culturele sporen van de koloniale ervaring*. Amsterdam: Bert Bakker, 2010.

Leonhard, Jörn and Ulrike von Hirschhausen, eds. *Comparing Empires: Encounters and Transfers in the Long Nineteenth Century*. Göttingen: Vandenhoeck & Ruprecht, 2011.

Lien, Sigrid. "Kolonial skam og borgerlig stolthet: historien om et ukjent maleri." *Tidsskrift for kulturforskning* 2–3 (2011): 96–108.

Lorenz, Chris. "Representations of Identity: Ethnicity, Race, Class, Gender and Religion: An Introduction into Conceptual History." *The Contested Nation: Ethnicity, Class and Gender in National Identities*. Eds. Stefan Berger and Chris Lorenz. Basingstoke: Palgrave Macmillan, 2008. 24–59.

MacGregor, Neil. *A History of the World in 100 Objects*. London: Allen Lane/the British Museum, 2010 [Based on the BBC Radio 4 Series].

MacKenzie, John M., ed. *European Empires and the People: Popular Responses to Imperialism in France, Britain, the Netherlands, Belgium and Italy*. Manchester: Manchester UP, 2011.

Mazower, Mark. *Dark Continent: Europe's Twentieth Century*. London: Penguin, 1998.

Mead, Matthew. "Plane Spotting, Military Portraiture, and Multiculturalism in the Imperial War Museum." *Photography & Culture* 5.3 (2012): 281–294.

Pattynama, Pamela. "*Tempo doeloe* Nostalgia and *Brani* Memory Community: The IWI Collection as a Postcolonial Archive." *Photography & Culture* 5.3 (2012): 265–280.

"Politische Umschau." *Deutsche Wochenzeitung für die Niederlande* 21 February 1942.

Raben, Remco, ed. *Beelden van de Japanse bezetting van Indonesië: persoonlijke getuigenissen en publieke beeldvorming in Indonesië, Japan en Nederland*. Zwolle: Waanders Uitgevers, 1999.

Scagliola, Stef. *Last van de oorlog: de Nederlandse oorlogsmisdaden in Indonesië en hun ver-werking.* Amsterdam: Uitgeverij Balans, 2002.

Seriese, Edy. *Finding History: The Inheritance of the IWI Collection.* Amsterdam 2011. Online Research report for photoCLEC. photoclec.dmu.ac.uk/content/project-funding (accessed 21 March 2014).

Shipway, Martin. *Decolonization and its Impact: A Comparative Approach to the End of Colonial Empires.* Oxford: Blackwell Publishing, 2008.

Short, Anthony. "Pictures at an Exhibition." *Imperial Policy and Southeast Asian Nationalism 1930–1957.* Eds. Hans Antlöv and Stein Tønnesson. Richmond: Curzon Press, 1995. 15–33.

Soerabaja/Surabaya. Dir. Peter Hoogendijk, Amsterdam: Stichting Damma Films, 2007. Film.

Stoler, Ann Laura. *Along the Archival Grain: Epistemic Anxieties and Colonial Common Sense.* Princeton: Princeton UP, 2009.

Sutomo (Bung Tomo). *Pertempuran 10 November 1945: Kesaksian & Pengalaman Seorang Aktor Sejarah.* 1951. Jakarta: Transmedia Pustaka, 2008.

Ter Keurs, Pieter. *Colonial Collections Revisited.* Leiden: CNWS, 2007.

Tønnesson, Stein. "Filling the Power Vacuum: 1945 in French Indochina, the Netherlands East Indies and British Malaya." *Imperial Policy and Southeast Asian Nationalism 1930–1957.* Eds. Hans Antlöv and Stein Tønnesson. Richmond: Curzon Press, 1995. 110–143.

Tygesen, Peter and Espen Wæhle. *Congospor: Norden I Congo – Congo I Norden.* Copenhagen and Stockholm: Nationalmuseet og Nordisk Kulturfond, 2006.

Van Dartel, Daan. *Indies Images of the Colonial Everyday in a Multi-Ethnic Postcolonial Society: Interviews.* Amsterdam 2012. Online Research report for photoCLEC. photoclec.dmu.ac. uk/content/project-funding (accessed 21 March 2014).

Van Dijk, Janneke, Rob Jongmans, Anouk Mansfeld, Steven Vink and Pim Westerkamp. *Photographs of the Netherlands East Indies at the Tropenmuseum.* Amsterdam: KIT Publishers, 2012 [with contribution by Wimo Ambala Bayang].

Van Kempen, Michiel, *Een geschiedenis van de Surinaamse literatuur. Band 1: 1596–1957 & de orale literatuur.* Breda: De Geus, 2003.

Welzer, Harald, and Claudia Lenz. "Opa in Europa: erste Befunde vergleichender Tradierungs-forschung." *Der Krieg der Erinnerung: Holocaust, Kollaboration und Widerstand im europäischen Vergleich.* Ed. Harald Welzer. Frankfurt: Fischer Taschenbuch Verlag, 2007. 7–40.

Wesseling, Hendrik Lodewijk. *Europa's koloniale eeuw: de koloniale rijken in de negentiende eeuw, 1815–1919.* Amsterdam: Bert Bakker, 2003.

Wiebenga, Jan Kees. "Toespraak uitgesproken door Mr Jan Kees Wiebenga, Voorzitter Stichting Herdenking 15 augustus 1945, op 15 augustus 2012." www.indieherdenking.nl/cms/publish/content/showpage.asp?pageid=255 (accessed 21 March 2014).

Willems, Wim. *De uittocht uit Indië 1945–1995.* Amsterdam: Bert Bakker, 2001.

Gal Kirn

Transnationalism in Reverse: From Yugoslav to Post-Yugoslav Memorial Sites

Articulating the past historically does not mean recognizing it 'the way it really was.' It means appropriating a memory as it flashes up in a moment of danger. Historical materialism wishes to hold fast that image of the past which unexpectedly appears to the historical subject in a moment of danger. (Benjamin [1940] 2003, 391)

The return of memory

In 1989, on the verge of the *end of history*, when the end of socialism was being celebrated as the triumph of liberal democracy, all big narratives were buried in society or dismissed as 'totalitarian' or 'essentialist.'[1] Within the academy there was also a re-orientation, away from the grand narrative of history towards micro-histories and the issue of memory. Indeed, the last two decades since the breakdown of state socialism in Europe have been marked by a veritable boom in the interdisciplinary field of memory studies. Some authors would even argue that our age is obsessed with memory (Huyssen 2003; Buden 2009).

Seen from a political perspective, the recent decades have also been crucial for the development of a newly expanded Europe including as members the new states that had emerged after the collapse of socialism. European expansion ran parallel to the internal consolidation of those newly-formed states, often with the help of multiple memorial projects. The latter answered to what Eric Hobsbawm has called the "re-invention of tradition" (Hobsbawm 1992), re-traditionalizing society and shaping its identity by an appeal to collective ties based on familiar categories and familiar values: ethnicity, the traditional family, religion, and the institutionalized Church. The major social transformation at stake also relied on a strong measure of historical revisionism, which played a strategic role in all post-socialist, and even more importantly for us here, in all post-Yugoslav societies.

---

1 This is an upgraded version of the lecture that I gave at WHW Nova Galerija in Zagreb (9 October 2012). The first two subsections are revised and extended parts of the article that I co-authored with Robert Burghardt (2012), to whom I express my indebtedness and gratitude for our long discussions.

Memorialization projects within nation-building since the 1990s, however, have been linked not to narratives of liberation, but to a discourse of trauma. It is by way of a working through of trauma that they evoke a new sense of community and sense of belonging that is both national and supra-national.

At least two ramifications of these post-socialist memorial practices deserve analysis, and I will explore them here. Firstly, the transition towards the post-Yugoslav and the post-socialist context brought a highly charged nationalistic memory to the fore, at the expense of – indeed to the point of erasing – the earlier antifascist, socialist, Yugoslav memory, which was transnationalist par excellence. Revisionism and erasure were applied with varying degrees of intensity in the different national contexts. But one can nevertheless extract at least one common denominator from these ambivalent processes: the ideological procedure I shall call 'nationalistic reconciliation.'

To clarify this procedure I will take a detour by way of Yugoslav times. Through the analysis of some of the modernist memorials built in the post-WWII period in Yugoslavia, I will outline the memorial imaginary that was operative in attempts to come to terms with the war while also giving closure (or not) to the revolution that had brought the socialist state into being. As I shall show, many of these transnational memorials have recently been either destroyed or revised so as to be incorporated into the newly-formed nationalist memory of WWII. A new series of nationalist monuments has signaled the end of transnationalism and the emancipatory project, echoed also in the new European memory politics, to which I will return at the end of the essay. This essay is highly critical of the recent resurgence of nationalist memories and is largely inspired by two intellectual sources. Firstly, I build on Walter Benjamin's thesis on the dialectics of memory and oblivion that emphasizes the asymmetrical relation between the oppressed and victors. Secondly, I follow the call of Susan Buck-Morss for a "de-nationalized and de-privatized structure of collective memory" (Buck-Morss 2012, 27), which is critical of dominant national narrative in the post-Yugoslav context.

Back to the future: transnational modernist monuments in Yugoslavia

Even if the territory of the former Yugoslavia is nowadays shattered into seven nation-states, one can find a vast and impressive collection of socialist modernist memorials scattered around the common territory. A popular album[2] with monuments to the revolution in the late 1970s included 190 famous memorials which, broadly speaking, shared in the specific aesthetic legacy of socialist modernism. These modernist objects involved much more than mourning the suffering of victims; they also celebrated the victory of the oppressed and hence incited in audiences cognition of universal gestures of reconciliation, resistance, revolutionary modernization, and transnationalism. Let us remember that Yugoslavia after WWII was not a nation and that there was no common Yugoslav language; this means that the memorialization of the resistance during WWII was based on the multinational or transnational solidarity that was the core of new socialist Yugoslavia. Nowadays, after the bloody destruction of Yugoslavia, the partisan struggle and victory in 1945 have been retrospectively turned into a defeat, and this new historical constellation renders the monumental sculptures into very ambiguous objects: beautiful, sad, powerful, strange, weak, bold, but also almost invisible and often misunderstood. Many were destroyed in the early 1990s by new nationalist forces, while others were vandalized, or at best abandoned and left in a state of decay. Nevertheless, for those who encounter them, they remain highly imaginative: they could be "ambassadors from far-away stars" (Burghardt 2009), witnesses of an unrealized future, and resources for progressive nostalgia and retro-utopia, but also specters that keep haunting the post-Yugoslav present. Yugoslavia is a country that does not exist anymore, the former historical referents of communism and transnationalism have been critically targeted, but its name nevertheless continues to yield effects in thought and memory. These modernist monuments trigger the memory of the historical drama and the wager of the Yugoslav transnational project. They stage it in front of us again, clashing with the newly nationalized post-Yugoslav archives (see Foucault 1986).

The memorial landscape in socialist Yugoslavia: how to represent the partisan struggle?

Between 1945 and 1985, several thousand monuments to the revolution and partisan struggle were erected. They can be divided into three politico-aesthetic types. Firstly, there were the "popular architectonic monuments,"[3] built already in the

---

2 This album (Mihajlović 1978) was conceived for children as a pedagogical tool and collection of facts and photos in a way similar to today's football players albums.
3 For an excellent visual analysis, see Silič-Nemec (1982).

Fig. 1. Memorial to the fallen of the People's Liberation Struggle in Lipa (1952); photograph from Nelida Silič-Nemec, *Javni spomeniki na Primorskem, 1945–1978* (1982, 137); reproduced courtesy N. Silič-Nemec.

1940s and 1950s, and dedicated to local villagers and partisans who had died in the struggle. The spontaneous erection of these memorials can be seen as an important part of ordinary people's mourning and a reflection of the empowerment of popular memory. Around 80% of the monuments erected in the first ten years after the war were built in this uncontrolled manner and were not ordered or monitored by the Party apparatus or other central agency. Often it was stonemasons who designed and built them, sometimes in cooperation with a local artist and other volunteers from the village. These self-initiated memorial practices resulted in a wide range of monuments: from simple plaques and small memorial rocks to sculptures of faces. Most frequently, the memorials simply commemorated the victims of the fascist terror by listing their names (Figure 1).[4]

Secondly, from the 1950s onwards a state realist genre of monument emerged, taking the form of partisan sculptures and large murals depicting historical battles, but also of larger pyramidal tombs to national heroes. This proliferation of realist monuments was largely promoted and coordinated by established organizations, especially the *Veterans Association of the People's Liberation Struggle*

---

4 One has to imagine that almost every village community lost a substantial part of its fellow villagers; almost 8% of the whole Yugoslav population lost their lives with an additional 2% being expelled or displaced. The number of casualties was highest in the rural areas.

and the official *Commission for Ensuring and Developing Further the Traditions of the People's Liberation War and the Achievements of the Revolution.* These institutions pursued more systematic memory politics besides financing larger projects in the cities and in the countryside. Their principal task was to initiate and publicly discuss new ideas for memorials which would be suitable in the affirming and formalizing of such abstract notions as revolution, the People's Liberation Struggle, the figure of the partisan, brotherhood, and unity. In general, however, the Commission failed to provide a clear answer as to how to represent these abstract notions, and did not prescribe a specific typology for the memorial sites.[5] Instead, their work yielded a massive proliferation of memorials in the 'realist' (figurative) mode, where pedagogical and historical inscriptions (content) were more important than the aesthetic form. These realist monuments imitated an already established genre of war memorial sites in the East and West, consisting of the realistic representation of victims and heroes, on the one hand, and more massive memorial plaques and tombs, on the other. All in all, one can conclude that the first phase of organized memorialization saw a mixture of popular architectonic forms and realist sculptural projects that did not differ much from the contemporary genre of war memorials in both Eastern and Western Europe. It is important to note, however, that it was very rare to find in Yugoslavia the massive socialist realist monuments typical of Eastern European countries or the Soviet Union. This difference had to do, on the one hand, with a shift in Party politics after the split with Stalin in 1948, when the gradual introduction of self-management as an independent road to socialism was launched. On the other hand, politico-artistic discussion among partisans and communists during WWII had already criticized the propagandistic use of art and the doctrine of socialist realism. In 1952, at the Yugoslav Congress of Writers in Ljubljana, for example, the Croatian writer Miroslav Krleža renounced socialist realism. Such attitudes marked a path towards socialist modernism, which became the prevailing trend not only in architecture, but also in sculpture and later on, in the other arts (theatre, cinema, performance art).[6]

Thirdly, a very heterogeneous memorial movement emerged between the mid-1960s and the 1980s that, following the trend mentioned above, could be named 'socialist modernist.' Those monuments to the revolution are not only modernist in terms of being aesthetically more abstract, but also because they combine features that are hard to find anywhere else in this historical period; they are monumental, symbolic (fists, stars, hands, wings, flowers, rocks), bold (sometimes

---

5 For details on the discussions in the Commission, see Karge (2010).
6 For details on the discussion on art autonomy, see Komelj (2009).

structurally daring), otherworldly and fantastic. The political system and official cultural policy of self-management supported a moderate modernism and thus organized financial and infrastructural support for various artists and sculptors.[7] Institutions of self-management, such as self-management interest groups, workers' councils/collectives, and cultural organizations commissioned the memorial projects, which were subsequently funded by the federal government as well as by the individual republics. This financial support indicates both the importance attached to cultural projects and the significant role played by the state and the self-management organizations in the development of *modernist* art (also monument art) in Yugoslavia. Going on the evidence of interviews, memoirs, and the monuments themselves, it is very clear that the artists were able to maintain their artistic freedom. Moreover, through the modernist memorial movement a new and powerful aesthetics emerged that in many ways criticized the existing canon of realist and popular memorials built after WWII.

The Kozara and Tjentište memorial sites: from resistant circle to formal break

Many modernist monuments in Yugoslavia are located in deep forests surrounded by mountains, and hence away from the important urban sites that would have made them easily accessible to the public. One could perhaps best describe them as memorial parks, where nature and the monument enter into a specific relationship. The monuments are staged within the beautiful landscape, while they in turn become 'agents' that stage the landscape surrounding them, making it more grandiose. Nature and the sculptural object enter into a dialogue, raising questions about the relationship between humans and the environment. This very plastic and spatial aspect is a constant feature of the modernist monuments, whose forms invite us to investigate the relationship between sculptural form and our bodies.

The monumental sites included cafés, restaurants or even hotels as well as picnic facilities. Adding to their function in remembrance, the memorial parks were conceived as hybrid complexes, merging leisure with education, architecture with sculpture, object with landscape. Sometimes museums and sculpture merge

---

7 Self-management was a specific form of socialist governance developed in Yugoslavia in the course of the 1950s. The central emphasis was on decentralization and the empowerment of workers' participation in enterprises, but also in cultural organizations.

Fig. 2. Kozara monument; Dušan Džamonja (1972); photograph Robert Burghardt, reproduced with permission.

into one. Sometimes the sculpture becomes part of an amphitheatre, combining form and political function in pregnant ways. Amphitheatres worked as open-air classrooms and discussion spaces, inviting people to congregate and enter into discussion with each other. The natural setting thus triggered different 'public uses' of the memorial sites by visitors, from tourism and nature trips to organized school excursions featuring short lectures and presentations.

The two memorial sites to be discussed in what follows were both built in the early 1970s, at a time when the modernist movement had reached maturity and the first nationalist voices were being heard in Yugoslavia. Importantly, both monuments conceptually and aesthetically refer to the historical experience of the fascist siege and the partisan resistance to it. The first example is the memorial site of Kozara, which is located in northern Bosnia on the highest point of the forested mountain range, and was built by Dušan Džamonja in 1972 (Figure 2). The monument takes the form of a cylinder consisting of 20 tall trapezoid pillars made of concrete, with conical gaps left between them. Visitors can enter the monument through these gaps, which are made exactly so as to allow human bodies to squeeze through them. The conical form of the gaps thus giving access to the monument makes it easier to get in than to get out; squeezing out of the monument is a physically unpleasing act. Inside the cylinder, visitors stand in a dark, chimney-like space from which they can glimpse the outside only via the vertical slits through which the light trickles in. The physical form thus produces an uneasy feeling of entrapment, which clearly refers to the horrific experiences that took place during WWII in the Kozara mountain range. Nazi troops surrounded the neighboring forests with the help of Ustasha collaborators and closed in on partisans and the villagers fleeing from fascist terror. Not many survived the fascist offensive, but those who did were sent to concentration camps, while others remained partisans. Kozara paid a big price for their antifascist uprising.

The strongest aesthetic feature of the Kozara monument is its use of concentric circular forms, which have a double echo in a contextual historical setting. The circle form immediately recalls and highlights the idea of the *Kolo* (circle dance), a traditional dance practiced by different people and nationalities around the Kozara mountains right up to the 1990s. The circle also refers to the claustrophobic experience of the partisans and villagers as they were encircled and besieged by the fascist forces. In this way, the monument brings together two mutually exclusive legacies; the circle as Kolo exemplifies the general cohesive bonds of multinational and antifascist solidarity that moves within and beyond the ethnic principle and, above all, embraces the possibility of living together as a multinational community in a different world. The second circle of the fascist siege attempts to destroy the first and is predicated on the hatred of the fascists and ethnic exclusivity. The encirclement and siege by the fascists can be broken only through the internal circle of solidarity and struggle.

Similarly, the Tjentište monument (also known as *Sutjeska* after the famous battle), my second example here, refers to the most tenuous moment of 1943, which was a turning point for the whole Yugoslav partisan movement in WWII. The core of the Yugoslav partisan resistance and the General Command was trapped in the high mountains on the edge of Montenegro and Herzegovina and was carrying along thousands of wounded fighters. Nazi, fascist, and other collaborationist troops outnumbered partisans by almost ten to one; this was the *to be or not to be* of the Yugoslav partisan resistance. Thousands of civilians and partisans were killed in the forests close to the village of Tjentište, but in the end the partisans, thanks to their military courage and persistence, were able to break through the siege.

A monument after a design by Miodrag Živković was built in 1971 near the village of Tjentište (Figure 3 and 4). It consists of two monumental rocks that mark the site of the breakthrough, and simultaneously form an artificial gorge. The sculpture reproduces the experience of marching through the mountains and of being exposed from both sides. But it also evokes the idea that even the hard rock of a siege can be broken. The configuration of the rocks constantly changes according to the point of view and the movement of the visitor. When approached from below, the rocks seem massive and monolithic. Once the passage between the rocks is crossed, however, the form opens up and becomes more sophisticated, changing the initial quasi-symmetrical and monolithic appearance. Upon climbing further up the path and looking down to the monument, the rocks seem to turn into wings. And if from there one keeps walking along the path leading down to the small museum, which houses a large mural on the events by Krsto Hegedušic, the rocks seem to dissolve into fingers. Shifting perspectives on the object thus produce very subtle effects; the first impression of symmetry given by a frontal view of the rocks gives way to an impression of fundamental asymmetry once one has passed through the monument. The rocks are similar, without being exact copies of one another. Tjentište thus points to the asymmetrical nature of the struggle in which the partisans managed to prevail over forces that were greatly superior in number and equipment.

Fig. 3. Tjentište monument; Miodrag Živković (1971); photograph Robert Burghardt, reproduced with permission.

Both the Kozara and the Tjentište monuments refer to historical events – the besieging that took place at these locations during WWII – but they use extremely different aesthetic strategies in order to promote the necessity of the partisan resistance and solidarity. If Kozara stresses the importance of the inner circle and partisan solidarity in order to break from another circle, the Tjentište monument

Fig. 4. Tjentište monument; Miodrag Živković (1971); photograph Robert Burghardt, reproduced with permission.

aesthetically portrays the break-through as a break with form that escaped annihilation and opened a path towards something new. This can be viewed as the central contribution of Yugoslav modernist memorials in rethinking the Yugoslav revolution.

Modernist memorials: how to represent the revolution, how to represent (Yugoslav) transnationalism?

Despite their formal heterogeneity, the modernist memorials share two central features: they are usually large in scale and they are also extremely ambitious in their development of new monumental, and even counter-monumental forms. My central argument is that these monuments not only instigated a retroactive affirmation of the partisan and antifascist past, but that they also succeeded in orienting the gaze of visitors towards the future. Their very form embodied a certain 'untimely timeliness' and it is not accidental that many of these monuments were called 'monuments to the revolution.' However, is the phrase 'monument to

the revolution' not already paradoxical at first glance? Since revolution is generally associated with the overthrow of government, the destruction of a certain heritage, and a real rupture with the past, how is it then possible to impose a memory,
something that would conserve and institutionalize the revolution? Why should
one remember a revolution as a past event, if revolution can be, perhaps should
be conceived as an unfinished task and a process that is open to the future? If
history is considered as open-ended, then the only meaningful memorial practice
in the case of revolutions is to keep the place of transformation open for further
change (and to do so without falling back on the avant-garde role of educators
leading the masses). The central task of a monument to the revolution is, to paraphrase Marx's. famous *11th Thesis on Feuerbach*, to re-invent a memorial form that
does not only interpret and memorialize the past, but also changes it in the light
of the future communist society (Marx 1845). My thesis is that the major contribution of the Yugoslav modernist monuments lies precisely in their investigation
and materialization of a revolutionary temporality in the spaces they occupy. Instead of sticking with the past event as a fixed and closed set of premises, and
with the realist memorial aesthetic, the monuments became much more of a contested field of cultural and political struggles. The privileged time of these monuments is the 'not-yet-existing,' the *futur antérieur* which is connected with the
real work of memory and politics in the community-to-come. If the partisan revolution is to exert its force on the present, it needs to be reactivated and reasserted
for the future also through cultural and memorial struggle. The major question
that was posed by 'modernist' artists in Yugoslavia was the following: how to formalize the revolution or, in other words, does revolution have its own memorial-
aesthetic form?[8] Can one formalize partisan antifascism in revolutionary terms?
These questions were often posed unconsciously or emerged *a posteriori* in the
discussions that came after the erection of the memorials. One thing was for sure,
they disturbed the established memorial regime of visibility. In Rancière's terms
(2006), their aesthetic gesture was not directly political, but it became so through
their invention of new visual strategies and new experiences of monumentality,
which helped to reshape and re-orient social attitudes and practices towards the
partisan past. The modernist movement developed in different directions over a
period of almost two decades (up to the mid 1980s) and followed a specific his-
torico-aesthetic sequence.

The Yugoslav modernist monuments were not the first to reflect on revolutionary temporalities, to be sure, since similar strategies had already been devised, for
example, by Wladimir Tatlin in 1919 (Figure 5). His famous *Monument to the Third*

---

8 See Karge (2010).

Fig. 5. Monument to the Third International; Wladimir Tatlin (1919); public domain.

International directly criticized the simplistic monuments of early Soviet times, where massive structures depicting historical personalities from the French (e.g. Danton, Robespierre) and Russian revolutions (e.g. Lenin, Marx, and Engels) were common. Tatlin's work attempted to move beyond such representations, which only imitated reality (in the mode of realism, later socialist realism) and did not contribute anything new. *Third International* was a 'monument' to a political organization that still existed at that time, and was very much in the centre of world history. The re-orientation of memorial work towards the future may have been initiated by Tatlin, then, but it was reinvented by the Yugoslav modernist memorial movement. It was re-invented in the sense that the idea of revolutionary form was materialized in reality at multiple locations (Tatlin's work was never put into practice), but also in the sense that the initial aesthetics of Constructivism was transformed into multiple forms. The difficult task of formalizing revolution was taken on, consciously or not, by a wide range of sculptors, artists, and architects in the Yugoslav context: Vojin Bakić, Bogdan Bogdanović, Dušan Džamonja, Slavko Tihec, Edvard Ravnikar, Gradimir Vedaković, and Miodrag Živković, to name just a few. Together they formed a heterogeneous group,[9] but they faced a common quandary: while remaining in deep agreement with the partisan legacy, how to

---

9 There were certainly many differences in artistic style ranging from romanticist influence, cubism, avant-gardism, late modernism, to very novel approaches to monuments that were linked to the new tendencies in Yugoslav architecture. However, they were not in any way anti-modernist

avoid mythologizing the past and simply repeating the dominant narrative of the socialist state? This was particularly urgent in the 1960s, the period that saw the first serious political and economic contradictions emerging within the project of socialist Yugoslavia, with the rise of unemployment, class differentiation, and the growing gap between richer and poorer regions. The effects of the new liberal orientation of the Party demonstrated a painstaking and even regressive course that might not lead to the future communist society.[10] For many critics it was necessary to assert the unfinished task of the revolution, something that would engage productively with the partisan legacy and its future.

The biggest challenge for the new generation of artists was to find a critical response to the existing monumental styles and a new aesthetic language. It was in their breaking with the two dominant traditions of memorialization mentioned earlier, the realist and the popular,[11] that we can locate a specific political dimension in the modernist movement. The new monuments did not heroicize the partisan struggle in the form of statues to heroic individuals. Nor did they offer simple figurations of the victims of fascist violence. Instead, their formal abstraction combined political and artistic innovation in a way that did not easily fit the dominant archive of monuments. What later on became known as the "counter-monument" in the West (Young 1992), was already being tried out in Yugoslavia during the 1960s and 1970s. As the example of Kozara has already shown, the role of the monument was located not in any didactic message, but in the experience it orchestrated through its innovative use of space. However, and paradoxically, the counter-monumental form in Yugoslavia was not so much a negative reaction to modernism. While later counter-monuments offered a critique of modernism by opting for smaller scales, along with interactivity, the Yugoslav examples remained large in scale even as they introduced aspects of interactivity. In this sense, they represented a productive upgrade in late modernism that experimented with form while also inscribing the emancipatory promise of the partisan past in less visible ways into their composition. For this reason these monuments cannot be separated from their historical context as mere exemplars of the international style of 'pure' artworks; even less can we read them as anti-systemic or anti-communist artistic gestures. I would suggest instead an alternative way of describing their radicality; they were *modernist counter-monuments* of and to Revolution. These modernist counter-monuments celebrated something that had

---

or anti-socialist; in terms of their political engagement through culture we could argue that they addressed the most important topic of Yugoslavia and its revolution: how to continue it later?
10 See Horvat (1976) and Kirn (2012b).
11 In my article (Kirn 2012a), I developed several Rancière-inspired theses regarding this specific rupture with the canon of realist monuments in the Yugoslav context (see also Rancière 2006).

been won by partisans in the past, but only on condition that this process would continue to exert its emancipatory universalist promise in the future.

Whereas art and politics are usually seen as separated in modernism, the Yugoslav monuments can be said to combine a transnational form of political life with aesthetic innovation in a mutually productive way. Abstraction was the most obvious strategy for representing universalism. This should not be read though in a 'postmodern' fashion, namely, as a way of hiding the political message, but rather as an indication of the tense relationship between the abstract and the universal. Hence, the memorial strategies deployed in these monuments formally avoided the concrete representation of a particular situation or the projection of one idealized and fixed image defining once and for all the image of Yugoslav revolution. Instead, they opened the memorial space to individual thinking and associations, facilitating multiple interpretative approaches and awakening political fantasies. Their abstract vocabulary allowed for appropriations of their meaning that could concur with the official narrative, while also allowing room for disagreement with the official political line.

To sum up, there is a strong correlation between the language of formal abstraction and political function. The idea of the communist revolution contained many universalist claims – to gender equality, the equal distribution of wealth, equality between different nations and nationalities – and hence invoked a specific form of transnationalism that transcended the Yugoslav perspective in the direction of a cosmic planetary construction of community. In post-war Yugoslavia, the communist revolution materialized not only in the abolition of private property and a more just distribution of surplus value, but also in projects relating to modernization, education, antifascism, and the creation of a common multiethnic space predicated on anti-nationalism. In what follows, I shall compare this politico-aesthetic development with later ones in the post-Yugoslav context that reveal how transnationalism gave way to nationalist memory.

Post-Yugoslavia: from 'pure art' to nationalist reconciliation

Many antifascist, partisan, and modernist monuments were destroyed in the 1990s, as mentioned earlier, or simply left to decay. Some of the regions of Croatia and Bosnia went through a rigorous 'monument cleansing' using dynamite, or by replacing red stars with Catholic crosses or the Yugoslav flag by a new national one.[12] The Yugoslav monuments invited destruction because they were a sign of a different future based on universalist claims and symbols of a shared Yugoslav past based on a non-national imaginary. Moreover, in some cases they were all the easier to forget because of the remoteness of their location. With some notable exceptions (linked to partisan celebrations and nostalgic tours), they have by and large lost their symbolic power in the collective imaginary.

Nevertheless, several articles, photo-reportages, and small exhibitions have recently been fuelling at least an academic turn to the archaeology of Yugo-modernism.[13] The renewed interest in these strange objects on many design blogs has been triggering both enthusiasm and negative commentary. This renewed interest may be helpful in saving some of the monuments from total demolition by insisting on their high artistic value without necessarily connecting them to communist ideology. From the position of critical research, however, such nostalgic modernism is extremely problematic because it assumes that art can be autonomous and divorced from politics. Moreover, by embracing the formalism of the monuments, it denies them an emancipatory social function and contributes to the widespread nostalgia[14] that is gradually abandoning Yugoslavia to commodification and musealization. Once we put things in a museum, they become fossils, part of a long-gone history. The argument I have been presenting here runs counter to this approach and urges the need to go beyond the museum by re-using and re-appropriating Yugoslav relics in a critical way. It is only when the partisan memorials become integrated into new social practices that the memory they hold can be re-activated. Thus, one of the chief tasks of a critical reading of such memory politics is to recuperate the re-de-nationalized partisan

---

12 The exhibition "Destruction of Monuments to the People's Liberation Struggle in Croatia" organized in October 2012 (Galerija Nova, Zagreb) demonstrated very nuanced and differentiated strategies of recuperation and destruction, see http://www.whw.hr/galerija-nova/izlozba-spomenici-u-tranziciji.html# (accessed 29 June 2014).

13 Jan Kampenaers' *Spomenik* (2010) is an important visual contribution to these monuments, though as a photo-reportage, it lacks a deeper interpretative background. In the accompanying text, Willem Jan Neutelings describes Kampenaers' photography as raising "the question of whether a former monument can ever function as a pure sculpture, an autonomous work of art, detached from its original meaning" (see www.jankempenaers.info/texts/03/, accessed 18 March 2014). I share the critical approach started with the exhibition on Vojin Bakić organized in Zagreb by the WHW women's art collective a few years ago that seriously tackled the question of the modernist legacy in memorials (see kuda.org/en/political-practices-post-yugoslav-art-exhibition-vojin-bakic-held-zagreb-2007-production-whw-zagreb, accessed 18 March 2014).

14 Yugo-nostalgia dwells on the construction of an idealized past (the good old times); for a detailed analysis, see Velikonja (2009).

so as to mobilize resources from a transnational and emancipatory past in order to intervene in the current nationalistic hegemony.[15]

There is yet another discourse on the Yugoslav past that is even more powerful and dominant at the present time than that of nostalgia. This discourse, which is supported by the dominant national institutions, approaches the memory of Yugoslavia in a very negative way and can best be labeled anti-totalitarian.[16] Anti-totalitarianism conceives history in black and white: on the one hand, there is the authoritarian bad state and the dictatorship of Tito, on the other hand, good art and true dissidents. Apart from being a simplified psychologization of complex historical processes, such an approach erases everything transnational and revolutionary in the Yugoslav past. The revolutionary kernel of the partisan experience and the socialist project is reduced to the totalitarian specter of terror, crimes, and the cult of personality. Obviously, anti-totalitarianism exists in various forms and degrees of intensity, ranging from attempts to reconcile the opposing sides in the civil war within the framework of particular nations (Slovenia, Croatia, Serbia, etc.) to a more aggressive and fundamentalist tendency that erases and demonizes anything connected with the name of Yugoslavia. This revisionist and nationalist tendency promotes the view that the 'artificial' entity of Yugoslavia should be forgotten and, instead, the history of new nations rewritten, starting most frequently in the Middle Ages (with 'national' nobilities, kingdoms) or, as in Macedonia today, even in Antiquity (Alexander the Great).

In the specific arena of memorial politics, the first signs of historical revisionism date back to the mid-1980s, a time of rising socio-economic insecurity[17] that reactivated extreme nationalism while undermining the official ideology of 'brotherhood and unity' and antifascism. In what was the most symptomatic of these ideological struggles, a bitter dispute took place about the extermination and concentration camp Jasenovac, in which the number of victims was either drastically inflated or toned down by the different sides. Running parallel to this discussion, the post-WWII killings became prominent in public discussions for the first time, and were now interpreted as acts of revenge and revolutionary terror on the part of communists and partisans. Within this context, Slovenian and Croa-

---

15 See also Buck-Morss (2012).

16 For a critique of the totalitarian discourse, see Žižek (2001).

17 Susan Woodward's *Balkan Tragedy* (1995) and Branka Magaš's *Destruction of Yugoslavia* (1993) both refer to the dramatic austerity measures that needed to be implemented in order to receive new loans from the International Monetary Fund and the World Bank and to pay off the interest rates on previous loans. With the demise of socialism, the geopolitical importance of Yugoslavia faded away and this meant high vulnerability in times of general economic crisis that was accompanied by high inflation and unemployment, see also Kirn (2012b).

tian nationalists and 'new historians' opened the case of Bleiburg and Kočevski Rog (as examples of communist violence), while Serbian nationalists pointed to the concentration camp of Jasenovac and interpreted it through a purely 'nationalist' lens as the elimination of Serbs by Croats. Unquestionably, the communist leadership carried its share of the blame for these developments; because it had never properly addressed these issues, they had remained one of the most crucial blind spots of socialist rule. This meant that the civil war of the 1940s became a politically-charged topic in the mid-1980s and *a fortiori* invested with strong anti-communist sentiments. In this way, national reconciliation became integrated into historical revisionism with new dissident and nationalist forces instrumentalizing the wounds of the civil war for new national causes. As one of its more extreme by-products, the discourse on nationalist reconciliation opened the way towards the rehabilitation of local fascisms in the past and, more tragically, in the present. Especially from the 1990s onwards, a whole range of new memorials was built to commemorate fascist collaborators. In turn, these monuments became crucial sites for the anti-communist gatherings that imagined new national communities and produced revised historical accounts of WWII which minimized or demonized the importance of the antifascist struggle. This new trajectory of nationalist memory, moreover, participated in setting the ideological stage for the coming civil war of the 1990s. In order to illustrate these developments, I will describe in the following section how this process of nationalistic reconciliation took shape in Slovenia, which was luckily exempted from most brutal aspects of the recent wars.

Nationalist reconciliation in Slovenia: the erection of memorials to fascist collaborators

From the outset, it needs to be pointed out that the re-emergence of a nationalist discourse went hand in glove with revising the history of the partisan struggle and Yugoslav transnationalism. Any nation-building project demands a major revision of history and this was also evident in Slovenia on the level of memorial policies and a new ritualization and celebration of the specifically Slovenian past. For right-wing forces and nationalist currents, the debate on national reconciliation was devised as a fantasmatic screen providing a path to the rehabilitation of the Home Guard (the Slovenian variant of fascism), who had been the losers in the socialist narrative. Now, it was believed, the wounds of the Slovenian nation ought to be healed. On the other hand, the advocates of the partisan struggle adopted a rather defensive position; they agreed on the necessity of national reconciliation, but attempted to integrate the partisan experience into the history of Slovenian nationhood. Partisans became construed as *Slovenian* partisans who first expressed Slovenian sovereignty. Both the right-wing and the (old) partisan groups wanted reconciliation, but since their diagnosis of WWII was different, a certain place for future political divisions was kept open. In my view, it is the revolutionary remainder that has been triggering the constant return to the past.

The Slovenian nation had long been divided along political lines, with partisan antifascists on the one hand, and local collaborationists on the other. For any true patriot in contemporary Slovenia, it seemed to be high time that these two parties and opposing political cultures be reconciled in linear progression leading to the emergence of a Slovenian nation that had buried old divisions. The first institution to venerate the local fascists (Home Guards) and anticommunism was the Catholic Church, which had the political support of the right-wing political parties in consecrating new memorial projects. Their quest for a new truth received a huge boost when new monuments to WWII were built that were largely dedicated to the Home Guard. History had to be made more objective, and the new victims, no matter their political affiliation or crimes in WWII, needed to be commemorated.

Fig. 6. Home Guard Memorial in Kočevski Rog (1998); photograph Manca Bajec, reproduced with permission.

Figure 6 shows a typical example of a Home Guard memorial. It was erected in 1998 and is located in Kočevski Rog, which was one of the major sites of the post-war execution of fascists in Yugoslavia, especially Serbian Chetniks, Croatian Ustasha and Slovenian Home Guards.[18] The memorial bears the inscription: *Odpusti* (Forgive) and invokes Christian morality and its symbols, a pattern that is repeated in all of the Home Guard memorials. The massive layering of crosses in front of the monument recalls a cemetery while the monument itself is shaped like a chapel and is ornamented with the figure of Jesus and with crosses that consecrate the victims in a variety of languages. The memorial site is shrouded in the silence of a forest, as a home for the fallen that lacks pomposity or heroism. Moreover, it seems to avoid any integral historical reference, by expressing the moral aspect of depoliticized suffering and by appealing to piety and forgiveness. The memorial seems intended to incite its audience to the humble glorification of the victims and to present fascists as normal human beings. The civil war is thus transformed into the seemingly transhistorical and eternal coordinates of tragedy. Apart from its attempts to universalize the victim and exclude the collaborator, one could also argue that the Home Guard memorial site addresses another collective subject: the crucified Slovenian nation and its tragic experience of a civil war.

Thus, instead of taking into consideration the importance and the novelty of antifascist solidarity and resistance that was so important for Yugoslav memory, the new memorials demand of people that they bear witness to the post-war executions on the part of a bad totalitarian regime. A series of small memorial graves and tombs share a number of short inscriptions, such as: "Mother, Homeland, God" and "To the Victims of Revolutionary Violence." The first slogan embodies the essence of a political ideology based on conservatism and the Catholic Church, while the second slogan directly introduces the critique of a totalitarian regime opposed to seemingly innocent victims. The memorial strategy presents Home Guard members not as active protagonists, but as victims who fought for homeland and God and who only by mere coincidence found themselves collaborating with Nazism. The Home Guard memorials are then read in two complementary ways: firstly, as a reflection of the (pessimistic) humanist assumption that choosing sides in the war was a matter of chance, and that peasants did not know what they were really fighting for; secondly, as an expression of adherence to fascism and the idea that it was morally right to fight on the side of Nazism since the anti-

---

18 My utmost sympathy with the partisan cause and criticality towards fascist rehabilitation does not preclude a fierce condemnation of the excesses of the Communist Party's repressive policies after the war. There were other ways to prevent violence and excesses in the social revolution.

communist struggle was primary. The latter does not explain how it is possible to be both a patriotic Slovenian and an ally of the Nazi army which had terrorized the civilian population – but that is already a secondary issue. Both readings pose a set of problems. The humanistic position claiming they were all just human beings (and Slovenians!) reduces the Home Guard members to passive and innocent victims outside of any historical context. The second reading implies a rehabilitation of fascist collaborationism, which consists of the annual commemorative pilgrimages accompanied by the speeches of bishops and other politicians. They provide new memorial places with a historical displacement of memory to the times after WWII. This memorial agenda pushed the advocates of the partisan struggle into a defensive position that more or less accepts the need for nationalist reconciliation. Even the old partisan veterans now largely adhere to the reconciliation of the *Slovenian nation* and agree on the importance of mourning rituals for the victims on both sides.

However, when one adopts a critical perspective on the recent memorial turn and nationalist reconciliation[19] and juxtaposes it to the earlier wave of modernist memorials in Yugoslavia, a series of rather disconcerting effects emerges: firstly, one witnesses the relativization of the antifascist struggle and its potential use for contemporary thought; secondly, the demonization of the transnationality of Yugoslavia, which comes at the expense of new national mythologies; thirdly, the erasure and oblivion of any emancipatory dimension of the socialist project. Then again, why should one naively expect that, in the context of new countries and their dominant institutions, state ideology would remember the dead project of Yugoslavia? Especially once it is clear that the partisan experience and transnationalism run against the very logic of the nation-building process. Above all, these nationalist memories seem to have become even stronger thanks to their sublation on the supranational level in the quest for a new Europe. The idea of a new European memory, as I shall argue in the next section, gives nationalist recuperations a particularly strong legitimacy and becomes complicit in downsizing the importance of the European antifascist past.

---

19 Miklavž Komelj (2009) has pointed out that 'national reconciliation' was a key dimension of Ciril Žabot's fascist national program of breaking up Yugoslavia. National reconciliation has a reactionary background, stemming from a biologistic conception of the nation, which was reactivated during the 1980s. A very interesting thesis on the contextualization of national reconciliation was put forward by Lev Centrih: "In the broadest sense, it has been understood as a call for the mutual recognition and respect of all sides engaged in the conflict, on the grounds that they all belong to the same motherland, to the same Nation, even though they may perceive their devotion differently and are marked by errors and crimes. Nation and motherland have been perceived as pre-given qualities of every individual, that is, as essentially separate from one's affiliations to political, production, or ideological practices" (2008: 70–71).

Instead of a conclusion: moving towards a new European memory, or anti-totalitarianism reloaded

It would not be exaggerated to claim that for many people from ex-Yugoslavia, the image of Europe was the light at the end of the Balkan tunnel of civil wars and the devastation of the 1990s. Liberal concerns about national parochialism and re-traditionalization could be overcome by entering into the frame of a European Union that would contain nationalist excesses and follow the celebrated image of a tolerant Europe: *all different all equal*.[20] The insistence on neutralizing nationalist excesses in the legal state was supported by liberal ideology and evidently favored one side. Either we will join the enlightened civilized Europe, or we shall remain forever in the backyard among backward barrels of Balkan gunpowder.[21] To paraphrase Žižek, it is not difficult to observe the (self) orientalizing discourse which portrayed the Balkans as an ideological screen onto which the dark fantasies of the Other could be projected. The process of shaping a new European identity in the wake of the Maastricht Treaty (1992) took place at the same time as the tragic civil wars that destroyed Yugoslavia. The policy of the European Union in dealing with the break-up of Yugoslavia was an utter failure; it was extremely divided about its first political task to mediate in the peace process in its own backyard. However, the wars in the Balkans were more successful in their impact, at least from the perspective of the mainstream liberal ideology; the Balkans needed Europe as much as Europe needed the Balkans in order to strengthen its future orientation and its identity.

The transition to liberal democracy and capitalism took a very tragic turn with brutal consequences for people in the Balkans, thus it is not surprising that the fear of Balkanization in Europe was so strong. Moreover, this fear was complemented by another important ideological frame, contributed largely by the post-socialist countries themselves. The specter of totalitarianism not only haunted Eastern Europe and ex-Yugoslavia, but gradually inhabited the core of the new European memory. The end of the twentieth century demanded a critical verdict on the past century, which was soon found in the collective condemnation of to-

---

20 The end of the grand narratives enabled the reign of plurality and a mosaic of micro-stories about the shared past and a possible common future strengthening the supranational layer, but not trying to over-determine the micro-stories.
21 See Todorova (2009). For a critique of the ideology of ruling classes and their political project to enter the European Union, see also Močnik (1999).

talitarian crimes. This anti-totalitarian turn is also reflected in a shift within European legal discourse, which adopted a declaration of totalitarian crimes as a common denominator for the future memory. This major memorial shift was reflected in the *Resolution on European Conscience and Totalitarianism*,[22] adopted in 2009 by the European Parliament and implemented in national parliaments, which settled on 23 August as a European day of commemoration for the victims of totalitarian crimes. The date of 23 August historically coincides with the Molotov-Ribbentrop pact, which divided Europe into two 'spheres of influence' in 1939. One could ironically add that the new historians perhaps forgot to acknowledge that these spheres of influence had later also been redistributed by Churchill and Stalin, and perpetuated in the construction of the Cold War divisions propelling American and Soviet imperialism. Yet the silence on these matters not only shows the privileging of one 'civilization' and one imperialism over others. The resolution also disavows its own fundamental ideological gesture: the fact that it boldly equates communism with fascism. As a result, 23 August is read, in some radical quarters, as a day to condemn communism.

Even if I am extremely critical of the new memorial promulgation of Europe, I would not like to downsize the cruelty of Stalinism in its various historical stages: this clearly deserves an important chapter in the history of socialism and its political critique. However, there are a few theoretical and historical issues that call for stricter analysis. Firstly, the 2009 resolution denies the relevance and existence of different political forms and affiliations that fought side by side against fascism in WWII. There were many resistance movements influenced and organized by socialist forces that played a crucial role in the antifascist struggle.[23] Nor may the role of the Soviet Union in WWII be overlooked, since the Eastern Front was one of the crucial sites where the power of Nazi Germany was broken. Secondly, the resolution blends together all the historical experiences of socialism behind the ideological screen of Stalinism, thus ignoring among other things the specificity of Yugoslav socialism. Moreover, even the various historical stages of Soviet socialism deserve a much more rigorous historical analysis and cannot be simply equated with Soviet imperialism or Stalinism. Thirdly, the resolution does not provide any analytical tools with which to tackle the superficial identification of fascism with communism. The historical and analytical differences between communism and

---

22 See www.europarl.europa.eu/sides/getDoc.do?pubRef=-//EP//TEXT+TA+P6-TA-2009-0213+0+DOC+XML+V0//EN (accessed 18 March 2014).
23 See the excellent study by Donny Gluckstein (2012) that develops the thesis of "two wars;" apart from being a struggle against fascism, WWII should be read in terms of imperialist wagers that were continued in the post-war period. The example of Greece, Eastern Europe, but also former colonies speaks in favor of this argument.

fascism relate to various dimensions: different political forms (the organization of the working class or the nation), ideas (social justice and equality or the purity of ethnic and racial subjects), the relationship between Party and masses, forms of terror. All of this cannot be reduced to the Molotov-Ribbentrop Pact.[24] Moreover, even if we were to take into account the fear of Russia in the context of Eastern states, where anti-communism was part of anti-Sovietism and consequently inscribed into the new national projects, it still remains highly questionable whether this paradigmatic frame can be simply imported into the Yugoslav experience.

For the purposes of my current argument on (post-)Yugoslav memory, let me only refer to two fundamental differences that have emerged from the above analysis. The difference between post-Yugoslav anti-totalitarian memory and the Yugoslav socialist modernist memory relates both to the subjectivity addressed in their respective memorials and to their temporality. Socialist modernism in general and modernist memorials in particular strove towards a future and the possibility of a different world; rather than asserting the fixed past, they remain open to history as a set of contingent processes. Moreover, they went beyond a subjectivity that is based on racist and nationalist categories (in post-socialist times, as we have seen, memorials address local fascists, the Slovenian nation, Christianity, European civilization – all denominators of the presupposed subjectivity). Subjectivity in the partisan memorials was centered instead around the rather abstract figuration of the community-to-come, working people and partisans who would re-activate the history of the oppressed (the latter conceived not simply as victims of this or that regime). Analysis of (post-)Yugoslav memory bring to the fore two, mutually exclusive models. The first is the memory of the antifascist struggle as revolution with its open temporality and transnational subjectivity. The second is nationalist reconciliation that focuses on the romantic teleological temporality of the Nation with its strong ethnic and religious form of identification. In its most extreme variant nationalist reconciliation takes the form of a defense of fascism (and local collaboration).

From the perspective of the decision to take 23 August as a new day of European remembrance, the presupposed subjectivity is performed through the intersection of the democratic regimes of Western Europe and the uneducated children of Eastern Europe. In other words, the new subjectivity becomes rooted, on the one hand, in victimization and the trauma of totalitarian crime and, on the other hand, in a democratic deficit that has to be overcome in the years of transition. Anything

---

24 For an important contribution on the distinction between fascism and communism, see Žižek (2001); more generally, the work of the Frankfurt School is here of analytical help.

hinting at revolution or communism is pre-emptively condemned as totalitarianism. Obviously, it remains extremely difficult to extract the shared experience of divided Europe so that making any sort of generalization on this score is academically dubious. Nevertheless, one can claim that the post-totalitarian universality of the new memorial project is bent in favor of a neo-conservative ideology of a democratic European civilization. The European memory project goes in the direction of the erasure of the antifascist legacy, which used to be the cornerstone of the idea of a united Europe. Moreover, today, in the time of crisis, antifascist experiences could regain particular importance in organizing and conceptualizing alternative and emancipatory potentialities for a future Europe based on more egalitarian and just principles. This perspective is close to the project that Étienne Balibar (2004) rightly termed a "Europe open for all," which should be based on an inclusive notion of citizenship that then overcomes racist and cultural borders. In this respect, Europe today is based on the anti-totalitarian project, which reinstates the logic of ethnic communities and imposes selective memorial strategies that reconcile fascism and communism. This mainstream neo-conservative perspective, resembles in part the period of economic crisis in the 1920s and 1930s, where strong anti-communism fed the rise of European fascism which produced its own way to exit the economic crisis. In contrast, antifascism held emancipatory promises constituted in the idea of a popular liberation front including communist and other democratic forces from the Centre and the Left, alongside the different religious groups and social organizations that had fought against the fascists. European transnationalism as such existed in specific moments of history, sometimes bent towards new colonial projects (the dark side of history), at other times linked to antifascist and anticolonial movements (emancipatory history). One thing is clear: the period of WWII brought the historical experience of antifascism to the level of a political alternative. Not only the struggle against fascism, but also a potential for a deeper social transformation. It is not only important to remember this today, but also to re-activate it in our present struggles for the future idea and community of Europe.

In this light, the discussion of the memory of the Yugoslav revolution can provide us with material resources for imagining a new Europe that is not prepared to be reconciled with the present state of affairs and remains open to a community that does not yet exist. Memory then becomes a thinking memory, an image that re-activates the past for the future. Recent attempts in the post-Yugoslav context to restore the 'transnationalist' character of the modernist memorials are noteworthy and necessary against the background of nationalist revisionisms that foster exclusions and marginalizations. Art collectives, critical journals, and historians have all been playing an important role in the process of opening society towards a different future, although the question remains: how much of a difference can they make in their local context without a stronger political organization? As importantly, it remains unanswered how these particular debates and mobilizations of resources can influence the building of new perspectives in European memory. This will not only be a matter of critical intellect and art, but also of a politics that will not rest easy with any simplistic regression into 'totalitarian' cliché and nationalist memory.

References

Balibar, Étienne. *We, the People of Europe? Reflections on Transnational Citizenship.* Trans. James Swenson. Princeton: Princeton UP, 2004.

Balibar, Étienne and Immanuel Wallerstein. *Race, Nation, Class: Ambiguous Identities.* London: Verso, 1991.

Benjamin, Walter. "On the Concept of History." *Selected Writings, Vol. 4: 1938–1940.* Cambridge: Harvard UP, 2003. 389–400.

Buck-Morss, Susan and Emily Jacir. *Notebook 4.* Ostfildern: Hantje Cantz, 2012.

Buden, Boris. *Zone des Übergangs: vom Ende des Postkommunismus.* Frankfurt: Suhrkamp, 2009.

Burghardt, Robert. "Partisan Memorials in Former Yugoslavia." *FZZ fanzine* 2009. fzz.cc/issue02PART.html (accessed 18 March 2014).

Centrih, Lev. "O pomenu Komunistične partije Slovenije med drugo svetovno vojno in po njej" [On the role of the Communist Party of Slovenia during and after WWII]. *Oddogodenje zgodovine: Primer Jugoslavije.* Special issue Borec (Ljubljana) 60 (2008).

Damnatio Memoriae. Dir. Bogdan Žižić. Zagreb: Gama studio and Zagreb film, 2001.

European Parliament. "Resolution of 2 April 2009 on European Conscience and Totalitarianism." *European Parliament,* 2 April 2009. www.europarl.europa.eu/sides/getDoc.do?pubRef=-//EP//TEXT+TA+P6-TA-2009-0213+0+DOC+XML+V0//EN (accessed 18 March 2014).

Foucault, Michel. "Of Other Spaces." *Diacritics* 16.1 (1986): 22–27.

Fukuyama, Francis. *The End of History and the Last Man.* London: Penguin Books, 1992.

Gluckstein, Donny. *A People's History of the Second World War.* London: Pluto Press, 2012.

Hobsbawm, Eric. *Nations and Nationalism since 1780: Programme, Myth, Reality.* Cambridge: Cambridge UP, 1992.

Horvat, Branko. *The Yugoslav Economic System: The First Labor-Managed Economy in the Making.* White Plains: International Arts and Sciences Press, 1976.

Huyssen, Andreas. *Present Pasts: Urban Palimpsests and the Politics of Memory.* Stanford: Stanford UP, 2003.

Kampenaers, Jan. *Spomenik.* Amsterdam: Roma Publications, 2010.

Karge, Haike. *Steinerne Erinnerung – versteinerte Erinnerung? Kriegsgedenken im sozialistischen Jugoslawien.* Wiesbaden: Harrassowitz, 2010.

Kirn, Gal. "Antifascist Memorial Sites: Pure Art or Mythologization of Socialist Yugoslavia?" *Art Always Has Its Consequences.* Ed. by WHW. Zagreb: Zelina, 2010. 120–135.

Kirn, Gal. "Transformation of Memorial Sites in the Post-Yugoslav Context." *Retracing Images: Visual Cultures after Yugoslavia*. Eds. Slobodan Karamanicì and Daniel Šuber. Leiden: Brill Publishers, 2012a. 252–281.

Kirn, Gal. *Conceptualising Reproduction and Politics in the Work of Louis Althusser: The Case of Socialist Yugoslavia*. Nova Gorica: PhD dissertation, 2012b.

Komelj, Miklavž. *Kako misliti partizansko umetnost?* [How to think partisan art?] Ljubljana: založba cf./*, 2009.

Magaš, Branka. *The Destruction of Yugoslavia*. London: Verso, 1993.

Marx, Karl, *Theses on Feuerbach*. 1845. *Marx-Engels Archive*. www.marxists.org/archive/marx/works/1845/theses/index.htm (accessed 18 March 2014.)

Mihajlović, Aleksandar, ed. *Spomenici Revolucije* [Monuments of Revolution]. Bela Crkva: Grafičko izdavačka Radna ogranizacija Sava Munčan, 1978.

Močnik, Rastko. *3 Teorije*. Ljubljana: založba /*cf, 1999.

Neutelings, Willem Jan. "Spomenik, The Monuments of Former Yugoslavia." 2008. www.jankempenaers.info/texts/03/ (accessed 18 March 2014).

Nora, Pierre. "Between Memory and History: *Les Lieux de Mémoire*." *Representations* 26.1 (1989): 7–24.

Rancière, Jacques. *The Politics of Aesthetics*. Trans. Gabriel Rockhill. New York: Continuum, 2006.

Silič-Nemec, Nelida. *Javni spomeniki na Primorskem, 1945–1978*. Koper: založba Lipa, 1982.

Todorova, Maria. *Imagining the Balkans*. Oxford: Oxford UP, 2009.

Velikonja, Mitja. *Titostalgia*. Ljubljana: Mirovni Inštitut, 2009.

Woodward, Susan. *Balkan Tragedy*. Washington DC: The Brookings institution, 1995.

Young, James. "Counter-Monument: Memory against Itself in Germany Today." *Critical Inquiry* 18.2 (1992): 267–296.

Žižek, Slavoj. *Did Somebody Say Totalitarianism? Five Interventions in the (Mis)Use of a Notation*. London: Verso, 2001.

Ann Rigney

Ongoing: Changing Memory and the European Project

Setting the scene

In December 2008, the European Parliament voted to establish under its aegis a "European House of History," and commissioned a committee of experts to develop it.[1] The stated purpose of this Museum, currently under construction in Brussels at a controversial cost of some 50 million euro and due to open at the end of 2015, is to ensure that a "shared view on the past, present and future of Europe can emerge" by creating "a place where a memory of European history and the work of European unification is jointly cultivated" (Committee 2008, 5). The "key message" to be "conveyed" by the new institution was described as follows:

> The overcoming, to a large extent, of nationalisms, dictatorship and war, coupled with, since the 1950s, a willingness to live together in Europe in peace and liberty, a supranational and civil union – these should be the key messages conveyed by the House of European History. The exhibitions should make it clear that, in a world of progress, a united Europe can live together in peace and liberty on the basis of common values.[2]

A recently published prospectus (European Parliament 2013) outlining the actual design of this new institution indicates that the permanent display will be organized around a central narrative with a distinctly classical, tri-partite structure. After a prologue on "mythical origins,"the story will begin with a section entitled "Ascendant Europe," which depicts the modernization of Europe in the nineteenth century, including as central themes the rise of social democracy at home and growing domination abroad. The middle section "Europe eclipsed" will describe Europe's "downward trajectory" through totalitarianism and the Two World Wars with the Shoah marking the nadir of the continent's fall. The final section

---

1 An earlier version of this article appeared as "Transforming Memory and the European Project," *New Literary History* 43.4 (2012): 607–628. I am very grateful for permission to re-use this material.
2 Committee of Experts 2008, 5. There have also been several non-governmental initiatives to establish a European museum of memory, with a mixed record of success; see, for example, Pomian (2004), Krakenhagen (2011). Various attempts have also been made to define a canon of European sites of memory: den Boer et al. (2012); also François (2006).

will deal with the slow emergence of a new Europe from the ashes of its self-destruction and "the search for a better life through an increasingly united Europe." This post-war period is described as a single phase in the summary at the beginning of the prospectus (European Parliament 2013, 6), but in the exhibition will actually break down into three subsections to be called successively "A House Divided," "Breaking Boundaries," and "Looking Ahead." While the mandate of the museum is to focus on "events and processes which originated in Europe" (European Parliament 2013, 24), the very slight attention paid to colonialism in the prospectus suggests that this will above all mean 'taking place in Europe' (see also Legêne and Eickhoff, this volume).

Whereas the 2008 outline is more top-down in its presentation (it seeks to "convey" and "make clear" a message), the recent prospectus insists that the museum is to be a place for debate, exchange, and the expression of multiple perspectives. Moreover, as a "Welcoming House," it will attempt to put the visitor at the centre of its concerns by offering an "experience for all the senses" and the possibility of interacting with the displays and expressing one's views. The use of the name 'House' itself suggests a domestic place where one can be at home rather than a merely public space controlled by authorities. At least in its rhetoric, the House of History is clearly concerned with reducing the democratic deficit with which the EU is often charged and plans to mobilize in the process all the latest technology at its disposal. However, it is clear from the summary above that any public debate stimulated by the Museum will use the foundational narrative as its central point of historical reference: from hubris, to downfall, to a redemptive dénouement in the ongoing process of European integration. Although the recent prospectus is much more 'bottom-up' in its discourse and is written more in the spirit of participatory culture than the original parliamentary decision, they share the same underlying commitment to celebrating the European project as an antidote to war and as part of a search for a better life. In light of this, it is not surprising that the awarding of the Nobel Prize to the EU in 2012 features very prominently in the plans for the permanent exhibition at the museum, since a comparable foundational narrative for the EU underpinned President Van Rompuy's acceptance speech, significantly titled "From War to Peace: A European Tale": "So, where there was war, there is now peace. But another historic task now lies ahead of us: keeping peace where there is peace."[3]

Much more could be said about *Building a House of European History*. Displaying a typically EU habitus of compromise and negotiation, this new institu-

---

3 Available at: europa.eu/rapid/press-release_SPEECH-12-930_en.htm (accessed 30 January 2014).

tion valiantly attempts to square the circle between top-down and bottom-up processes, between a centralized narrative and interpretive diversity, between "history" as established by professionals and a "shared memory" associated with divergent opinions and bottom-up involvement: "the concept of a 'shared memory' should contribute to the development of a critical perspective, one that seeks to uncover the intentions and motives which lead to the construction of history" (European Parliament 2013, 24).

It would be unfair to judge such an enterprise merely on the basis of its prospectus, and only time will tell if the new museum can live up to its own aspirations and justify its costs. I refer to it here in the first place as a powerful illustration of the fact that there is ongoing discussion about Europe and memory at the highest institutional levels in the EU, and that it has been going on for quite some time now. Indeed, developing a shared relation to the past was formally enshrined in article 167 of the Lisbon Treaty (2007), which established a common governmental commitment to the "improvement of the knowledge and dissemination of the culture and history of the European peoples" and to "bringing the common cultural heritage to the fore" while also respecting differences.[4] Various other documents and initiatives could be adduced, including the research agenda of the European Research Council (ERC), as testimony to a continuous balancing act between respect for differences and a search for communalities, and all pointing to the importance of 'dealing with memory' to the future of Europe and, as the ERC recently added, to a "secure and inclusive society."[5] Striking as it may seem in the case of what is so often described as a future-oriented 'project', 'memory' is continuously being invoked at the top echelons of the EU both as a path to a more democratic future and as something standing in the way.

Against this background, the recent economic crisis in Europe has brought to a new level of visibility the challenge at the heart of the European project; the fact that, as Jürgen Habermas once put it, "the citizens of one nation must regard the citizens of another nation as 'fundamentally one of us'" (Habermas and Derrida 2003, 293; see also Beck 2012). For those living across the continent, other

---

4 Available at www.lisbon-treaty.org (accessed 30 January 2014).

5 See, for example, SSH-2009 5.2.2: Socio-Economic Sciences and Humanities, Work program 2009; European Commission C (2009)10074; available at www.cordis.eu (accessed 13 June 2012). The EU has subsequently also funded various initiatives relating to the exploration of the role of memory in impeding or advancing integration: for example, www.cost.eu/domains_actions/ isch/Actions/IS1203 (accessed 18 March 2014). The most recent research agenda Horizon 2020 has shifted focus slightly from the issue of integration as such to the understanding of heritage in relation to the making of a "secure" Europe that is also "inclusive, innovative, and reflective:" ec.europa.eu/programmes/horizon2020/ (accessed 18 March 2014).

Europeans have become 'one of us' where they used to be merely 'other;' they are becoming both domestic and foreign, in an ongoing extension of identity-frames that, as various neo-nationalist and neo-fascist movements illustrate, is often experienced as a threat – one that is apparently all the more threatening when the foreigners becoming "fundamentally one of us" happen to be immigrants from other continents (see Paci's *Centro di Permanenza Temporanea* below). No matter where one is located in that complex system we call Europe, European citizenship has become intimately linked to a willingness (or unwillingness, as the case may be) to 'become different;' to adopt a new memory and a new identity on a much larger scale; to continue to change while still retaining some sense of connection to the past.

It is well known that nineteenth-century nation-building entailed the subsuming of local identities into national ones (turning "Peasants into Frenchmen;" as Weber (1976) called it) through the cultivation of national sites of memory and the help of a battery of newly established memory institutions (Nora 1984–1992; Leerssen 2006). It would appear that the EU is aiming to replicate and extend this process at European level so as to stimulate the integration of national identities into a larger framework. Yet these governmental initiatives can themselves be seen as simply one symptom among many of a complex dynamic affecting all of society in which the traditional relationship between nationality, citizenship, and memory is in the process of shifting. The deep-rooted importance of nationalist thought on the 'old' continent, and the nexus between national identity and memory established in the nineteenth century, means that there are conditions and path dependencies particular to Europe that determine the rate and nature of this change. Since a strong sense of (threatening) interdependence between strangers is not unique to Europe, however, but rather an integral part of globalization, the particular and even provincial (Chakrabarty 2000) case of Europe may help us as academics to articulate more clearly the complex relationship between memory and identity in an increasingly inter-related and multi-scalar world.

Remembering Europe

In contrast to other confederative projects like that of the United States, 'pastness' has always played a key role in imagining the futures of Europe (Assmann 2007, 11). The sheer length of the documented pre-history of modern Europe and its entanglements, as well as the legacy of nineteenth-century nationalism, goes a long way to explain this. Nevertheless, the importance of the past to the current European project has to be linked above all to the legacy of the immensely bloody conflicts that took place within Europe itself in the twentieth century (François 2006, 293). The fact that the EU selected *Ode an die Freude* as its official anthem (searching for common symbols in the manner of nineteenth-century nations) is an ironic mirror of this deep history of hostility. Overcoming the legacy of the past, in the first instance by creating the conditions in which France and Germany could no longer go to war with each other, has been a key element in discourses about European integration since the foundation of the Council of Europe in 1949 and the formation of the European Coal and Steel Community in 1952. Thus Winston Churchill, in his famous Zurich speech in 1948, promoted the idea of a United States of Europe (modeled on the idea of 'family') specifically as a way of transcending the negativity of the past:

> We must all turn our backs upon the horrors of the past. We must look to the future. We cannot afford to drag forward across the years that are to come the hatreds and revenges which have sprung from the injuries of the past. If Europe is to be saved from infinite misery, and indeed from final doom, there must be an act of faith in the European family and an act of oblivion against all the crimes and follies of the past.[6]

At first sight, this combination of future-building with memory politics seems to replicate Ernest Renan's analysis of the dynamics of nation-building in his classic essay "Qu'est-ce qu'une nation?" (1947–1961 [1882]). Outlining his performative model of identity, Renan argued that nations were on-going referenda ("everyday plebiscites") in which members continuously confirm their willingness to work together towards a common future while sharing the sense of a shared past. As Renan recognized, in ways that resonate with recent discussions of controlled amnesia, shared pasts are the product both of selective remembering (of the things that connect people) and of selective forgetting (of the things that divide them).[7] In the case of France, for example, he pointed out that people needed to forget the Saint Bartholomew's Day Massacre of 1572 in order to envisage living together in the future. Although people come to believe that their nation was always already there, in fact national unity always depends on the occlusion of differences fed by the desire of different groups at particular moments in history to overcome their divisions. In reality, Renan continued, most nations of Europe are hybrids originating in two different groups, although they are now doing their best to forget this fact. Following this logic of integration, he then predicted that the current division of Europe into nations could be replaced in time by a new confederation

---

6 www.churchill-society-london.org.uk/astonish.html (accessed 18 March 2014).
7 Among the growing body of literature on historical acts of oblivion and post-conflict forgetting, see in particular: Weinrich (1997); Ricoeur (2000); Passerini (2003); Connerton (2008); Immler et al. (2012).

in which presumably the same process of overcoming divisions through future-oriented remembering and forgetting will simply be repeated on a larger scale.

There were certainly many attempts made in the second half of the twentieth century by politicians and intellectuals to formulate a master narrative that would underpin the European project and help generate the sense of a common past. Its main outlines have been evoked above. From the outset, the attempt to create this common narrative was fed by the unprecedented scale of intra-European slaughter in the twentieth century, but also mortgaged to it since recollecting war would inevitably open up old wounds and old divisions. Against this background, both European integration and European memory became linked to the idea of reconciliation, that is, to the possibility of generating new alliances and identities based on a new 'shared memory' rather than the older divisive ones. The challenge of such "reparative remembering" (Dawson 2007, 77–81; see also Ricoeur 2011 on critical recollection) has been to recollect conflict in a transformative way by acknowledging its reality while changing its affect and meaning.

As various historical studies of memory discourses have shown, the first Europeanized narrative to develop in the immediate post-war period was that of collective, transnational resistance to fascism (Lagrou 2000, 262–63), with this defense of democratic principles becoming enshrined, as guarantor of a different future, in the European Convention on Human Rights ratified in 1950 by the recently formed Council of Europe. However, as awareness grew in the 1960s both of the enormity of the Holocaust and the prevalence of collaboration under Nazi occupation, the foundational narrative of successful resistance to tyranny gave way to a new concern with genocide and with culpability in its many forms.[8] As a result, the need for transnational cooperation became refigured as a way of moving beyond the Holocaust – taken to be the 'Other' of European values and an indication of where pathological nationalism and unbridled racism can lead. The central importance of the Holocaust, as a figure of memory (Assmann 1997) for the "Dark Continent" that Europe became in the twentieth century (Mazower 1998), is reflected in the fact that the European Parliament has officially marked Holocaust Remembrance Day since 2005.

The Holocaust as a negative benchmark for European identity has also generated variations on a neo-Enlightenment narrative identifying Europe as a global defender of democratic values whose present and future investment in universal human rights is, and should continue to be, all the greater precisely because of the extent to which it had violated them in the past. Thus Jürgen Haber-

---

8 This summary is based on Banchoff (1997); Müller (2002); Olick, (2003); Kansteiner et al. (2006); Meier (2010); Leggewie (2011, especially 15–21).

mas argued in 2003, in an essay co-signed by Jacques Derrida at the time of the American-led invasion of Iraq, that 'old' Europe (primarily, the French-German axis) should develop its own foreign policy so as to bring a distinctive voice to the international table that would be committed to "defend and promote a cosmopolitan order on the basis of international law" (Habermas and Derrida 2003, 293). Crucially, according to the two philosophers, it was the Europeans' historical experience of dealing with dictatorships that made them now particularly well-equipped to defend a cosmopolitan rule of law; their own mistakes had taught them a painful lesson about "how differences can be communicated, contradictions institutionalized, and tensions stabilized" (294). Writing a year later, Derrida again linked the "bad conscience" of Europe specifically to the "memory of the Enlightenment" and outlined its future role in terms of a heightened responsibility to promote human rights globally because of its own violations of them, not only in Europe itself, but also elsewhere under colonialism (Derrida 2004).

In the first instance, the collapse of communism in the late 1980s and the major expansion of the European Union that followed in 2004 undermined this emerging consensus about the centrality of the Holocaust and the idea of a "bad conscience" to any master narrative of Europe. Revivified nationalism in countries only recently emancipated from foreign dominance, together with the "defrosting" (Judt 2005) of unprocessed memories of WWII, brought other variations back into play (see also Kirn, this volume). At a time of "disappearing customs barriers and single currencies," Tony Judt wrote, "the frontiers of memory stay solidly in place" (Judt 2005, 173). After all, where 1945 meant liberation for 'old' Europe, it had marked the beginning of a new dictatorship for the countries in the East. Where there had been an intensive production in 'old' Europe of all sorts of narratives re-interpreting the events of 1914–1945, state censorship, the inaccessibility of archives, and other priorities in the former East meant that the process of critical recollection in the public sphere was delayed. In the decade after 1989, and especially during the Yugoslav Wars, there was a tendency among commentators in the former West (echoes of which are to be found in the 2008 document on the House of History) to view the 'new' members of Europe as belonging to an earlier stage of development in an implicitly stadial narrative in which 'overcoming' ethnic and political conflict was taken to be an inevitable stage in modernization and European integration (Leggewie 2011, 134; also Assmann 2012). Critically, the difficulty of integrating the former communist countries into the larger European master narrative was compounded by the fact that the legacy of Stalinist dictatorship introduced a new focus of memory that offered serious competition to the Holocaust as the dominant site of atrocity and victimhood (Leggewie 2011, 127–143).

With the passing of time, however, new conceptual frameworks have allowed stories from the 'new' Europe to be integrated into the dominant narrative, with the idea of negotiation and the very ability to reconcile differences becoming a key element in the dominant self-image. In line with this, memory scholar Aleida Assmann has recently summarized European identity discourses in terms of an ability to reach a point of reconciliation where enemies turn into neighbors; this is an even broader framework than the Holocaust-based one and, as such, can accommodate narratives brought (back) into play in Eastern and Central Europe after 1989 and the war in the former Yugoslavia (while also 'forgetting' international socialism; see Kirn, this volume). The European 'dream,' Assmann argued, is based on a proven capacity to bury the hatchet so that past enemies become present neighbors as well as on an historical awareness that it is all too easy for the process to be reversed:

> The European dream … consists of the conviction that former deadly enemies can become peacefully co-existing neighbors. In the last decades we have seen how the opposite can happen and how formerly peaceful neighbors can turn into deadly enemies and mass murderers, which means that the European dream has become a cultural legacy of the highest significance and undiminished relevance. (Assmann 2012, 19, translation AR; also Assmann 2007)

This particular combination of "cultural legacy" and "dream" suggests that the European master narrative has morphed into a meta-narrative of memory itself: out of multiple bitter experiences Europeans have been forced to learn the art of reconciliation and how to transcend the past while also remembering it.

A variety of other sources can be adduced to support the idea that the willingness to admit responsibility for past actions and to assume the burden of guilt inherited from an earlier generation has itself become a marker of a distinctively European set of values. Even where Europeans do not yet share a common narrative, it is believed that they increasingly share a common memory culture (Levy et al. 2011, 211). In this regard, Chancellor Willy Brandt's public performance of apology in kneeling at the Warsaw ghetto in 1970 can be seen retrospectively as having initiated a "politics of regret," in which demonstrations of repentance became signs of moral strength (Olick 2007). In short: an increasingly dominant discourse links European identity and integration precisely to an ability to deal with divisive and troublesome pasts for the sake of a better future, by allowing stories to be told from different perspectives (as we have seen, a key theme in the museum prospectus), but above all through performances of remorse which help transform the affective charge of grievous events and hence help the parties involved to transcend their enmity. The same master narrative echoed very strongly in the awarding of the Nobel Peace Prize to the European Union in October 2012 and in its acceptance by Van Rompuy, whose "From War to Peace" narrative included the idea that Europeans had managed to convert violence into the boring, but far less bloody art of negotiation around a conference table.[9]

It is not without irony that this particular repentance-based identity has also been seen as expressing German hegemony within European memory culture, a mark of that country's success in providing a template for dealing with WWII (and, as at least one critic complained, a way of Europeanizing a culpability that is primarily that of Germany, see Novick 2007).[10] One way or another, "the politics of regret" has become widespread as a cultural template across Europe for dealing with bilateral conflicts and, though still only hesitantly and very unevenly, with the legacy of colonialism and slavery.[11] Indeed, participation in what is now a global culture of apology has, at the regional level of Europe, become a semi-official passport for entry into the European community at least as far as certain human rights violations are concerned: hence the pressure on Serbia to apologize for the massacre of Srebrenica as a prelude to accessions talks, hence also the fact that the debate concerning the qualifications of Turkey to become a member of the European Union has crystallized around that country's readiness to admit to the Armenian genocide.

Given the plans for a Parliament-sponsored House of European History and the 'canonization' of its master narrative in the form of the Nobel prize, it would seem that this "From Peace to War" metanarrative of European integration is enjoying some success, at least among politicians. There is no denying the enormous and very real achievements of the integration project in helping to turn the awful 'bloodlands' of Europe into a largely peaceful, prosperous, and lawful region with a strong social model.[12] However, the idea of integrating European memory into a single master narrative, supported and disseminated by a centrally-located museum (on a par with the European Central Bank), seems uncomfortably like a

---

9 See www.nobelprize.org/nobel_prizes/peace/laureates/2012/ (accessed 18 March 2014).

10 The very naming of the 'House of European History' is symptomatic of this Germanization in that its most obvious precedent is the *Haus der Geschichte der Bundesrepublik Deutschland* in Bonn (which opened in 1994).

11 On the international culture of apologies, including many European cases, see, for example, Barkan and Karn (2006); Nobles (2008). Its particular resonance in Europe is discussed in Olick (2007). Apologies for colonialism are emerging as sites of new controversy but also of new forms of political opportunism: see, for example, De Cesari (2012).

12 On the necessity of actively teaching history as a critical counterforce to cultural memory, see Judt (2005): 830–31. The impressive collaborative project Cliohres (2005–2010), funded by the EU, has been developing new educational materials aimed to go beyond nationalism in the teaching of history in the various member states by showing international cross-currents and entanglements; www.cliohres.net/ (accessed 18 March 2014).

348 — Ann Rigney

throw-back to nationalist models rather than a long-term vision on how a 'shared memory' could contribute to meeting the challenges facing European society today. It risks foreclosing memory by reducing it to an inherited problem that is to be resolved once and for all, rather than as a starting point for an ongoing debate about the future or as a resource for imagining alternatives (see also Kirn, this volume). Even more fundamentally perhaps, it risks perpetuating a nineteenth-century habitus in which the identity of citizens was articulated through a monumental narrative that served, by an appeal to origins and continuities, to differentiate those who belonged from those who did not and that, by an appeal to an exclusive past, created a symbolic, but nonetheless powerful obstacle to the integration of newcomers. The fact that the House of European History stipulates that its remit is confined to "events and processes which have originated in Europe" seems symptomatic of a way of thinking that links becoming European to the idea of having 'always been so,' making memory a resource for exclusion as much as for integration.

The very experimental character of the European project, however, coupled with the insights developed in the earlier chapters of this book, seems to call for a more dynamic way of looking at the relationship between memory, citizenship, and culture in Europe today. Ideally, such a view would be less monolithic and monumental, more forward-looking and, to echo arguments advanced by Étienne Balibar (2004), more in tune with the shifting alliances and material realities of lived experience at local level and hence more capable of mobilizing people. How to talk about memory in Europe in other terms than that of a monumental integrated narrative relating to an irreversible past?

Europe as borderland

As we have set out in greater detail in our introduction, the present volume is an attempt to find new ways of conceptualizing memory in relation to citizenship in a globalized world. This is not the place to rehearse again the details of these discussions, but simply to note the fact that attempts to go beyond methodological nationalism in memory studies have generally gravitated either towards an open, global horizon (Levy and Sznaider 2002; 2006; Assmann and Conrad 2010) or towards the incomparably intimate – witness the renewed interest in family memory (Hirsch 1997; Hirsch and Miller 2011). The former tendency is understandable given that cosmopolitanism and the rule of universal human rights have become cherished ideals in the contemporary world. The latter is understandable given the renewed interest among scholars in embodied, localized experience and in the formation of subjectivities as a key to citizenship. Between the global and the intimate (Pratt and Rosner 2012), however, there has so far been a singular lack of interest in Europe.

This is understandable in view of the history of Eurocentrism and the fear of reinstating a border in a world that, seen from the perspective of cosmopolitan values, should aspire ultimately to have no boundary except that of humanity itself (see Levy and Sznaider 2007). Yet it is precisely the importance of borders which makes the case of 'Europe' theoretically so fascinating. It represents neither the national nor the global, but a social formation – a legal as well as imagined frame – that occupies an intermediary position between the regional and the global scale, between past and future. As an intermediary structure, it challenges us to think about solidarity, frictions, and community-building at lower levels of aggregation than that of humanity but at higher levels than the nation. In the process, it also challenges us to take into account the borders, in the first instance national ones, which regulate the flow of stories and create differentiated zones of solidarity in a world that is not only not seamless, but cut through by multiple fault lines and marked by multiple thresholds. Where nation-building supposed a convergence between culture and statehood, a convergence that the master narrative of Europe discussed above aspires to replicate, the European project in practice can be said to run constantly into an agonistic divergence between cultural production and governmental regulation.

For Europe is defined, for better or worse, by multiple borders, both internal and external. Whereas the 'global' or 'universal' knows no horizon, since everybody is in principle included on the basis of their common humanity, the very term 'Europe' will always designate a bounded space, even if no-one quite knows where those boundaries lie (see also Balibar 2003). To begin with, Europe is circumscribed by the legal borders that constitute the often fortress-like interface of the EU with the outside world as well as the fuzzier cultural borders demarcating its horizon as an imagined community. Within that bounded area, moreover, Europe is made up of a spaghetti-like entanglement of interfaces that run along administrative, linguistic, cultural, and mnemonic lines both vertically (within any given society) and horizontally (across space). It represents less a monolithic container, than a multi-dimensional system of 'translation zones' (Apter 2007), thresholds that both link and divide people.

The coming of various forms of European cooperation has, if anything, increased the complexity of the landscape. By now, 'Europe' refers to multiple, if overlapping realities: a geographical area (circumscribed more broadly, narrowly, or imprecisely depending on whether one is talking about the European Union, the Eurozone, or Google maps); a conglomerate of Euro-institutions involving consortia of variable geographical reach (the European Union, the Schengen area, the

European football association, the European Broadcasting Union, and so on); an imagined community based on shared values and traditions against a background of linguistic and ethnic diversity; a bastion that keeps out non-Europeans from less prosperous parts of the world; the home of former colonial powers with an extra-territorial history on other continents; an increasingly small province within a world stage whose centre of power is shifting eastwards; a trajectory; a community to come.[13]

Much could be said about these overlapping and multiplying Europes. Suffice it here to argue that there is a structural difference (a *différance* in the Derridean sense) between all of these entities, in particular between the European Union as a legal entity with defined boundaries, Europe as a cultural space with much more fuzzy edges, and Europe as an imagined community. Historical research has shown just how frequently those borders have shifted across time (Davies 2011), and they continue to do so as the EU itself expands. Among the most recent boundaries to emerge are those around the zones of otherness occupied by immigrant communities in cities across the region; these new ethnoscapes (Appadurai 1996) serve as a reminder of Europe's extra-territorial colonial past and of a future at home that will be colored differently. The growing visibility of Lampedusa as a memory site for migration from Africa also offers a daily reminder that the Mediterranean has become a treacherous frontier and that all EU citizens are "implicated subjects" (Rothberg 2013) when it comes to its policing.

In short, 'Europe' is continuously 'under construction' on the ground in a dialectical relation with existing imaginaries: images of European unity hit off against the memory of conflict and the reality of linguistic differences; images of a monolithically white-skinned continent united by virtue of having overcome the past exist in tension with more ethnically diverse realities on the ground, and the fact of social inequalities. The differences between these 'Europes' should be and, in many ways already are, the subject of critical debate. In light of this, it seems best to think of 'Europe,' not as a monolithic container, but as a horizon that can be continuously displaced and whose boundaries are subject to reconfiguration. Picking up on the generative model of memory proposed in the introduction, I want to consider in what follows how the performance itself of memory might have a role to play in renegotiating these borders, in creating new lines of affiliation as well as new possibilities for critical debate. Reconceptualizing memory as a cognitive and imaginative resource, rather than as a fixed legacy that is inher-

---

13 For a wide-ranging exploration of the many overlapping images of Europe, see Leerssen (2011). For shifting visualizations of Europe as territory, see Wintle (2009). On Europe as an aspirational community of values, see especially Habermas (2011).

ited or owned by particular groups could provide a better, more inclusive model for Europe and, more generally, for new forms of post-national citizenship based on the principle of affiliation rather than of descent (Said 1984).

Subtitling memory

Hayden White once argued that the desire to narrate history arises from the possibility that someone else might tell the 'same' story differently and that it is hence inherently agonistic (White 1980, 19). Although White was referring specifically to the genre of historiography, his basic point could be applied to all modes of recollecting the past, which are then seen as less about the self-expression of a particular group than as a way of relating to others (see also Olick 2007). It is the energy generated by frictions (Tsing 2005) and possible differences in perspective which gives public acts of remembrance their raison d'être and power to reconfigure identities (see also Rigney 2007). Indeed, the many cases presented in Claus Leggewie's *Der Kampf um die europäische Erinnerung* (The Struggle for European Memory, 2011) bear out the point that controversy, rather than consensus, has been driving the on-going production of memory narratives and their multimedia expression in the European public sphere. Recollection becomes important if it is under threat from another perspective, not when there is agreement.

Placing the useful concept of *geteilte Erinnerung* (memory that is both shared and divided) at the centre of his analysis, Leggewie offers a multi-sited account of memory practices at particular flashpoints in contemporary Europe, analyzing the interfaces where controversies about the meaning of the past are played out in multiple media and cultural forms (Leggewie 2011, 7). These controversies take place at close quarters in specific locations (for example, a hotly disputed monument to the Russian army in Tallin or debates among Turkish immigrants in Germany relating to the Armenian genocide), but may also play out across longer distances (the claims by Ukrainians that the Holodomor they suffered under Stalinism was on a par with the suffering of the Jews in the Holocaust; or the discussions about how best to renovate the colonial museum near Brussels which have played out both locally and transnationally). Although the controversies are sometimes very fraught, Leggewie argues (in line with Mouffe 2012) that dissensus too has a value; in this case, in articulating and, in the process, gradually transforming the relations between the opposing parties by producing, if not newly integrated stories, then at least mutual recognition of grievances and aspirations through the multidirectional interaction of opposing narratives. Through various forms of sometimes heated dialogue, the boundaries of imagined communities can be seen to be very slowly shifting at local level and old enemies gradually transformed into co-implicated neighbors who can live together even if they will never see the past or even the future from the same point of view (on Polish-German relations, see also Assmann 2012, 50–61).

As important as all of this is, the core of the issue of European memory may not actually lie in the 'divided/shared' memories of old enemies. The real challenge for the future may actually lie elsewhere: in creating solidarity or at least a sense of mutual implication and a sense of neighborliness among people who have *not* been former enemies in any direct way, who have long been indifferent to each other, rather than at loggerheads. How does one generate a sense of connectedness between groups who have not traditionally figured prominently in each other's identity narratives or have been excluded from them, but who now belong together for better or for worse as 'intimate others' and fellow residents within the European Union? Michael Rothberg writes strikingly above with respect to Turkish-German relations within Germany about "unscripted" linkages, and describes the difficulties but also the stakes involved in developing new identity narratives which could 'articulate' Turkish-Germans with their German fellow-citizens and transform the memory narratives of both groups. Versions of the same dilemma can be found elsewhere, affecting relations at local, national, and transnational level. What memory narrative might connect/divide the debt-ridden Portuguese and Greeks and their prosperous fellow-citizens in Germany and Great Britain? Or the indigenous Dutch and 'new' fellow citizens from Morocco, or non-citizens newly arrived from Sub-Saharan Africa? Rothberg shows how some Turkish immigrants to Germany have been laying claim to recognition as full German citizens through the platform of Holocaust memory (Rothberg, this volume). The jury is out as to how this will pan out elsewhere. It is unlikely, however, that a master narrative of Europe based on a regional transcendence of conflict or on the Holocaust as benchmark will be enough to sustain these transnational linkages and interfaces at a more localized and specific level (see also Kirn, this volume). Community-building at home and at a European scale will also call for new and as yet unheard stories, ones based on the creative re-activation of the archive and on multidirectional dialogue about long-term memories, but also on experiences of the recent past and aspirations for the future.

As several essays in this volume have illustrated, the production of cultural memory today is intimately linked to the power of the media in circulating stories across borders. This point has been brought out by Rosanne Kennedy, for example, in her analysis of the 'travels' of the Goldstone Report and its mobilizing impact, specifically in the US. Kennedy's analysis highlights the importance of the documentary and the testimonial in breaching the boundaries between imagined communities (albeit sometimes at the cost of seeing the other primarily as victim), and her point about "moving testimony" would presumably be borne out by other examples taken from the European public sphere. In what follows, however, I want to concentrate not on documentary and testimonial per se, the genres with which discussions of memory are usually associated, but on the role of the arts. I argue that creative writing and the other narrative arts have a singularly important role to play in the production of new forms of connectedness across the boundaries of imagined communities. Although this is usually either overlooked or taken for granted in public discussions about memory in Europe, the arts are powerful in slowly and quietly laying the basis for new publics and counter-publics (Warner 2002).

As I have argued elsewhere, creative writing and film-making travel more easily than historiography and documentaries do because they invite voluntary participation in a story and offer aesthetic and emotional rewards (Rigney 2009). In contrast, top-down memory narratives offered by institutions (even those that, like the House of European History, promise to appeal to all of the senses) arguably lack the lure and transformative power of the arts and their capacity to mobilize individuals through imagination and affect. Since at least the emergence of the historical novel and related genres at the beginning of the nineteenth century (a time that is usually seen as the beginning of modern memory culture), fiction has acted in crucial ways as a mediator or 'connector' between different mnemonic communities, be these defined nationally, ethnically or in other terms (Rigney 2009). Recent research has shown how novels, thanks to the surplus aesthetic pleasure offered by art along with the possibility of becoming immersed in singular stories (Attridge 2004), have had a key role to play in shaping public perceptions of a larger geopolitical world in Europe and beyond (Moretti 1998) and in the emergence of the discourse of human rights (Hunt 2007; Slaughter 2007). This suggests that the arts, precisely because of their unscripted character and imaginative appeal, can more easily break away from inherited models and identity-ruts than other genres, and hence provide an experimental space bringing into play new actors and unfamiliar voices that fall outside dominant discourses.

Not all fiction has this effect, of course, but its influence is significant and observable. In multilingual Europe, envisaged here as the site of a dense network of exchanges across various borders, literature and the audio-visual arts have long been involving people voluntarily in "the lives of others" (to invoke the translated title of the 2006 film which played ambassador for East-German history both across Germany and abroad). To name just a few illustrative examples of this informal and non-institutionalized circulation of translated or subtitled narratives across national borders: Ivo Andrić's *Bridge on the Drina* (1945) on Ottoman Bosnia-Herzegovina; Javier Cercas' *Soldiers of Salamis* (2001) on the Spanish Civil War; *La graine et le mulet* (dir. Abdellatif Kechiche, 2007) and *In-*

digènes (dir. Rachid Bouchareb, 2006) on the lives of Algerians in France; and Andrzej Wajda's *Katyn* (2007) which played a role in recalibrating Russian-Polish relations at a local level, while also conveying the story of the massacre of Polish officers in 1940 across Europe. Many other examples of the circulation of what can best be called 'subtitled memories' – memories that cross borders while retaining their alterity – could be offered. But the basic point is hopefully clear: that the translation of narratives from one European zone to another can create a new memory at the point of destination that is prosthetic, but that nevertheless has the power to convert a 'distant' reading of other European countries or migrant groups into a 'closer' reading by staging a virtual contact with the singular experiences of individuals in another zone in moments both of crisis and of routine. In this way, creative narratives help to create 'thick' (Margalit 2002) relations with other groups with whom one is already economically and politically connected but with whom one does not (yet) share a cultural memory (see also Rothberg, this volume). This imaginative thickening, along lines that transcend those of traditional memory narratives, helps lay the basis for shared points of reference and remembrance in the future. Given the nature of artistic production, this 'thickening' of relations between individuals across cultures and distances is a largely unplanned and non-institutionalized process. But it is nevertheless crucial to the creation of what might be called a 'banal' Europeanism (in line with Billig 1995) that reaches from the intimate preferences of individual readers and viewers to a larger sense of implication in the lives of others as part of a shared world and, in some cases, a shared involvement in 'Europe' and the making of its future. In view of this, as the philosopher Paul Ricoeur once wrote: "It is no extravagance to formulate the future of Europe in terms of imagination" (Ricoeur 1996).

Going by the distribution of movies and the translation of literary works, there are closely-knit patterns in the circulation and exchange of narratives within the European cultural space, just as there is a particularly dense network of flight paths across our skies. If we follow Astrid Erll's point that memory narratives and cultural templates "travel" outside of their original social formations, however, then there is no reason to think that the multilateral trafficking mentioned above should stop at the borders of the European Union, any more than weather systems or flight paths do. Transactions also occur between European cultural space and the world outside, although arguably at a lower level of intensity and reciprocity than those within Europe.[14] Reference could be made here, for example, to the Turkish movie *Once Upon a Time in Anatolia* (dir. Nuri Bilge Ceylan, 2011) which

---

14 This view of cultural borders as a series of thresholds marking reduced ease of communication is based on Lévi-Strauss (1974, 352–353).

recently brought a haunting sense of life in Eastern Turkey to cinemagoers in Europe, or to Amitav Ghosh's *River of Smoke* (2011), originally written in a combination of English and pidgin and, like Ghosh's earlier works, set for translation into many European languages, which vividly depicts the world of nineteenth-century Canton at the height of European imperialism and the opium wars. The circulation of such works undoubtedly helps extend the borders of imaginative communities in different directions, creating forms of virtual solidarity that exceed the boundaries of Europe as a political and economic configuration – in the case of Ghosh by recalling Britain's extra-territorial colonial history from a multiplicity of indigenous perspectives. Echoing White's point about the link between dissensus and narration, I argue that new memory narratives, and hence new points of reference for the future, emerge precisely from the systemic and continuously contested gap between such imagined communities and hard-wired, legal borders.

This productive discrepancy can be illustrated in a very concrete way with reference to the self-presentation of European art-house cinemas belonging to the International Network for the Circulation of European Films: an organization supported financially by the European Union which aims to promote the showing of European movies (defined very broadly) outside their country of origin using subtitles (example inspired by Leerssen 2011). Each showing at a member cinema accordingly begins with a rhythmical, fast-paced visual presentation of the names of the cities participating in the network: Dublin, Amsterdam, Paris ... but also Ramallah, Algiers, Istanbul and Baku. Every time these opening credits are played in any of the member cinemas, an imagined network of cities is projected that overlaps with, but also extends beyond, the legal and geographical borders of Europe as these are currently defined. In this way, the networked cinemas work to circulate subtitled memories across translation zones, while also producing continuous reflection on where the outer reaches of Europe are located, and on what lies beyond.

"The peoples of Europe are a work in progress and always must be," Patrick Geary wrote in his *Myth of Nations* (2002):

> the history of European peoples ... is a history of constant change, of radical discontinuities, and of political and cultural zigzags, masked by the repeated re-appropriation of old words to define new realities. (Geary 2002, 157)

The historian was referring here to the Middle Ages, but his point about Europe being a locus of continuous change seems also to apply to Europe today. In the process, it provides a salutary reminder of the fact that many issues discussed in this chapter are not new and that long-term memory should remain an important resource for critical reflection on the world today – alongside imagination.

Circulation, articulation, scales

Since 'Europe' is indeed a work in progress, it is impossible to draw any definitive conclusions from this case study. Nor does my analysis yield any practical guidelines that might be used by EU decision-makers (beyond the recommendation that investment in translation and subtitling is as important as any museum in Brussels). The case of Europe does, however, provide a very good illustration of the issues and complexities at hand in the study of transnational memory and of what in our Introduction we referred to as its multi-layered, multi-sited, and multi-scalar dynamic. What the case of Europe adds to the other chapters is a final illustration of the many levels and locations at which memory narratives are produced, circulated, and transformed. Having started with the EU Parliament and ended with movie-makers and their audiences, it leaves us with a new challenge. This is the challenge of mapping the articulation of memories, not just between different media and locations, but between different spheres of activity and spheres of influence: between academics, politicians, journalists, educators, artists, the mythical man/woman in the street, the would-be citizen and, finally, the future Visitor envisaged at the centre the House of European History.

References

Appadurai, Arjun. *Modernity at Large: Cultural Dimensions of Globalization.* Minneapolis: University of Minnesota Press, 1996.
Apter, Emily. *The Translation Zone: A New Comparative Literature.* Princeton: Princeton UP, 2006.
Assmann, Aleida and Sebastian Conrad, eds. *Memory in a Global Age: Discourses, Practices and Trajectories.* London: Palgrave Macmillan, 2010.
Assmann, Aleida. "Response to Peter Novick." *Bulletin of the German Historical Institute* 40 (2007): 33–38.
Assmann, Aleida. *Auf dem Weg zu einer europäischen Gedächtniskultur.* Vienna: Picus Verlag, 2012.
Assmann, Jan. *Das kulturelle Gedächtnis: Schrift, Erinnerung und politische Identität in frühen Hochkulturen.* 1992. Munich: C. H. Beck, 1997.
Attridge, Derek. *The Singularity of Literature.* London: Routledge, 2004.
Balibar, Étienne. "Europe, an Imagined Frontier of Democracy." Trans. Frank Collins. *Diacritics* 33.3–4 (2003): 36–44.
Balibar, Étienne. *We, the People of Europe? Reflections on Transnational Citizenship.* Trans. James Swenson. Princeton: Princeton UP, 2004.
Banchoff, Thomas. "German Policy towards the European Union: The Effects of Historical Memory." *German Politics* 6.1 (1997): 60–76.

Barkan, Elazar and Alexander Karn, eds. *Taking Wrongs Seriously: Apologies and Reconciliation*. Stanford: Stanford UP, 2006.

Beck, Ulrich and Ciaran Cronin. "The European Crisis and the Context of Cosmopolitization." *New Literary History* 43.4 (2012): 641–663.

Billig, Michael. *Banal Nationalism*. London: Sage, 1995.

den Boer, Pim, Heinz Duchhardt, Georg Kreis, and Wolfgang Schmale, eds. *Europäische Erinnerungsorte*. 3 vols. Munich: Oldenbourg Verlag, 2012.

De Cesari, Chiara. "The Paradoxes of Colonial Reparation: Foreclosing Memory and the 2008 Italy–Libya Friendship Treaty." *Memory Studies* 5.3 (2012): 316–326.

Chakrabarty, Dipesh. *Provincializing Europe: Postcolonial Thought and Historical Difference*. Princeton: Princeton UP, 2000.

Committee of Experts. *Conceptual Basis for a House of European History*. Brussels, October 2008. www.europarl.europa.eu (accessed 18 March 2014).

Connerton, Paul. "Seven Types of Forgetting." *Memory Studies* 1.1 (2008): 59–71.

Davies, Norman. *Vanished Kingdoms: The History of Half-Forgotten Europe*. London: Allen Lane, 2011.

Dawson, Graham. *Making Peace with the Past? Memory, Trauma and the Irish Troubles*. Manchester: Manchester UP, 2007.

Derrida, Jacques. "A Europe of Hope." *Epoché* 102 (2004): 407–412.

Erll, Astrid and Ann Rigney, eds. *Mediation, Remediation, and the Dynamics of Cultural Memory*. Berlin: De Gruyter, 2009.

Erll, Astrid. "Travelling Memory." *Transcultural Memory*. Ed. Rick Crownshaw. Special Issue *Parallax* 17.4 (2011): 4–18.

European Parliament. *Building a House of European History*. Brussels: European Parliament, 2013. www.europarl.europea.eu (accessed 18 March 2014).

François, Étienne. "Europäische Lieux de mémoire." *Transnationale Geschichte: Themen, Tendenzen und Theorien*, ed. Gunilla Budde. Göttingen: VandenHoeck and Ruprecht, 2006. 290–303.

Geary, Patrick J. *The Myth of Nations: The Medieval Origins of Europe*. Princeton: Princeton UP, 2002.

Habermas, Jürgen and Jacques Derrida. "February 15, or What Binds Europeans Together: A Plea for a Common Foreign Policy, Beginning at the Core of Europe." *Constellations* 10.3 (2003): 291–297.

Habermas, Jürgen. *Zur Verfassung Europas: Ein Essay*. Frankfurt: Suhrkamp, 2011.

Hirsch, Marianne. *Family Frames: Photography, Narrative, and Postmemory*. Cambridge: Harvard UP, 1997.

Hirsch, Marianne and Nancy K. Miller, eds. *Rites of Return: Diaspora Poetics and the Politics of Memory*. New York: Columbia UP, 2011.

Hunt, Lynn. *Inventing Human Rights: A History*. New York: Norton, 2007.

Immler, Nicole, Ann Rigney, and Damien Short, eds. *Memory and Reconciliation: Critical Perspectives*. Special Issue of *Memory Studies* 5.3 (2012).

Judt, Tony. *Post-War: A History of Europe Since 1945*. New York: Vintage, 2005.

Kansteiner, Wulf, Claudio Fogu, and Ned Lebow, eds. *Memory and Identity in Postwar Europe*. Durham: Duke UP, 2006.

Krankenhagen, Stefan. "Exhibiting Europe: The Development of European Narratives in Museums, Collections, and Exhibitions." *Culture Unbound* 3 (2011): 269–278.

Lagrou, Peter. *The Legacy of Nazi Occupation: Patriotic Memory and National Recovery in Europe 1945–65.* Cambridge: Cambridge UP, 2000.

Leerssen, Joep. "Nationalism and the Cultivation of Culture." *Nations and Nationalism* 12.4 (2006): 559–578.

Leerssen, Joep. *Spiegelpaleis Europa.* Nijmegen: Van Tilt, 2011.

Leggewie, Claus with Anne Lang. *Der Kampf um die europäische Erinnerung: Ein Schlachtfeld wird besichtigt.* Munich: C. H. Beck, 2011.

Lévi-Strauss, Claude. *Anthropologie structurale.* Paris: Plon, 1974.

Levy, Daniel, Michael Heinlein and Lars Breuer. "Reflexive Particularism and Cosmopolitanization: The Reconfiguration of the National." *Global Networks* 11.2 (2011): 139–159.

Levy, Daniel and Natan Sznaider. *The Holocaust and Memory in the Global Age.* Trans. Assenka Oksiloff. Philadelphia: Temple UP, 2006.

Levy, Daniel and Natan Sznaider. "Memories of Europe: Cosmopolitanism and its Others." *Cosmopolitanism in Europe.* Ed. Chris Rumford. Liverpool: Liverpool UP, 2007. 158–177.

Levy, Daniel and Natan Sznaider. "Memory Unbound: The Holocaust and the Formation of Cosmopolitan Memory." *European Journal of Social Theory* 5.1 (2002): 87–106.

Margalit, Avishai. *The Ethics of Memory.* Cambridge: Harvard UP, 2002.

Mazower, Mark. *Dark Continent: Europe's Twentieth Century.* London: Allen Lane, 1998.

Meier, Christian. *Das Gebot zu vergessen und die Unabweisbarkeit des Erinnerns: Vom öffentlichen Umgang met schlimmer Vergangenheit.* Bonn: BPB, 2010.

Moretti, Franco. *Atlas of the European Novel 1800–1900.* London: Verso, 1998.

Mouffe, Chantal. "An Agonistic Approach to the Future of Europe." *New Literary History* 43. 4 (2012): 629–640.

Müller, Jan-Werner ed. *Memory and Power in Post-War Europe: Studies in the Presence of the Past.* Cambridge: Cambridge UP, 2002.

Nobles, Melissa. *The Politics of Official Apologies.* Cambridge: Cambridge UP, 2008.

Nora, Pierre, ed. *Les lieux de mémoire.* 3 vols. 1984–1992. Paris: Gallimard, 1997.

Novick, Peter. "Comments on Aleida Assmann's Lecture." *Bulletin of the German Historical Institute* 40 (2007): 27–32.

Olick, Jeffrey K. *The Politics of Regret: On Collective Memory and Historical Responsibility.* London: Routledge, 2007.

Olick, Jeffrey K., ed. *States of Memory: Continuities, Conflicts, and Transformations in National Retrospection.* Durham: Duke UP, 2003.

Passerini, Luisa. "Memories Between Silence and Oblivion." *Memory, History, Nation: Contested Pasts.* Eds. Katherine Hodgkin and Susannah Radstone. London: Routledge, 2003. 238–254.

Pomian, Krzysztof. "Pour un musée de l'Europe: Visite commentée d'une exposition en projet." *Le Débat* 129 (2004): 89–100.

Pratt, Geraldine and Victoria Rosner, eds. *The Global and the Intimate: Feminism in our Time.* New York: Columbia UP, 2012.

Renan, Ernest. "Qu'est-ce qu'une nation?" 1882. *Oeuvres complètes d'Ernest Renan.* Vol. 1. Ed. Henriëtte Psichari. Paris: Calmann-Lévy, 1947–61. 886–907.

Ricoeur, Paul. "Reflections on a New Ethos for Europe." *Paul Ricoeur: The Hermeneutics of Action.* Ed. Richard Kearney. London: Sage, 1996. 3–14.

Ricoeur, Paul. *La mémoire, l'histoire, l'oubli.* Paris: Seuil, 2000.

Ricoeur, Paul. "Memory – History – Forgetting." *Collective Memory Reader.* Eds. Jeffrey K. Olick, Vered Vinitzky-Seroussi, and Daniel Levy. Oxford: Oxford UP, 2011. 475–480.

Rigney, Ann. "Plenitude, Scarcity and the Circulation of Cultural Memory." *Journal of European Studies* 35.1 (2005): 209–226.

Rigney, Ann. "Divided Pasts: A Premature Memorial and the Dynamics of Collective Remembrance." *Memory Studies* 1.1 (2007): 89–97.

Rigney, Ann. "Fiction as a Mediator in National Remembrance." *Narrating the Nation: The Representation of National Narratives in Different Genres*. Eds. Stefan Berger, Linas Eriksonas, and Andrew Mycock. Oxford: Berghahn, 2009. 79–96.

Rothberg, Michael. *Multidirectional Memory: Remembering the Holocaust in the Age of Decolonization*. Stanford: Stanford UP, 2009.

Rothberg, Michael. "Implicated Subjects." Utrecht University. June 2013. Lecture.

Said, Edward W. *The World, The Text, and the Critic*. Cambridge: Harvard UP, 1984.

Slaughter, Joseph R. *Human Rights, Inc.: The World Novel, Narrative Form, and International Law*. New York: Fordham UP, 2007.

Tsing, Anna Lowenhaupt. *Friction: An Ethnography of Global Connection*. Princeton: Princeton UP, 2005.

Warner, Michael. "Publics and Counterpublics." *Public Culture* 14.1 (2002): 49–90.

Weber, Eugen. *Peasants into Frenchmen: The Modernization of Rural France, 1870–1914*. Stanford: Stanford UP, 1976.

Weinrich, Harald. *Lethe: Kunst und Kritik des Vergessens*. Munich: C. H. Beck, 1997.

White, Hayden. "The Value of Narrativity in the Representation of Reality." *Critical Inquiry* 7.1 (1980): 5–27.

Wintle, Michael. *The Image of Europe: Visualizing Europe in Cartography and Iconography throughout the Ages*. Cambridge: Cambridge UP, 2009.

Adrian Paci
Envoi: Centro di permanenza temporanea[1]

1 Temporary Stay Center, 2007; 16:9 video projection 5′30″; courtesy of the artist and Kaufmann Repetto, Milan, Italy.

Notes on Contributors

Marie-Aude Baronian is Associate Professor of Film and Visual Culture at the University of Amsterdam and a member of the Amsterdam School for Cultural Analysis. She has published extensively on filmmaking and visual arts in relation to issues of memory, archive, testimony, and diaspora. Recent publications include *Mémoire et Image: Regards sur la Catastrophe arménienne* (L'Age d'Homme, 2013), *Cinéma et mémoire: Sur Atom Egoyan* (Editions Académie Royale Belgique, 2013) and *La Caméra à la nuque: Penser l'image filmique avec Emmanuel Lévinas* (forthcoming). Her current project relates to fashion and costume in film practices and cultural theory.

Chiara De Cesari is a cultural anthropologist and Assistant Professor in European Studies and Cultural Studies at the University of Amsterdam. Her research focuses on heritage, memory, and broader cultural politics and the ways in which these change under conditions of globalization. She has published in numerous journals including *American Anthropologist, Memory Studies,* and *Studies in Ethnicity and Nationalism*. She is currently finishing a book titled *Heritage and the Struggle for Palestine*. Her most recent project explores the making of a new European collective memory in relation to its blind spots, with particular reference to the heritage of colonialism.

Paulla Ebron is Associate Professor of Anthropology at Stanford University. She is the author of *Performing Africa* (Princeton UP, 2002), a work based on her research in The Gambia that traces the significance of West African praise-singers in transnational encounters. Her current research focuses on tropicality and regionalism as it ties West Africa and the US Georgia Sea Islands in a dialogue about landscape, memory, and political uplift.

Elizabeth Edwards is Research Professor and Director of the Photographic History Research Centre at De Montfort University, Leicester. An historical and visual anthropologist she has worked extensively in the field of cross-cultural photography, and on the relationship between photography, history, and anthropology. Her numerous publications include the monographs *Raw Histories: Photographs, Anthropology and Museums* (2001) and *The Camera as Historian: Amateur Photographs and Historical Imagination 1885–1918* (2012), and the edited volumes *Anthropology and Photography 1860–1920* (1992), *Photographs Objects Histories* (2004), *Sensible Objects: Colonialism, Museums and Material Culture* (2006), and *Photographs, Anthropology and History: Expanding the Frame* (2009).

Martijn Eickhoff is Senior Researcher at the NIOD (Netherlands Institute for War, Holocaust and Genocide Studies) in Amsterdam and a lecturer in cultural history at the Radboud University Nijmegen (RUN). His research focuses on the politics of memory and archaeology particularly in times of regime change and political violence. He has published widely on the role of academics in the Third Reich and Nazi-occupied Europe. He is currently preparing, in collaboration with Marieke Bloembergen, a book on archaeology and heritage in colonial and post-colonial Indonesia.

Astrid Erll is Professor of Anglophone Literatures and Cultures at Goethe-University Frankfurt am Main. She has written monographs on memories of the First World War and of British colonialism in India. She is co-editor (with A. Nünning) of *A Companion to Cultural Memory Studies* (De Gruyter, 2010) and (with A. Rigney) of *Mediation, Remediation, and the Dynamics of Cultural Memory* (De Gruyter, 2009). She is author of *Memory in Culture* (Palgrave 2011)/*Kollektives Gedächtnis und Erinnerungskulturen* (2005, 2nd ed. 2011), widely-used introductions to memory studies.

Stephan Feuchtwang is Professor Emeritus in the Department of Anthropology, London School of Economics. He has published books on Chinese popular religion, feng-shui, and (with Wang Mingming) on grassroots charisma in southern Fujian and northern Taiwan. His comparative study of the transmission of great events of state violence in China, Taiwan, and Germany was published in *After the Event* (Berghahn Books, 2011). Together with Michael Rowlands he is completing a long-term comparative project which reworks the notion of civilizations in terms of polycentric spreads and mixtures rather than as cultures that clash.

Slawomir Kapralski is Professor of Sociology in the Center for Social Studies at the Graduate School for Social Research, Warsaw and a researcher at the Institute of Philosophy and Sociology, Polish Academy of Sciences. His research focuses on Roma memory and the memory of the Holocaust in Poland. He has published in *History & Memory* and *Studies in Ethnicity and Nationalism* among other journals. His most recent book (2012, in Polish, English title: *A Nation from the Ashes: Memory of Genocide and Roma Identity*) examines the consequences of the Holocaust for Roma communities in Europe. He also co-authored *Roma in Auschwitz* (2011), published (in English) by the Auschwitz-Birkenau State Museum.

Rosanne Kennedy is Associate Professor of Literature and Gender, Sexuality and Culture at the Australian National University. Her research interests include trauma, testimony, and memory and its remediations in cultural, literary, and human rights texts and contexts. Her articles have appeared in numerous journals including *Comparative Literature Studies, Biography, Studies in the Novel, Women's Studies Quarterly, Australian Humanities Review* and *Profession*. She edited with Susannah Radstone a special issue of *Memory Studies* on "Memory Studies in Australia" (July 2013). She is currently leading a Go8/DAAD project on "Memory and its Media."

Gal Kirn is currently a Humboldt Postdoctoral Fellow at Humboldt Universität in Berlin. His dissertation in political philosophy at the University of Nova Gorica combined contemporary French philosophy with the history of the emergence of socialist Yugoslavia and its tragic break-up. He is co-editor of the books *Encountering Althusser* (Bloomsbury, 2012) and *Yugoslav Black Wave Cinema and its Transgressive Moments* (JvE Academie, 2012), and editor of *Postfordism and its Discontents* (JvE Academie, 2010).

Susanne Küchler is Professor of Anthropology and Material Culture at University College London. She has conducted ethnographic fieldwork in Papua New Guinea and Eastern Polynesia over the past 25 years, studying memory, creativity, innovation and futurity in political economies of knowledge from a comparative perspective. Her publications include *Malanggan: Art, Memory and Sacrifice* (Berg, 2002) and *Tivaivai: The Social Fabric of the Cook Islands* (British Museum Press, 2009). She is currently working on a new book entitled *The Material Mind*.

Susan Legêne is Professor of Political History at the Free University, Amsterdam, and former head of the Curatorial Department at the Tropenmuseum in Amsterdam. As leader of the CLUE-program "Global History and Heritage in a Post-Colonial World," her research focuses on citizenship and the cultural meaning of the colonial past in processes of nation-building since the nineteenth century, and on the impact and meaning of digitally mediated public history (see www.ghhpw.com). In *The Netherlands East-Indies at the Tropenmuseum: A Colonial History* (Amsterdam KIT Publishers, 2011), co-edited with Janneke van Dijk, she explores the museum's many cultural sources for political history.

Adrian Paci is one of the most active artists in the contemporary international art scene. Born in 1969 in Shkoder, Albania, in 1997 he moved to Milan where he currently lives and works. He has held solo shows in institutions such as Trondheim Kunstmuseum, Norway (2014); MAC, Musée d'Art Contemporain de Montréal (2014); Padiglione d'Arte Contemporanea – PAC, Milan (2014); Jeu de Paume, Paris (2013); Kunsthaus Zurich (2010); and MoMA PS1, New York (2006). Among many group shows, Paci's work has been featured in the 14th International Architecture

Exhibition – La Biennale di Venezia (2014); and in the 48th and the 51st edition of the International Art Exhibition La Biennale di Venezia (in 1999 and 2005).

Ann Rigney is Professor of Comparative Literature at Utrecht University, and has published widely in the field of narrative theory, theories of cultural memory, and modern memory cultures, including *The Rhetoric of Historical Representation* (Cambridge UP, 1990), *Imperfect Histories* (Cornell UP, 2001), *Mediation, Remediation, and the Dynamics of Cultural Memory* (co-edited with Astrid Erll, De Gruyter 2009), and *The Afterlives of Walter Scott: Memory on the Move* (Oxford UP, 2012).

Michael Rothberg is Professor of English and Head of the Department of English at the University of Illinois at Urbana-Champaign, where he is also Director of the Holocaust, Genocide, and Memory Studies Initiative. His latest book is *Multidirectional Memory: Remembering the Holocaust in the Age of Decolonization* (Stanford UP, 2009). He is also the author of *Traumatic Realism: The Demands of Holocaust Representation* (U of Minnesota Press, 2000), and has co-edited *The Holocaust: Theoretical Readings* (Rutgers UP, 2003) and special issues of the journals *Criticism, Interventions, Occasion*, and *Yale French Studies*.

Christina Schwenkel is Associate Professor of Anthropology at the University of California Riverside. She has conducted extensive ethnographic research in Vietnam since the late 1990s on transnational co-productions of postwar memory. Her work is concerned with the relationships between visuality, historical memory, affect, and knowledge production – from representations of war and suffering to post-reform politics of "reconciliation" and "healing." She is the author of *The American War in Contemporary Vietnam: Transnational Remembrance and Representation* (Indiana UP, 2009) and a co-edited special issue of *positions: asia critique* (with Ann Marie Leshkowich) on Neoliberalism in Vietnam (2012). She is currently writing a book entitled, *Revitalizing the City: Socialist Architecture, Postwar Memory, and Urban Renewal in Vietnam*.

List of Illustrations

Index of Names

Made in the USA
Lexington, KY
11 May 2018